InDesign® CS2 For Dummies

Best InDesign Keyboard Shortcuts

	Macintosh	Windows
Opening/closing/saving		
New document	⌘+N	Ctrl+N
Open document	⌘+O	Ctrl+O
Close document	⌘+W	Ctrl+W or Ctrl+F4
Save document	⌘+S	Ctrl+S
Export document to PDF or EPS	⌘+E	Ctrl+E
Place text and graphics	⌘+D	Ctrl+D
Viewing		
Zoom in	⌘+=	Ctrl+=
Zoom out	⌘+– (hyphen)	Ctrl+– (hyphen)
Fit page/spread in window	⌘+0	Ctrl+Alt+=
Display actual size	⌘+1	Ctrl+1
Display at 50%	⌘+5	Ctrl+5
Display at 200%	⌘+2	Ctrl+2
Show/hide rulers	⌘+R	Ctrl+R
Show hidden characters	Option+⌘+I	Ctrl+Alt+I
Guides		
Show/hide guides	⌘+; (semicolon)	Ctrl+; (semicolon)
Lock/unlock guides	Option+⌘+; (semicolon)	Ctrl+Alt+; (semicolon)
Snap to guides on/off	Shift+⌘+; (semicolon)	Ctrl+Shift+; (semicolon)
Show/hide baseline grid	Option+⌘+"	Ctrl+Alt+"
Show/hide document grid	⌘+"	Ctrl+"
Moving objects		
Bring object to front	Shift+⌘+]	Ctrl+Shift+]
Bring object forward	⌘+]	Ctrl+]
Send object to back	Shift+⌘+[	Ctrl+Shift+[
Send object backward	⌘+[	Ctrl+[
Object commands		
Paste into	Option+⌘+V	Ctrl+Alt+V
Paste in place	Option+Shift+⌘+V	Ctrl+Alt+Shift+V
Clear	Backspace	Backspace or Del
Step and repeat	Shift+⌘+U	Ctrl+Shift+U
Resize proportionately	Shift+drag	Shift+drag

For Dummies: Bestselling Book Series for Beginners

InDesign® CS2 For Dummies®

Cheat Sheet

Text/paragraph formats		
Bold	Shift+⌘+B	Ctrl+Shift+B
Italic	Shift+⌘+I	Ctrl+Shift+I
Normal	Shift+⌘+Y	Ctrl+Shift+Y
Underline	Shift+⌘+U	Ctrl+Shift+U
Strikethrough	Shift+⌘+/	Ctrl+Shift+/
Superscript	Shift+⌘+=	Ctrl+Shift+=
Subscript	Option+Shift+⌘+=	Ctrl+Alt+Shift+=
Text alignment and spacing		
Align left	Shift+⌘+L	Ctrl+Shift+L
Align right	Shift+⌘+R	Ctrl+Shift+R
Align center	Shift+⌘+C	Ctrl+Shift+C
Justify left	Shift+⌘+J	Ctrl+Shift+J
Justify right	Option+Shift+⌘+R	Ctrl+Alt+Shift+R
Justify center	Option+Shift+⌘+C	Ctrl+Alt+Shift+C
Align to grid on/off	Option+Shift+⌘+G	Ctrl+Alt+Shift+G
Table editing		
Insert table	Option+Shift+⌘+T	Ctrl+Alt+Shift+T
Insert column	Option+⌘+9	Ctrl+Alt+9
Insert row	⌘+9	Ctrl+9
Special characters		
Bullet (•)	Option+8	Alt+8
Copyright (©)	Option+G	Alt+G
Registered trademark (®)	Option+R	Alt+R
Trademark (™)	Option+2	Alt+2
Switch between keyboard and typographic quotes	Option+Shift+⌘+"	Ctrl+Alt+Shift+"
Em dash (—)	Option+Shift+– (hyphen)	Alt+Shift+– (hyphen)
En dash (–)	Option+– (hyphen)	Alt+– (hyphen)
Discretionary hyphen	Shift+⌘+– (hyphen)	Ctrl+Shift+– (hyphen)
Em space	Shift+⌘+M	Ctrl+Shift+M
En space	Shift+⌘+N	Ctrl+Shift+N
Insert current page number	Option+Shift+⌘+N	Ctrl+Alt+Shift+N
Miscellaneous		
Print document	⌘+P	Ctrl+P
Help	Help	F1
Undo	⌘+Z	Ctrl+Z
Redo	Shift+⌘+Z	Ctrl+Shift+Z

InDesign® CS2 FOR DUMMIES®

by Barbara Assadi and Galen Gruman

Wiley Publishing, Inc.

InDesign® CS2 For Dummies®

Published by
Wiley Publishing, Inc.
111 River Street
Hoboken, NJ 07030-5774
www.wiley.com

Published by Wiley Publishing, Inc., Indianapolis, Indiana

Published simultaneously in Canada

For general information on our other products and services, please contact our Customer Care Department within the U.S. at 800-762-2974, outside the U.S. at 317-572-3993, or fax 317-572-4002.

For technical support, please visit www.wiley.com/techsupport.

Wiley also publishes its books in a variety of electronic formats. Some content that appears in print may not be available in electronic books.

Library of Congress Control Number: 2005923416

ISBN-13: 978-0-7645-9572-1

ISBN-10: 0-7645-9572-5

Manufactured in the United States of America

10 9 8 7 6 5 4 3 2

1B/RS/QV/QV/IN

About the Authors

Barbara Assadi is the co-founder and principal of BayCreative, a research-based advertising and marketing services firm in San Francisco. In that capacity, she manages marketing and creative content for client companies. Previously, she was marketing programs manager and editor-in-chief of Oracle Corporation's Web site and managing editor at Quark, Inc. Barbara has collaborated with coauthor Galen Gruman on several other books on publishing software and has been a contributor to *Oracle Magazine, Macworld, Publish,* and *InfoWorld*. She has edited software books for Adobe Systems and Peachpit Press and has taught university-level courses on publishing topics.

Galen Gruman is the principal at The Zango Group, an editorial and marketing consulting firm, and senior editorial associate at BayCreative, as well as editorial director at EmergeMedia, publisher of *IT Wireless.* Currently a frequent contributor to *SBS Digital Design, CIO,* and *InfoWorld,* he has also been editor of *Macworld* and *M-Business,* executive editor of *Upside,* West Coast bureau chief of *Computerworld,* and vice president of content for ThirdAge.com. He is coauthor of 18 other books on desktop publishing, most with Barbara Assadi. Gruman led one of the first successful conversions of a national magazine to desktop publishing in 1986 and has covered publishing technology since then for several publications, including the trade weekly *InfoWorld,* for which he began writing in 1986, *Macworld,* whose staff he joined in 1991, and most recently *SBS Digital Design*.

Dedication

To my nephew, Ali Ghezelbash, with my deepest respect and admiration.

—Barbara

To a group of dear friends — Cameron and Anita Crotty, Steve and Denise Kazan, Rosey Machado, Kevin McGee, and Missie McCarthy — whose friendship I all too often take for granted.

—*Galen*

Authors' Acknowledgments

Bianca Wolf designed the sample documents shown in Figures 1-1 and 1-2. Arne Hurty, of San Francisco–based agency BayCreative, designed the brochure shown in Figure 1-3.

Publisher's Acknowledgments

We're proud of this book; please send us your comments through our online registration form located at www.dummies.com/register/.

Some of the people who helped bring this book to market include the following:

Acquisitions, Editorial, and Media Development

Project Editor: Beth Taylor

Acquisitions Editor: Bob Woerner

Copy Editor: Andy Hollandbeck

Technical Editor: Dan Ogle

Editorial Manager: Leah Cameron

Media Development Manager: Laura VanWinkle

Media Development Supervisor: Richard Graves

Editorial Assistant: Amanda Foxworth

Cartoons: Rich Tennant (www.the5thwave.com)

Composition Services

Project Coordinator: Adrienne Martinez

Layout and Graphics: Carl Byers, Andrea Dahl, Kelly Emkow, Lauren Goddard, Joyce Haughey, Barry Offringa, Lynsey Osborn, Melanee Prendergast, Ron Terry

Proofreaders: Leeann Harney, Jessica Kramer, Carl William Pierce

Indexer: TECHBOOKS Production Services

Publishing and Editorial for Technology Dummies

Richard Swadley, Vice President and Executive Group Publisher

Andy Cummings, Vice President and Publisher

Mary Bednarek, Executive Acquisitions Director

Mary C. Corder, Editorial Director

Publishing for Consumer Dummies

Diane Graves Steele, Vice President and Publisher

Joyce Pepple, Acquisitions Director

Composition Services

Gerry Fahey, Vice President of Production Services

Debbie Stailey, Director of Composition Services

Contents at a Glance

Table of Contents

Introduction

What is Adobe InDesign and what can it do for you? InDesign is a powerful publishing application that lets you work the way *you* want to work. You can use InDesign as a free-form but manual approach to layout, or as a structured but easily revised approach. The fact that you can choose which way to work is important for both novice and experienced users, because there isn't a single, correct way to lay out pages. Sometimes (for example, if your project is a single-instance publication), creating a layout from scratch — almost as if you were doing it by hand on paper — is the best approach. And sometimes using a highly formatted template that you can modify as needed is the way to go, because there's no need to reinvent the wheel for documents that have a structured and repeatable format.

InDesign can handle sophisticated tasks, such as magazine and newspaper page layout, but its simple approach to publishing also makes it a good choice for smaller projects, such as one-off ads and flyers. InDesign is also a good choice for corporate publishing tasks, such as proposals and annual reports. Plug-in software from other vendors adds extra capabilities.

But that's not all. InDesign was designed from the ground up as an *electronic* publishing tool. That means that you can easily send documents to service bureaus and printing presses for direct output, which saves you lots of time and money. It also means that you can create documents for electronic distribution, particularly using the Adobe Portable Document Format (PDF). These electronic files can include interactive features, such as fill-in-the-blank forms.

Once you get the hang of it, InDesign is quite easy to use. At the same time, it's a powerful publishing program with a growing following among the ranks of professional publishers — and the latest InDesign CS2 version is certain to accelerate that trend. Part of its success is due to the fact that its interface is not unlike that of its sister applications, Adobe Illustrator and Adobe Photoshop, which are also components of the Adobe Creative Suite.

If you are just getting started with InDesign, welcome! We hope you'll find the information in these pages to be helpful in getting you started.

How to Use This Book

Although this book has information that any level of publisher needs to know to use InDesign, this book is primarily for those of you who are fairly new to the field, or who are just becoming familiar with the program. We try to take the mystery out of InDesign and give you some guidance on how to create a bunch of different types of documents. Here are some conventions used in this book:

- **Menu commands** are listed like this: Window➪Pages.

  If we describe a situation in which you need to select one menu and then choose a command from a secondary menu or list box, we use, for example: press Shift+⌘+P or Ctrl+Shift+P. Note that the Macintosh sequence comes first, followed by the Window equivalent.

- **Key combinations:** If you're supposed to press several keys together, we indicate that by placing plus signs (+) between them. Thus Shift+⌘+A means press and hold the Shift and ⌘ keys, and then press A. After you've pressed the A key, let go of the other keys. (The last key in the sequence does not need to be held down.) We also use the plus sign to join keys to mouse movements. For example, Alt+drag means to hold the Alt key when dragging the mouse.
- **Pointer:** The small graphic icon that moves on the screen as you move your mouse is a pointer (also called a cursor). The pointer takes on different shapes depending on the tool you select, the current location of the mouse, and the function you are performing.
- **Click:** This means to quickly press and release the mouse button once. On most Mac mice, there is only one button, but on some there are two or more. All PC mice have at least two buttons. If you have a multi-button mouse, click the leftmost button when we say to click the mouse.
- **Double-click:** This tells you to quickly press and release the mouse button twice. On some multi-button mice, one of the buttons can function as a double-click. (You click it once, the mouse clicks twice.) If your mouse has this feature, use it; it saves strain on your hand.
- **Right-click:** A Windows feature, this means to click the right-hand mouse button. On a Mac's one-button mouse, hold the Control key when clicking the mouse button to do the equivalent of right-clicking in programs that support it. On multi-button Mac mice, assign one of the buttons to the Control+click combination.
- **Dragging:** Dragging is used for moving and sizing items in an InDesign document. To drag an item, position the mouse pointer on the item, press and hold down the mouse button, and then slide the mouse across a flat surface.

How This Book Is Organized

We've divided this book into seven parts, not counting this introduction. Note that the book covers InDesign on both Macintosh and Windows. Because the application is almost identical on both platforms, we only point out platform-specific information when we need to, or when we remember to, or both.

We have also included some bonus content on the InDesignCentral Web site (`www.InDesignCentral.com`).

Part I: Starting at the Beginning

Designing a document is a combination of science and art. The science is in setting up the structure of the page: How many places will hold text, and how many will hold graphics? How wide will the margins be? Where will the page numbers appear? And so on. The art is in coming up with creative ways of filling the structure to please your eyes and the eyes of the people who will be looking at your document.

In this part, we tell you how to navigate your way around InDesign using the program's menus, dialog boxes, palettes, and panes. We give you a test drive of the application so you can see how it works. We also show you how to set up the basic structure of a document and then how to begin filling the structure with words and pictures. We also tell you how to bring in text and graphics created in separate word processing and graphics applications.

Part II: Document Essentials

Good publishing technique is about more than just getting the words down on paper. It's also about opening, saving, adding, deleting, numbering, and setting layout guidelines for documents. This part shows you how to do all that and a lot more, including tips on setting up master pages that you can use over and over again.

Part III: Object Essentials

This part of the book shows you how to work with *objects:* the lines, text frames, picture frames, libraries, and other odds and ends that make up a publication.

Part IV: Text Essentials

When you think about it, text is a big deal when it comes to publishing documents. After all, how many people would want to read a book with nothing but pictures? In this part, we show you how to create and manipulate text, in more ways than you can even imagine.

Part V: Graphics Essentials

Very few people would want to read a book with nothing but text, so this part is where we show you how to handle graphics in InDesign. We include some nifty special effects that can add visual pizzazz to your work.

Part VI: Printing and Output Essentials

Whether you're printing a publication or simply creating a PDF file for readers to download from a Web site, you still need to understand the basics of outputting an InDesign document. This part is where we show you how to set up your files, manage color, and work with service bureaus.

Part VII: The Part of Tens

This part of the book is like the chips in the chocolate chip cookies; you could eat the cookies without them, but you'd be missing a really good part. It's a part that shows you some important resources that will help you make the most of InDesign. It also gives some pointers on switching to InDesign from QuarkXPress and Adobe PageMaker.

Icons Used in This Book

So that you can pick out parts that you really need to pay attention to (or, depending on your taste, to avoid), we've used some symbols, or *icons*, in this book.

When you see this icon, it means we are pointing out a feature that's new to InDesign CS 2.

If you see this icon, it means that we're mentioning some really nifty point or idea that you may want to keep in mind as you use the program.

This icon lets you know something you'll want to keep in mind. If you forget it later, that's fine, but if you remember it, it will make your InDesign life a little easier.

If you skip all the other icons, pay attention to this one. Why? Because ignoring it could cause something really, really bad or embarrassing to happen, like when you were sitting in your second-grade classroom waiting for the teacher to call on you to answer a question, and you noticed that you still had your pajama shirt on. We don't want that to happen to you!

This icon tells you that we are about to pontificate on some remote technical bit of information that might help explain a feature in InDesign. The technical info will definitely make you sound impressive if you memorize it and recite it to your friends.

Part I
Starting at the Beginning

"Remember, your Elvis should appear bald and slightly hunched. Nice Big Foot, Brad. Keep your two-headed animals in the shadows and your alien spacecrafts crisp and defined."

In this part . . .

You have your copy of InDesign and you'd like some basic information on how to get started, right? Well, you have come to the right place. Read along with us and, before you know it, you'll be sailing smoothly through InDesign. This part of the book gives you a general idea of what InDesign can do. We explain the layout approaches you can take, and how to set up InDesign to work the way *you* work. Plus, we take you on a test drive, where you can see the steps involved in creating your first document in InDesign. Along the way, we help you navigate the plethora of panes, palettes, tools, and shortcuts that can seem overwhelming at first, but which soon become second nature as you gain experience using the program. Welcome aboard!

Chapter 1

Finding Out How InDesign Works

In This Chapter

- Understanding what InDesign can do for you
- Finding out how InDesign works
- Defining InDesign terms

Page layout programs have been around for the past couple of decades, so you'd think that software in this category is mature and past its innovative prime. But that's not true: Adobe InDesign has revitalized the category with a raft of powerful, unique capabilities. Yet Adobe InDesign, the new kid on the block, actually has a history that goes back way before its appearance on the scene. InDesign is the modern-day successor to PageMaker. PageMaker was an early — and popular — page layout program created by a no-longer-existing company by the name of Aldus, which was acquired by Adobe in 1994. To its credit, InDesign is also taking over market share from a market-leading competing product: QuarkXPress.

Why mention this history? Because if you're reading this, there's a good chance that you are already using a page layout program — perhaps QuarkXPress or PageMaker. If so, you'll find some features of InDesign to be familiar, others to be fairly easy to assimilate, and still others to be just about as confusing as can be. If you are new to page layout programs and are taking your first steps with InDesign, that's fine, too. You can get up and going with the program after a very short time.

If you're well-versed in how to use previous versions of InDesign, you already know the basics. Feel free to skip this chapter and move right ahead. If not, settle in for a nice conversation about how to get started using a very comprehensive page layout program.

Lots of Capabilities

Before InDesign, layout designers chose from two predominant software programs. PageMaker offered an unstructured approach to layout in which the designer had lots of flexibility but needed to manually position text and graphics on the print (or, later, online) page. A slightly later addition to the desktop publishing scene, QuarkXPress, offered structural elements to help construct the page while still making it easy to revise layouts. InDesign, which tries — successfully, for the most part — to be more things to more people, lets you choose from both approaches. This flexibility means that you can create a layout from scratch, or you can use a formatted template that helps you position text and graphics into a predetermined spot in the layout, with prearranged look-and-feel specifications. And if you want to deviate from the formatted template, InDesign lets you do that as well.

What kinds of layouts can InDesign handle? Pages for magazines, newspapers, marketing brochures, and ads to start with. InDesign is also an excellent choice for more structured documents, such as corporate reports, newsletters, white papers, and annual reports. The program's intuitive approach to publishing also makes it a good choice for smaller projects, such as newsletters and informational flyers. After you get the hang of it, you'll find InDesign simple to use. But don't forget that it is full-featured enough to handle the most complex page-layout tasks, everything from a magazine ad to an annual report. Figures 1-1 through 1-3 show a few examples of InDesign's range.

Finding Out What InDesign Can Do

Seeing as how InDesign is a leading, if not *the* leading, page layout program, it makes sense that it is a whiz at helping you lay out pages quickly and easily. InDesign offers a strong set of features for professional publishers working on brochures, magazines, advertisements, and similar publications. Although it lacks specialized tools for database publishing (such as for catalogs), it offers many unique features, such as a multiline composer, glyph scaling, and customer character strokes, some of which we talk about later in the chapter.

InDesign's use of both the free-form and structured layout metaphors — which we also explain later in the chapter — makes it very flexible, letting you pick the layout style that works best for you and for your document's specific needs.

Among InDesign's most useful and innovative capabilities are the following:

- Styles let you perform complex formatting quickly and easily. Use nested styles to handle tricky text formatting, such as a drop cap with its own character style nested inside a paragraph with its own style, or to make sure all sidebar frames have the same background.
- InDesign's support for sophisticated OpenType fonts (in addition to more standard PostScript and TrueType fonts) and its ability to highlight missing fonts in a document let you handle font issues easily.

- The multiline composer adjusts the spacing and hyphenation over several lines of text at once — rather than the typical one-line-in-isolation of other programs — to achieve the best possible spacing and hyphenation.

Figure 1-1: Get your message out with posters created in InDesign.

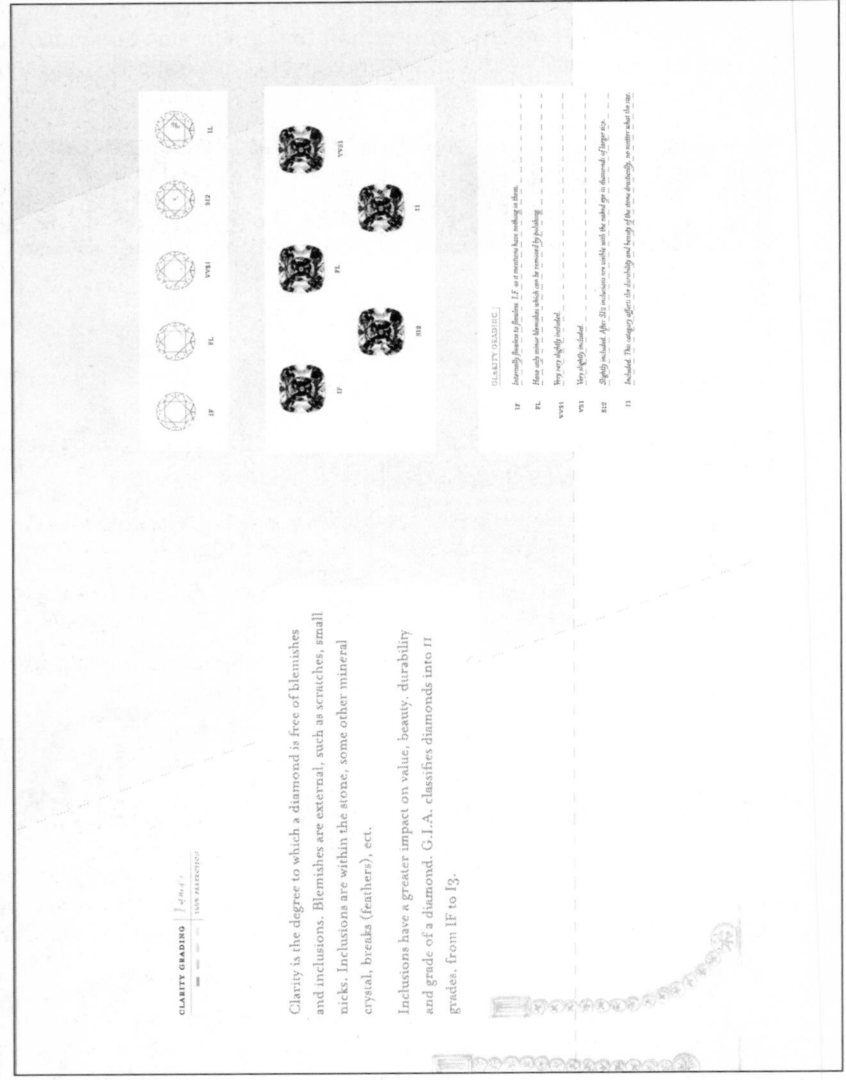

Figure 1-2: InDesign is great for producing product brochures, like this brochure about diamonds.

- Custom strokes for characters let you change the look of characters by making their outlines (*strokes*) thicker or thinner. You can also give the part of the characters inside the stroke a different color to create an outline effect. (Normally, the part inside the stroke is the same color as the stroke, so the reader sees a normal, solid character.)
- Illustrator and Photoshop file import lets you place these graphics files directly into your layout.

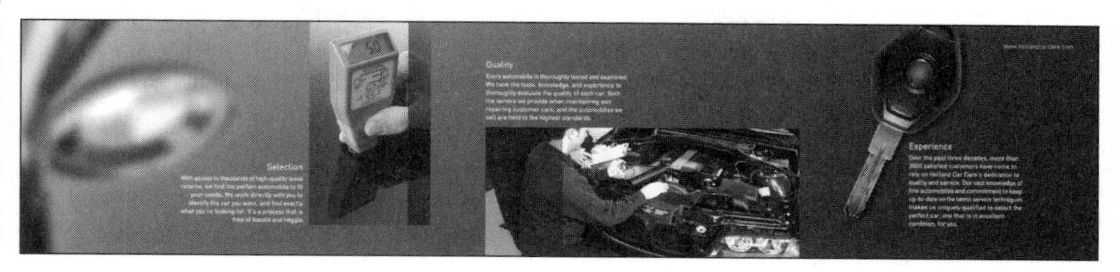

Figure 1-3: InDesign lets you design layouts with abnormal page sizes, like this brochure.

- Multiple views of the document let you see different sections at the same time.
- Transparency can make objects fade for ghost-like visuals or to create special effects as the objects overlap.
- InDesign offers automated spell checking and text correction similar to Microsoft Word's noninvasive correction tools.
- Object styles let you apply a range of attributes (such as fill and stroke) to an object and reuse those same settings on other objects.
- Follow-me anchored objects let you keep items such as figures and sidebars with text as it flows throughout a document.

Discovering the InDesign Approach

Publishing programs have some similarities and some differences in their various approaches to the publishing task. One way to describe a program's approach to publishing is to talk about its *metaphor,* or the overall way that it handles publishing tasks.

Some programs use a *free-form* metaphor, which means that the method used to craft a document is based on assembling page elements as you would if they were placed on a pasteboard until ready for use. This is also called the *pasteboard* metaphor, which is an imprecise term because software that uses other metaphors can still include a pasteboard. PageMaker is the best-known example of the free-form approach.

Other programs approach page layout by using a *frame-based* metaphor, in which frames (or boxes) hold both the page elements and the attributes that control the appearance of those elements. QuarkXPress is the best-known example of the frame-based approach.

InDesign is the best of both worlds because it incorporates both the free-form and the frame-based metaphors.

The frame-based metaphor

When you work with a frame-based metaphor, you build pages by assembling a variety of frames that will contain your text and graphics. First, you set up the basic framework of the document — the page size and orientation, margins, number of columns, and so on. You then fill that framework with text, pictures, and lines.

These frames and lines need not be straight or square. With InDesign, you can create frames that are shaped by *Bézier curves.* (In the 1970s, French engineer Pierre Bézier created the mathematics that make these adjustable curves work.)

Why would you want to use frames? Publishers find several reasons why frames come in handy:

- **To create a template for documents, such as newsletters and magazines, that use the same basic layout elements across many articles.** You create the frames and then add the text and graphics appropriate for each specific article, modifying, adding, and deleting frames as necessary for each article.
- **To get a sense of how you want your elements to be placed and sized before you start working with the actual elements.** This is similar to sketching a rough layout on paper with a pen or pencil before doing a formal layout with InDesign.
- **To set up specific size and placement of elements up front.** You often work with a template or with guidelines that limit the size and placement of elements. In many cases, you can copy an existing frame because its size is the same as what you use in several locations of your layout. For structured or partly structured documents, such as newsletters and magazines, we find it easier to set up documents up front so that elements are sized and placed correctly; the less favorable alternative is resizing elements one at a time later on.

Whether you start by creating frames to hold graphics or text or you simply place the text and graphics directly on your page, you're using frames. When you directly place elements on the page, InDesign creates a frame automatically for each element. The frame InDesign creates is based on the amount of text or the size of the graphic, rather than on your specific frame specifications. Of course, in either case, you can modify the frames and the elements within them.

The free-form metaphor

Working under a free-form (pasteboard) metaphor, you draw a page's content as if you're working on paper. If you've been in the publishing business for a while, you might once have used wax to stick strips of type, camera-ready line drawings, and halftone pictures to a pasteboard. You would then assemble and reassemble all those pieces until you got the combination that looked right to you. The free-form metaphor encourages a try-as-you-go, experimental layout approach, which is particularly well suited to one-of-a-kind documents such as ads, brochures, annual reports, and marketing materials.

If you use a frame-based approach to page layout, you can experiment with using the frames as placeholders for actual text and graphics. Visual thinkers like to work with actual objects, which is why the free-form metaphor works much better for them. With InDesign, you pick the metaphor that works for your style, your current situation, and your mood. After all, both approaches can lead to the same great design.

Understanding Global and Local Control

The power of desktop publishing in general, and InDesign in particular, is that it lets you automate time-consuming layout and typesetting tasks while, at the same time, letting you customize each step of the process according to your needs.

This duality of structure and flexibility — implemented via the dual use of the frame-based and free-form layout metaphors — carries over to all operations, from typography to color. You can use global controls to establish general settings for layout elements, and then use local controls to modify those elements to meet specific publishing requirements. The key to using global and local tools effectively is to know when each is appropriate.

Global tools include:

- General preferences and application preferences (see Chapter 4)
- Master pages and libraries (see Chapter 8)
- Character and paragraph styles (see Chapters 16 and 17)
- Object styles (see Chapter 13)
- Sections and page numbers (see Chapter 6)
- Color definitions (see Chapter 10)
- Hyphenation and justification (see Chapter 17)

Styles and master pages are the two main global settings that you can expect to override locally throughout a document. You shouldn't be surprised to make such changes often because, although the layout and typographic functions that styles and master pages automate are the fundamental components of any document's look, they don't always work for a publication's entire specific content.

Local tools include:

- Frame tools (see Part III, as well as Chapters 18 and 20)
- Character and paragraph tools (see Chapters 16 and 17)
- Graphics tools (see Part V)

Choosing the right tools for the job

Depending on what you're trying to do with InDesign at any given moment, you may or may not know right away which tool to use. If, for example, you maintain fairly precise layout standards throughout a document, then using master pages is the way to keep your work in order. Using styles is the best solution if you want to apply standard character and paragraph formatting throughout a document. When you work with one-of-a-kind documents, such as the poster shown in Figure 1-1, it doesn't make much sense to spend time designing master pages and styles — it's easier just to format elements as you create them.

For example, you can create *drop caps* (large initial letters set into a paragraph of type, like the drop cap that starts each chapter in this book) as a paragraph option in the Paragraph pane, or you can create a *paragraph style* (formatting that you can apply repeatedly to whole paragraphs, ensuring that the same formatting is applied each time) that contains the drop-cap settings, and then apply that style to the paragraph containing the drop cap. Which method you choose depends on the complexity of your document and how often you need to perform the action. The more often you find yourself taking a set of steps, the more often you should use a global tool (like character and paragraph styles) to accomplish the task.

Fortunately, you don't need to choose between global and local tools while you're in the middle of designing a document. You can always create styles from existing formatting later. You can also add elements to a master page if you start to notice that you need them to appear on every page.

Specifying measurement values

Another situation in which you can choose between local or global controls is specifying measurement values. Regardless of the *default measurement unit* you set (that is, the measurement unit that appears in all dialog boxes, panes, and palettes), you can use any unit when entering measurements in an InDesign dialog box. For example, if the default measurement is picas, but you're new to publishing and are more comfortable with working in inches, go ahead and enter measurements in inches.

InDesign accepts any of the following codes for measurement units. Note that the *x* in the items listed below indicates where you specify the value, such as **2i** for 2 inches. It doesn't matter whether you put a space between the value and the code: Typing **2inch** and **2 inch** are the same as far as InDesign is concerned:

- *x*i or *x* inch or *x*" (for inches)
- *x*p (for picas)
- *x*pt or 0p*x* (for points)
- *x*c (for ciceros)
- *x*cm (for centimeters)
- *x*mm (for millimeters)

You can enter fractional picas in two ways: in decimal format (as in **8.5p**) and in picas and points (as in **8p6**). Either of these settings results in a measurement of 8½ picas (there are 12 points in a pica).

Basic InDesign Vocabulary

Not too long ago, only a few publishing professionals knew — or cared about — what the words *pica, kerning, crop,* and *color model* meant. Today, these words are becoming commonplace because almost everyone who wants to produce a nice-looking report, a simple newsletter, or a magazine encounters these terms in the menus and manuals of their layout programs. Occasionally, the terms are used incorrectly or are replaced with general terms to make non-professional users feel less threatened, but that substitution ends up confusing professional printers, people who work in service bureaus, and Internet service providers. Throughout this book, we define other publishing terms as we go.

Like all great human endeavors, InDesign comes with its own terminology, much of it adopted from other Adobe products. Some general terms to know include the following:

- **Frame:** The container for an object. A frame can hold text, a graphic, or a color fill.
- **Link:** The connection to a file that you import, or *place* (defined below), into an InDesign document. The link contains the file's location, and its last modification date and time. A link can reference any image or text file that you have imported into a layout. InDesign can notify you when a source text or graphics file has changed so you can choose whether to update the version in your layout.

- **Package:** The collection of all files needed to deliver a layout for printing or Web posting.
- **PDF:** The Adobe Portable Document Format, which has become the standard for sharing electronic documents. No matter what kind of computer it is viewed on (Windows, Macintosh, Palm, or Unix), a PDF document displays the original document's typography, graphics representation, and layout. With InDesign, you can place PDF files as if they were graphics, and you can also export its InDesign pages to PDF format.
- **Place:** To import a picture or text file.
- **Plug-in:** A piece of software that loads into, and becomes part of, InDesign to add capabilities to the program.
- **Stroke:** The outline of an object (whether a graphic, line, or individual text characters) or frame.
- **Thread:** The connections between text frames that let a story flow from one frame to another.

Chapter 2

Taking a Quick Lap around the Track

In This Chapter

- Creating a new document
- Working with frames
- Creating lines
- Working with text and pictures
- Creating and applying colors
- Printing a composite

If InDesign were an automobile, it would be more like a Formula 1 racecar than an economy sedan. InDesign is a complex program that lets you do everything from creating ads to designing brochures and magazines to indexing a book to generating separation plates for professional printing. Yet, for all its inherent complexity, InDesign is also designed to get novice publishers up and running quickly. In fact, you can get started building documents with just a few simple skills.

In this chapter, we walk you through the process of creating a simple document. Don't worry if it all doesn't make sense — the goal is to give you a basic taste of InDesign's approach and interface, so when we get into the details in the rest of this book, you can relate them to a real publication and to the bigger picture.

If you've used other page layout programs, you can skip this chapter and move on to the chapters in the book that explore the full functionality of the program. But if you're just getting started, you've come to the right place.

To give you an idea of how to use InDesign's basic tools, we will guide you through the creation of a fictitious newsletter for an equally fictitious desert park in Arizona. To follow these steps on your computer, you need InDesign, a text file from a word-processing program, a graphics file, and a printer. You can follow the steps closely — either using the components we provide (available at www.InDesignCentral.com) or substituting your own text, graphic, and fonts — or you can make variations along the way. In any case, fasten your seat belts. It's sure to be an interesting ride.

Creating a New Document

When you create a new document in InDesign, you specify the size and setup of the pages in the document. Note that in this chapter, measurements are in picas (a *pica* is a typesetting measurement equal to one-sixth of an inch and is a standard measure in the layout world) with the equivalent measurement given in inches. Follow these steps to create a new document:

1. **Open InDesign.**
2. **Choose File⇨New⇨Document, or press ⌘+N or Ctrl+N.**

   The New Document dialog box appears (see Figure 2-1).

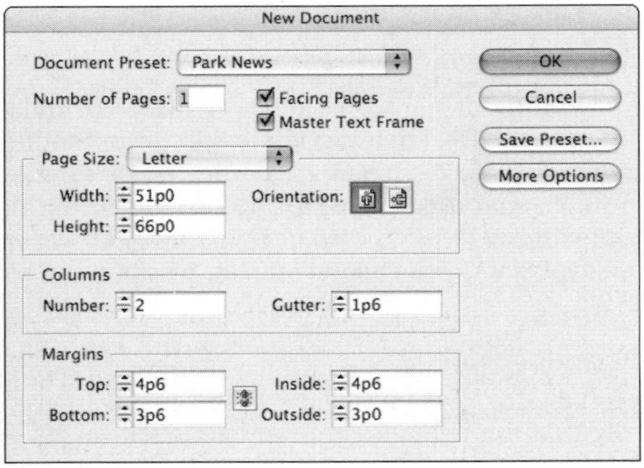

New Document

Document Preset: Park News | OK
Number of Pages: 1 | ☑ Facing Pages | Cancel
☑ Master Text Frame | Save Preset...
Page Size: Letter | More Options
Width: 51p0 | Orientation:
Height: 66p0
Columns
Number: 2 | Gutter: 1p6
Margins
Top: 4p6 | Inside: 4p6
Bottom: 3p6 | Outside: 3p0

Figure 2-1: Set up the document's page size and other attributes in the New Document dialog box.

3. **In the Page Size drop-down menu, choose Letter.**
4. **Select the Facing Pages option because this is a newsletter printed on two sides, thus needing both left-hand and right-hand pages.**
5. **Select Master Text Frame.**
6. **Set the number of columns to** 2, **with a gutter width of** 1p6 **(0.25 inches).**

7. **Set the margin guides to** 4p6 **(0.75 inches) for the top and inside,** 3p6 **(0.583 inches) for the bottom, and** 3p **(0.5 inches) for the outside.**

8. **Click the Save Preset button and give these specifications a name.**

   The example uses **Park News**. Assigning a name to a set of document specifications lets you select these exact settings for future documents. For example, to create future issues of the *Park News* newsletter, you choose the Park News preset name from the Document Preset pop-up menu.

9. **Click OK to create the new document's layout.**

   InDesign creates one 8½-by-11-inch page.

10. **Choose File⇨Save As or press Shift+⌘+S or Ctrl+Shift+S.**

    In the Save As field, type the name of the document you are saving; we name our example document `ParkNewsSpring.indd`. Choose a location for the file and then click Save.

Working with Frames

By using the Master Text Frame feature when you open a new, InDesign creates the frame for the text. But we want our newsletter to have colored frames at the top for the newsletter title and logo. Here's how you can create those frames.

1. **Select the Rectangle Frame tool.**

   To see the name of a tool, hover your mouse over it until a Tool Tip appears.

   Look at the control points in the Control palette —they're the group of nine squares at the palette's far left. All the coordinates in this chapter are based on the upper-left corner of frames and objects, but InDesign lets you base the coordinate on other corners or even on the center of objects. If your active control point—that's the one in black— is not the upper-left corner, nothing will be positioned where you expect when you follow the steps in this chapter. You can easily change the active control point: Just click the one you want to be active, and it becomes black (the others become white).

2. **Click and drag to create a frame that is approximately 21p (3.5 inches) wide and 4p (0.667 inches) tall, as shown in Figure 2-2.**

   You fine-tune the size and placement in the next steps. The new frame is selected, as indicated by the white handles on its corners. If the frame becomes deselected in the following steps, click it to select it.

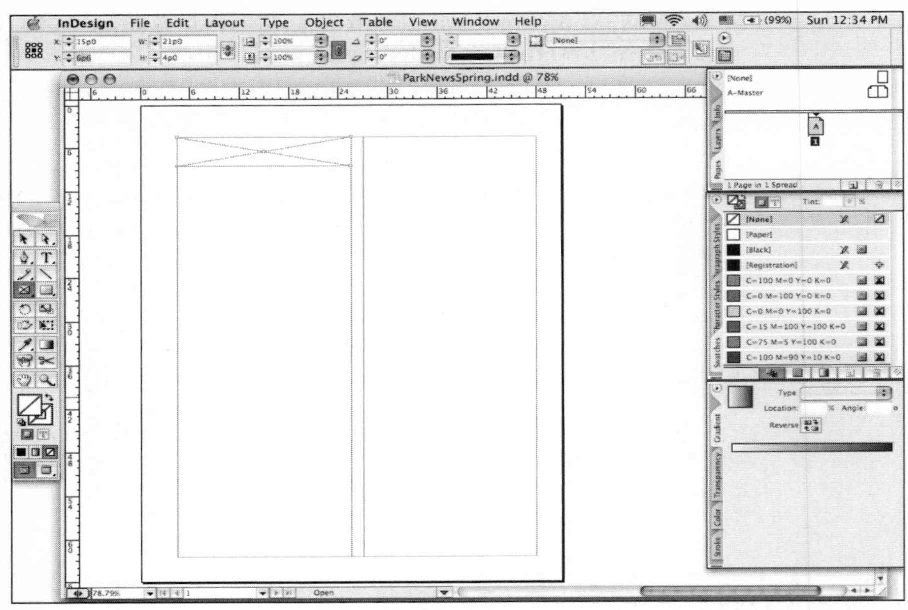

Figure 2-2: Build a frame for your title.

3. **Highlight the X: field in the Control palette and enter** 15p. **(If the Control palette is not visible, choose Window➪Control or press Option+⌘+6 or Ctrl+Alt+6 to open it.)**

   Doing so specifies the item's origin across (placement from the left edge of the page).

   For the X:, Y:, W:, and H: fields, you can also experiment with clicking the arrows near each field to change position, size, and other attributes.

4. **Tab to the Y: field, which specifies the item's origin down (placement from the top of the page), and type** 6p6.
5. **Tab to the W: field, which specifies the item's width, and type** 21p.
6. **Tab to the H: field, which specifies the item's height, and type** 4p.
7. **Press Return or Enter to reposition and resize the frame according to the values you enter, as shown in Figure 2-3.**

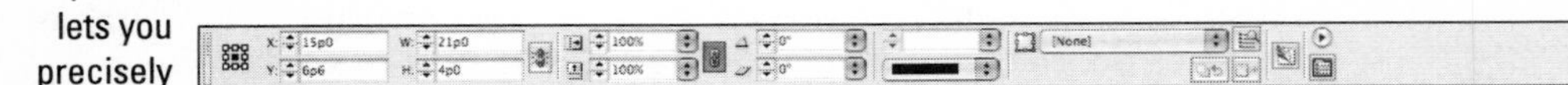

Figure 2-3: The Control palette lets you precisely position and size items.

8. **Be sure the frame is selected with the Selection tool, then choose Edit⇨Duplicate, or press Option+Shift+⌘+D or Ctrl+Alt+Shift+D.**

   Doing this makes a copy of the frame. (If there are no open squares on the corners of the new frame, you need to click the frame with the Selection tool to select it before you go on.)

9. **To size and place the second frame precisely, we typed the following values in the Control palette:**
   - X: 36p9
   - Y: 6p6
   - W: 22p6
   - H: 4p

10. **Press Return or Enter to reposition and resize the second frame.**

For more information about working with frames, see Chapter 10.

Working with Text

To get text onto a page, you first create a text frame and then fill the frame with text. You can type text directly into the frame or import a text file from another application, most commonly Microsoft Word. After the frame is filled with text, you can change the font, size, color, and many more characteristics of both the text and the frame itself. But the first step is to create the text frame. Here's how:

1. **Select the Rectangle Frame tool.**
2. **Click and drag to create a frame that is approximately the size you want.**

   In our example, we created a frame 45p (7.5 inches) wide and 4p (.667 inches) tall, as shown in Figure 2-4.

   The new frame is selected, as indicated by the white handles on the edges of the frame. If the frame becomes deselected in the following steps, simply click it to select it.

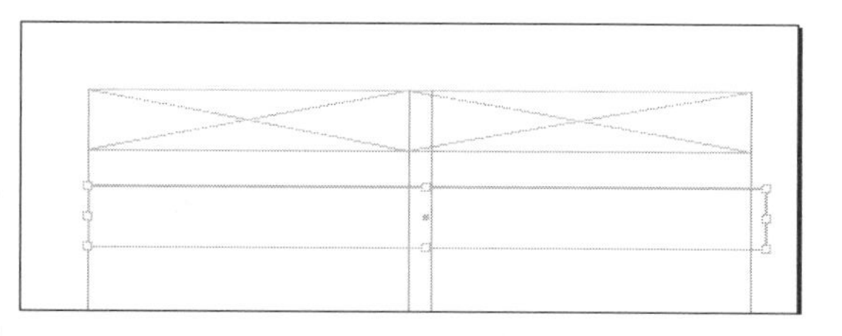

Figure 2-4: Use the Rectangle Frame tool to give your text a place to live.

3. **To size and place the frame precisely, we typed the following values in the Control palette:**
   - X: 4p6
   - Y: 9p6
   - W: 43p6
   - H: 5p0
4. **Select the Type tool, then click the new frame to hold the story's headline.**
5. **Type the word you want to appear in the frame.**

   In our example, we typed **Blooming Cactus: Sure Sign of Spring** in the frame.
6. **Highlight the entire phrase and choose a different font from the Control palette's Font Family menu.**

   The example in Figure 2-5 uses the font Century Old Style Std.
7. **Choose 24 pt from the Font Size list in the Control palette, as shown in Figure 2-5.**

   If you don't see the Font Size list, click the A button at the left side of the Control palette to display character-formatting options, as opposed to the paragraph-formatting options.

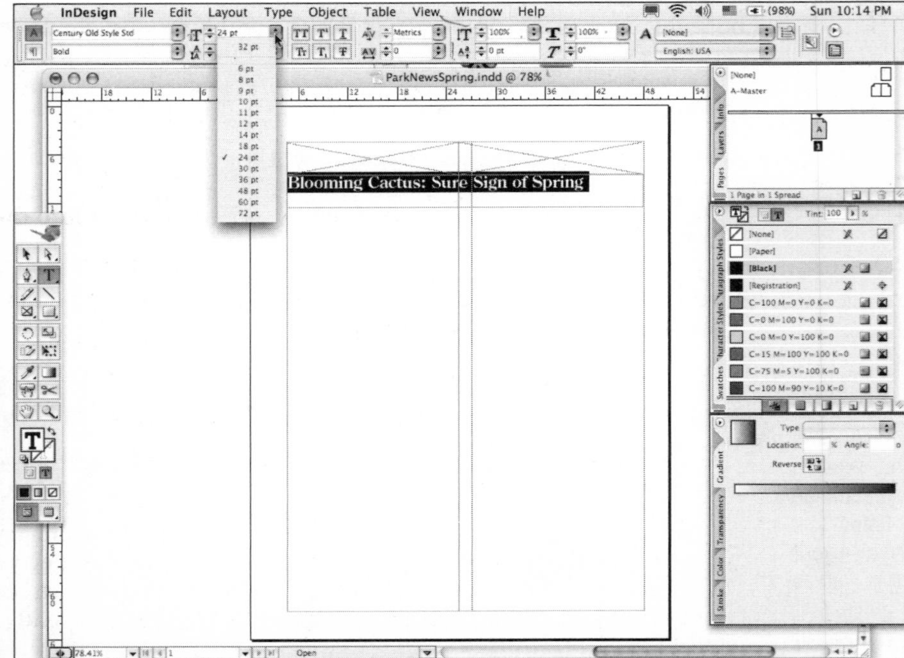

Figure 2-5: When text is highlighted, you can apply different fonts and sizes to it.

8. **Select the frame in the upper-right corner of your document and enter two paragraph returns and the words** Spring 2005.
9. **Highlight the text Spring 2005 and apply a font to it; make the point size 12 pt.**

   Here, we used the font Times.

Now you put text into the text frame that was created through the Master Text Frame feature earlier:

1. **Choose File⇨Place, or press ⌘+D or Ctrl+D.**

   The Place dialog box (shown in Figure 2-6) appears.

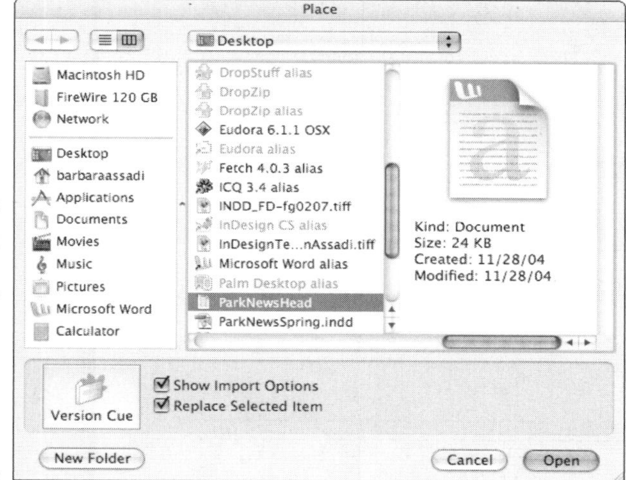

Figure 2-6: You can import your magnum opus from a word processing program.

2. **Locate and select the text file that you want to import into the text frame.**

   In our example, we use a Microsoft Word text file.
3. **Select the Show Import Options check box.**
4. **Click Open.**

   The Microsoft Word Import Options dialog box appears.
5. **Be sure that Use Typographer's Quotes is checked, and then click OK to import the file.**

   Typographer's quotes are the curly quotes used in publishing; if you don't check this box, you'll get the keyboard quotes that peg you as a beginner. After you click OK, InDesign shows the loaded-text icon (it looks like a tiny paragraph), which indicates that a file is ready to be placed into a frame.

6. **Click the two-column master text frame to pour the text into it.**

   Figure 2-7 shows the result.

   If the text file you import is too big to fit in the text frame, a red square will appear in the lower-right corner of the frame. For this example exercise, you needn't worry about that. If you do not have a text file to place, you can simply type sentences in the text frame.

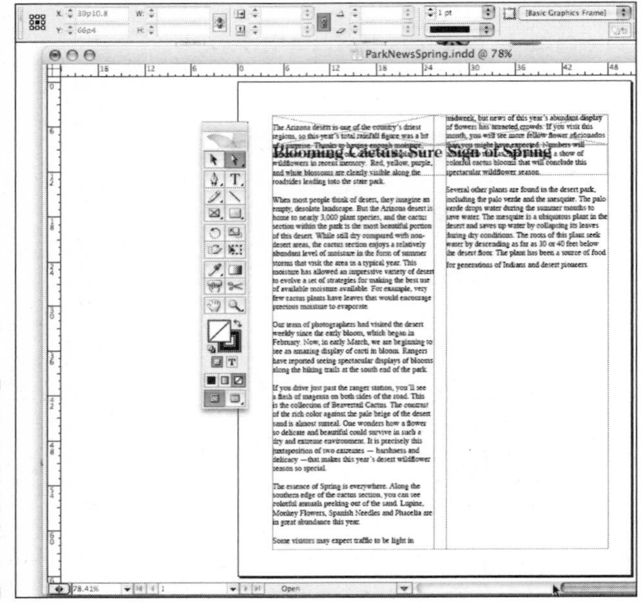

Figure 2-7: Your text is placed, but something is still not quite right.

   Because the first page of the article has the two empty frames at top as well as the headline frame, you want to resize the master text frame for this page so the story text doesn't overprint the other frames.

7. **To resize the frame, click the middle frame handle at the top of the selected frame and drag it below the three other frames.**

   You can also set text wrap for each of those frames by using the Text Wrap pane, which we cover later in this chapter.

After the text is placed, you need to format it:

1. **With the Type tool, click anywhere in the text and highlight all the text by pressing ⌘+A or Ctrl+A.**
2. **Choose Type⇨Character, or press ⌘+T or Ctrl+T, to open the Character pane; select a font family (the example uses Berthold Baskerville Book), select a type style (Regular is fine), set the font size (our example uses 11 pt), and set the leading (the leading in our example is set at 13 pt).**

Leading (pronounced "ledding") is a typographical term that refers to the space between lines of text.

You can also use the Control palette to adjust these settings. Figure 2-8 shows the Character pane and the results.

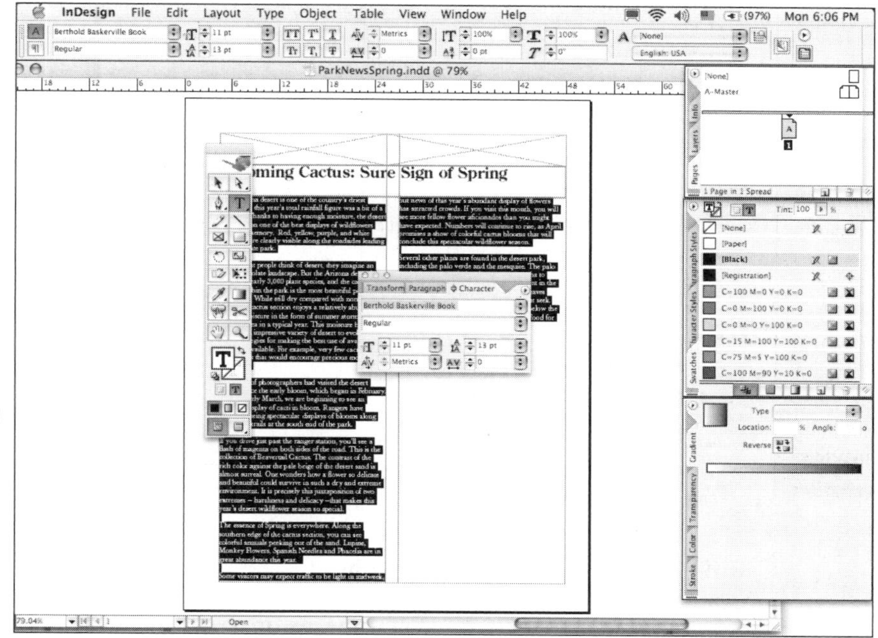

Figure 2-8: Go crazy with fonts, type styles, point sizes, and leading.

3. **Make sure all the text is still selected and then choose Type➪Paragraph, or press Option+⌘+T or Ctrl+Alt+T, to open the Paragraph pane.**
4. **Make sure the alignment is set to Justified (any of the group of four buttons in the center and the top of the Paragraph pane) and the First Line Indent (the second field on the left) is set to 0p10, as shown in Figure 2-9.**

   You can also use the Control palette to make these adjustments.

   Figure 2-10 shows the drop cap.

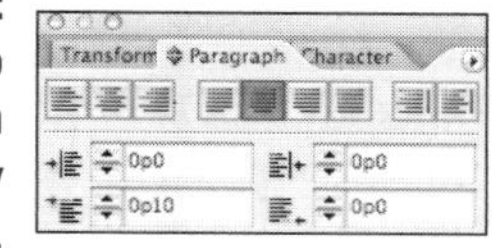

Figure 2-9: You need no justification to justify your text.

The Arizona desert is one of the country's driest regions, so this year's total rainfall figure was a bit of a surprise. Thanks to having enough moisture, the desert is putting on one of the best displays of wildflowers in recent memory. Red, yellow, purple, and white blossoms are clearly visible along the roadsides leading into the state park.

When most people think of desert, they imagine an empty, desolate landscape. But the Arizona desert is home to nearly 3,000 plant species, and the cactus section within the park is the most beautiful portion of this desert. While still dry compared with non-desert areas, the cactus section enjoys a relatively abundant level of moisture in the form of summer storms that visit the area in a typical year. This moisture has allowed an impressive variety of desert to evolve a set of strategies for making the best use of available moisture available. For example, very few cactus plants have leaves that would encourage precious moisture to evaporate.

Our team of photographers had visited the desert weekly since the early bloom, which began in February. Now, in early March, we are beginning to see an amazing display of cacti in bloom. Rangers have reported seeing spectacular displays of blooms along the hiking trails at the south end of the park.

If you drive just past the ranger station, you'll see a flash of magenta on both sides of the road. This is the collection of Beavertail Cactus. The contrast of the rich color against the pale beige of the desert sand is almost surreal. One wonders how a flower so delicate and beautiful could survive in such a dry and extreme environment. It is precisely this juxtaposition of two extremes – harshness and delicacy –that makes this year's desert wildflower season so special.

The essence of Spring is everywhere. Along the southern edge of the cactus section, you can see colorful annuals peeking out of the sand. Lupine, Monkey Flowers, Spanish Needles and Phacelia are in great abundance this year.

Some visitors may expect traffic to be light in midweek, but news of this year's abundant display of flowers has attracted crowds. If you visit this month, you will see more fellow flower aficionados than you might have expected. Numbers will continue to rise, as April promises a show of colorful cactus blooms that will conclude this spectacular wildflower season.

Several other plants are found in the desert park, including the palo verde and the mesquite. The palo verde drops water during the summer months to save water. The mesquite is a ubiquitous plant in the desert and saves up water by collapsing its leaves during dry conditions. The roots of this plant seek water by descending as far as 30 or 40 feet below the desert floor. The plant has been a source of food for generations of Indians and desert pioneers.

Figure 2-10: If you are following our example, the drop cap in your document looks something like this.

5. **If you plan to create pages with the same type specifications, create styles from the formatted text. Start with character styles (styles applied to specific text selections, as opposed to whole paragraphs). In this example, the only character style is for the drop cap's text.**

   a. With the Type tool, highlight the drop-cap text and choose New Character Style from the Character Styles pane's palette menu. (Choose Type➪Character Styles or press Shift+F11 to open the pane.)

   b. Provide a name at the top of the New Character Style dialog box and then verify the attributes in the Basic Character Formats pane.

   c. Click OK when you're done.

6. **Now follow a similar process to create the paragraph styles from the formatted text. Start with the regular story text.**

   a. With the Type tool, click anywhere in the text and choose New Paragraph Style from the Paragraph Styles pane's palette menu. (Choose Type➪Paragraph Styles or press F11 to open the pane.)

   b. Provide a name at the top of the New Paragraph Style dialog box and then verify the attributes in the Basic Character Formats, Indents and Spacing, Hyphenation, and Justification panes. (For the drop-capped paragraph, also verify the settings in the Drop

Cap & Nested Styles pane, such as making sure it uses the correct character style — defined in Step 5 — for the drop cap text.)

c. Click OK when you're done.

Repeat steps 7a through 7c for each different type of paragraph. You should end up with one character style (perhaps called Drop Cap text) and five paragraph styles (they could be called Main Headline, Internal Headline, Body Text, Drop Cap Body Text, and First Body Text).

Apply the paragraph styles to your text by clicking anywhere in a paragraph and then clicking the appropriate name in the Paragraph Styles pane. You can also highlight a range of paragraphs and format them all at once by clicking the desired style name in the Paragraph Styles pane. To apply character styles, you would first highlight the text you want to format and then click the desired style name in the Character Styles pane.

7. **Choose File⇨Save, or press ⌘+S or Ctrl+S, to save your work.**

For more information about creating and handling text, see Part IV.

Working with Lines

You can create lines of any shape, size, style, width, and color. In our example, we add a line at the bottom of the first page. You can also add lines to master pages if you want the lines to always appear when you create a document based on a master page. To work on a master page, double-click a master page icon in the Pages pane (choose Window⇨Pages or press F12 to open the Pages pane). Figure 2-11 shows the pane. A *master page* is essentially a template page in your document to which you can add objects, then have InDesign create new pages based on the master page, with all those objects added automatically to those new pages. When you selected Master Text Frame earlier, you were telling InDesign to place a text frame on the default master page, called A-Master.

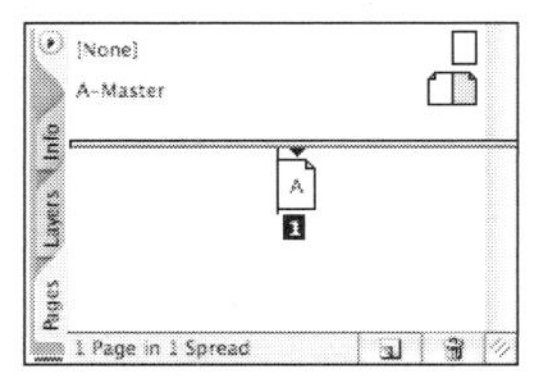

Figure 2-11: The Pages pane lets you work on master pages as well as create new pages.

1. **To begin drawing a line, select the Line tool.**
2. **Be sure the Stroke button in the Tools palette is set to black — click the Stroke button and then click the small black button in the row below.**
3. **Position the mouse where you want to draw the line (in our example, just below the text frame) and then click and drag to create a line, as shown in Figure 2-12.**

   If you don't want an uneven line, press the Shift key while you drag to constrain the tool to drawing a horizontal or vertical line. The new line is selected, as indicated by the white handles. If the line becomes deselected in the following steps, just click it to select it.

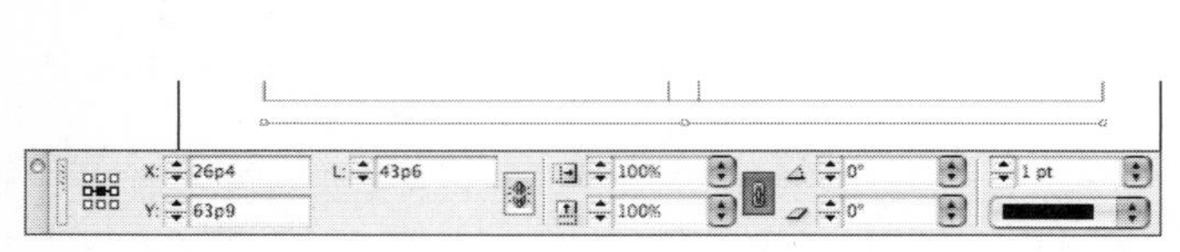

Figure 2-12: Put away your straight-edge; the Line tool draws straight lines for you!

4. **Precisely place and size the line by using the Control palette. In our example, we placed and sized the line as follows:**
   - X: 26p4
   - Y: 63p9
   - L: 43p6
   - Stroke: 1p0
5. **Choose File⇨Save, or press ⌘+S or Ctrl+S, to save your work.**

   For more information about working with lines, see Chapter 10.

Working with Graphics

In InDesign, any image that you import into a layout — whether it's a digital photograph, chart, or line drawing — is referred to as a *graphic.* A graphic goes inside a *graphics frame* — either one that you create before you place a picture or one that InDesign creates automatically when you import a graphic but have no frame selected. Once a graphic is inside a frame, you can change its size and placement.

1. **Click the Rectangle Frame tool.**
2. **Position the pointer on the page and then click and drag to create a rectangular graphics frame of any size.**

   The new frame is selected, as indicated by the white square handles. If the frame becomes deselected in the following steps, click it to select it.
3. **To import a picture, choose File⇨Place or press ⌘+D or Ctrl+D.**
4. **Locate and select a graphic file, such as a TIFF, JPEG, GIF, or EPS file, and click Open.**

   Your new graphic is placed in your newsletter, in that selected frame, as shown in Figure 2-13.

Park News

Blooming Cactus: Sure Sign of Spring

The Arizona desert is one of the country's driest regions, so this year's total rainfall figure was a bit of a surprise. Thanks to having enough moisture, the desert is putting on one of the best displays of wildflowers in recent memory. Red, yellow, purple, and white blossoms are clearly visible along the roadsides leading into the state park.

When most people think of desert, they imagine an empty, desolate landscape. But the Arizona desert is home to nearly 3,000 plant species, and the cactus section within the park is the most beautiful portion of this desert. While still dry compared with non-desert areas, the cactus section enjoys a relatively abundant level of moisture in the form of summer storms that visit the area in a typical year. This moisture has allowed an impressive variety of desert to evolve a set of strategies for making the best use of available moisture available. For example, very few cactus plants have leaves that would encourage precious moisture to evaporate.

Our team of photographers had visited the desert weekly since the early bloom, which began in February. Now, in early March, we are beginning to see an amazing display of cacti in bloom. Rangers have reported seeing spectacular displays of blooms along the hiking trails at the south end of the park.

If you drive just past the ranger station, you'll see a flash of magenta on both sides of the road. This is the collection of Beavertail Cactus. The contrast of the rich color against the pale beige of the desert sand is almost surreal. One wonders how a flower so delicate and beautiful could survive in such a dry and extreme environment. It is precisely this juxtaposition of two extremes – harshness and delicacy –that makes this year's desert wildflower season so special.

The essence of Spring is everywhere. Along the southern edge of the cactus section, you can see colorful annuals peeking out of the sand. Lupine, Monkey Flowers, Spanish Needles and Phacelia are in great abundance this year.

Some visitors may expect traffic to be light in midweek, but news of this year's abundant display of flowers has attracted crowds. If you visit this month, you will see more fellow flower aficionados than you might have expected. Numbers will continue to rise, as April promises a show of colorful cactus blooms that will conclude this spectacular wildflower season.

Several other plants are found in the desert park, including the palo verde and the mesquite. The palo verde drops water during the summer months to save water. The mesquite is a ubiquitous plant in the desert and saves up water by collapsing its leaves during dry conditions. The roots of this plant seek

Figure 2-13: You don't have to go through Customs to import a graphic into a frame.

5. **If necessary to make the graphic fit, switch to the Direct Selection tool and highlight the Scale X Percentage field in the Control palette and enter a new scale, such as** 80%.

   The Scale Y Percentage field should change to the same value as long as the two fields are locked (a chain button appears to their right). If the chain is open (unlocked), click the button to lock the two fields.

   You can also resize the image to fit the frame by choosing Object➪Fitting➪Fit Content Proportionally (Option+Shift+⌘+E or Ctrl+Alt+Shift+E).

6. **Add a runaround to the image so text does not run through the image:**

   a. Choose Window➪Text Wrap or press Option+⌘+W or Ctrl+Alt+W to get the pane shown in Figure 2-14.

   b. Click the Wrap Around Bounding Box button (the second from the left) and set the wrap margins in the four fields (there's one for each side) to **0p6**.

7. **Import a logo graphic for the newsletter's top left frame and size it to fit, as shown in Figure 2-14.**

   It doesn't have to fill the whole width of that frame.

Figure 2-14: Set text wrap with the Text Wrap pane.

Creating Colors

To apply a color to an item or text, you first want to create that color. InDesign provides a few very basic colors: cyan, magenta, yellow, [Black], red, blue, green, [Paper] (white), [None], and [Registration]. (The names that InDesign puts in brackets are colors that cannot be deleted or modified.) In most cases, you create additional colors to suit your documents:

1. **To open the Swatches pane, where you create, modify, and apply colors, choose Window⇨Swatches or press F5.**

   In the following steps, we create a color based on a color in our imported logo.

2. **Select the Eyedropper tool and then click the background color in that logo.**

   The Park News logo shown in Figure 2-14 uses a beautiful moss green. Of course, in this black-and-white book all you see is a dull cubicle gray. Unless you're creating a "Welcome to Dullsville" newsletter, choose a vibrant, interesting color.

3. **Choose New Color Swatch from the pane's palette menu.**

4. **From the Color Mode pop-up menu, choose CMYK.**

   Doing this creates a color based on the four process colors widely used in commercial printing: cyan, magenta, yellow, and black.

   Because you selected a color with the Eyedropper tool, the New Color Swatch dialog box shows the values, as Figure 2-15 shows. If you had not first selected a color with the Eyedropper tool, you would enter values or slide the four sliders to select a desired color. If the Name with Color Value option is checked, InDesign will name the color automatically; if it is unchecked, you can give it a more memorable name, such as *Soylent Green.*

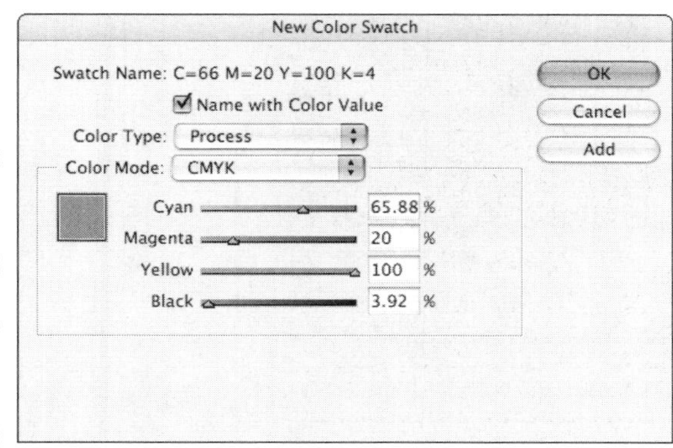

Figure 2-15: Creating Soylent Green in the New Color Swatch dialog box.

5. **Click OK to create the color and close the dialog box.**

   If you want to create more colors, click Add instead of OK. Click OK only when you want to close the dialog box.

Applying Colors

The InDesign Swatches palette, combined with the Tools palette, makes it easy to experiment with different colors. You can apply colors to frame backgrounds, lines, strokes, some imported images, and text.

1. **Be sure the Swatches pane is open (select Window⇨Swatches or press F5).**
2. **Using the Selection tool, select the two frames at the top of the page.**

   To select both, click one, then Shift+click the other.
3. **Make sure the Fill button is selected in the Tools palette, as it is in Figure 2-16.**

   This tells InDesign that you want to color the object, not any strokes it may have.

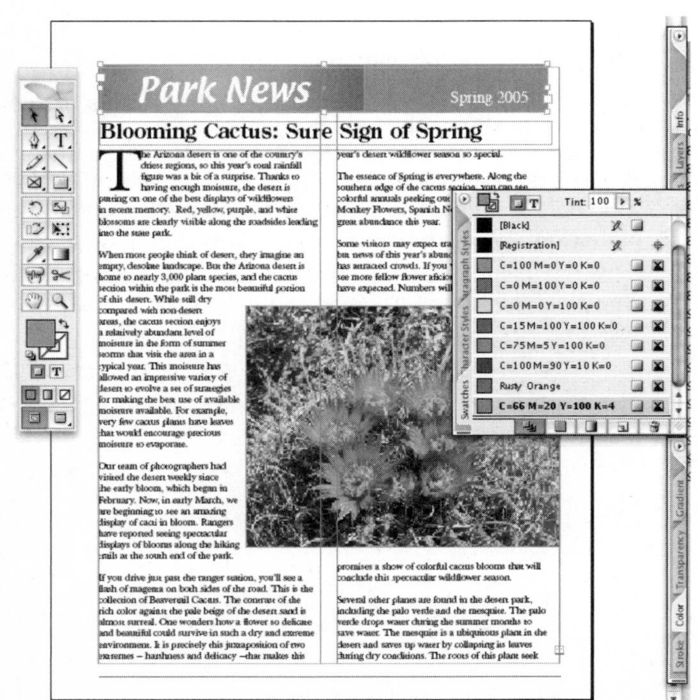

Figure 2-16: Click a color to give new life to a frame.

4. **Click the name of the color you want to use.**

   The selected frames will now fill with the color.

5. **Highlight the text *Spring 2005* in the upper-left frame.**

6. **Again ensuring that the Fill button is selected in the Tools palette, click the color [Paper] in the Swatches pane.**

   Clicking [Paper] makes the text white. You can also adjust the font and size of the text if you wish to, either through the Type menu or by using the Control palette.

7. **Choose File⇨Save or press ⌘+S or Ctrl+S to save your work.**

Printing a Composite

Whether you're designing a document for black-and-white photocopying, color printing, professional printing, or even for PDF, you need to review drafts.

1. **Choose File⇨Print or press ⌘+P or Ctrl+P.**

   If you press Return or Enter as soon as the Print dialog box appears, chances are that InDesign will print a usable draft on your printer. However, if you select a different page size, orientation, or other option, you might want to confirm the other settings.

2. **At the top of the dialog box, the Printer pop-up menu is usually set to your system's default printer.**

   You can leave this setting alone or locate and select the printer you're actually using.

3. **Go to the Output pane and make sure the Color pop-up menu is set to Composite Grayscale, if you're printing to a black-and-white laser printer, or to Composite CMYK, if you're printing to a color inkjet or laser printer.**

4. **Look at the page preview at the lower-left corner of the dialog box and make sure the page (you'll see this indicated by a light-gray rectangle) fits within the printer paper (indicated by the blue line), as shown in Figure 2-17.**

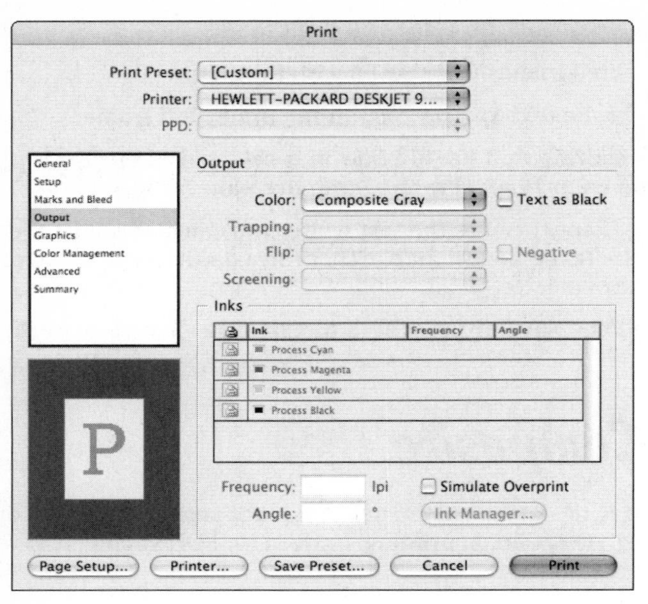

Figure 2-17: Confirm that your document fits on the paper and adjust the settings for your printer.

5. **Click Print.**

   You should end up with a printed version of your newsletter. Check to make sure that your colors printed out how you expected them to, and that all of the different page elements are in their correct places. If you find any problems, go back to your InDesign file and do some tweaking; then print yourself another copy and check it again.

For more information about printing, see Chapters 22 and 23.

Chapter 3

Understanding InDesign Ingredients

In This Chapter

- Discovering the document window
- Surveying the top tools
- Becoming familiar with tools, palettes, and panes

Starting to use a new software application is not unlike meeting a new friend for the first time. You take a long look at the person, maybe ask a few questions, and begin the process of becoming acquainted. Just as it's worthwhile to learn the likes and dislikes of a new friend, it's also worth your time to wrap your head around InDesign's unique style and approaches. Once you do so, you'll find it much easier to start using InDesign to get work done.

This chapter explains where to look in InDesign for the features and capabilities you need to master. We'll introduce you to the unique interface elements in the document window, survey the most commonly used tools, and explain how InDesign packages much of its functionality through an interface element called a *tabbed pane*.

Discovering the Document Window

In InDesign, you spend lots of time working in document windows — the "containers" for your documents. Each document, regardless of its size, is contained within its own document window.

The best way to get familiar with the InDesign document window is by opening a blank document. Simply choosing File⇨New⇨Document, or press ⌘+N or Ctrl+N, and click OK opens a new document window. Don't worry about the settings for now — just explore.

Figure 3-1 shows all the standard elements of a new document window. We won't bore you by covering interface elements that are standard to all programs. Instead, the rest of this section focuses on InDesign-specific elements.

The Version Cue pop-up menu lets you see the current status of a document in a shared workgroup setup. These are expert features you can ignore.

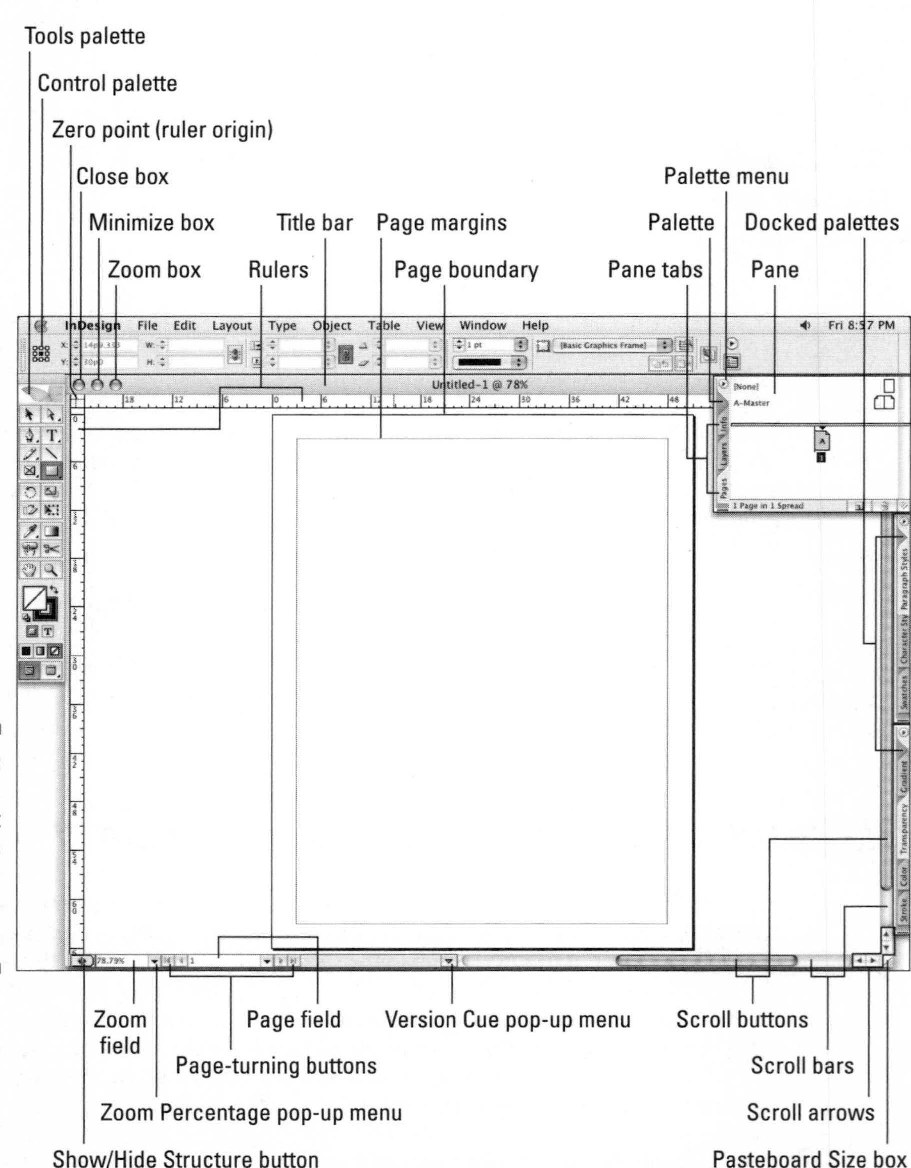

Figure 3-1: The document window is where you work on documents.

Rulers

Document windows display a horizontal ruler across the top and a vertical ruler down the left side. As shown in Figure 3-2, the horizontal ruler measures from the top-left corner of the page across the entire spread, and the vertical ruler measures from the top to the bottom of the current page. These rulers are handy for judging the size and placement of objects on a page. Even experienced designers often use the rulers while they experiment with a design.

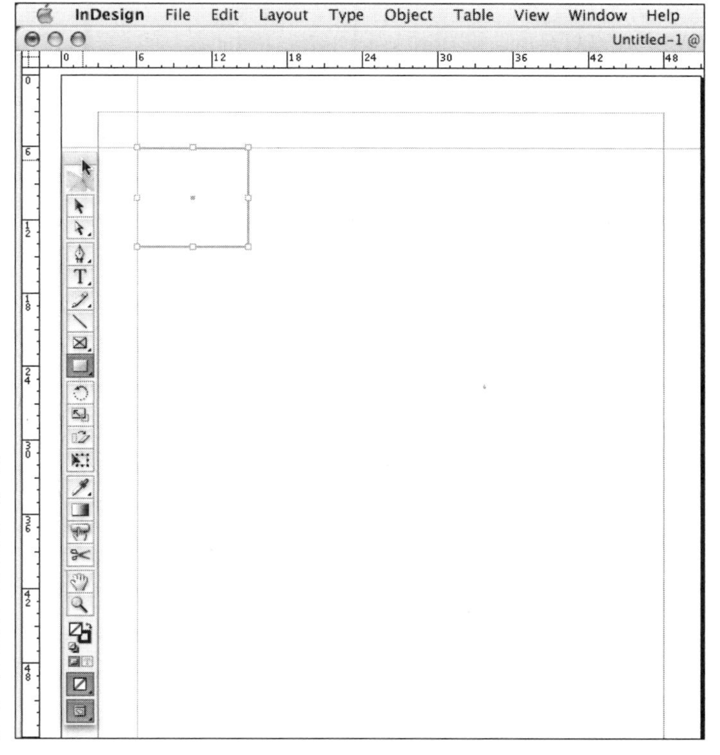

Figure 3-2: The horizontal and vertical rulers help you size and position boxes.

Both rulers display increments in picas unless you change the measurement system for each ruler in the Units & Increments pane of the Preferences dialog box. Choose InDesign⇨Preferences on the Mac or Edit⇨Preferences in Windows, or press ⌘+K or Ctrl+K to open the Preferences dialog box. Your choices include inches, points, decimal inches, ciceros, millimeters, and centimeters. If you change the ruler measurement system when no documents are open, the rulers in all new documents will use the measurement system you selected. If a document is open, the rulers are changed only in that document.

If your computer has a small monitor and the rulers start to get in your way, you can hide them by choosing View⇨Hide Rulers or by pressing ⌘+R or Ctrl+R.

Zero point

The point where the rulers intersect in the upper-left corner of the page is called *the zero point.* This is the starting place for all horizontal and vertical measurements. If you need to place items in relation to another spot on the page (for example, from the center of a spread rather than from the left-hand page), you can move the zero point by clicking and dragging it to a new location. Notice that the X: and Y: values in the Control palette update as you drag the zero point so you can place it precisely. If you change the zero point, it changes for all pages or spreads in the document. You can reset the zero point to the upper-left corner of the left-most page by double-clicking the intersection of the rulers in the upper-left corner.

If you move the zero point, all the objects on the page display new X: and Y: values even though they haven't actually moved. Objects above or to the left of the zero point will show negative X: and Y: values, and the X: and Y: values of other objects will not relate to their actual position on the page or spread.

You can lock the ruler origin (the zero point), making it more difficult to accidentally change it. Control+click or right-click the ruler origin and choose Lock Zero Point from the menu that appears. (The Unlock Zero Point command is right there as well, so you can just as easily unlock it.) Locking the zero point is a good idea because it will remind anyone working on your document that you prefer that they not fiddle with the zero point.

Pasteboard

The white area that surrounds the page is called the *pasteboard.* It is a workspace for temporarily storing objects. Above and below each page or spread is about an inch of pasteboard, and on the left and right a pasteboard space as wide as a page. For example, a spread of two 8-inch-wide pages will have 8 inches of pasteboard to the left and 8 inches of pasteboard to the right.

Pages and guides

Pages, which you can see onscreen surrounded by black outlines, reflect the page size you set up in the New Document dialog box (File⇨New⇨Document, or ⌘+N or Ctrl+N). If it looks like two or more pages are touching, you're looking at a *spread.*

InDesign uses nonprinting guides, lines that show you the position of margins and that help you position objects on the page. *Margins* are horizontal guides, and *columns* are vertical guides. Magenta lines across the top and bottom of each page show the document's top and bottom margins. Violet lines show left and right columns (for single-page documents) or inside and outside columns (for spreads).

You can change the location of guides by choosing Layout➪Margins and Columns, and you can create additional guides by holding down your mouse button on the horizontal or vertical ruler and then dragging a guide into the position you want.

Zoom field and pop-up menu

At the lower-left corner of the document window dwells the Zoom field, which shows the current zoom percentage. You can type in a new value any time. Immediately to its right is the Zoom pop-up menu that also lets you change the document's view. The view can be between 5 percent and 4,000 percent in 0.01-percent increments.

To change the view without taking your hands off the keyboard, press Option+⌘+5 or Ctrl+Alt+5, enter a new zoom value, and press Return or Enter. Or press ⌘+= or Ctrl+= to zoom in, or ⌘+– or Ctrl+– to zoom out.

Page controls

If you feel like flipping through pages of the document you are creating, InDesign makes it easy with page-turning buttons and the Page field and pop-up menu. Controls for entering prefixes for the page numbers of sections, and for indicating absolute page numbers in a document that contains multiple sections, are also handy. (An absolute page number indicates a page's position in the document, such as +1 for the first page, +2 for the second page, and so on.)

Next to the Zoom pop-up menu is a combined page-number field and pop-up menu encased by two sets of arrows. These arrows are page-turning buttons that take you to, from left to right, the first page, the previous page, the next page, and the last page. Just click an arrow to get where you want to go.

You can also jump directly to a specific page or master page. To jump to a specific page, highlight the current number in the page number field (by selecting it with your cursor, or by pressing ⌘+J or Ctrl+J), enter a new page number, and press Return or Enter. (To jump to a master page, select the Page Number field and enter the first few characters of the master page's name.)

Opening Multiple Document Windows

If you like to work on more than one project at once, you've come to the right program. InDesign lets you open several documents at once. It also lets you open multiple windows simultaneously for individual documents. A large monitor makes this multi-window feature even more useful. By opening multiple windows, you can:

- **Display two (or more) different pages or spreads at once.** You still have to work on the documents one at a time, but no navigation is required — you have only to click within the appropriate window.
- **Display multiple magnifications of the same page.** For example, you can work on a detail at high magnification in one window and display the entire page — and see the results of your detail work — at actual size in another window.
- **Display a master page in one window and a document page based on that master page in another window.** When you change the master page, the change is reflected in the window in which the associated document page is displayed.

To open a new window for the active document, choose Window➪Arrange➪New Window. The new window is displayed in front of the original window. To show both windows at once, choose Window➪Arrange➪Tile. When you choose the Tile command, all open windows are resized and displayed side by side. (If you choose Window➪Arrange➪Cascade, all open windows are displayed stacked and staggered on top of each other. The front-most document window is visible; the title bars of the other windows are visible above the front-most document.)

When multiple windows are open, you activate a window by clicking on a window's title bar or anywhere within the window. Also, the names of all open documents are displayed at the bottom of the Window menu. Choosing a document name from the View menu brings that document to the front. If multiple windows are open for a particular document, each window is displayed (they're displayed in the order in which you created them) in the Window menu.

To close all windows for the currently displayed document, press Shift+⌘+W or Ctrl+Shift+W. To close all windows for all open documents, press Option+Shift+⌘+W or Ctrl+Alt+Shift+W.

Tooling around the Tools Palette

You can move the InDesign Tools palette — the control center for InDesign's 30 tools and 13 additional functions — by clicking and dragging it into position. The Tools palette usually appears to the left of a document (see Figure 3-3).

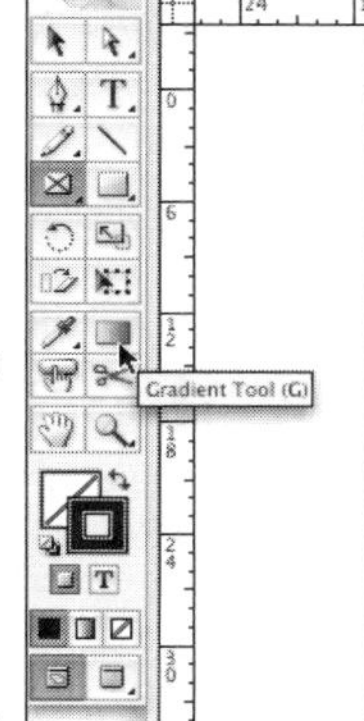

Figure 3-3: The InDesign Tools palette.

To discover each tool's "official" name, hover the mouse pointer over a tool for a few seconds, and a Tool Tip will appear, telling you the name of that tool (as shown with the Gradient tool in Figure 3-3). If the Tool Tips do not display, make sure that the Tool Tips pop-up menu is set to Normal or Fast in the General pane of the Preferences dialog box (choose InDesign➪Preferences on the Mac or Edit➪Preferences in Windows, or press ⌘+K or Ctrl+K).

InDesign gives you one — and only one — tool for each specific job. The Tools palette includes tools for creating and manipulating the objects that make up your designs. The tools in the Tools palette are similar to those in other Adobe products (such as Photoshop, Illustrator, and PageMaker). We cover what each tool does in the following sections.

The small arrow in its lower-right corner of some tools is a pop-out menu indicator. A tool that displays this arrow is hiding one or more similar tools. To access these "hidden" tools, click and hold a tool that has the pop-out menu indicator, as shown in Figure 3-4. When the pop-out displays, click one of the new tools.

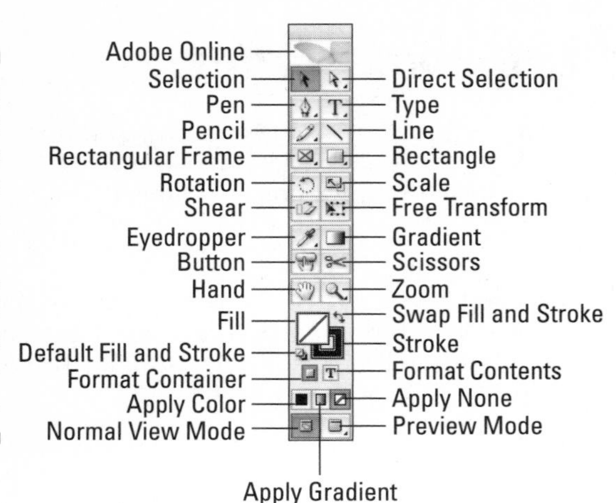

Figure 3-4: If a small triangle appears in the lower-right corner of a tool, click and hold it to display pop-out tools.

You don't need to worry about all the tools, so we highlight just those that you'll need to know to start using InDesign. You'll likely come across the others as you work on specific tasks, so we cover those in the chapters that introduce those functions. For example, you'll learn all about the Scissors tool in Chapter 21.

Using the Selection tools

To work with objects, you have to select them. InDesign provides three tools to do that, letting you select different aspects of objects.

Selection tool

This is perhaps the most-used tool in InDesign. With the Selection tool, you can select objects on the page and move or resize them. You might want to think of this tool as the Mover tool because it's the only tool that lets you drag objects around on-screen.

After you've selected the Selection tool, here's how it works:

- **To select any object on a document page,** click it. If you can't seem to select it, the object might be placed by a master page (a preformatted page used to format pages automatically), or the object might be behind another object.
- **To select an object placed by a master page,** press Shift+⌘ or Ctrl+Shift while you click.
- **To select an object that is completely behind another object,** ⌘+click it or Ctrl+click it.

Direct Selection tool

The Direct Selection tool is what you use to work on the contents of a frame, not the frame itself. For example, you can use the Direct Selection tool to select individual handles on objects to reshape them, or to move graphics within their frames.

Here's how the Direct Selection tool works:

- **To select an object to reshape it,** click the object to display anchor points on the edges (the anchor points are hollow handles that you can select individually, as shown in Figure 3-5). You can drag the anchor points to reshape the object.
- **To select objects placed by a master page,** Shift+⌘+click or Ctrl+Shift+click, as with the Selection tool. The Direct Selection tool lets you easily select objects behind other objects and to select items within groups.
- **To move a graphic within its frame,** click inside the frame and drag the graphic.
- **To move a frame but leave the graphic in place,** click an edge of the frame and drag it.

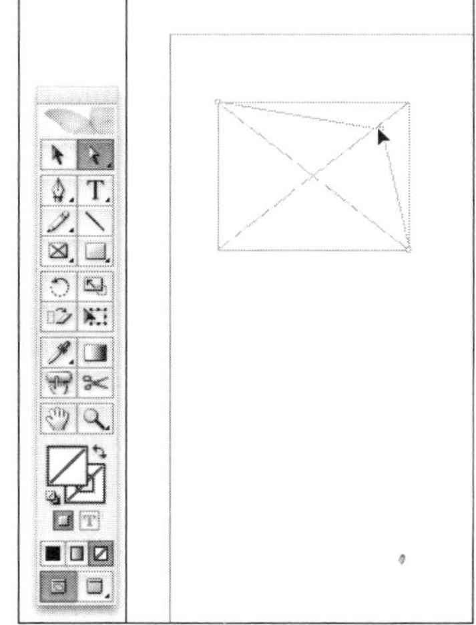

Figure 3-5: Reshape an item with the Direct Selection tool by clicking and dragging an anchor point.

Position tool

The InDesign CS2 Tools palette adds the Position tool, which acts like PageMaker's Crop tool.

The Position tool, which you access from the pop-out menu in the Direct Selection tool, combines some aspects of the Selection tool with some aspects of the Direct Selection tool:

- As with the Selection tool, you can resize an object's frame by dragging its handles.
- As with the Direct Selection tool, you can click a graphic and reposition it within the frame by dragging — and that has the effect of cropping the graphic.

Using the Type tool

A very frequently used tool, the Type tool lets you enter, edit, and format text. The Type tool also lets you create rectangular text frames.

Here's how the Type tool works:

- **To create a rectangular text frame,** click and drag; hold the Shift key to create a perfect square.
- **To begin typing or editing text,** click in a text frame or in any empty frame and type away.

  We discuss stories and threaded text frames in Chapter 14.

Using the object-creation tools

InDesign has a bunch of tools for creating shapes. Part V covers them in more depth, but you should know about a few of them now, since they create objects that can contain either text or graphics. Plus, you can also use them to draw your own shapes that you then color or otherwise embellish in your layout.

Pen tool

With the Pen tool, you can create simple illustrations. You use the Pen tool, which is modeled after the pen tools in Illustrator and Photoshop, to create paths (both open, such as lines, and closed, such as shapes) consisting of straight and curved segments. Give it a try — it's fun!

Here's how the Pen tool works:

- **To create straight lines,** click to establish an anchor point, then move the mouse to the next location, click again, and so on. To move an anchor point after clicking, press the spacebar and drag the anchor point.
- **To create curved lines,** click and drag, then release the mouse button to end the segment.

- **To close a path and create a frame,** click the first anchor point created (the hollow one).
- **To leave a path open and create a line,** ⌘+click or Ctrl+click away from the path or select another tool.

Type tool

The Type tool lets you draw rectangular text frames, as well as type text inside them.

Line tool

The Line tool lets you draw freestanding lines (rules) on your page. After selecting this tool, simply click and drag the mouse to draw the line. Holding the Shift key while you click and drag constrains the line angle to 45-degree increments, which is useful for creating straight horizontal and vertical lines.

Frame and shape tools

InDesign has three frame tools — Rectangle Frame, Ellipse Frame, and Polygon Frame — and three shape tools — Rectangle, Ellipse, and Polygon. The frame and shape tools are redundant, since both frames and shapes can hold text or graphics or be empty.

To create a rectangle or ellipse, choose the appropriate tool and click somewhere in the document window and drag the mouse to another location. The rectangle or ellipse fills the area. But creating a polygon works differently:

1. **Double-click the Polygon or Polygon Frame tool to display the Polygon Settings dialog box,** shown in Figure 3-6.
2. **Enter a value between 3 and 100 in the Number of Sides field** to specify the number of sides on your polygon.
3. **To create a star shape,** use the Star Inset field to specify the size of the spikes.

   The percent value specifies the distance between the polygon's bounding box and the insides of the spikes (for example, entering **50%** creates spikes that are halfway between the bounding box and the center of the polygon).
4. **Click OK to close the Polygon Settings dialog box.**

   The settings are saved with the active document for the next time you use the Polygon or Polygon Frame tool.
5. **Click and drag to create the polygon,** using the rulers or the Transform pane or Control palette to judge the size and placement. To create a symmetrical polygon, in which all the sides are the same size, press the Shift key while you click and drag the Polygon or Polygon Frame tool.

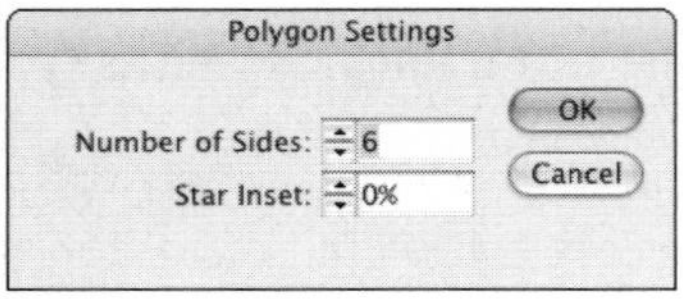

Figure 3-6: Double-clicking the Polygon or Polygon Frame tool displays the Polygon Settings dialog box, which you can use to specify the number of sides on a polygon.

Using the navigation tools

Hand tool

The Hand tool lets you move a page around to view different portions of it or another page entirely. After selecting the Hand tool, click and drag in any direction. You can access the Hand tool temporarily without actually switching tools by pressing Option+spacebar or Alt+Spacebar.

Zoom tool

With the Zoom tool, you increase and decrease the document view scale. You can highlight a specific area on a page to change its view or you can click onscreen to change the view scale within InDesign's preset increments, which is the same as pressing ⌘+= or Ctrl+= to zoom in.

View buttons

The very bottom of the Tools palette has two view buttons: Normal View Mode and Preview Mode. The first shows the document's pasteboard, margins, and guidelines; the second hides those so you can get a better idea of how the document will look when it's printed or saved as a PDF.

A pop-up menu in the Preview Mode button has two preview options: Bleed mode and Slug mode. Bleed mode shows any objects that bleed (extend) beyond the page boundaries, while Slug mode shows the space reserved for information such as crop marks and color separation names used in final output. You can read more about these in Chapters 5 and 6. You set these options when you create new documents or by choosing File⇨Document Setup.

Using contextual menus

InDesign's contextual menu interface element is very useful. By Control+clicking or right-clicking the document, an object, the rulers, and so on, you can display a menu of options for modifying whatever it is you clicked. InDesign provides a lot of options this way, and it is often easier to use the contextual menus to access InDesign functions than to hunt through the many regular menu options and panes.

Working with Panes and Palettes

Both panes and palettes are "windows" of options to consider when working in InDesign. Palettes — often made up of multiple panes — provide an interactive method of working with features, one that lets you access the controls quickly. In many cases, palettes offer the only method for performing many tasks.

Is it a pane? Is it a palette?

InDesign's palettes usually contain two or more panes. Each pane has a tab; to select a pane, click its tab. To better suit your working style, you can drag panes from one palette to another, as well as to anywhere on-screen (creating a new palette with just the one pane). That makes the distinction between a palette and a pane somewhat artificial. In this book, we use *palette* to refer to the entity that holds one or more panes, or for entities like the Tools and Control palettes that are self-contained floating objects. We use *panes* as anything that can be made a pane, even if you might have made it into its own palette (for example, we still call the Transform pane *the Transform pane,* even if we move it into its own palette).

Almost every palette (whether it contains one pane or many panes) has a palette menu, which provides a pop-up menu of options specific to that pane. The palette menu's options are specific to the current pane.

As if the distinction between pane and palette wasn't obscure enough, the word *pane* has another use in InDesign. A pane is also a specific area in a dialog box. Such multipane dialog boxes also have tabs (and in some cases, option lists) that let you switch among the panes. Having multiple panes in a dialog box lets Adobe fit more functionality into the same space on-screen.

You can tell that the developers of InDesign have a passion for panes. Because there are so many of them, you might want to consider hooking up a second monitor for displaying them. As with the tools, if you make sure Tool Tips are enabled in the General pane of the Preferences dialog box (choose InDesign⇨Preferences or press ⌘+K on the Mac, or choose Edit⇨Preferences or Ctrl+K in Windows), you'll get some ideas as to what the pane icons and fields do.

InDesign CS2 adds the PageMaker Toolbar palette, the Quick Apply palette, Object Styles pane, and the Data Merge pane.

Managing palettes and panes

To further confuse you, InDesign has two kinds of palettes: docked and floating. Docked palettes appear at the left or right side of the monitor window; double-clicking a tab in the palette will expand or minimize the palette, depending on whether the palette is already expanded or not. Floating palettes can be anywhere on your screen. You open them by choosing them from the Window menu or, for those that have them, typing their keyboard shortcuts. You close palettes and panes by clicking the Close box (in the upper-left corner on the Mac and in the upper-right corner in Windows).

Whether docked or floating, InDesign's palettes can be rearranged to suit your needs:

- **To combine the panes of different palettes,** drag and drop a pane's tab into another palette.
- **To pull a pane out of a palette into its own,** drag and drop its tab out of the palette into its own palette.

To manage InDesign's palettes, you can create workspaces, which are essentially memorized palette collections. You can create different combinations of panes to customize the palettes. Display the palettes you want, where you want them, and create a new workspace by choosing Window⇨Workspace⇨Save Workspace. Give the workspace a name that makes sense, such as Text Palettes. That workspace is now available via Window⇨Workspace⇨*workspace name,* automatically displaying just those saved palettes in their saved locations. By having several such workspaces, you can quickly switch among collections of palettes based on what you're working on.

A few palettes contain arrows in the lower-right corner that you can drag to resize the palette. Some palette menus let you change the orientation of the palette from horizontal to vertical. A few palettes also use a double-arrow character next to the pane name to indicate that there is more to the pane than may be displayed; click the pane title to expand or collapse those extra options.

Unless you have a wall-sized monitor, you probably won't have all the palettes open at all times. As you become familiar with the palettes, you'll discover which ones you want to keep open.

Using panes

To use a pane, first you need to activate it by clicking its tab (if the palette containing it is open) or by choosing its menu command in the Window menu (if the pane is not open or if another pane in that palette is active).

When a pane is active, controls in panes have the following characteristics:

- **To display and select an option,** click a pop-up menu; the changes take effect immediately.
- **To place a new value in a field,** highlight the value that's already in the field and enter the new value. Note that fields accept values in all different measurement systems (see Chapter 3). To implement the new value, press Shift+Return or Shift+Enter. To get out of a field you've modified, leaving the object unchanged, press Esc.
- **To increase or decrease the value in the field** use the clickable up and down arrows (available for some fields).
- **To use math to perform changes,** enter calculations in the field. You can add, subtract, multiply, and divide values in fields by using the following operators: +, –, * (multiply), and / (divide). For example, to reduce the width of a frame by half, type **/2** after to the current value in the Width field. Or, to increase the length of a line by 6 points, you can type **+6** next to the current value in the Length field. You can also use percentages in fields, such 50%, which adjusts the current value by that percentage.
- **To display a pane's full menu**, click the arrow in the upper-right corner of a floating pane and in the upper-left of a docked pane. The palette menu provides commands related to the current pane's contents. Most panes include palette menus that provide access to related features (see Figure 3-7).

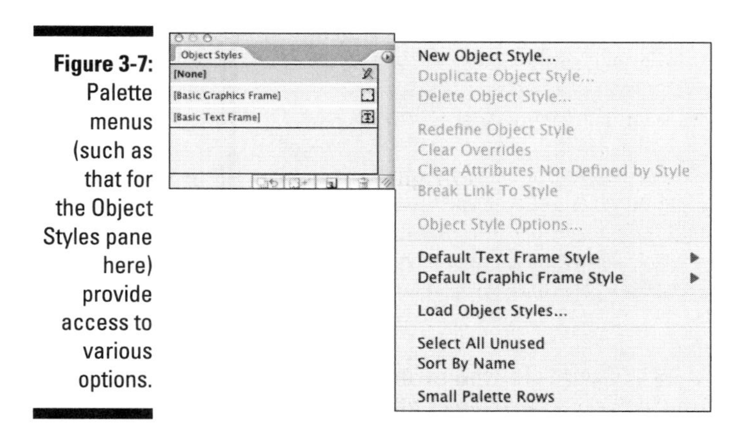

Figure 3-7: Palette menus (such as that for the Object Styles pane here) provide access to various options.

Chapter 4

Making It Work Your Way

In This Chapter

- Setting document preferences
- Setting measurement standards
- Changing text and object defaults
- Working with view defaults
- Setting color and style defaults

Giving credit where credit is due, we can safely say that the nice people who created InDesign did their best. They put their smart heads together and made educated guesses about how most people would like to work and, in doing so, established defaults for various settings in the program. When you're just starting out, it's not a bad idea to simply stick with the default settings and see how they work for you. But after you become more familiar with InDesign and start putting it through its paces, you can change default preferences, views, and measurements, making them better suited to your way of working.

Preferences are program settings that dictate how InDesign will act in certain instances. InDesign provides extensive preference settings for everything from how objects appear on-screen to how text is managed for spelling and hyphenation.

Setting InDesign to work your way is easy, and this chapter explains how. And we promise not to numb you by covering every single option. Instead, we focus on just those preferences you are likely to change. As for the rest, feel free to explore their effects once you've gotten more comfortable using InDesign. (And in other chapters, we'll sometimes recommend specific preferences changes for the specific actions explained there.)

InDesign stores some preferences in the documents that govern how the document works as you work on it, or as it is transferred to other users. Other preference settings reside on your computer. Knowing how InDesign manages preferences is important if you share preferences with others or want to make sure that all your documents are updated with a new preference setting.

Setting Document Preferences

Preferences are settings that affect an entire document — such as what measurement system you use on rulers, what color the guides are, and whether substituted fonts are highlighted. To access these settings, open the Preferences dialog box by choosing InDesign⇨Preferences or pressing ⌘+K on the Mac, or by choosing Edit⇨Preferences or pressing Ctrl+K in Windows.

The Type and Advanced Type panes are new, splitting the options from the old Text pane. The Appearance of Black pane takes the Print Options section from the old General pane and adds additional control. The Autocorrect pane is new to InDesign CS2. The Updates pane has gone away, and its settings are now handled by clicking the Preferences button in the Updates dialog box (Help⇨Updates).

InDesign has two methods for changing preferences: You can change preferences when no documents are open to create new settings for all future documents, or you can change preferences for the active document, which affects only that document.

When you open the Preferences dialog box, InDesign automatically opens the General pane, as shown in Figure 4-1. To access one of the other 13 preferences panes, just click its name from the list at the left of the dialog box. After you've changed the desired preferences settings, just click OK to save those settings.

You cannot reverse changes to preferences by using the Undo command (Edit⇨Undo or ⌘+Z or Ctrl+Z). If you change your mind about a preference setting, reopen the Preferences dialog box and change the setting again.

Type preferences

The Type pane of the Preferences dialog box, shown in Figure 4-2, includes settings that affect character formats, controls whether you use typographer's quotes, and manages how text appears on-screen. You're likely to adjust these settings, so let's go through the main ones.

- If Use Typographer's Quotes is checked, InDesign inserts the correct typographer's quotes (often called *curly quotes*) for the current language in use whenever you use quotation marks. For example, for U.S. English, InDesign inserts typographic single quotes (‘ ’) or double quotes (“ ”) rather than straight quotes. For French, InDesign inserts guillemets (« »).
- Check Triple Click to Select a Line if you want to be able to select an entire line of text by triple-clicking it.
- When the Adjust Text Attributes When Scaling box is checked, InDesign changes text size and proportional scaling when you resize the text box or path that contains the text. If this box is unchecked, the text formatting is

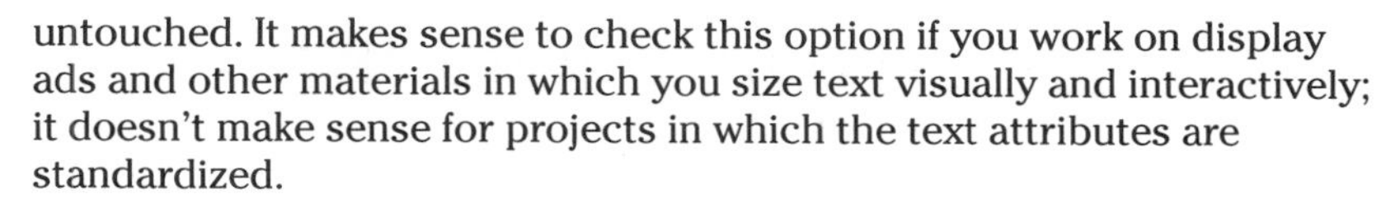

untouched. It makes sense to check this option if you work on display ads and other materials in which you size text visually and interactively; it doesn't make sense for projects in which the text attributes are standardized.

- When the Apply Leading to Entire Paragraph box is checked, leading changes apply to the entire paragraph, as opposed to the current line. In most cases, you want the leading to be applied to all paragraphs, so it's a good idea to check this box.

- Adjust Spacing Automatically When Cutting and Pasting Words, which is checked by default, will add or delete spaces around words when you cut and paste.

- When Font Preview Size is checked, menus let you preview in your font choice before you actually select it. The pop-up menu at right of the check box lets you select the size of the preview.
- The options in the Drag and Drop Text Editing section of the Type pane control whether you can drag and drop text selections within a document. By default, Enable in Story Editor is checked and Enable in Layout View is unchecked, which means that you can drag and drop text in the Story Editor but not when working on a layout. You'll probably want to check them both.
- The When Pasting Text and Tables from Other Applications area lets you choose how formatting is handled when you paste textual objects from other applications. The default is Text Only, which means that you want copied text to assume the formatting of the destination location's text in InDesign. The All Information option retains the original formatting when you copy the text into InDesign.

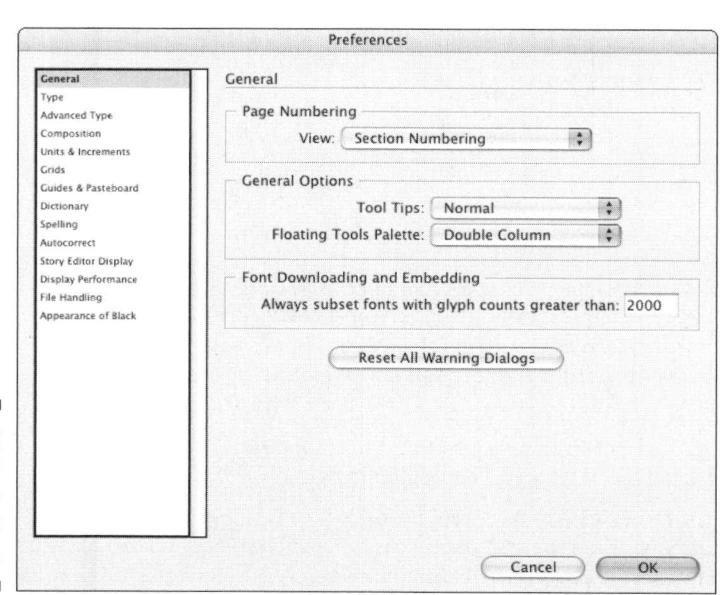

Figure 4-1: The General pane of the Preferences dialog box.

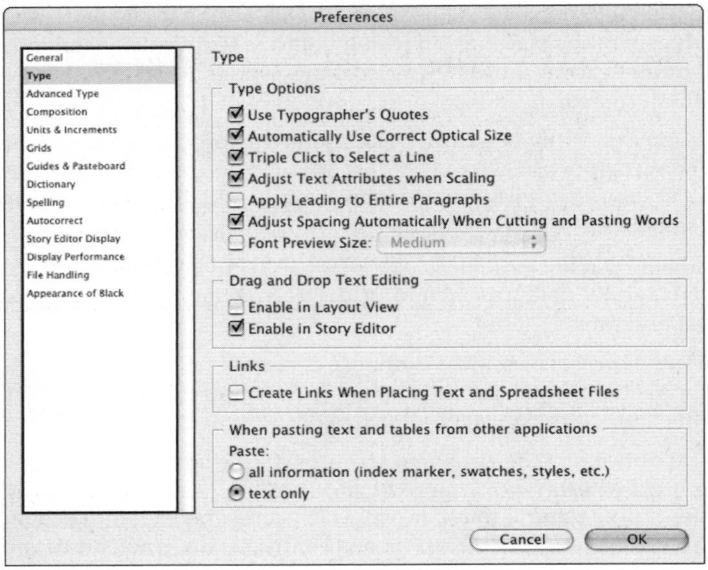

Figure 4-2: The Type pane of the Preferences dialog box.

The Advanced Type pane includes additional typographic settings, as Figure 4-3 shows.

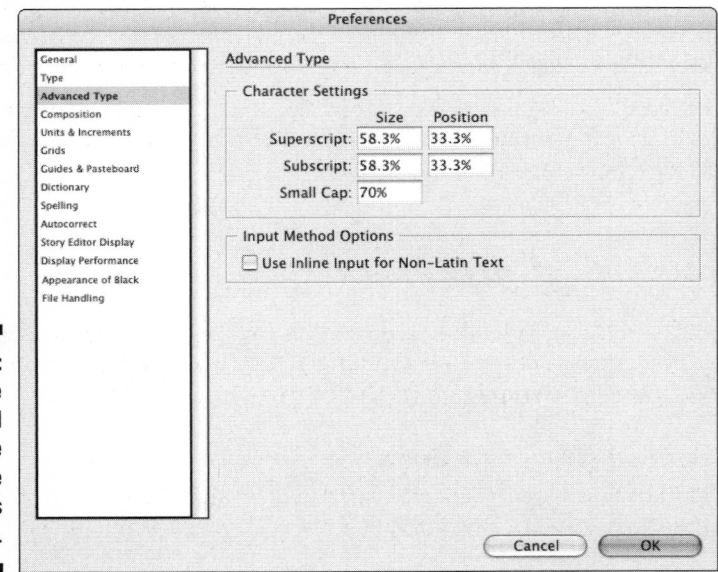

Figure 4-3: The Advanced Type pane of the Preferences dialog box.

Working with stored preferences

Some preferences in InDesign are stored in files that you can share with other users, so the preferences can be consistently used in a workgroup. These include keyboard shortcut sets, color swatch libraries, document setups, workspaces, and scripts.

These types of preferences are called *presets,* and the files that store them reside in the Presets folder within the InDesign application folder. When you save a preset, InDesign automatically updates the presets file. You can then copy that preset file to another user's Presets folder.

In the Character Settings section of the Advanced Type pane, you control precisely how superscript, subscript, and small-caps characters are placed and sized:

- The Size fields let you specify the percentages to which superscript and subscript characters are reduced (or even enlarged). The default is 58.3 percent, but you can enter a value between 1 and 200 percent. We prefer 60 or 65 percent, depending on the type size and font.
- The Position fields let you specify how much to shift superscript characters up and subscript characters down. The default is 33.3 percent, but you can enter a value between –500 and 500 percent. We prefer 30 percent for subscripts and 35 percent for superscripts. Note that negative values move text in the opposite directions: down for superscripts and up for subscripts. The percentage is relative to the top of a lowercase letter (the *x height*) for superscripts and to the baseline for subscripts.
- The Small Cap field lets you specify the scale of Small Caps characters in relation to the actual capital letters in the font. The default is 70 percent, but you can enter a value between 1 and 200 percent.

Composition preferences

Preferences in the Composition pane, shown in Figure 4-4, do two things: highlight potential problems on-screen while you're working, and establish the behavior of text wrap in certain situations.

Highlighting potential problems

The Highlight check boxes control whether InDesign calls attention to possible typesetting problems by drawing a highlighter pen effect behind the text:

- Keep Violations, which is unchecked by default, highlights the last line in a text frame when it cannot follow the rules specified in the Keep Options dialog box in the Paragraph pane's palette menu (Window⇨Type & Tables⇨Paragraph, or Option+⌘+T or Ctrl+Alt+T), as explained in Chapter 17. For example, if the Keep Options settings require at least three lines of text in the text frame, but only two lines fit and thus bump all the text in a frame to the next text frame in the chain, the Keep Options rules are violated, and the last line of text is highlighted.

- When H&J Violations is checked, InDesign uses three shades of yellow (the darker the shade, the worse the problem) to mark lines that might be too loose or too tight due to the combination of spacing and hyphenation settings. (H&J refers to hyphenation and justification.) Chapter 17 covers this, too.
- Custom Tracking/Kerning, if checked, highlights custom tracking and kerning (essentially, anywhere you overrode the defaults) in a bluish green. Chapter 16 covers kerning and tracking in more detail.
- Substituted Fonts, which is checked by default, uses pink highlights in pink to indicate characters in fonts that are not available and thus for which InDesign has substituted a different font. For output purposes, it's important that you have the correct fonts, so you probably want to leave this checked.
- Substituted Glyphs highlights, in pink, any glyphs (special characters) that were substituted. This usually occurs when you have multiple versions of the same font, with different special characters in each version. For example, a file that uses the euro (€) currency symbol might have been created in the newest version of a font, but a copy editor working on the same file may have an older version of the font that is missing the euro symbol.

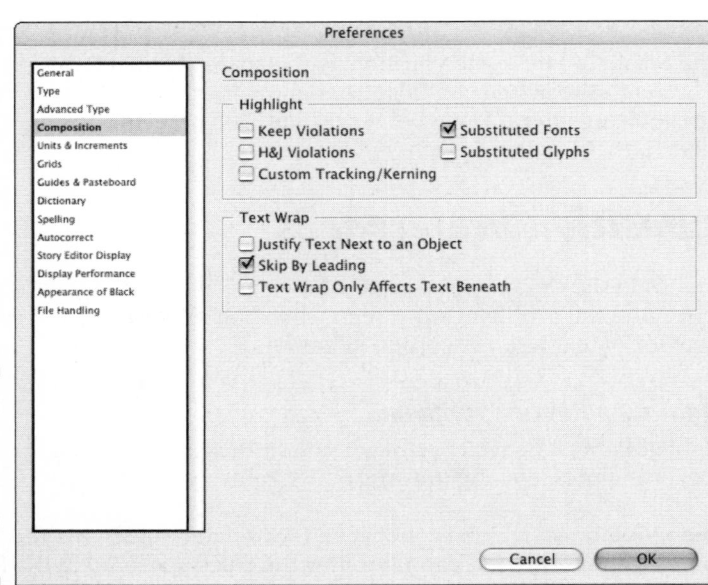

Figure 4-4: The Composition pane of the Preferences dialog box.

Setting text-wrap rules

The three options in the Text Wrap area affect how text flows (wraps) around images and other frames:

- Selecting the Justify Text Next to an Object check box overrides any local justification settings to make text wrapping around an object justified. That means the text will smoothly follow the object's shape, rather than keep any ragged margins that can make the wrap look strange. This option comes into play when you wrap ragged (left-aligned or right-aligned) text around objects.
- Skip by Leading, if checked, uses the text's leading to determine how much space follows an object around which text wraps. This has an effect is used only if you choose the Jump Object text-wrap option in the Text Wrap pane (Window➪Text Wrap, or Option+⌘+W or Ctrl+Alt+W).
- Text Wrap Only Affects Text Beneath, if checked, causes only text below (behind) an object to wrap around that object.

Chapter 18 covers text wrap in detail.

Measurement preferences

The Units & Increments pane, shown in Figure 4-5, is where you choose the measurement systems for positioning items.

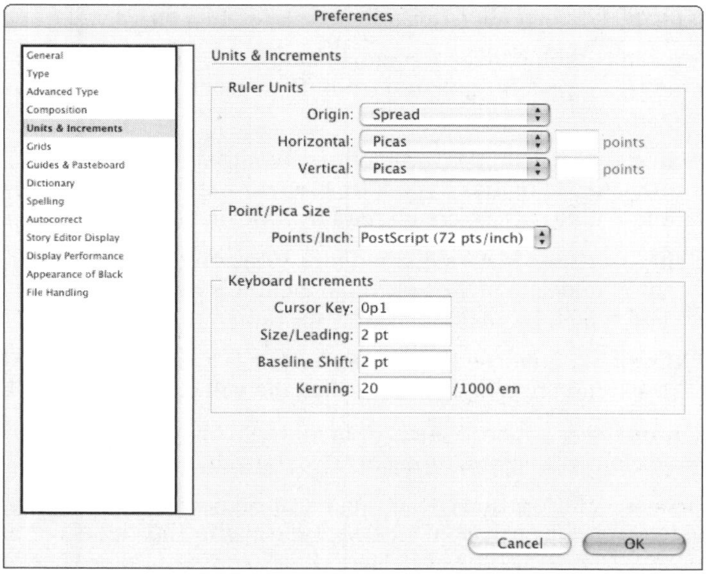

Figure 4-5: The Units & Increments pane of the Preferences dialog box.

Ruler Units area

The Ruler Units area affects three things: the zero point (by page, by spread, or by the spine), the measurement system displayed on the horizontal and vertical rulers in the document window, and the default values in fields used for positioning objects.

The Origin pop-up menu determines the zero point (typically, the upper-left corner of the page) for object positions. If you choose Page, the positions of objects are relative to each page's upper-left corner. If you choose Spread, the positions of objects are relative to the current spread's upper-left corner. If you choose Spine, objects' positions are relative to the binding spine of each spread — the very top and center of where the two pages meet.

With the Vertical and Horizontal pop-up menus, you specify one measurement system for the horizontal ruler and measurements, and the same or different measurement system for the vertical ruler and measurements. For example, you might use points for horizontal measurements and inches for vertical measurements.

To specify the measurement systems you want to use, choose an option from the Horizontal pop-up menu and from the Vertical pop-up menu. You have the following options:

- **Points:** A typesetting measurement equal to $\frac{1}{72}$ of an inch (or $\frac{1}{12}$ of a pica). To enter values in points, type a **p** before the value or **pt** after the value (for example, **p6** or **6 pt**).
- **Picas:** A typesetting measurement equal to $\frac{1}{6}$ of an inch. To enter values in picas, type a **p** after the value (for example, **6p**).

  You can combine measurements using both picas and points. Keeping in mind that 1 pica is equal to 12 points, you can enter 1$\frac{1}{2}$ picas as either **1.5p** or **1p6**.

- **Inches:** An English measurement system that is divided into 16ths. To enter values in inches, type **i**, **in**, **inch**, or **"** after the value. For example, **3i**, **3in**, **3 inch**, and **3"** are all read by InDesign as "3 inches."
- **Inches decimal:** Inches divided into 10ths on the ruler rather than 16ths. To enter values in inches decimal, include a decimal point as appropriate and type **i**, **in**, **inch**, or **"** after the value.
- **Millimeters:** A metric measurement that is $\frac{1}{10}$ of a centimeter. To enter values in millimeters, type **mm** after the value. For example, **14mm**.
- **Centimeters:** A metric measurement that is about $\frac{1}{3}$ of an inch. To enter values in centimeters, type **cm** after the value. For example, **2.3cm**.
- **Ciceros:** A European typesetting measurement that is slightly larger than a pica. To enter values in ciceros, type **c** after the value. For example, **2c**.

Typographic terminology 101

Publishing tools like InDesign use specialized terms, some of which appear in the Preferences dialog box:

- **Baseline:** This term refers to the invisible line that text sits on in each line. Except for a few characters like *g* and *p* that poke below it, all characters rest on this baseline.
- **Kerning:** This refers to an adjustment of the space between two letters. You kern letters to accommodate their specific shapes. For example, you probably would use tighter kerning in the letter pair *to* than in *oo* because *to* looks better if the *o* fits partly under the cross of the *t*.
- **Leading:** This term, also called line spacing, refers to the space from one baseline to another.
- **Tracking:** Tracking determines the overall space between letters within a word.

- **Custom:** This option lets you set a customer number of points as your measurement unit, placing a labeled tick mark at every point increment you specify. You get to customize the number of tick marks between the labeled marks by entering a value in the Points field. For example, if you enter **12** in the field, you get a tick mark at each pica because there are **12** points in a pica.

Keyboard Increments area

This area lets you customize the way the keyboard arrow keys work. You can use the arrow keys to move selected objects right, left, up, or down. You can also use the arrow keys and other keyboard shortcuts to change some text formatting. The options are:

- **Cursor Key field:** When you select an object with the Selection tool or the Direct Selection tool, you can move it up, down, left, or right by using the arrow keys on the keyboard. By default, the item moves 1 point with each key press. You can change the increment to a value between 0 (which would be useless) and 8p4 (1.3888 inches). If you use a document grid, you might change the increment to match the grid lines.
- **Size/Leading field:** The value in this field specifies by how many points the leading or font size is increased or decreased when done with keyboard commands. You can enter a value between 0.001 and 100 (the default is 2).
- **Baseline Shift field:** To shift the baseline of highlighted text up or down, you can click in the Baseline Shift field on the Character pane, then click the up or down arrow on the keyboard. The default for the Baseline Shift increment value is 2 points, which you can change to any value between 0.001 and 100.

- **Kerning field:** To kern text with keyboard commands, you position the cursor between two letters and then Option+press or Alt+press the right arrow button to increase kerning or the left arrow to decrease kerning. By default, each click changes kerning by 1⁄50 of an em. You can change this value to anything between 1 and 100.

Document defaults

InDesign also lets you change the default page size, margins, and columns in new documents; the default attributes of guides; and the way layouts are adjusted. You don't modify these settings in the Preferences dialog box; instead, to modify document defaults, first make sure that no documents are open and then choose the following:

- **File⇨Document Setup (Option+⌘+P or Ctrl+Alt+P).** The Document Setup dialog box lets you change the default settings in the New Document dialog box for the Number of Pages, Page Size, Facing Pages, and Master Text Frame, as well as for bleeds and slugs if you click the More Options button.
- **Layout⇨Margins and Columns.** The Margins and Columns dialog box lets you change the default settings in the New Document dialog box for the Margins and Columns areas.
- **Layout⇨Ruler Guides.** This opens the Ruler Guides dialog box where you adjust the View Threshold and Color for all new guides.
- **Layout⇨Layout Adjustment.** The Layout Adjustment dialog box lets you resize entire layouts and modify how they are resized.

If you are unhappy with the preferences and defaults you have established, you can revert InDesign to all its default settings. To revert all preferences and defaults, press Control+Option+Shift+⌘ or Ctrl+Alt+Shift when launching InDesign.

Modifying Defaults for Text and Objects

When you create a new document, start typing, or create a new object, your work conforms to default settings. You can change these settings. For example, by default, a new document is always letter-sized, but if you design only posters, you can change the default.

You may need to work with InDesign for a while to figure out which settings you prefer. When you identify a problem — for example, you realize that you always end up changing the inset for text frames — jot down a note about it or close all documents right then. When no documents are open, change the setting for all future documents.

Text defaults

When you start typing in a new text frame, the text is formatted with default Character formats, Paragraph formats, and Story attributes. You can also choose to show invisible characters such as spaces and tabs by default; otherwise you need to manually activate character visibility in each text-heavy document. To modify text defaults:

- **Choose default options for character formats** such as Font Family, Font Size, and Leading from the Character pane. Choose Type⇨Character (⌘+T or Ctrl+T).
- **Choose defaults for paragraph formats,** such as alignment, indents, spacing, and so on, from the Paragraph pane. Choose Type⇨Paragraph (Option+⌘+T or ⌘+M, or Ctrl+Alt+T or Ctrl+M).
- **Choose defaults for the [Basic Paragraph] style**, which is what all unstyled imported text, as well as text entered in a new text frame in InDesign, will use. Choose Type⇨Paragraph Styles (F11).
- **Activate Optical Margin Alignment.** Choose Type⇨Story. This adjusts the left position of characters along the left margin to make the left edges look more pleasing, by letting the top of a *T*, for example, hang slightly to the left of the margin, even if that means the characters aren't strictly aligned. (Since optical margin alignment works best for display type rather than body type, it's unlikely that you'll activate optical margin alignment as your default setting.)
- **Show Hidden Characters** is a good thing to activate if you always end up turning on Show Hidden Characters when you are editing a document. Choose Type⇨Show Hidden Characters (⌘+Option+I or Ctrl+Alt+I).

InDesign versus Exposé: End the conflict

The Mac OS X Exposé utility usurps three commonly used InDesign shortcuts: F10 (which opens the Stroke pane), F11 (which opens the Paragraph Styles pane), and F12 (which opens the Pages pane). Exposé provides a quick way to change your display of windows on-screen, but its usage of keyboard shortcuts long employed by other programs is annoying.

We recommend that you change Exposé shortcuts to ones that won't interfere with InDesign and other programs. To change the shortcuts, open the System Preferences dialog box (⇨System Preferences), double-click the Exposé button, and change or disable the Exposé shortcuts in the Keyboard section of the Exposé dialog box.

Object defaults

When you create new objects, they're based on default settings. For example, you can specify how text wraps around objects. To modify object defaults, use the following commands:

- **Specify the default Columns, Inset Spacing, First Baseline, and Ignore Text Wrap settings** for new text frames using the Text Frame Options dialog box. Choose Object⇨Text Frame Options (⌘+B or Ctrl+B).
- **Choose defaults for the [Normal Graphics Frame] and [Normal Text Frame] styles,** which are what all new frames created in InDesign will use. Choose Window⇨Object Styles (⌘+F7 or Ctrl+F7).
- **Specify how text will wrap around all new objects.** Choose Window⇨Text Wrap (⌘+Option+W or Ctrl+Alt+W).
- **Choose a style for the corners of all new frames except those created with the Type tool.** Choose Object⇨Corner Effects (⌘+Option+R or Ctrl+Alt+R).
- **Specify the default attributes of clipping paths imported into graphics frames.** Choose Object⇨Clipping Path (Option+Shift+⌘+K or Ctrl+Alt+Shift+K).
- **Specify other default properties of objects.** For example, if all objects you create are stroked (framed), specify a weight in the Stroke pane. Choose Window⇨Stroke (F10), Window⇨Swatches (F5), Window⇨Gradient (F6), or Window⇨Attributes.
- **Specify the default number of sides and the inset for the first new polygon in a new document.** Double-click the Polygon or Polygon Frame tool to open the Polygon Settings dialog box (there is no menu command or keyboard shortcut).

Modifying Defaults for Views

You can also control which layout tools display by default. Selections in the View menu let you do this. If you prefer not to view the edges of frames, you can hide them by default. Or if you always want to start with a document-wide grid (see Chapter 11), you can show that by default. Other defaults you can modify in the View menu include:

- **Show the links between text frames.** Choose View⇨Show Text Threads (Option+⌘+Y or Ctrl+Alt+Y).
- **Hide the edges of frames.** Choose View⇨Hide Frame Edges (⌘+H or Ctrl+H).

- **Hide the horizontal and vertical ruler.** Choose View⇨Hide Rulers (⌘+R or Ctrl+R).
- **Hide margin, column, and layout guides.** View⇨Grids & Guides⇨Hide Guides (⌘+; [semicolon] or Ctrl+; [semicolon]).
- **Show the baseline grid established in the Grids pane of the Preferences dialog box.** Choose View⇨Grids & Guides⇨Show Baseline Grid (Option+⌘+' [apostrophe] or Ctrl+Alt+' [apostrophe]).
- **Show the document-wide grid established in the Grids pane of the Preferences dialog box.** Choose View⇨Grids & Guides⇨Show Document Grid (⌘+' [apostrophe] or Ctrl+' [apostrophe]).

InDesign has another place to set view settings: in the Pages pane's palette menu, choose View⇨Show/Hide Master Items. When you choose Show Master Items, any objects on the currently displayed document page's master page are displayed. When you choose Hide Master Items, master objects on the currently displayed page are hidden. This command is page-specific, so you can show or hide master objects on a page-by-page basis.

Adding Default Colors and Styles

If you are a creature of habit, you may find yourself creating the same colors, paragraph styles, character styles, and object styles over and over again. Save yourself some steps by creating these features when no documents are open; when you do so, the features will be available to all future documents.

To set up these often-used items, use the New command in the palette menus for the following panes: Swatches (F5), Character Styles (Shift+F11), Paragraph Styles (F11), and Object Styles (⌘+F7 or Ctrl+F7). You can also use the palette menus' Load commands to import colors and styles from existing documents instead of creating them from scratch.

Chapter 10 covers color swatches, Chapter 13 covers object styles, Chapter 16 covers character styles, and Chapter 17 covers paragraph styles in more detail.

Part II
Document Essentials

"No, it's not a pie chart; it's just a corn chip that got scanned into the document."

In this part . . .

The reader sees your text and images, but as a layout artist, you know there's a lot more going on behind the scenes. Your documents contain all sorts of elements — the publishing equivalent of the girders and beams and so forth of a building — that are essential to delivering the final text and graphics. This part covers those document essentials, showing you how to work with the document files, pages, layers, templates, libraries, and sections — the basic organizing elements and containers. You'll also find out how to put together books and similar documents that have special needs such as automatic table of contents and indexing.

Chapter 5

Opening, Viewing, and Saving Your Work

In This Chapter

- Creating a new document
- Opening documents
- Saving and exporting documents
- Recovering information after a crash
- Working with templates

You're eager to create a new document and get started with InDesign. So you launch InDesign, create or open a new document, and begin working. Right? Wrong, sort of. You can just plunge in, but you're best served if you have an idea before you start of what you want to accomplish. That way, you won't be staring at a blank screen with no brilliant ideas in mind.

Once you have an idea of what you want to do, you need to create the document that will hold those brilliant ideas. InDesign lets you apply those ideas from the very start of creating the document, and also lets you make changes later on, as you refine your ideas.

This chapter shows you the basics of working with document files, from creating and opening them to saving them, as well as how to make a template for easy reuse later on.

Setting Up a New Publication

After you launch InDesign, you have two options: You can choose File➪Open (or press ⌘+O or Ctrl+O) to open a previously created document or template, or you can choose File➪New➪Document (or press ⌘+N or Ctrl+N) to create a new document.

Creating a new document is where all the fun is, since you get to create something yourself, from scratch. Here's how to create a new document:

1. **Choose File➪New➪Document or press ⌘+N or Ctrl+N.**

   The New Document dialog box appears, as shown in Figure 5-1. It is here that you will have to make many up-front decisions about how you want your new document set up — including page size, number of pages, number of columns, and margin width. Although you're free to change your mind later, you'll save yourself time and potential headaches by sticking with the basic page parameters you establish in the New Document dialog box.

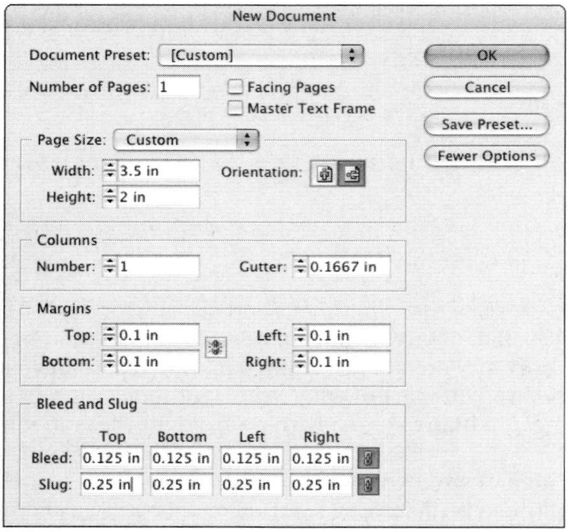

Figure 5-1: The New Document dialog box establishes the basic framework for your pages.

2. **If you know exactly how many pages your publication will have, enter the number in the Number of Pages field.**

   If you don't know for sure, you can always add or delete pages later. So guesstimate, since it's easy to add or delete pages later.

3. **Decide whether to lay out your documents in a spread or as separate pages.**

   - If you're creating a multi-page publication that will have a spine, such as a book, catalog, or magazine, select Facing Pages.
   - If you're creating a one-page document, such as a business card, an ad, or a poster, don't select Facing Pages.
   - Some publications, such as flip charts, presentations, and three-ring bound documents, have multiple pages but use only one side of the page. For such documents, don't check Facing Pages, either.

4. **If you want to flow text from page to page in a multi-page document, such as a book or a catalog, check Master Text Frame.**

   If you check this box, InDesign automatically adds a text frame to the document's master page and to all document pages based on this master page. Doing this saves you the work of creating a text frame on each page and manually threading text through each frame. (See Chapter 6 for more information about using master text frames.)

5. **In the Page Size area, you can choose one of the predefined sizes from the pop-up menu.**

6. **Specify margin values in the Margins area.**

   If Facing Pages is checked, Inside and Outside fields are available in the Margins area. Designers often specify larger inside margins for multi-page publications to accommodate the fold at the spine. If Facing Pages is not checked, Left and Right fields replace the Inside and Outside fields. You can also specify margin values by clicking the up/down arrows associated with the fields.

7. **To specify how many columns your pages have, enter a value in the Columns field.**

   You can also specify the number of columns by clicking the up/down arrows associated with the Column field.

8. **Specify a gutter distance (the gutter is the space between columns) in the Gutter field.**

   You can also specify a gutter width value by clicking the up/down arrows associated with the Gutter field.

9. **Click the More Options button to access the Bleed and Slug area of the New Document dialog box (refer to Figure 5-1).**

   The More Options button provides options to set bleed and slug areas. A *bleed area* is a margin on the outside of the page for objects you want to extend past the edge of the page — you want them to extend at least ⅛ inch so if there is any shifting of the paper during printing, there's no white space where the image should be (touching the edge of the page). The slug area is an area reserved for printing crop marks, color plate names, and other such printing information — some output devices will cut these off during printing unless a slug area is defined. For both bleed and slug areas, you can set the top, bottom, left, and right margins independently.

10. **Click OK to close the New Document dialog box.**

    Your new, blank document appears in a new document window. Figure 5-2 shows the window of a newly created document (a business card) that uses the settings shown in Figure 5-1.

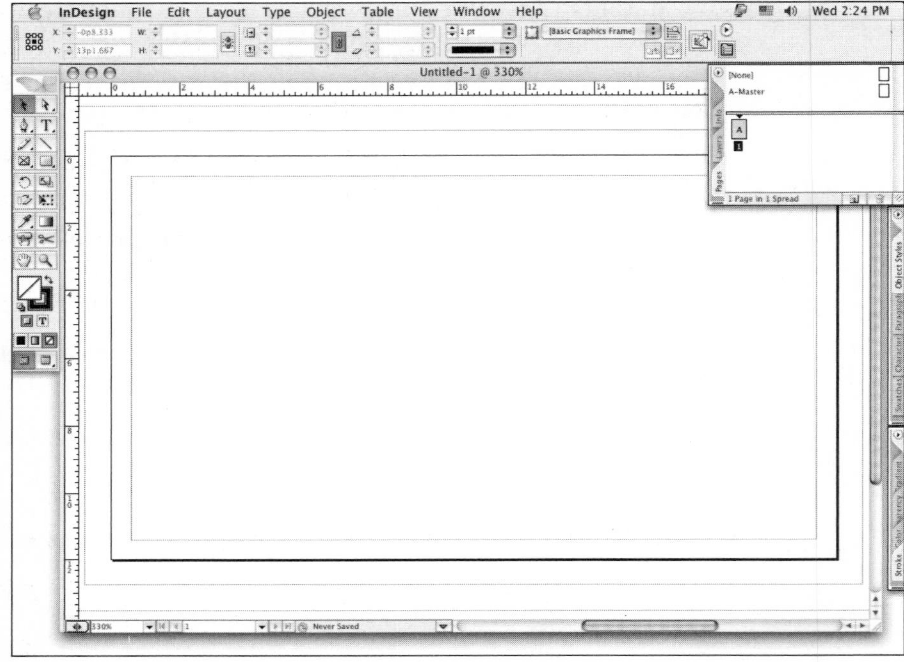

Figure 5-2: The results of the settings in the New Document dialog box shown in Figure 5-1.

You can bypass the New Document dialog box by pressing Shift+⌘+N or Ctrl+Shift+N. When you use this method, the most recent settings in the New Document dialog box are used for the new document.

Opening documents

Opening documents with InDesign is pretty much the same as opening documents with any program. Simply choose File➪Open (or press ⌘+O or Ctrl+O), select the document you want to work on, and then click the Open button. But InDesign offers a few options for opening documents that you don't find in every program. For example, you can:

- **Open more than one document at a time.**
- **Open a copy of a document instead of the original.** This keeps the original file from being overwritten accidentally — very helpful if you're making several variations of one document.
- **Open a template under its own name.** This makes editing templates easier than it is with other programs, specifically QuarkXPress.
- **Open documents created with Versions 6.0, 6.5, and 7.0 of PageMaker and Versions 3.3, 4.0, and 4.1 of both QuarkXPress and QuarkXPress Passport.**

Opening InDesign files

To open an InDesign file (any version from 1.0 to CS2), follow these steps:

1. **Choose File⇨Open, or press ⌘+O or Ctrl+O.**

   The Open a File dialog box, shown in Figures 5-3 and 5-4, appears. The Open a File dialog box will differ based on whether you are using Adobe's Version Cue file-management system or the standard Mac or Windows interface. (This book's screen shots assume that you are not using Version Cue, so this is the only time we'll show you the Version Cue interface.) The sidebar "Banishing Version Cue" later in this chapter explains how to turn Version Cue off.

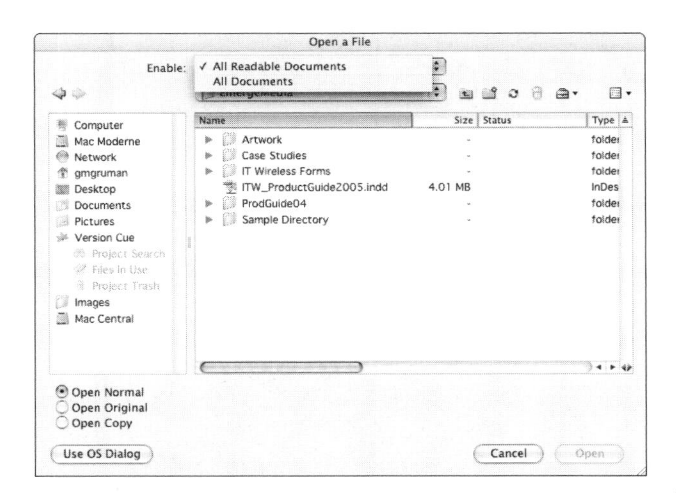

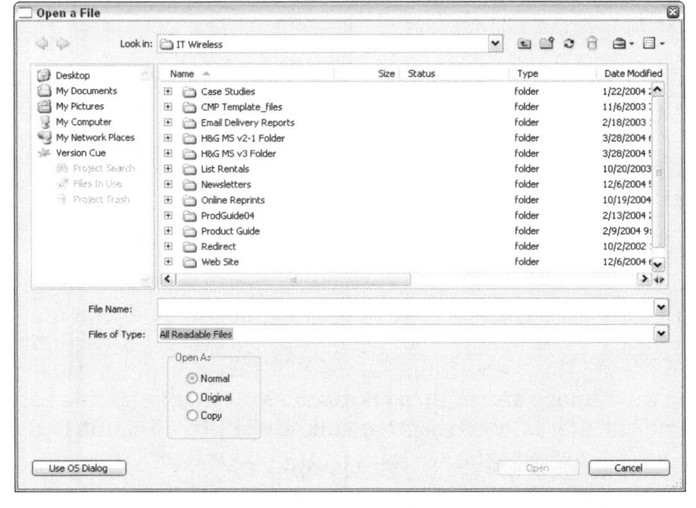

Figure 5-3: The Open a File dialog box with Version Cue enabled (Mac at top, Windows at bottom).

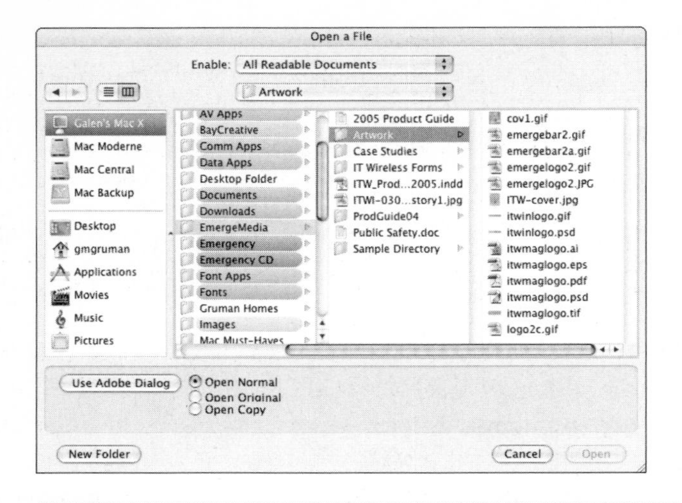

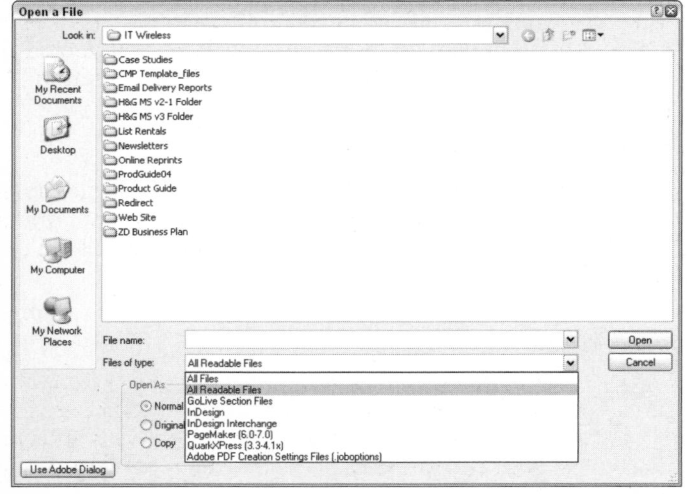

Figure 5-4: The Open a File dialog box with Version Cue disabled (Mac top, Windows at bottom).

2. **Locate and open the folder that contains the document(s) you want to open.**

   Select a single filename or hold down the ⌘ or Ctrl key and select multiple filenames.

   In Windows, the Files of Type pop-up menu offers several options: PageMaker 6.0–7.0 files, QuarkXPress 3.3–4.1 files, InDesign files, InDesign Interchange, GoLive Section, Adobe PDF Creation Settings Files, and All Formats. Choose any of these options to display a specific file format in the file list. (The GoLive Section and Adobe PDF Creation Settings Files options are for experts, so don't worry about them for now.)

On a Mac, the Open a File dialog box will display any supported file formats that have a Mac icon, and the dialog box includes a Preview pane that displays a thumbnail version of the selected file or, more commonly, its icon. Use All Documents in the Enable pop-up menus to display files without the expected icons (typically, those transferred from a PC or perhaps via e-mail).

In Windows, the Open a File dialog box will display any supported file formats that have a supported filename extension. Use All Files in the Files of Type pop-up menu to display files with no filename extensions (typically, these are files created on a Mac).

3. **Select Normal under Open As to open the original version of the document; click Open Copy if you just want to open a copy of it.**

   When you open a copy of a document, it's assigned a default name (Untitled-1, Untitled-2, and so on).

   If you are opening a template to create a new version of a publication, also select Normal; InDesign will create a document based on the template. To open a template under its own name so that you can edit it, click Open Original. (Templates are explained in the section "All about Templates" later in this chapter.)

4. **Click OK to close the dialog box.**

   Each document you opened is displayed in a separate document window. The page and view magnification used when the document was last saved is also used when you open the document, as we discuss in Chapter 4.

Opening foreign formats

One of InDesign's hallmarks is its ability to open documents from other programs and convert them into InDesign documents. You can open documents created in PageMaker 6.0, 6.5, and 7.0 as well as QuarkXPress and QuarkXPress Passport 3.3, 4.0, and 4.1. (Chapters 25 and 26 cover conversion issues in greater detail.)

But beware: InDesign's ability to open a foreign-format file doesn't mean you get a perfect translation. The other programs' formats and capabilities are so different from InDesign's that you should expect to spend time cleaning up the converted files by hand. In some cases, you might find that the amount of cleanup work is greater than if you simply re-create the document from scratch in InDesign — don't panic when this is the case. And be happy when your documents convert effortlessly. The good news is that InDesign will alert you to any import issues of PageMaker and QuarkXPress files with a dialog box that appears after the import is complete, as Figure 5-5 shows.

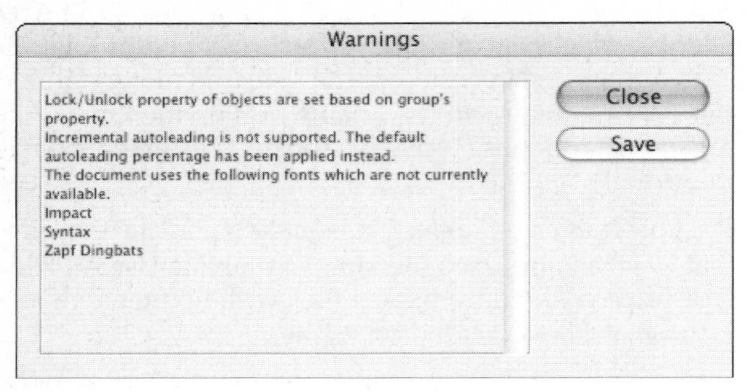

Figure 5-5: InDesign shows a Warnings dialog box if there are any issues in importing foreign file formats.

When opening QuarkXPress files, here are some common conversion issues to pay attention to:

- If your QuarkXPress document relies on XTensions (a type of plug-in) to add capabilities (such as table creation), it will not convert correctly into InDesign and may not even import at all. Examples include any documents built with the QuarkXPress indexing and book features.
- QuarkXPress's line-spacing (leading) model is different than InDesign's, so expect leading to sometimes vary significantly, especially if you use additive leading (such as **+2pt** to add two points to whatever the current font size is) as the automatic leading method in QuarkXPress.
- InDesign won't retain kerning-table adjustments in QuarkXPress files. (Like InDesign CS, InDesign CS2 does retain any kerning applied manually — but InDesign 2 did not.)
- The customizable dashes in QuarkXPress are converted to solid and dashed lines — note that stripes do convert properly.
- Special gradient blends, such as the diamond-pattern, are converted to linear gradients or circular gradients.
- Text on a curved path is converted to regular text in a rectangular frame, even though InDesign supports text on paths.
- H&J (hyphenation and justification) sets don't have an equivalent in InDesign, so they do not convert, although any H&J settings are carried over into the converted paragraph styles.
- Rotated items may lose their rotation when converted to InDesign.
- Libraries won't convert.
- Printer styles won't convert.

Banishing Version Cue

Adobe's Version Cue feature is meant to help people collaborate in a workgroup, so you can share a master file with multiple people, each working on it in turn. Version Cue even lets you save different versions of a file, so you can experiment and then decide which one to keep. But Version Cue is complicated and too difficult to use in most environments. You can accomplish similar functions simply by saving common files to a network server and saving new versions with slightly different names, so you can later choose the version you want.

But with InDesign CS2, Adobe forces you to use Version Cue, at least at first. That's because Version Cue is turned on automatically for you. To get rid of it, you have a few options:

- The easiest way is to turn off Version Cue itself. Just choose InDesign⇨Preferences⇨File Handling or press ⌘+K on the Mac, or choose Edit⇨Preferences⇨File Handling or press Ctrl+K in Windows, then uncheck the Version Cue option. Click OK. Voilà! Version Cue is disabled for all your Adobe software.
- You can also go to the Macintosh System Preferences dialog box (⇨System Preferences) or the Windows Control Panel (Start⇨Settings⇨Control Panels) and double-click the Version Cue CS2 button to open a pane that has an option to turn off Version Cue. Again, this turns off Version Cue for all your Adobe software.
- In some cases, you might want to leave Version Cue on (maybe because you use it occasionally in a workgroup setting) but not use its unique dialog boxes for opening, saving, exporting, and importing until you're ready to use the Version Cue tools. That's also easy: Click the Use OS Dialog button in the Open a File, Save As, Export As, Load, and other dialog boxes that work with filenames. Clicking OS Dialog brings you to the standard Mac or Windows dialog boxes, which will continue to display until you later click Use Adobe Dialog button in any of those dialog boxes. Clicking Use Adobe Dialog button in any of those dialog boxes brings back the Version Cue interface for all of those dialog boxes. Note that these changes affect only InDesign CS2, not your other Adobe software.

When opening PageMaker files, take note of the following:

- Fill patterns aren't supported.
- Libraries won't convert.
- Printer styles won't convert.

Saving documents

When you open a new document, it's assigned a default name — Untitled-1, Untitled-2, and so on — and the first page is displayed in the document window. At this point, you're like a painter in front of a blank canvas. You can work on your layout without giving it a name, but it's best to give it a name by saving it as soon as possible so you don't lose any changes to a power outage or other system problem.

The second group of commands in InDesign's File menu — Close, Save, Save As, Save a Copy, Save a Version, and Revert — provide options for saving the active (frontmost) document. Here's a rundown of what each command does:

- **Close** (⌘+W, or Ctrl+W or Ctrl+F4) closes the active document. If the document has never been saved or if it has been changed since it was last saved, a dialog box lets you save, close without saving, or cancel and return to the document.
- **Save** (⌘+S or Ctrl+S) saves changes you've made to the active document since you last saved. (If you choose Save for a document that hasn't yet been saved, the Save As dialog box is displayed.)
- **Save As** (Option+⌘+S or Ctrl+Alt+S) lets you save a copy of the active document using a different name (or with the same name in a different folder). When you choose Save As — and when you choose Save for an unsaved document — the Save As dialog box, shown in Figure 5-6, appears. This dialog box lets you create or choose a folder for the document, as well as name the document.
- **Save a Version** saves the current document as a version within a Version Cue project. This latest save will be considered a version of the previously saved file. (This expert option is available only if Version Cue is enabled.)
- **Save a Copy** lets you create a copy of the active document in a different (or in the same) folder using a different (or the same) name. When you use the Save a Copy command, the original document remains open and retains its original name. It differs from Save As only in that it keeps the original document open.
- **Revert** undoes all changes you've made to a document since you last saved it.

Knowing how to not save changes

InDesign is a very forgiving program. If you make a mistake, change your mind, or work yourself into a complete mess, you don't have to remain in your predicament or save your work. InDesign offers several escape routes. You can:

- **Undo your last action by choosing Edit⇨Undo or pressing ⌘+Z or Ctrl+Z.** (Some actions, particularly actions such as scrolling that do not affect any items or the underlying document structure, cannot be undone.) You can undo multiple actions in the reverse order in which they were done by repeatedly choosing Edit⇨Undo or pressing ⌘+Z or Ctrl+Z — each time you undo, the previous action is undone.

- **Redo an action you've undone by choosing Edit⇨Redo or pressing Shift+⌘+Z or Ctrl+Shift+Z.** Alternately choosing Undo and Redo is a handy way of seeing a before/after view of a particular change. As with undo, you can redo multiple undone actions in the reverse of the order in which they were undone.
- **To undo all changes you've made since last saving a document, choose File⇨Revert.** There is no way to undo this action and reinstate all your changes after you revert, so be careful.

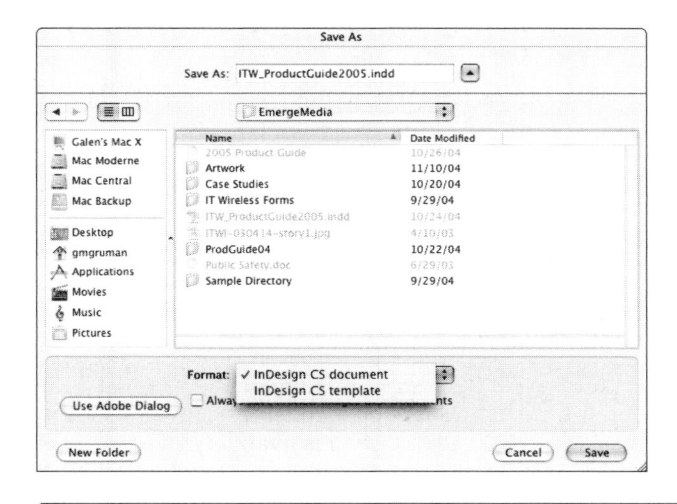

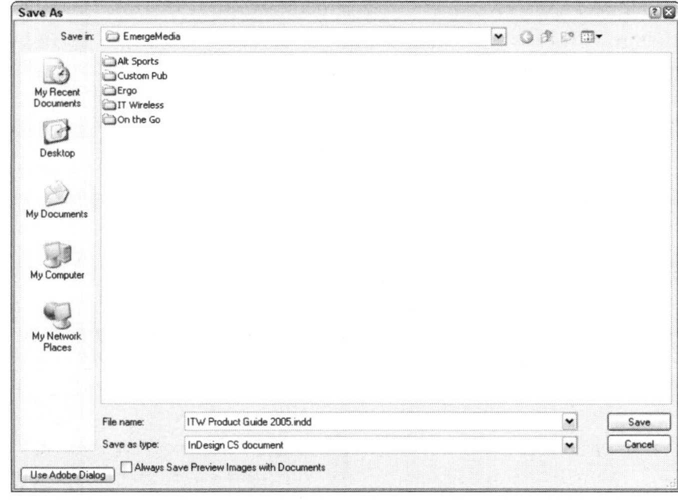

Figure 5-6: The Mac version of the Save As dialog box (top) and the Windows version (bottom) are slightly different.

Saving files in other formats

InDesign's Save commands (Save, Save As, and Save a Copy) let you save documents and templates in InDesign's native file format. But the Export command (File➪Export) lets you save the stories — and in some cases stories and whole layouts — from InDesign documents in several formats: InDesign Interchange, Rich Text Format (RTF), Text Only, InDesign Tagged Text, Encapsulated PostScript (EPS), Portable Document Format (PDF), JPEG, and Scalable Vector Graphics (SVG).

Note that when exporting a file, you need to choose a format from the Format menu (Mac) or Save as Type menu (Windows).

Here are your format options in more detail:

- **InDesign CS format:** You can make your InDesign CS2 files readable by InDesign CS users by saving your files in the InDesign Interchange format. (There is no way for users of InDesign 2 or previous versions to open InDesign CS2 or CS files.)
- **Word-processing formats:** If you place the text cursor into a story, you can export its text (select a range of text if you want to export only that selection) into one of two formats: RTF, for import into word processors with only basic formatting retained; and Text Only, for import into word processors that don't support RTF (with Text Only, note that no formatting is retained).

  You can save only one text file at a time. If you need to export several stories from the same document, you must do so one at a time.
- **InDesign workflow formats:** If text is selected via the Type tool, you can save the story in the InDesign Tagged Text format (for editing in a word processor and later reimport into InDesign CS2 with all InDesign formatting retained) or in the InDesign CS Interchange format (for import into InDesign CS).
- **Production formats:** Whether or not anything is selected, you can save the document — not just the story — in EPS or PDF formats for use by prepress tools and service bureaus or for import into other applications as pictures.
- **Online formats:** Whether or not anything is selected, you can save the document — not just the story — in XML format for use in online database-oriented content-management systems, as well as a specific page, spread, or text selection into JPEG or SVG formats for use as online graphics.

Recovering from Disaster

Make sure that when you work on InDesign documents, you follow the first rule of safe computing: Save early and often.

InDesign includes an automatic-recovery feature that protects your documents in the event of a power failure or a system crash. As you work on a document, any changes you make after saving it are stored in a separate, temporary file. Under normal circumstances, each time you choose Save, the information in the temporary file is saved to the document file. The data in the temporary file is important only if you aren't able to save a document before a crash. (A word of warning: Although InDesign's automatic recovery feature is a nice safety net, you should still be careful to save your work often.) If you suffer a system crash, follow these steps to recover your most recent changes:

1. **Relaunch InDesign or, if necessary, restart your computer and then launch InDesign.**
2. **If automatic-recovery data is available, InDesign automatically opens the recovered document and displays the word "Recovered" in the document's title bar.**

   This lets you know that the document contains changes that were not included in the last saved version.
3. **If you want to save the recovered data, choose File⇨Save; "Recovered" is removed as part of the filename, and InDesign will ask if you want to overwrite the old file.**

   Overwriting the old file is easier than using File⇨Save As and entering a name — unless you do want to save a copy of the file in case you want to go back to the old version later. If you want to use the last saved version of the document (and disregard the recovered data), close the file (File⇨Close, or ⌘+W or Ctrl+W) without saving, then open the file (File⇨Open, or ⌘+O or Ctrl+O).

Sometimes, InDesign can't automatically recover the documents for you. Instead, it gives you the choice of recovering any files open during a crash or power outage, saving the recovery data for later, or deleting the recovery data. You typically want to recover the files immediately.

All about Templates

Whenever you save a document, you have the option of saving a standard document file or a template (more on saving templates later in this chapter). A *template* is an InDesign file that's used to create multiple iterations of the same publication. For example, if you produce a monthly newsletter, you save gobs of time and ensure consistency from issue to issue by using a template as the starting point for each edition of the newsletter. A template is essentially the shell of a publication that contains the basic framework — page layout, master pages, styles, and so on — but doesn't contain any actual content.

When you open a template, you have two choices: You can either open a copy of the file and use it to create a new publication, or you can open the original file, make changes, and then save an updated version of the template.

If you want to use a template as the starting point for a new publication, choose File⇨Open or press ⌘+O or Ctrl+O, locate and select the template, and make sure Open Normal is selected in the Open a File dialog box (refer to Figures 5-3 and 5-4) before you click Open. Clicking Open opens a new document window and assigns the document a default name, Untitled-1, Untitled-2, and so on.

If you want to modify a template file, select Open Original. Clicking Open opens the original file and displays the original name in the title bar. Be careful, because you're now editing the template file itself, not a copy of it.

Whenever you save a document for the first time or you use the Save As or Save a Copy command, the Save As or Save a Copy dialog boxes let you save a standard InDesign document file or a template: You choose a format (document or template) in the Format menu (Mac) or Save as Type menu (Windows). By default, InDesign saves your layout as a document.

If you forget to save a document as a template, it will open under its actual name. If you then make any changes and choose File⇨Save (⌘+S or Ctrl+S), the changes are saved with the original document. If this happens, simply save the document again and choose the InDesign CS2 Template option.

Chapter 6

Discovering How Pages Work

In This Chapter

- Adding and removing document pages
- Adjusting page numbers and creating sections
- Navigating through a document
- Adjusting page layouts and objects

It's a rare InDesign user who creates only one-page documents. Even if you spend your time working on business cards, ads, and posters, you probably produce at least a few multi-page documents. And if you create newsletters, newspapers, books, catalogs, or any other such multi-page publications, you must know how to add pages to your document, move pages around if you change your mind, and delete pages if necessary. InDesign also lets you divide multi-page documents into independently numbered sections.

As documents grow in size, getting around can be a real drag — on your time, that is. The longer you spend getting to the page you want, the less time you have to work on it. Fortunately, InDesign provides several navigation aids that make it easy to move around on a page or in a document.

Understanding the Pages Pane

The Pages pane is where you do most of your page actions, so you get to know it well the more you use InDesign.

If you intend to create a multi-page document, you want to display the Pages pane (Window⇨Pages or F12), shown in Figure 6-1, because it provides the controls that let you add pages (both document and master), delete and move pages, apply master pages to document pages, and navigate through a document.

For more information about using the Pages pane to work on master pages, see Chapter 8.

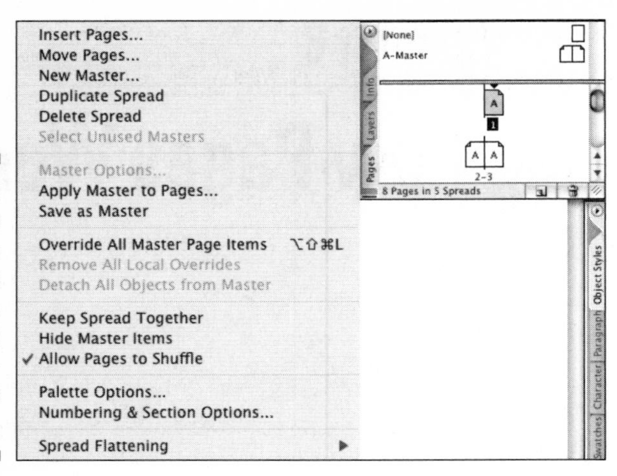

Figure 6-1: The Pages pane and its palette menu showing a new, facing-pages document.

Keep in mind that the overwhelming majority of multi-page documents are facing-pages publications such as books, catalogs, and magazines. Some exceptions are flip charts and three-hole-punched publications printed on only one side. In this chapter, the figures show examples of a facing-pages document. If you create a single-sided multi-page document, the techniques are the same as for facing-pages documents, but the icons in the Pages pane show only single-sided page icons (the icons aren't dog-eared).

Adding pages

A document can contain as many as 9,999 pages — more than anyone would ever want to have in one file. In general, try to break up long publications into logical pieces. For example, if you're creating a book, it's a good idea to create separate documents for the front matter, each chapter, the index, and any other parts (appendixes and so on). Also, if you're producing a long document, you want to take advantage of master pages (covered in Chapter 8), which save you the work of building each page from scratch.

When you create a multi-page document, you're free to add however many pages you want. But be careful: Even though InDesign will let you create a seven-page newsletter, in real life, facing-page publications always have an even number of pages — usually a multiple of 4 and often a multiple of 16 because of the way printers arrange multiple pages on a single sheet of paper before folding and cutting them into the final document.

Here's how to add pages to a document:

1. **If it's not displayed, open the Pages pane by choosing Window➪Pages or pressing F12.**

2. **From the Pages pane's palette menu, choose Insert Pages.**

   The Insert Pages dialog box, shown in Figure 6-2, appears.

Figure 6-2: The Insert Pages dialog box.

3. **In the Pages field, type the number of pages you want to add.**
4. **Select an option from the Insert pop-up menu: After Page, Before Page, At Start of Document, or At End of Document.**

   Be careful: If you've already started working on page 1, for example, make sure you add new pages *after* page 1. Otherwise, it won't be page 1 anymore, and you'll have to move the objects you already created.
5. **Type a page number in the field next to Insert or use the arrows to increase or decrease the value in one-page increments.**
6. **From the Master pop-up menu, select the master page you want to apply to the new pages.**
7. **When you're finished, click OK to close the dialog box.**

InDesign CS2 offers a faster way to add and manipulate pages if you don't happen to have the Pages pane already open: Choose Layout⇨Pages, and then select the appropriate option, such as Add Pages, from the submenu. The resulting dialog boxes match those accessed from the Pages pane.

If you want to quickly add just one page after the current page, click Layout⇨Pages⇨Add Page or just press Shift+⌘+P or Ctrl+Shift+P.

You can also add new pages or spreads one at a time at the end of a document by clicking the Create New Page button at the bottom of the Pages pane. (Spreads are added if a spread is selected in the Pages pane.) When you use this method, the master page applied to the last document page is applied to each new page. Pages are added after the currently selected page in the pane.

You can also click and drag a master page icon (or both pages in a facing-pages spread to add a spread) from the top of the Pages pane to add a page using a master page's settings (use the [None] page for a plain page) between any pair of document page spreads or to the right of the last document spread. If a vertical bar appears when you release the mouse button, the spread is placed between the spreads on either side of the bar. If a vertical bar does not appear between document page spreads when you release the mouse button, the new spread is placed at the end of the document.

When you insert new pages, existing pages are automatically changed from left-hand pages to right-hand pages, and vice versa, as needed when individual pages are added and removed in a facing-pages document. You can prevent this for selected spreads by first selecting them in the Pages pane and then clicking Keep Spread Together in the palette menu. You might do this for a spread, such as a two-page table, that you don't want to have broken apart when other pages are added or deleted. Of course, for proper printing, you might need to move that spread when you're done adding or deleting pages so that it follows a complete spread.

Selecting pages

InDesign offers several choices for selecting pages from a document, so you can move, delete, copy, or otherwise manipulate them:

- Click a page's icon in the Pages pane to select it.
- To select both pages in a spread, the easiest way is to click a spread's page numbers to select both pages.
- To select a range of pages, you can click a page icon or spread number beneath it and then Shift+click another page icon or spread number.
- To select multiple, noncontiguous pages, hold down the ⌘ or Ctrl key and click page icons or spread numbers.

Copying pages

You can copy pages from one document to another by clicking and dragging the page icon(s) from the source document's Pages pane to the target document's Pages pane. Any master page(s) associated with the copied document pages(s) are copied as well.

You can also duplicate the current spread within the current document by clicking Duplicate Spread from the Pages pane's palette menu or by choosing Layout⇨Pages⇨Duplicate Spread.

Deleting pages

The fastest way to delete selected pages is either click and drag them to the pane's Delete Selected Pages button (the trashcan icon) or simply click the Delete Selected Pages button.

Moving pages

Although you can move pages around in a document, do so only with great care — if at all. Generally, if you want to move the objects on one page to another page, it's safer to cut (Edit⇨Cut or ⌘+X or Ctrl+X) or copy (Edit⇨Copy, or ⌘+C or Ctrl+C) the objects than to move the page, which might cause subsequent pages to shuffle.

What's the big deal about shuffling? Shuffling will move pages around to make space for the moved page, and that can move what had been left-hand pages to the right-hand side of the spread and vice versa. If you have different alignments on left and right pages — such as having page numbers on the outside of pages — this shuffling can wreak havoc with that alignment.

If you absolutely must move a single page, it's safer to move its spread. (Of course, if you're working on a single-sided facing-page document, shuffling is not an issue.)

To move a page, drag its icon between two spreads or between the pages of a spread. A vertical bar indicates where the selected page will be placed. Release the mouse button when the vertical bar is where you want to move the page. To move a spread, drag the page numbers beneath the icons (rather than the page icons themselves).

Alternatively, you can select the page(s) you want to move in the Pages pane and then click Move Pages from the Pages pane's palette menu. (If you don't want to work through the Pages pane, you can also choose Layout⇨Pages⇨Move Pages.) In that dialog box, you can specify where to move the page(s): after a specific page, before a specific page, at the beginning of the document, or at the end of the document.

Starting documents on a left page

By default, InDesign starts all documents on the right page, which makes sense because the first sheet in a document is always a right-hand page. But sometimes you want documents to start on a left-hand page, particularly if they are a chapter or section in a larger document. For example, magazine articles often start on a left page, giving the introduction a full spread. To start a document on a left page:

1. **Select the first page in the Pages pane and then choose Numbering & Section Options from the pane's palette menu or choose Layout⇨Numbering & Section Options.**
2. **Select the Start Section option.**

3. **Select the Start Page Numbering At option and enter an even number in the field.**

4. **Click OK.**

   The Pages pane will update, showing the start page on the left of the spine.

   You may not want to assign a starting page number (for example, if the starting page number is unknown because the number of pages that precede this document is unknown and you let the Book feature determine the page numbers later). In this case, repeat Step 1, but deselect Start Section. Doing so leaves the page as a left-hand page but let the Book feature figure out the page number.

See Chapter 9 for more information on the Book feature and long-document creation. Sections are covered later in this chapter.

Working with Page Numbers

By default, pages are numbered automatically starting at 1, but you can change the page numbering from Arabic numerals to Roman numerals or letters, as well as change the start page to something other than 1. To do so, select the first page in the document in the Pages pane and choose Layout⇨Numbering & Sections or choose Numbering & Section Options from the Pages pane's palette menu. You get the dialog box shown in Figure 6-3.

To change the initial page number, select the Start Page Numbering At option and type a new starting page number in its field. To change the page numbering style from the default of Arabic numerals (1, 2, 3, 4 . . .), use the Style pop-up menu and choose from I, II, III, IV . . . ; i, ii, iii, iv . . . ; A, B, C, D . . . ; and a, b, c, d. . . .

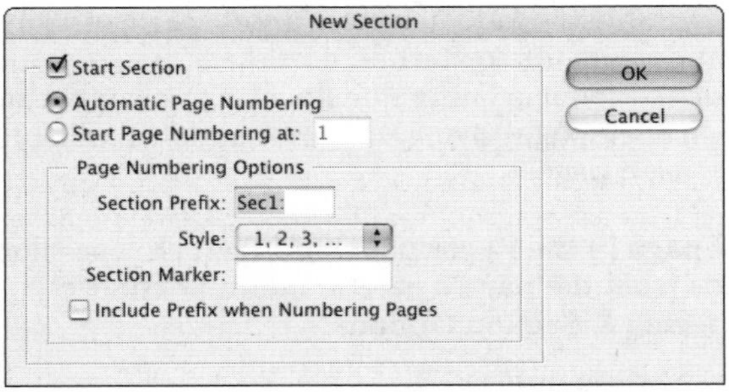

Figure 6-3: The Numbering & Section Options dialog box lets you change the starting page number and the types of numerals used.

New Section
Start Section
Automatic Page Numbering
Start Page Numbering at: 1
Page Numbering Options
Section Prefix: Sec1:
Style: 1, 2, 3, ...
Section Marker:
Include Prefix when Numbering Pages
OK
Cancel

To have a facing-pages document start on a left-hand page, the starting page number must be even.

Entering page references in text

You often want page references in text — the current page number, for example, or the target page number for a "continued on" reference. You could type in a page number manually on each page of a multi-page document, but that can get old fast. As we mention earlier in this chapter, if you're working on a multi-page document, you should use master pages. And if you use master pages, you should handle page numbers on document pages by placing page-number characters on the master pages.

If you want to add the current page number to a page, you can choose Type➪Insert Special Character➪Auto Page Number or press Option+Shift+⌘+N or Ctrl+Shift+Alt+N whenever the Type tool is active and the text cursor is flashing. If you move the page or the text frame, the page-number character is automatically updated to reflect the new page number.

To create "continued on" and "continued from" lines, choose Type➪Insert Special Character➪Next Page Number to have the next page's number inserted in your text, or choose Type➪Insert Special Character➪Previous Page Number to have the previous page's number inserted. That next or previous page will be the next or previous page in the story.

One flaw in InDesign's continued-line approach is that the text frames must be linked for InDesign to know what the next and previous pages are. Thus, you're likely to place your continued lines in the middle of your text. But if the text reflows, so do the continued lines. Here's a way to avoid that: Create separate text frames for your continued-on and continued-from text frames. Now link just those two frames, not the story text. This way, the story text can reflow as needed without affecting your continued lines.

Dividing a document into sections

Some long documents are divided into parts that are numbered separately. For example, the page numbers of book introductions often use Roman numerals, while standard Arabic numerals are used for the body of the book. If the book has appendixes, a separate numbering scheme could be applied to these pages. In InDesign, such independently numbered parts are referred to as *sections.*

A multi-page document can contain as many sections as you want (a section has to contain at least one page). If each section of a document uses a different page layout, you probably want to create a different master page for each section. Here's how to create a section:

1. **If it's not displayed, open the Pages pane by choosing Window⇨Pages or pressing F12.**
2. **Click the icon of the page where you want to start a section.**
3. **Choose Numbering & Section Options from the pane's palette menu.**

   The Numbering & Section Options dialog box appears (refer to Figure 6-3). By default, the Start Section option is selected. Leave it selected.

   You can also create a section starting at the current page in your document by choosing Layout⇨Numbering & Section Options.

4. **In the Section Prefix field, type up to eight characters that identify the section in the page-number box at the lower-left corner of the document window.**

   For example, if you type **Sec2**, the first page of the section will be displayed as Sec2:1 in the page-number box. This prefix won't appear as part of the actual page numbers when you print — it's really just a way for you to keep track of sections while you work.

5. **From the Style menu, choose the Roman numeral, Arabic numeral, or alphabetic style you want to use for page numbers.**
6. **For Page Numbering, select the Automatic Page Numbering option if you want the first page of the section to be one number higher than the last page of the previous section.**

   The new section will use the specified style; the previous section may use this style or another style.

7. **Select the Start Page Numbering At option and type a number in the accompanying field to specify a different starting number for the section.**

   For example, if a book begins with a section of front matter, you could begin the body section of a book on page 1 by choosing Start At and typing **1** in the field. If you select Continue from Previous Section, the first page of the body section begins one number higher than the numeral on the last page of the front matter.

8. **In the Section Marker field, type a text string that you can later automatically apply to pages in the section.**

   You might want to enter something straightforward like **Section 2** or, if the section is a chapter, the name of the chapter.

   You can insert the section marker name in folios, chapter headings, and story text by choosing Type⇨Insert Special Character⇨Section Marker. This is a great way to get a chapter name (if you use it as the section marker) in your folio or to have cross-references in text to a section whose name might later change. (A *folio* is the collection of a page number, magazine or chapter name, section name, or issue date, and so forth that usually appears at the top or bottom of pages.)

9. **Click OK to close the dialog box.**

When you create a section, it's indicated in the Pages pane by a small, black triangle over the icon of the first page in the section, as shown in Figure 6-4. (If you move the mouse pointer over the black triangle, the name of the section appears.) The page-numbering scheme you specify is reflected in the page numbers below the page icons. When you begin a section, it continues until the end of the document or until you begin a new section.

By default, the Pages pane displays section numbers beneath the icons of document pages. If you want to display absolute page numbers — the first page is page 1 and all other pages are numbered sequentially — you can do so by choosing InDesign➪Preferences➪General or pressing ⌘+K on the Mac or by choosing Edit➪Preferences➪General or pressing Ctrl+K in Windows and choosing Absolute Numbering from the View pop-up menu.

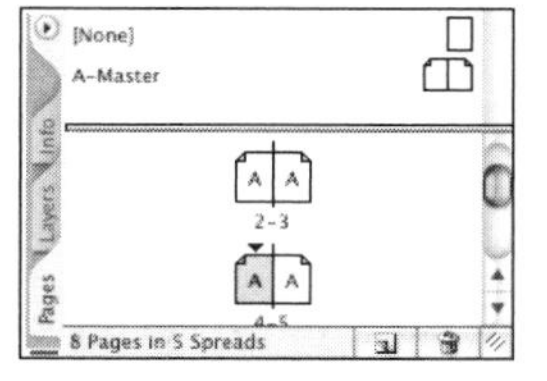

Figure 6-4: The small triangle above a page icon represents a section start.

Removing a section start

If you decide that you want to remove a section start, navigate to the page that begins the section, choose Numbering & Section Options from the Pages pane's palette menu, or choose Layout➪Numbering & Section Options, and deselect the Section Start option. That's it! The pages in the former section will remain, but their numbering will now pick up from the previous pages.

Navigating Documents and Pages

Moving from page to page in a long document and scrolling around a large or magnified page are among the most common tasks you perform in InDesign. The more time you spend navigating to the page or page area you want to work on, the less time you have to do the work you need to do. Like most trips, the less time you spend between destinations, the better.

For navigating through the pages of a document, the Pages pane (Window➪Pages or F12) offers the fastest ride. For navigating around in a page, you may want to switch to the Navigator pane (Window➪Object & Layout➪Navigator).

Navigating with the Pages pane

When the Pages pane appears, you can use it to quickly move from page to page in a multi-page document and to switch between displaying master pages and document pages. To display a particular document page, double-click its icon. The selected page is centered in the document window. To display a master spread, double-click its icon in the lower half of the pane.

The Fit Page in Window command (View➪Fit Page in Window, or ⌘+0 or Ctrl+0) and Fit Spread in Window command (View➪Fit Page in Window or Option+⌘+0 or Ctrl+Alt+0) let you enlarge or reduce the display magnification to fit the selected page or spread in the document window. Related view options are View➪Fit Spread in Window (Option+⌘+0 or Ctrl+Alt+0) and View➪Entire Pasteboard (Option+Shift+⌘+0 or Ctrl+Alt+Shift+0). (Note that the shortcuts use the numeral *0,* not the letter *O.*)

Navigating with the menus and shortcuts

InDesign also offers several menu commands and keyboard shortcuts to quickly navigate your layout, as Table 6-1 details.

Table 6-1 Page Navigation Menus and Shortcuts

Navigation	*Menu Sequence*	*Macintosh Shortcut*	*Windows Shortcut*
Go to first page	Layout➪First Page	Shift+⌘+PgUp	Ctrl+Shift+ Page Up
Go back one page	Layout➪Previous Page	Shift+PgUp	Shift+Page Up
Go forward one page	Layout➪Next Page or Layout➪Go Forward	Shift+PgDn or ⌘+PgDn	Shift+Page Down or Ctrl+keypad PgDn
Go to last page	Layout➪Last Page	Shift+⌘+PgDn	Ctrl+Shift+ Page Down
Go to last page viewed	Layout➪Go Back	⌘+PgUp	Shift+Page Up or Ctrl+keypad PgUp

Navigation	Menu Sequence	Macintosh Shortcut	Windows Shortcut
Go forward one spread	Layout➪Next Spread	Option+PgDn	Alt+Page Down
Go back one spread	Layout➪Previous Spread	Option+PgUp	Alt+Page Up

Using the Navigator pane

Although it's possible to use the Navigator pane (Window➪Object & Layout➪Navigator) to move from page to page in a long document, the Pages pane is better for this task. The Navigator pane is more useful for scrolling within a page, particularly for doing detail work on a page that's displayed at a high magnification. If you're an Illustrator, PageMaker, or Photoshop user, you may already be familiar with the Navigator pane, which works the same in all three applications.

Figure 6-5 shows the Navigator pane and its palette menu.

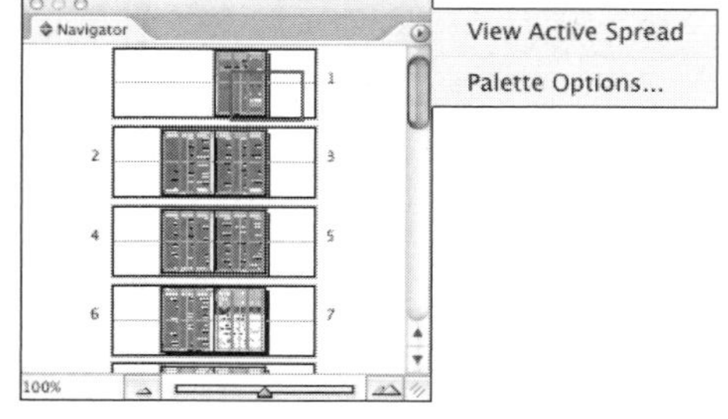

Figure 6-5: The Navigator pane and its palette menu.

You can also use the scroll bars at the right and bottom of the document window to move to different areas of a page or to a different page in a document.

Adjusting Page Layouts and Objects

If you've ever created and worked with a document all the way to the finishing touches and then discovered that the page size was wrong from the beginning, you know the meaning of frustration. Manually adjusting the size and placement of all the objects in a document is an ugly chore, one you want to avoid at all costs. However, should the unthinkable happen — you have to modify the size, orientation, or margins of a document that is partially or completely finished — InDesign can automatically resize and reposition objects when you change its basic layout.

For example, maybe you created a magazine for an American audience that subsequently needs to be converted for publication in Europe. Most newsletters in the United States use letter-sized pages (8½ × 11 inches), while in Europe the standard page size for such publications is A4 (210 × 297 mm), which is slightly narrower and slightly taller than U.S. letter size. Of course, you have to change *color* to *colour, apartment* to *flat,* and so on, but you also have to both squeeze (horizontally) and stretch (vertically) every item on every page to accommodate the A4 page's dimensions. The Layout Adjustment command (Layout⇨Layout Adjustment) gives you the option of turning this chore over to InDesign, which will automatically adjust object shape and position according to the new page size, column guides, and margins.

The Layout Adjustment dialog box lets you turn layout adjustment on or off and specify the rules used to adjust objects when you change page size or orientation, margins, or columns. To adjust a layout, follow these steps:

1. **Choose Layout⇨Layout Adjustment to display the Layout Adjustment dialog box, shown in Figure 6-6.**

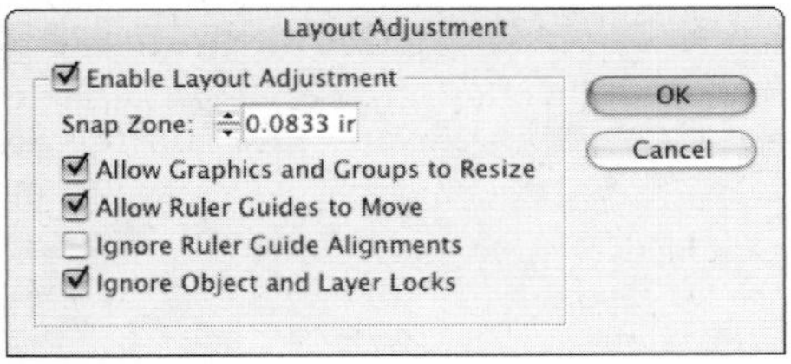

Figure 6-6: The Layout Adjustment dialog box.

2. **Select the Enable Layout Adjustment option to turn on the feature; deselect it to turn it off.**
3. **In the Snap Zone field, type the distance within which an object edge will automatically snap to a guideline when layout adjustment is performed.**
4. **Select the Allow Graphics and Groups to Resize option if you want InDesign to resize objects when layout adjustment is performed.**

   If you don't select this option, InDesign will move objects but not resize them (the preferred option, so you don't get awkward sizes).

5. **Select the Allow Ruler Guides to Move option if you want InDesign to adjust the position of ruler guides proportionally according to a new page size.**

   Generally, ruler guides are placed relative to the margins and page edges, so you probably want to select this option.

6. **Select the Ignore Ruler Guide Alignments option if you want InDesign to ignore ruler guides when adjusting the position of objects during layout adjustment.**

   If you think that objects might snap to ruler guides that you don't want them to snap to during layout adjustment, select this option. If selected, InDesign will still snap object edges to other margin and column guides.

7. **Select the Ignore Object and Layer Locks option to let InDesign move locked objects (either objects locked directly via Object⇨Lock Position or ⌘+L or Ctrl+L, or objects that reside on a locked layer).**

   Otherwise, locked objects will not be adjusted.

8. **When you're done, click OK to close the dialog box.**

The Layout Adjustment feature works best when there's not much work for it to do. But if you radically change a document that you've already done considerable work on, the Layout Adjustment feature usually creates more work than it saves. For example, the switch from a U.S. letter-sized page to an A4-sized page is a relatively minor change and the layout adjustments will probably be barely noticeable. But if you decide to change a tabloid-sized poster into a business card in midstream, well, you're probably better off starting over.

Here are a few things to keep in mind if you decide to use InDesign's Layout Adjustment feature:

- If you change page size, the margin widths (the distance between the left and right margins and the page edges) remain the same.
- If you change page size, column guides and ruler guides are repositioned proportionally to the new size.
- If you change the number of columns, column guides are added or removed accordingly.
- If an object edge is aligned with a guideline before layout adjustment, it remains aligned with the guideline after adjustment. If two or more edges of an object are aligned with guidelines, the object is resized so that the edges remain aligned with the guidelines after layout adjustment.
- If you change the page size, objects are moved so that they're in the same relative position on the new page.

- If you used margin, column, and ruler guides to place objects on pages, layout adjustment will be more effective than if you placed objects or ruler guides randomly on pages.
- Check for text reflow when you modify a document's page size, margins, or column guides. Decreasing a document's page size can cause text to overflow a text frame whose dimensions have been reduced.
- Check *everything* in your document after the adjustment is complete. Take the time to look over every page of your document. You never know what InDesign has actually done until you see it with your own eyes.

If you decide to enable layout adjustment for a particular publication, you might want to begin by using the Save As command (File⇨Save As or Shift+⌘+S or Ctrl+Shift+S) to create a copy. That way, if you ever need to revert back to the original version, you can simply open the original document.

Chapter 7

Layers and Layers

In This Chapter

- Discovering what layers can do for you
- Setting up layers
- Working with individual objects on layers
- Manipulating entire layers

If you've ever seen a series of clear plastic overlays in presentations, understanding layers is easy. In one of those old overhead presentations, the teacher could choose to start with one overlay containing a graphic, then add another overlay with descriptive text, and then add a third overlay containing a chart. Each overlay contained distinct content, but you could see through each one to the others to get the entire message. InDesign's layers are somewhat like this, letting you isolate content on slices of a document. You can then show and hide layers, lock objects on layers, rearrange layers, and more.

And unlike those old overhead slides, you can selectively turn layers on or off, so you can use layers for other purposes as well, such as having multiple languages in one document, with each language's text frames on their own layers. Or you could have production notes on their own layer, so you can see them when desired but otherwise keep them out of the way.

What Layers Can Do for You

If you never looked at the Layers pane, you could continue to do your work in InDesign. But take a look at the possibilities and see whether they fit into your workflow. In the long run, using layers can save you time and help you prevent mistakes that can result when you need to track changes across multiple documents. It's the kind of feature that, once discovered, can help you work much easier.

Say you've created an ad with the same copy in it but a different headline and image for each city where the ad runs. You can place the boilerplate information on one layer and the information that changes on other layers. If any of the boilerplate information changes, you need to change it only once. To print different versions of the ad, you control which layers print.

You might use layers in the following situations (and in many others):

- **A project with a high-resolution background image:** For example, a background such as a texture might take a long time to redraw. You can hide that layer while designing other elements, and then show it occasionally to see how it works with the rest of the design.
- **A document that you produce in several versions:** For example, a produce ad may have different prices for different cities, or a clothing catalog may feature different coats depending on the climate in each area. You can place the content that changes on separate layers, and then print the layers you need.
- **A project that includes objects you don't want to print:** If you want to suppress printout of objects for any reason, the only way you can do this is to place them on a layer and hide the layer. You might have a layer that's used for nothing but adding editorial and design comments, which can be deleted when the document is final.
- **A publication that is translated into several languages:** Depending on the layout, you can place all the common objects on one layer, and then create a different layer for each language's text. Changes to the common objects need to happen only once — unlike creating copies of the original document and flowing the translated text into the copies, which you would need to do for each language's version.

Layer Basics

Each document contains a default layer, Layer 1, which contains all your objects until you create and select a new layer. Objects on the default layer — and any other layer for that matter — follow the standard *stacking order* of InDesign. (What's the stacking order? Well, the first object you create is the backmost, the last one you create is the frontmost, and all the other objects fall somewhere in between. This is how InDesign knows what to do with overlapping objects.)

Like the clear plastic overlays, the order of the layers also affects the stacking order of the objects. Objects on the bottom layer are behind other objects, and objects on the top layer are in front of other objects. In Figure 7-1, the Default layer toward the bottom of the list contains the business card's standard graphics and the main text. An additional layer contains a different set of contact information — in separate text frames — for a different person. Each new person would have his or her information on his or own new layer. Each layer has its own color, and frames will display in that color if frame edges are visible (choose View⇨Show Frame Edges or press ⌘+H or Ctrl+H).

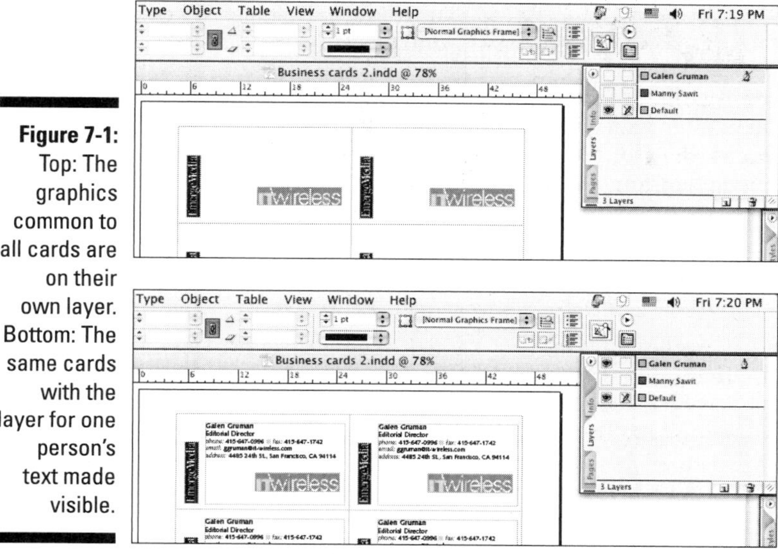

Figure 7-1: Top: The graphics common to all cards are on their own layer. Bottom: The same cards with the layer for one person's text made visible.

Although people often compare layers to plastic overlays, one big difference exists: Layers aren't specific to individual pages. Each layer encompasses the entire document, which doesn't make much difference when you're working on a one-page ad but makes a significant difference when it comes to a 16-page newsletter. When you create layers and place objects on them, you must consider all the pages in the document.

The Layers pane (choose Window➪Layers or press F7) is your gateway to creating and manipulating layers (see Figure 7-2).

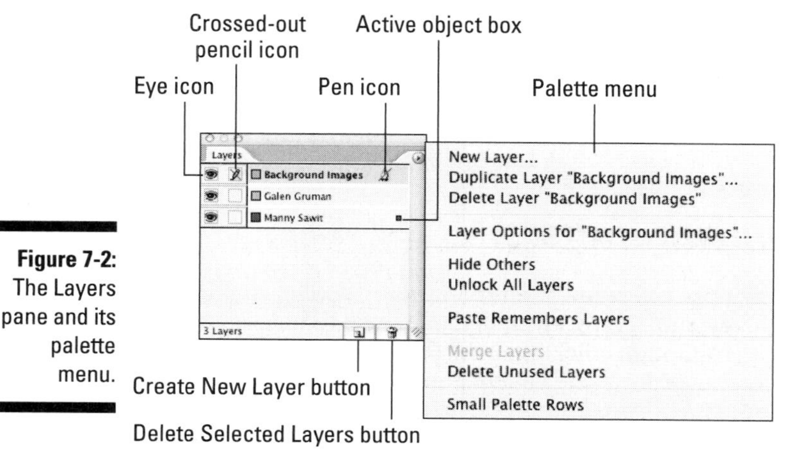

Figure 7-2: The Layers pane and its palette menu.

Working with Layers

Each document contains a default layer, Layer 1, that contains all the objects you place on master pages and document pages. You can create as many layers as you need. After you create a new layer, it's activated automatically so you can begin working on it.

Creating a layer

The Layers pane (choose Window➪Layers or press F7) provides several methods for creating new layers. It doesn't matter which document page is displayed when you create a layer, because the layer encompasses all the pages in the document. To create a layer, do one of the following:

- **To create a new layer on top of all existing layers,** click the New Layer button on the Layers pane to open the New Layer dialog box. The layer receives the default name of Layer *x*.
- **To create a layer above the selected layer,** ⌘+click or Ctrl+click the New Layer button. The layer receives the default name of Layer *x*.
- **To create a new layer on top of all existing layers but customize its name and identifying color,** Option+click or Alt+click the New Layer button, or choose New Layer from the Layers pane's palette menu. Use the New Layer dialog box to specify options for the layer. (The New Layer dialog box — set with a custom name and color — is shown in Figure 7-3.)

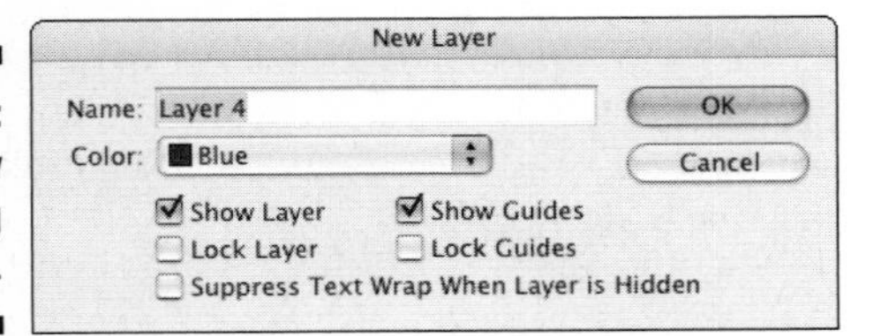

Figure 7-3: The New Layer dialog box.

Customizing layers

You can customize the name, identifying color, guides, and lock status of objects on a new or existing layer. If you choose to customize the layer when you create it (by Option+clicking or Alt+clicking the New Layer button or by choosing New Layer from the Layers pane's palette menu), the New Layer dialog box appears. If you choose to customize an existing layer, double-click it to display the Layer Options dialog box. (You can also choose Layer Options for *Layer Name* from the palette menu on the Layers pane.)

Whether you're using the New Layer dialog box shown in Figure 7-3 or the nearly identical Layer Options dialog box, the options all work the same:

- **Name field:** Type a descriptive name for the layer. For example, if you're using layers for multilingual publishing, you might have a United States English layer, a French layer, and a German layer. If you're using layers to hide background objects while you're working, you might have a Background Objects layer.
- **Color pop-up list:** Choose a color from the list. A layer's color helps you identify which layer an object is on. The color appears to the left of the layer name in the Layers pane and appears on each object on that layer. The color is applied to frame edges, selection handles, bounding boxes, text ports, and text wraps. By default, InDesign applies a different color to each new layer, but you can customize it to something meaningful for your document and workflow.
- **Show Layer check box:** Selected by default, this control lets you specify whether objects on a layer display and print. If you want to suppress printout of the objects on a layer (for example, to hide a different version of a document or to hide pictures while proofing), deselect the Show Layer check box. The Show Layer option has the same effect as clicking the Eye icon on the Layers pane.
- **Lock Layer check box:** Deselected by default, this option lets you control whether objects on a layer can be edited. Select Lock Layer if you don't want to be able to select items and modify them. For example, in a document containing multiple versions of text on different layers, you might lock the layer containing background images and other objects that stay the same. The Lock Layer option has the same effect as clicking the Pencil icon on the Layers pane.
- **Suppress Text Wrap When Layer Is Hidden check box:** Deselected by default, this option prevents text wrapping around the layer's objects when the layer is hidden. Be sure to select this option when you use multiple layers for variations of the same content, such as multilingual text or different contacts for business cards. Otherwise, your layer's text can't display because it is wrapping around a hidden layer with an object of the same size in the same place.

  The Suppress Text Wrap When Layer Is Hidden check box is new to InDesign CS2.
- **Show Guides check box:** This check box lets you control the display of guides that were created while the selected layer was active. When selected, as it is by default, you can create guides while any layer is active and view those guides on any layer. When deselected, you can't create guides. Any guides you create while that layer is active are not displayed, but you can still see guides that you created while other layers were active. Note that when guides are hidden entirely (choose View➪Grids & Guides➪Hide Guides, or press ⌘+; [semicolon] or Ctrl+; [semicolon]), this command has no apparent effect.

- **Lock Guides check box:** This works similarly to Show Guides in that it affects only the guides that you created while the layer is active. When deselected, as it is by default, you can move guides on any layer for which Lock Guides is deselected. When selected, you cannot move guides created while that layer was active. You can, however, move guides on other layers for which Lock Guides is deselected. Note that when all guides are locked (choose View⇨Grids & Guides⇨Lock Guides, or Option+⌘+; [semicolon] or press Ctrl+Alt+; [semicolon]) this command has no apparent effect.

You can select multiple layers and customize them all at once. However, because each layer must have a different name, the Name field isn't available in the Layer Options dialog box when multiple layers are selected.

Working with Objects on Layers

Whether you're designing a magazine template from the ground up or modifying an existing ad, you can isolate specific types of objects on layers. You can create objects on a layer, move objects to a layer, or copy objects to a layer.

The active layer

The *active layer* is the one on which you're creating objects — whether you're using tools, importing text or graphics, clicking and dragging objects in from a library, or pasting objects from other layers or other documents. A Pen icon to the right of a layer's name means it's the active layer (refer to Figure 7-2). Although more than one layer can be selected at a time, only one can be active. To switch the active layer to another layer, click to the right of the layer name that you want to be active; the Pen icon moves, making that the new active layer. Keep in mind that to activate a layer, it must be visible.

Selecting objects on layers

Regardless of the active layer, you can select, move, and modify objects on any visible, unlocked layer. You can even select objects on different layers and manipulate them.

The Layers pane (choose Window⇨Layers or press F7) helps you work with selected objects in the following ways:

- To determine which layer an object belongs to, match the color on its bounding box to the color that appears to the left of a layer name.

- To determine which layers contain active objects, look to the right of the layer names. A small square to the right of a layer name (refer to Figure 7-2) indicates that you have selected an object on that layer.
- To select all the objects on a layer, Option+click or Alt+click the layer's name in the Layers pane. The layer must be active, unlocked, and visible.

To select master-page objects as well as document-page objects on a layer, you need to Option+Shift+click or Altl+Shift+click the layer name.

Placing objects on layers

To place objects on a layer, the layer must be active as indicated by the Pen icon. Anything you copy, import, or create in InDesign goes on the active layer.

When you create objects on master pages, they are placed on the Default layer and are therefore behind other objects on document pages. To create objects on master pages that are in front of other objects, place the objects on a different layer while the master page is displayed.

You can cut and paste objects from one page to another, but have the objects remain on their original layer — without concern about the active layer. To do this, be sure the Paste Remembers Layers is selected in the Layers pane's palette menu before choosing Edit➪Paste or pressing ⌘+V or Ctrl+V.

Moving objects to different layers

When an object is on a layer, it isn't stuck there. You can copy and paste objects to selected layers, or you can move them by using the Layers pane. When you move an object to a layer, it's placed in front of all other objects on a layer. To select multiple objects, remember to Shift+click them, and then move them in one of the following ways:

- **Paste objects on a different layer.** First cut or copy objects to the Clipboard. Activate the layer on which you want to put the objects, and then use the Paste command (by choosing Edit➪Paste or by pressing ⌘+V or Ctrl+V). This method works well for moving objects that are currently on a variety of layers.
- **Move objects to a different layer.** Click and drag the active object square (to the right of a layer's name) to another layer. When you use this method, it doesn't matter which layer is active. However, you can't move objects from several different layers to the same layer using this method. (If you select multiple objects that reside on different layers, dragging the box moves only objects that reside on the first layer on which you selected an object.)

- **Move objects to a hidden or locked layer.** Press ⌘ or Ctrl while you click and drag the active object box.
- **Copy rather than move objects to a different layer.** Press Option or Alt while you click and drag the active object box.
- **Copy objects to a hidden or locked layer.** Press Option+⌘ or Ctrl+Alt while you drag the active object box.

Locking objects on layers

After you lock a layer, you can't select or modify objects on it — even if the locked layer is active. You might lock a layer that contains boilerplate text or a complex drawing that you don't want altered. Locking and unlocking layers is easy, so you might lock one layer while focusing on another, and then unlock it. To lock or unlock layers with the Layers pane, do one of the following:

- Click the blank box in the column immediately to the left of a layer's name. When the crossed-out Pencil icon appears, the layer is locked. Click the crossed-out Pencil icon to unlock the layer. You can also double-click a layer and select or deselect the Lock Layer option in the Layer Options dialog box.
- If no layers are locked, you can lock all but the active layer by choosing Lock Others from the palette menu.
- If any layers are locked, you can unlock all layers by choosing Unlock All Layers from the palette menu.
- You can toggle between Lock Others and Unlock All Layers by Option+clicking or Alt+clicking the blank box or the crossed-out Pencil icon.

When you lock an object to a page (by choosing Object⇨Lock Position, or ⌘+L or Ctrl+L), the object's position stays locked regardless of its layer's lock status.

Manipulating Entire Layers

In addition to working on objects and their layer positions, you can also select and manipulate entire layers. These changes affect all the objects on the layer — for example, if you hide a layer, all its objects are hidden; if you move a layer up, all its objects appear in front of objects on lower layers. Functions that affect an entire layer include hiding, locking, rearranging, merging, and deleting. You work on entire layers in the Layers pane.

Selecting layers

The active layer containing the Pen icon is always selected. You can extend the selection to include other layers the same way you multiple-select objects: Shift+click for a continuous selection and ⌘+click or Ctrl+click for a noncontiguous selection.

Hiding layers

When you hide a layer, none of the objects on that layer display or print. You might hide layers for a variety of reasons, including to speed screen redraw, to control which version of a publication prints, and to simply focus on one area of a design. Be careful when you hide layers with actual content — InDesign won't print, package, or export hidden layers, so you need to unhide any needed layers before printing, packaging, or exporting.

To show or hide layers by using the Layers pane, do one of the following:

- Click the Eye icon in the first column to the left of a layer's name. When the Eye's column is blank, the layer is hidden. Click in the column again to show the layer. You can also double-click a layer and select or deselect the Show Layer option in the Layer Options dialog box.
- If no layers are hidden, you can show only the active layer by choosing Hide Others from the palette menu.
- Regardless of the state of other layers, you can show only one layer by Option+clicking or Alt+clicking in the leftmost column next to its name. All other layers will be hidden.
- If any layers are hidden, you can show all layers by choosing Show All Layers from the palette menu. You can also Option+click or Alt+click twice in a box in the first column to show all layers.

Rearranging layers

Each layer has its own front-to-back stacking order, with the first object you create on the layer being its backmost object. You can modify the stacking order of objects on a single layer by using the Arrange commands on the Object menu. Objects are further stacked according to the order in which the layers are listed in the Layers pane. The layer at the top of the list contains the frontmost objects, and the layer at the bottom of the list contains the backmost objects.

If you find that all the objects on one layer need to be in front of all the objects on another layer, you can move that layer up or down in the list. In fact, you can move all currently selected layers up or down, even if the selection is noncontiguous. To move layers, click the selection and drag it up or down. When you move layers, remember that layers are document-wide, so you're actually changing the stacking order of objects on all the pages.

Combining layers

When you're just discovering the power of layers, you might create a document that is unnecessarily complex (for example, you might have put each object on a different layer and realized that the document has become too difficult to work with). The good news is that you can also merge all the layers in a document to *flatten* it to a single layer. To flatten all layers

1. **Select the *target layer* (the layer where you want all the objects to end up) by clicking it.**
2. **Select the *source layers* (the layers that contain the objects you want to move) in addition to the target layer.**

   Shift+click or ⌘+click or Ctrl+click to add the source layers to the selection.
3. **Make sure the target layer contains the Pen icon and that the target and source layers are all selected.**
4. **Choose Merge Layers from the Layers pane's palette menu.**

   All objects on the source layers are moved to the target layer, and the source layers are deleted.

When you merge layers, the stacking order of objects doesn't change, so the design looks the same, but with one notable exception: If you created objects on a layer while a master page was displayed, those objects go to the *back* of the stacking order with the regular master-page objects.

Deleting layers

If you carefully isolate portions of a document on different layers and then find that you don't need that portion of the document, you can delete the layer. For example, if you have a United States English and an International English layer and you decide that you can't afford to print the different versions, you can delete the unneeded layer. You might also delete layers that you don't end up using to simplify a document.

When you delete layers, all the objects on the layer throughout the document are deleted.

Using the Layers pane, you can delete selected layers in the following ways:

- Click and drag the selection to the Delete Selected Layers button.
- Click the Delete Selected Layers button. The currently selected layers are deleted.
- Choose Delete Layer from the Layers pane's palette menu.

If any of the layers contain objects, a warning reminds you that they will be deleted. And, of course, the ubiquitous Undo command (choose Edit⇨Undo or press ⌘+Z or Ctrl+Z) lets you recover from accidental deletions.

To remove all layers that don't contain objects, choose Delete Unused Layers from the Layers palette.

Chapter 8

Creating Layouts Right the First Time

In This Chapter

- Making layouts easy with master pages
- Applying master pages
- Using templates
- Using libraries

Unless you enjoy continually reinventing the wheel, you'll want to take full advantage of the features that InDesign offers to help you work more productively. After you make some important decisions about elements in your document that will repeat, page after page, in the same spot (such as page numbers, graphics, headers and footers, and so on), you want to set up mechanisms that make the process simple.

Fewer activities in life are less rewarding than doing the same job over and over, and publishing is no exception. Fortunately, InDesign includes some valuable features that let you automate repetitive tasks. In this chapter, we focus on three of them — master pages, templates, and libraries.

Creating and Using Master Pages

A *master page* is a preconstructed page layout that you can use to create new pages — it is the starting point for document pages. Typically, master pages contain text and graphic elements, such as page numbers, headers, footers, and so on, which appear on all pages of a publication. Master pages also include guidelines that indicate page edges, column boundaries, and margins, as well as other manually created guidelines to aid page designers in placing objects. By placing items on master pages, you save yourself the repetitive work of placing the same items one by one on each and every document page.

It may surprise you to know that every InDesign document you create already contains a master page, called A-Master. Whether you use the default master page or create and use additional master pages depends on what kind of document you want to create. If it's a single-page document, such as a flyer or an ad, you don't need master pages at all, so you can just ignore them. However, if you want to create a document with multiple pages — a brochure or booklet, for example — master pages will save time and help ensure consistent design.

Creating a new master page

When you're ready to create a new master page, here's what you do:

1. **If the Pages pane is not displayed, choose Windows⇨Pages or press F12.**

   The Pages pane is covered in more detail in Chapter 6.

2. **From the Pages pane's palette menu, choose New Master.**

   You can also hold Option+⌘ or Ctrl+Alt and click the Create New Page button at the bottom of the pane. The New Master dialog box, shown in Figure 8-1, appears.

Figure 8-1: The New Master dialog box.

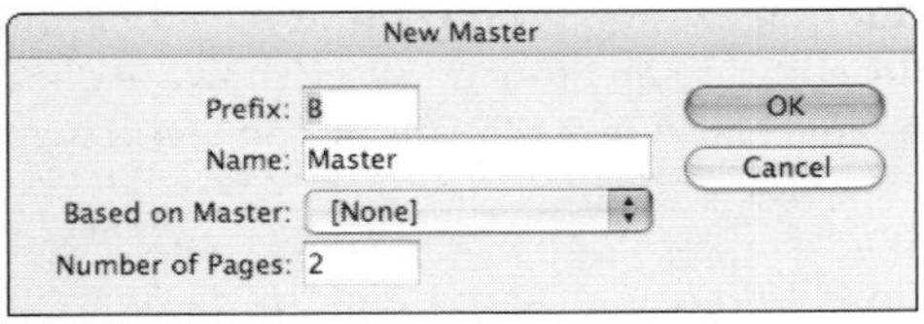

3. **In the Prefix field, specify a one-character prefix to attach to the front of the master page name and displayed on associated document page icons in the Pages pane.**

   The default will be a capital letter, such as the *B* in Figure 8-2.

4. **In the Name field, give your new master page a name.**

   It's a good idea to use a descriptive name, such as `Title Page`.

5. **To base the new master page (the *child*) on another master page (the *parent*), choose the parent master page from the Based on Master pop-up menu.**

6. **In the Number of Pages field, enter the number of pages you want to include in the master spread.** For a document with a single-page design, enter **1**; if the document will have facing pages, enter **2**.

7. **Click OK to save the page and close the dialog box.**

Your new master page will appear in the document window. The name of the master page will appear in the Page Number field in the bottom-left corner of the document window. To make changes to a master page's attributes, simply click its icon at the top of the Pages pane, choose Master Options from the pane's palette menu, and then change settings in the Master Options dialog box.

When you're building a master page, you should think more about the overall structure of the page than about details. Keep the following in mind:

- **To build a document with facing pages,** create facing-page master spreads. The facing pages are somewhat like mirror images of each other. Typically, the left-hand master page is for even-numbered document pages, and the right-hand master page is for odd-numbered document pages.
- **To have page numbers automatically appear on document pages,** add a page number character on each page of your master spreads by drawing a text frame with the Type tool where you want the page number to appear and then choosing Type⇨Insert Special Character⇨Auto Page Number or pressing Option+Shift+⌘+N or Ctrl+Alt+Shift+N. The prefix of the master page (A, B, C, and so on) appears on the master page, but the actual page number is what appears on document pages. Don't forget to format the page number on the master page so that page numbers will look the way you want them to in the document.
- **Specify master page margins and columns** by first making sure that the page is displayed in the document window and then choosing Layout⇨Margins and Columns. The Margins and Columns dialog box, shown in Figure 8-2, is displayed. The controls in this dialog box let you specify the position of the margins, the number of columns, and the gutter width (space between columns).

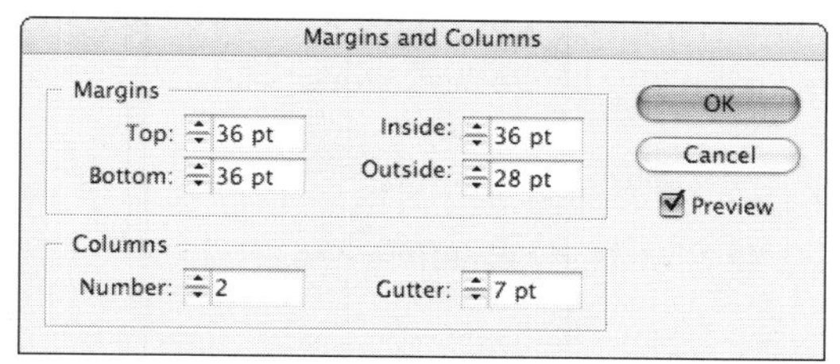

Figure 8-2: The Margins and Columns dialog box.

You can place additional guidelines on a master page — as many custom guidelines as you want. (Guidelines are covered later in this chapter.)

To copy a master page from one document to another, just drag the master page's name from Pages pane to the target document.

Basing one master page on another

Some publications benefit from having more than one master page. If you're building a document with several pages that are somewhat similar in design, it's a good idea to start with one master page and then use it as a basis for additional master pages.

For example, if the brochure you're working on uses both two-column and three-column page layouts, you can create the two-column master spread first and include all repeating page elements. You can then create the three-column master page spread, basing it on the two-column master, and simply specify different column formats. The "child" master page will be identical to the parent except for the number of columns. If you later change an element on the original master page, the change will apply automatically to the child master page.

When you create a new master page, the New Master dialog box provides the option to base it on an existing master page. To help you keep things straight, when you base a master page on another master page, InDesign displays the prefix of the parent page on the icon of the child page.

If you base a master spread on another master spread, you can still modify the master objects (that is, the objects inherited from the parent master) on the child master page. As with regular document pages, you have to Shift+⌘+click or Ctrl+Shift+click the object inherited from a parent master to release it before you can edit it on a child master.

Basing a master spread on a document spread

You might be talented enough to create an effective spread, one that is so handsome that you want to create a master page from it to use on future documents. Simply highlight the spread by clicking the page numbers below the relevant page icons in the Pages pane and choose Save as Master from the Pages pane's palette menu. The new master is assigned a default name and prefix. To change any of its attributes, click its name in the Pages pane and then choose Master Options from the pop-up menu.

Duplicating a master spread

Create a copy of a master spread by selecting its icon and then choosing Duplicate Master Spread from the Pages pane's palette menu or simply by dragging its icon onto the Create New Page button at the bottom of the pane. If you duplicate a master spread, the duplicate loses any parent/child relationships.

Deleting a master

To delete a master page, select its name and then choose Delete Master Page from the Pages pane's palette menu. You can also drag the master icon to the Delete Pages button at the bottom of the Pages pane.

Applying a master page to document pages

After you build a master page, you can apply it to new or existing document pages. (See Chapter 6 for information about adding and removing document pages.) For documents with facing pages, you can apply both pages of a master spread to both pages of the document spread or you can apply one page of a master spread to one page of the document spread. For example, you can apply a master page with a two-column format to the left-hand page of a document spread and apply a master page with a three-column format to the right-hand page.

To apply a master page to a document page, select the name or icon of the page in the top part of the Pages palette and then drag it onto the icon of the document page you want to format. When the target document page is highlighted (framed in a black rectangle, as shown in the left side of Figure 8-3), release the mouse button. If both document pages are highlighted, and if you are applying a master page to the document, both sides of the master spread are applied to the document spread.

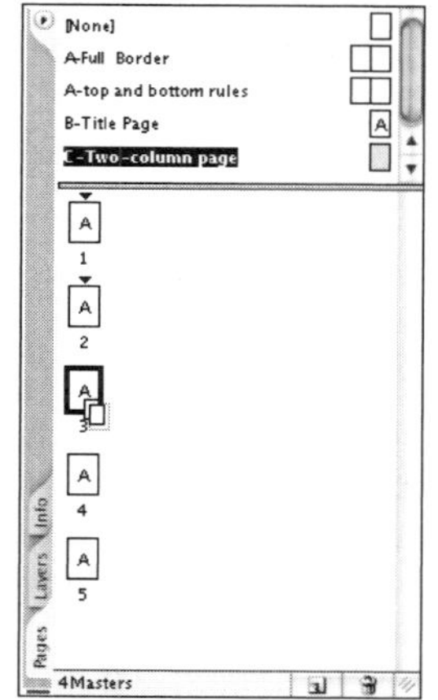

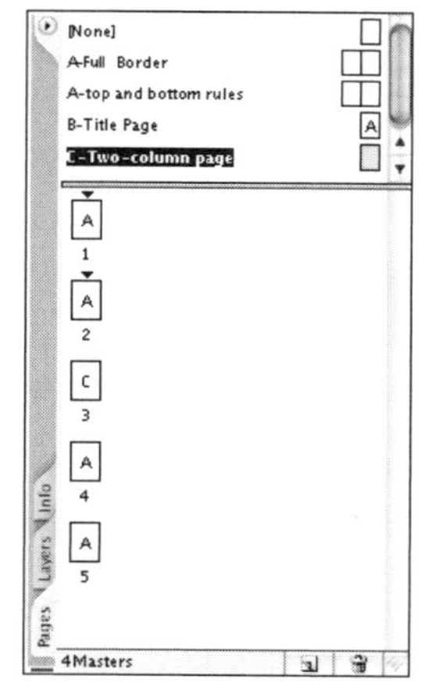

Figure 8-3: Applying a single master page to a document page.

InDesign CS2 lets you apply a master page to the currently displayed page(s) by choosing Layout➪Pages➪Apply Master to Page(s).

Changing master items on document pages

As you work on a document page that's based on a master, you may find that you need to change, move, or delete a master object. Any change you make to a master object on a local page is referred to as a *local override*.

Whenever you remove a master object from a document page, you sever the object's relationship to the master-page object for that document page only. If you subsequently move or modify the object on the master page, it won't affect the deleted object on the document page — it remains deleted on that particular document page.

The Show/Hide Master Items command in the Pages pane's palette menu lets you show or hide master objects on document pages.

To change a master object on a document page, you must first select it, and doing so can be a bit tricky. To select a master object on a document page, hold down Shift+⌘ or Ctrl+Shift when you click the object with one of the selection tools. After you select a master object on a document page, you can modify it just as you would objects that are not part of a master page.

If you modify one or more master objects on a document page and then decide you want to revert back to using the original master objects, you can remove the local overrides. To do so, display the document page that contains the master objects you've modified, select the objects, and then choose Remove Selected Local Overrides from the Pages pane's palette menu. If no objects are selected, the command name changes to Remove All Local Overrides. If the selected spread doesn't have any modified master objects, the command is not available.

Building a Template

A *template* is a pre-built InDesign document that you use as the starting point for creating multiple versions of the same design or publication. For example, if you create a monthly newsletter that uses the same layout for each issue, but with different graphics and text, you begin by creating a template that contains all the elements that are the same in every issue — placeholder frames for the graphics and text, guidelines, and so on.

Creating a template is very similar to creating a document. You create character, paragraph, and object styles, master pages, repeating elements (for example, page numbers), and so on. The only thing you don't add to a template is actual content.

Most often, you create a template after building the first iteration of a document. Once you have that document set up the way you like, you simply strip out the content (that first issue's stories and graphics in our newsletter example) and save it as a template.

Here are the steps for creating a template:

1. **Choose File➪Save As or press Shift+⌘+S or Ctrl+Shift+S to display the Save As dialog box, shown in Figure 8-4.**
2. **Choose a folder and specify a name for the file.**
3. **Choose InDesign CS2 Template in the Format pop-up menu (Mac) or Save as Type pop-up menu (Windows).**
4. **Click Save to close the Save As dialog box and save the template.**

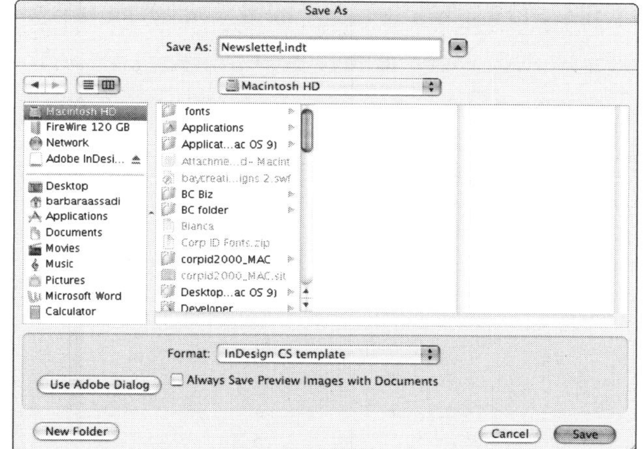

Figure 8-4: Saving a template.

If you're designing a template that will be used by others, you might want to add a layer of instructions. When it's time to print a document based on the template, simply hide the annotation layer. (See Chapter 7 for more information about working with layers.)

If you didn't know better, you might think that a template is exactly the same as a regular InDesign document. It is, with one major exception: A template is a bit more difficult to override. When you open a template, it receives a default name (Untitled-1, Untitled-2, and so on). The first time you choose File➪Save or press ⌘+S or Ctrl+S, the Save As dialog box appears.

As you use a template over time, you might discover that you forgot to include something — perhaps a paragraph style, a repeating element on a particular master page, or an entire master page. To modify a template, you must open it, make your changes, and then use the Save As command to save it again as a template.

Using Libraries

An InDesign *library* is a file — similar in some ways to a document file — where you can store individual objects (graphics, text, and so forth), groups and nested objects, ruler guides, and grids. Once an item is in a library, every time you need a copy, you simply drag one out of the library.

Creating a library is easy:

1. **Choose File➪New➪Library.**

   The New Library dialog box appears, as shown in Figure 8-5.

2. **Choose a location in which to save the library.**
3. **Give the library a name.**
4. **Click OK.**

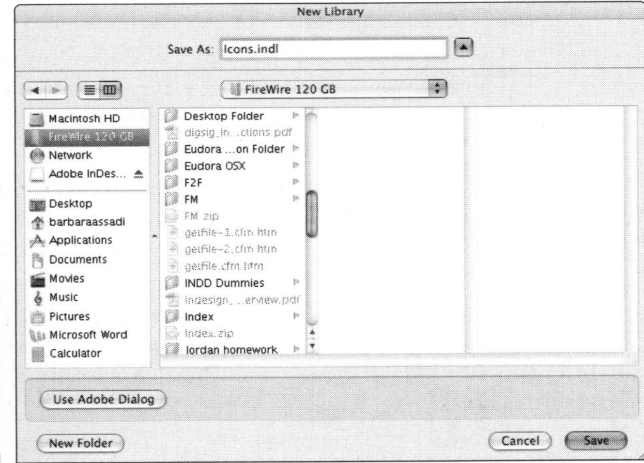

Figure 8-5: The New Library dialog box.

You can create as many libraries as you want and store them wherever is most convenient, including on a networked server so that other InDesign users can share them. You can also open libraries created on a Mac from a Windows computer, and vice versa.

Right after you create a new library, you see an empty library pane, as shown in Figure 8-6. The title bar displays the name you assigned to the library (*Icons,* in our example). To add items to the library, you drag them to the pane. You can group the pane with other panes (by dragging its tab onto another pane) or close it by clicking its close box or choosing Close Library from its pop-up menu.

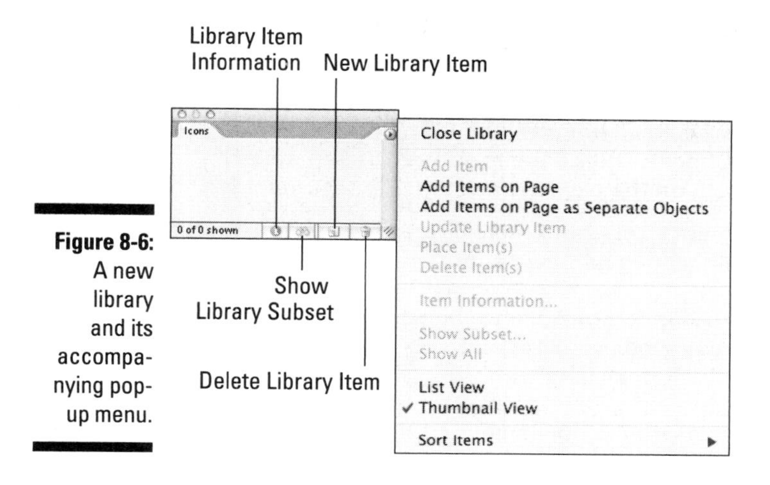

Figure 8-6: A new library and its accompanying pop-up menu.

Here is an explanation of some of the controls and commands shown in Figure 8-6:

- The numbers in the lower-left corner of the pane indicate the number of items currently displayed in the pane and the number of items in the library. In our example in Figure 8-6, these numbers are zeroes because we just opened a new library.
- The Library Item Information button displays the Item Information dialog box. Here you can give each library item a name, a type (for example, image or text), and a description. Later, you can search for library items based on these attributes.
- The Show Library Subset button displays a dialog box that lets you locate and display items that meet certain search criteria.
- The Delete Library Item button lets you delete highlighted items in the library.

Putting items into a library

You can place individual items, such as text and graphics frames, into a library. You can also place multiple selected objects, groups, nested frames, ruler guides, guidelines, and all items on a document page.

To add items to a library:

- Select one or more items and then drag and drop them into an open library pane. (Open an existing library by choosing File➪Open or by pressing ⌘+O or Ctrl+O.)

- Select one or more items and then choose Add Item from the pop-up menu of an open Library pane.
- Choose Add All Items on Page from the pop-up menu of an open Library pane to add all items on the current page or spread *as one library item.* Choose Add All Items on Page as Separate Objects to add each object on the page in one step *as a separate library item.*
- Select one or more items and then click the New Library Item button at the bottom of an open Library pane.

If you hold down the Option or Alt key when adding an item to a library, the Item Information dialog box is displayed. This dialog box lets you add searchable attributes to the library item.

If you import a graphic into a document and then place a copy of the graphic into a library, the path to the original graphics file is saved, as are any transformations you've applied to the graphic or its frame (scale, rotation, shear, and so on). If you save text in a library, all formats, including styles, are retained.

Tagging library items

A library can hold as many items as you want. As a library grows, locating a particular item can become increasingly difficult. To make InDesign library items more easily found, tag them with several searchable attributes.

To tag a library element, select it and then choose Item Information from the library pane's palette menu. You can also display the Item Information dialog box by double-clicking a library item or by clicking once on a library item and then clicking the Library Item Information icon at the bottom of the Library pane. (It's the *i* in a circle.) Specify a Name, Object Type, and/or Description. In the Description field, use a few words that describe the object; this will make it easier to find later. Click OK to close the dialog box and return to the document.

Searching for library items

You can search for library items based on the information specified in the Item Information dialog box. For example, if you place several different icons into a library that includes many other items, and if you use the term *icon* in the Name or Description field, a search of these fields that includes *icon* will find and display those items stored in your library.

Follow these steps to search a library:

1. **Choose Show Subset from a library pane's palette menu or click the Show Library Subset button at the bottom of the pane.**
2. **Decide whether to search the entire library or only the items currently displayed in the page and select the appropriate radio button.**

3. **In the Parameters area, choose the Item Information category you want to search.**

   Your choices are Item Name, Creation Date, Object Type, and Description.

4. **From the next pop-up menu, choose Contains if you intend to search for text contained in the chosen category; choose Doesn't Contain if you want to exclude items that contain the text you specify.**

5. **In the Parameter's area text-entry field, type the word or phrase you want to search for (if you selected Contains in Step 4) or exclude (if you selected Doesn't Contain).**

6. **Add more search criteria by clicking the More Choices button; reduce the number of search criteria by clicking Fewer Choices.**

   You can create up to five levels of search criteria. If you select two or more levels of search criteria, you will be able to choose whether to display items that match all search criteria (by selecting Match All) or to display items that match any of the search criteria (by selecting Match Any One).

7. **Click OK to conduct the search and close the dialog box.**

The library items that match the search criteria are displayed in the pane (unless no items matched the search criteria). To display all items after conducting a search, choose Show All from the Library pane's palette menu.

Deleting items from a library

To delete a library item, drag its icon to the Delete Library item (trashcan icon) at the bottom of the pane or select the item and then choose Delete Item(s) from the library pane's palette menu. You can select a range of items by clicking the first one and then Shift+clicking the last one. You can select multiple, noncontiguous items by holding down the ⌘ or Ctrl key and clicking each icon.

Copying library items onto document pages

Once an item is in a library, you can place copies of that library item into any document or into another library. To place a copy of a library item onto the currently displayed document page, drag the item's icon from the library pane onto the page. As you drag, the outline of the library item is displayed. Release the mouse button when the outline of the item is positioned where you want it to end up. You can also place a library item onto a document by clicking its icon and then choosing Place Item(s).

Copy an item from one library to another by dragging its icon from the source library pane onto the target library pane. To move (rather than copy) an item from one library to another, hold down the Option or Alt key when dragging and dropping an item between libraries.

Chapter 9

Working with Books

In This Chapter

- Adding chapters
- Numbering pages and sections
- Generating tables of contents and indexes
- Adding footnotes

Not only is InDesign useful for short documents like ads and newsletters, but it's also able to comfortably handle longer, multi-chapter documents. The most common and easiest way to build longer documents, especially those created by more than one author or contributor, is to create multiple InDesign documents and then assemble them into a larger book.

If you follow the advice in this chapter, you can use the InDesign Book feature to manage document files, update page numbers across chapters, and maintain consistency throughout the book. You can also use the Table of Contents feature to create and update tables of contents (TOCs). And we also show you how to add an index using InDesign's Index feature.

Managing Chapters and Books

A *book* in InDesign is a specific type of file that you create to track chapters or multiple documents that make up the book. Using InDesign's book panes, you can add, open and edit, rearrange, and print chapters of the book. The book palette is nice for workgroups because multiple users can open the same book and access different chapters; it also works well if you are a single user working on a multi-chapter book.

InDesign's Book feature lets you:

- See who is working on each chapter and when.
- Update paragraph styles, character styles, object styles, colors, and TOC styles across documents for consistency.
- Update page numbers across multiple documents.

- Create a table of contents and an index for multiple documents.
- Easily print all the chapters of a book.

Creating a new book

To create a new book, choose File➪New➪Book. The New Book dialog box lets you specify a location for the book and give it a name. Click Open to create and open the book.

Opening and closing a book

Open an existing book by using the File➪Open command (⌘+O or Ctrl+O). The book will appear in its own pane in the palette (the palette has no title and will appear automatically if you open a book when no other books are open). You can also double-click a book's icon to open it.

To close a book's pane, and any book documents that are in it, simply click its close box.

Adding chapters to books

A new book pane is empty — you need to add chapter documents to fill it up. To do this, click the Add Document button — the + button on the bottom-right of the book's pane (see Figure 9-1) — or use the Add Document option in the book pane's palette menu. Use the Add Chapter dialog box to locate and select the first chapter you want to add. Click the Add button to make this the first chapter in the book. Repeat this process to add to the book all the chapters you have ready (you can also add more later).

Chapters are listed in the book pane in the order in which you add them. You may want to rearrange them to match the actual order of the book project — especially if you are numbering the book automatically from start to finish, since InDesign will number them based on their order in the book pane. To rearrange the relative position of chapters, just click and drag chapter names up or down within the pane to put them in the desired order.

Working on chapters

To work on a chapter in a book, first open the book and then double-click the chapter name in the book's pane. The chapter opens in InDesign just like any other InDesign document. For a chapter to be opened, it must be Available, as discussed in the next section. When you finish editing a chapter, save and close it as usual.

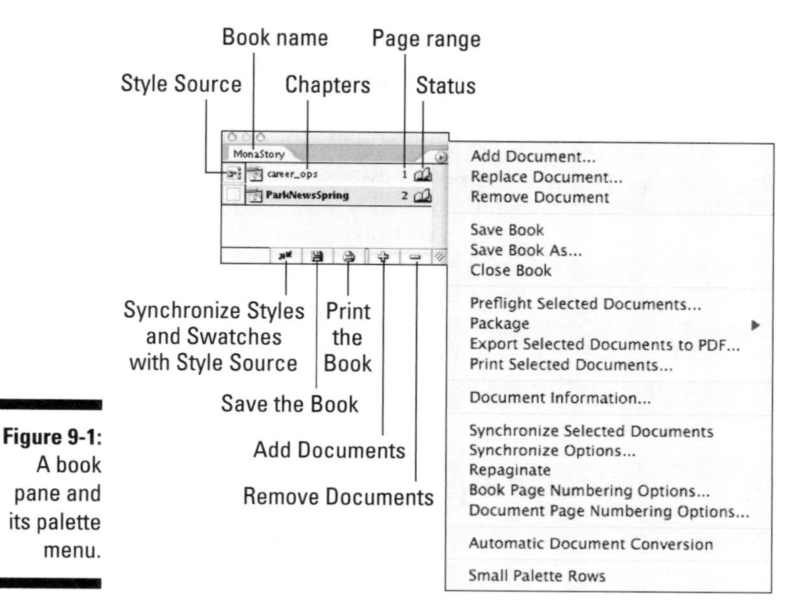

Figure 9-1: A book pane and its palette menu.

Replace an existing chapter with another document by selecting the chapter in the book pane and choosing Replace Document from the palette menu. Navigate to a new document, select it, and click the Open button. InDesign will replace the selected chapter with the new document.

Delete chapters from a book by choosing Remove Document from the palette menu or by clicking the Remove Document button (the – icon) from the bottom of the pane.

InDesign offers three other menu options in the palette menu that come in handy for managing a book: You can save books by choosing Save Book, save to a new name by choosing Save Book As, and close the book by choosing Close Book (any changes to the book are not saved, though a warning box gives you the chance to save any unsaved changes).

Finding out about chapter status

When you use the book palette in a workgroup, it provides helpful status reports about each chapter. The statuses are:

- **Available:** The chapter can be opened, edited, or printed. Only one user at a time can open a chapter.
- **Open:** You have the chapter open and can edit it or print it. Nobody else can open the chapter at this time.

- **In Use:** Another user has the chapter open. In this case, you cannot edit or open the chapter.
- **Modified:** The chapter has been changed since the last time you opened the book palette. Simply click the book pane to update it.
- **Missing:** The chapter's file has been moved since it was added to the book. Double-click the chapter name to open a Find File dialog box and locate it.

The Document Information menu option in the book pane's palette menu provides useful information. When you select a chapter and choose this option, you can see the file's modification date, location, and page range, and you can replace the chapter with a different document.

Taking advantage of style sources

The first chapter you add to the book is, by default, the style source. You can tell which chapter is the style source by the icon to the left of the chapter name. In most cases, you want the text formatting, object styles, colors, and so on to remain the same from chapter to chapter. The style source in an InDesign book defines the styles and swatches that are common to all the chapters in the book. When you use the Synchronize feature, InDesign makes sure that the paragraph styles, character styles, object styles, trap presets, TOC styles, and swatches in each chapter in the book match those in the style source.

If you decide to make a different chapter the style source, all you need to do is (in the book pane) click in the column to the left of that chapter's filename. This moves the icon indicating the style source to that chapter.

Synchronizing formatting

When formatting is synchronized, chapters maintain a consistent appearance. The book pane includes a Synchronize button, as well as a Synchronize Selected Documents or Synchronize Book menu item in the palette menu. Before you synchronize, make sure that you're happy with the styles you've established in the style source and then follow these steps to synchronize:

1. **Be sure that all chapters are available for editing.**
2. **Choose the style source (the document that contains the styles you want to use throughout the book) by clicking the box to the left of the source chapter so that the style-source icon appears.**

3. **Choose Synchronize Options from the book pane's palette menu, which opens a dialog box.**

   Make sure that every type of item you want to synchronize — Object Styles, TOC Style, Character Styles, Paragraph Styles, Trap Presets, and Swatches — is checked. You can click All Styles to ensure that all are synchronized across a book's chapters.

4. **Select the chapters you want to synchronize and either click the Synchronize button or choose Synchronize Selected Documents from the palette menu.**

   If no chapters are selected, InDesign assumes you want to synchronize all chapters; the menu option Synchronize Book will appear in the palette menu rather than Synchronize Selected Documents in that case.

5. **Compare the styles (character, paragraph, object, and TOC), swatches (color, tint, and gradient), and trap styles in the style source to those in each chapter.**

   If anything is different, the information in each chapter will be updated to match the style source. If someone changed the typeface in a paragraph style in a chapter, it will revert to the typeface specified in the style source. If anything is missing from a chapter — for example, if you just added a swatch to the style source but not to other chapters — that information is added to each chapter.

By using the Synchronize feature, you give each chapter the same basic set of styles and swatches as the style source, although you can still add more of these specifications to individual chapters. Keep in mind that synchronizing doesn't repair the formatting fiascos that can happen when multiple users work on the same book. Be sure everyone who needs to know the standards for the design has access, ahead of time, to that information.

Printing chapters and books

Using the book pane, you can print any chapters with the status of Available or Open. Here's how:

1. **To print the entire book, make sure no chapters are selected. To print a contiguous range of chapters, Shift+click the first and last chapters that you want to print. To print noncontiguous chapters, ⌘+click or Ctrl+click the chapters to select them.**

2. **Click the Print Book button or choose Print Book or Print Selected Documents in the book pane's palette menu (the option will depend on whether chapters are selected in the book pane).**

   The standard InDesign Print dialog box opens. Note that the option to choose all pages or a range of pages is grayed out — you must print all chapters in the selected chapters.

3. **Make any adjustments in the Print dialog box.**
4. **Click Print to print the chapters.**

You can also output a book to PDF by using the Export Book to PDF or Export Selected Documents to PDF menu items in the palette menu. These menu items work like their equivalent Print versions.

Working with sections in chapters

Section-based page numbering is fairly common in long documents because it lets you, for example, restart page numbering in each new section, such as 4.1, 4.2, and so on. Creating a section start is also the only way to start a document on a left-facing page. InDesign gives you two choices for numbering book pages: You can let the book pane number pages consecutively from one chapter to the next, or you can add sections of page numbers, which carry through the book until you start a new section.

Numbering pages consecutively

If your book chapters don't have sections, use consecutive page numbering, in which the first page number of a chapter follows the last page number of the previous chapter (for example, one chapter ends on page 224, and the next chapter starts on page 225).

Consecutive page numbering is applied by default in InDesign. If for some reason a document resets its numbering, go to that document, open the Numbering & Section options dialog box (choose Numbering & Section Options in the Pages pane's palette menu), and select Automatic Page Numbering.

Consecutive page numbering works as follows:

- Whenever you add a chapter that contains no sections, or that has section numbering set to Automatic Page Numbering, InDesign numbers pages consecutively throughout the book.
- As you add and delete pages from chapters, InDesign updates all the page numbers in the chapters that follow.
- You can force InDesign to renumber all the pages by choosing Repaginate from the book pane's palette menu — this is handy if you changed section options in some chapters and want the book to see those changes.

Numbering pages with sections

When chapters you add to books already contain sections of page numbers (implemented through the Numbering & Section dialog box, which you access via the Numbering & Section Options menu option in the Pages pane's palette

menu), section page numbering overrides the book's consecutive p
bering. The section page numbering carries through chapters of th
InDesign encounters a new section start. So if one chapter ends on page
next chapter starts on page *v* unless you start a new section for that chapter.

For more in-depth information about section numbering, see Chapter 6.

Creating Tables of Contents

A table of contents (TOC) is useful in a long document because it helps readers locate information quickly. A TOC is simply a list of paragraphs that are formatted with the same styles. This means that if you want to use the Table of Contents feature, you have to use paragraph styles. Not only do styles guarantee consistent formatting, they also tell InDesign what text you want to include in your TOC.

After you've created a book (or even a single document), InDesign can build a table of contents by scanning pages for the paragraph styles you specify. For example, if you create a book, you might use paragraph styles named *Chapter Title, Section,* and *Subsection.* Using the Table of Contents feature, InDesign can generate a table of contents that includes all three levels.

TOC styles manage the text that you want in a table of contents, the order in which it appears, how page numbers are added, and how the various TOC elements are formatted. To create a TOC style, choose Layout⇨Table of Contents Styles, which opens the dialog box shown in Figure 9-2.

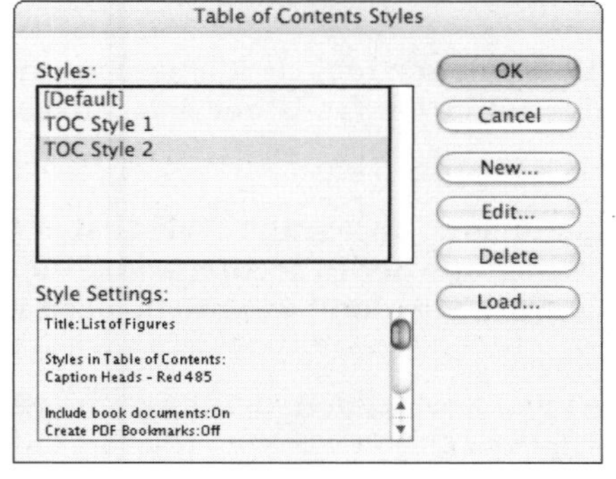

Figure 9-2: The Table of Contents Styles dialog box.

In the Table of Contents Styles dialog box, click New to create a new TOC style. You can also edit an existing TOC style via the Edit button, delete one via the Delete button, and import one from another InDesign document via the Load button.

Here's how to create a TOC style after clicking the New button:

1. **Enter a name for the TOC style in the TOC Style field (shown in Figure 9-3).**

   The default is TOC Style 1.

2. **In the Title field, enter a heading for the TOC.**

   This text appears in your table of contents.

   If you don't want a title, leave the Title field blank, but note that you still get an empty paragraph at the top of your TOC for this title. You can always delete that paragraph.

3. **Use the Style pop-up menu to choose the paragraph style that this title will have.**

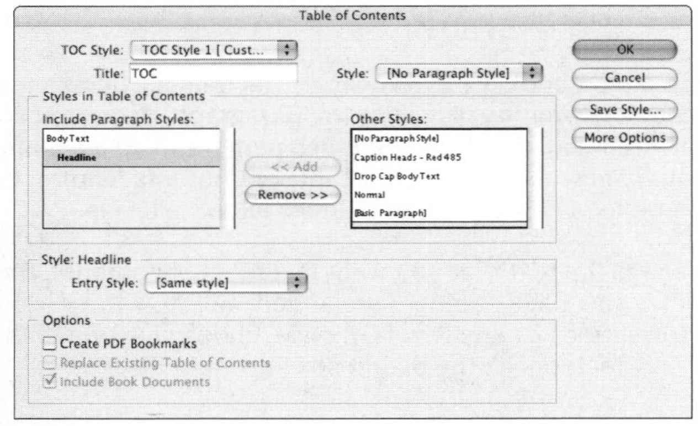

Figure 9-3: The Table of Contents dialog box.

4. **In the Styles in Table of Contents section, click a paragraph style that you want to appear in your TOC from the Other Styles list at right.**

   For example, you might click Chapter Title.

5. **Click<<Add to add it to the Include Paragraph Styles list at left. (Select a style from the Include Paragraph Styles section and click Remove>> to remove any paragraph styles you don't want to be used in the TOC.)**

6. **Repeat Steps 4 and 5 until you have added all of the paragraph styles that you want to include in the TOC.**

7. **Use the Entry Style pop-up menu to select a TOC level and then choose the paragraph formatting for that style.**

   If the Entry Style, Page Number, and other options don't display, click the More Options button to see them.

- Use the Page Number pop-up menu to determine how page numbers are handled: After Entry, Before Entry, and No Page Number. If you want the page numbers to have a character style applied, choose that style from the Style pop-up menu to the right of the Page Number pop-up menu.
- Use the Between Entry and Number field and pop-up menu to choose what appears between the TOC text and the page number. You can enter any characters you want; use the pop-up menu to select special characters such as bullets and tabs. In most cases, you should select a tab; the paragraph style selected earlier for the TOC entry includes leader information, such as having a string of periods between the text and the number. You can also apply a character style to the characters between the text and the page numbers via the Style pop-up menu at right.
- To sort entries at this level alphabetically, such as for a list of products in a brochure, select the Sort Entries in Alphabetical Order check box.
- To change the level of the current TOC entry, use the Level pop-up menu. If you change the level of entries, InDesign will correctly sort them when it creates the TOC, even if the levels seem out of order in the Include Paragraph Styles list.
- In the Options section of the dialog box, choose the appropriate options. Check Create PDF Bookmarks if you're exporting the document to PDF format and want the PDF TOC file to have *bookmarks* (a clickable set of TOC links). Check Run-in if you want all entries at the same level to be in one paragraph. (This is not common for TOCs but is used in indexes and lists of figures.) Check Replace Existing Table of Contents if you want InDesign to automatically replace an existing TOC if the TOC style is changed. Check Include Text on Hidden Layers if you want text on hidden layers to be included in the TOC. Finally, check Include Book Documents if you have a book open and want InDesign to generate a TOC based on all chapters in that book. (InDesign will show the current open book's name.)

8. **Continue this process for each paragraph style whose text should be in the TOC.**

   Note that the order in which you add these styles determines the initial levels: The first paragraph style added is level 1; the second is level 2, and so on. But you can change the order by changing the Level setting, as described earlier.

To make changes to a TOC style, go to the Edit Table of Contents Style dialog box. Choose Layout⇨Table of Contents Styles, select the TOC style to edit, and click Edit.

With a TOC style in place and your document properly formatted with the paragraph styles that the TOC style will look for when generating a TOC, you're ready to have InDesign create the actual TOC for you.

To generate a TOC, choose Layout⇨Table of Contents. You get a dialog box that is identical to the Table of Contents dialog box shown in Figure 9-4. In this dialog box, you can make changes to the TOC style settings. (If you want to save those TOC style changes, be sure to click the Save Style button.) Then click OK to have InDesign generate the TOC. You might also get a dialog box asking whether you want to include items in *overset text* (text that didn't fit in your document after you placed it) in your TOC. It may take a minute or two for the program to generate the TOC. (See Chapter 15 for more details on overset text.)

Be sure you allow enough space (a single text frame, a series of linked text frames, or one or more empty pages) for the TOC before generating a final TOC because if you end up adding or deleting pages based on the TOC length, the TOC will display the old page numbers. To update page numbering after flowing a TOC, simply rebuild the TOC by selecting the text frame holding the TOC and then choosing Layout⇨Update Table of Contents.

If you select a text frame, InDesign will place the TOC text in it when you generate the TOC. If you don't select a text frame, you see the familiar loaded-text icon (the paragraph pointer) that you see when you place a text file. Click a text frame to insert the TOC text in that frame or click in an empty part of your document to create a text frame in which the TOC text will flow.

The feature that creates TOCs is actually a list generator, and you can use it to create other kinds of lists. Basically, anything that is tagged with a paragraph style can be used to create a list. For example, if your figure captions all use their own paragraph style, you can generate a list of figures by creating a TOC style that includes just the Caption Title paragraph style. An InDesign document can have more than one TOC, so you can include multiple lists in your document.

Creating Indexes

When trying to locate information in a book, nothing is as wonderful as a good index. Once upon a time, book indexing was a labor-intensive process involving piles of index cards. InDesign makes indexing much easier, while still allowing you to make key decisions about how the index is formatted.

But be warned: Indexing is complicated business and is, by and large, an expert feature. So we cover just the basics here.

Choosing an indexing style

Before you begin indexing your document, ask yourself the following questions:

- Do you want to initial-cap all levels of all entries, or do you just want sentence case?
- Should index headings appear in boldface?
- What type of punctuation will you use in your index?
- Will you capitalize secondary entries in the index?
- Should the index be nested or run-in style? (A nested index is an indented list, with each entry on its own line. A run-in index puts all related entries in one paragraph, separated by semicolons.)

After you make these decisions, it's a good idea to make a small dummy index. From the dummy, create a master page for index pages, paragraph styles for index headings (the letters *A, B, C,* and so on), paragraph styles for each level of the index (including indents as appropriate), and character styles for any special formatting you want on page numbers or cross-reference text. InDesign doesn't do any of this for you.

Inside the Index pane

When you want to index a chapter or document, open the Index pane by choosing Window➪Type & Tables➪Index or by pressing Shift+F8. Use this pane to add words to the index in up to four indent levels, edit or delete index entries, or create cross-references. The Index pane is shown in Figure 9-4.

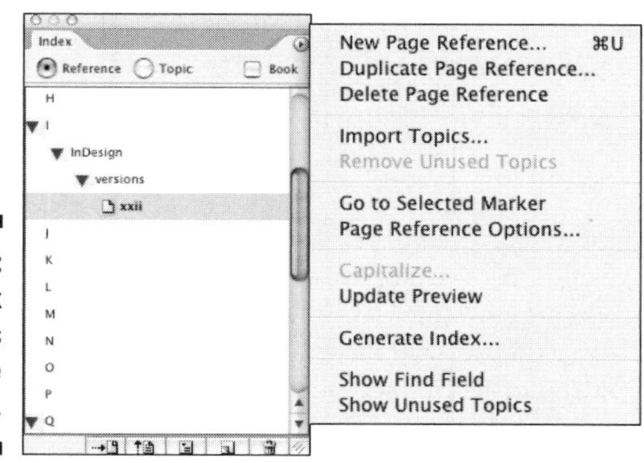

Figure 9-4: The Index pane and its palette menu.

Two radio buttons appear at the top of the Index pane: Reference and Topic. You use Reference mode to add and edit entries from selected text. If you're creating an index in a book, be sure to click the Book check box as well in the Index pane. (Although it is a well-intentioned feature meant to help standardize index entries, the Topic mode's use is not intuitive, and most indexers simply ignore it and add entries manually from selected text or type phrases into the Index pane in Reference mode. You should ignore it, too.)

Select the Book check box if you are creating an index for multiple chapters in a book. You must have a book open for this option to be available. If you have a book open and do not select the Book box, the index is saved with the current document and not opened when you open other chapters of the book.

Adding index items via the Index pane

To add entries to the index, be sure the Type tool is active, then choose New Page Reference from the Index pane's palette menu, or press ⌘+U or Ctrl+U, to get the dialog box shown in Figure 9-5.

If the Type tool is not active when you open the dialog box, the palette menu option will be called New Cross-Reference instead, letting you add a cross-reference entry to the index. The resulting New Cross-Reference dialog box is identical to the New Page Reference dialog box, except the various options default to ones appropriate for a cross-reference.

Here's how the controls work:

Figure 9-5: The New Page Reference dialog box.

- If you selected text first in your document, the text is entered automatically into Topic Level 1. Otherwise, type in the text that you want to add to the index. In Figure 9-5, you can see that we typed **keyboard**. The text will be added to the Topic list and to the list of index entries.

- You can enter text that controls how the entry is sorted in the Sort By column. For example, if the selected text you're indexing is *The A-Team,* but you want it sorted as if it were *A-Team, The* (so it appears with the A entries in the index), enter **A-Team, The** in the Sorted By column.
- If you want a more complex index, you might want to use some or all of the four possible entry levels. You may want an index entry to appear under a higher-level topic. For example, you may want *Border Collies* to appear in the index under *Herding Dogs,* in which case you would enter **Herding Dogs** the Topic Level 1 field and **Border Collies** in the Topic Level 2 field.
- Use the Type pop-up menu, shown in Figure 9-7, to determine the page entries for the index entry. For instance, if you select To End of Section, the page numbers for the selected text in the index will cover the range from the index entry to the end of the section it is in.
- To add just the selected text as an index entry, click Add. (If no text is selected, the text will be added to the Topic list, but no index entry will appear for the it.) To add all occurrences of the text in the book, click Add All.
- To change previously defined index entries, select an entry and then choose Page Reference Options in the Index pane's palette menu.
- At the bottom of the New Page Reference dialog box is a list of letters as well as the entry Symbols (where entries that begin with numbers and other non-letter characters will be grouped in the index). You can scroll through this list of headings to see what is already in the index under each letter. Although you might think clicking a letter would force the current index entry to appear in that letter's section of the index, it does not.

InDesign CS2 changes how multi-paragraph text selections are indexed. InDesign CS2 now indexes each paragraph in that selection as separate entries.

To quickly add a word or text selection to an index, highlight the text and press ⌘+U or Ctrl+U to add the text to the New Page Reference dialog box. To index a word without opening that dialog box, just press Option+Shift+⌘+[or Ctrl+Alt+Shift+[. This adds the text to the index using the index's default settings. (You can always edit them later.) And to enter an index entry as a proper name (last name, first name), use the shortcut Option+Shift+⌘+] or Ctrl+Alt+Shift+].

Polishing and generating the index

The Index pane's palette menu has several options useful for generating and fine-tuning an index:

- **Duplicate Topic** lets you duplicate a topic entry so you can use the settings from one entry without having to re-enter those settings in a new entry.

- **Delete Topic** removes a topic (and any associated entries) from the index.
- **Import Topics** lets you import topic lists from other InDesign documents.
- **Go to Selected Marker** causes InDesign to jump to the text that contains the selected index entry in the Index pane.
- **Topic Options** lets you edit the Level and Sort By settings for topic entries; these affect all index entries that use them.
- **Capitalize** lets you standardize the capitalization of topic entries — you can choose Selected Topic, Selected Topic and All Subtopics, All Level 1 Topics, and All Topics.
- **Update Preview** updates the index entries in the Index pane to reflect page-number changes, new occurrences of index text occurrences, and deleted occurrences of indexed text.
- **Generate Index** creates the index via the dialog box shown in Figure 9-6. In this dialog box, you specify the following: title for the index, the paragraph style sheet for that title, whether a selected index is replaced with the new one, whether an entire book is indexed, whether text on hidden layers is indexed, whether the index is nested or run-in, whether empty index headings and sections are included, what paragraph styles are applied to each level of index entry, what character styles are applied to different portions of index entries, and which characters will be used as separators within index entries. (Click the More Options button to see the nested/run-in and later options.) After you generate an index, you get the standard InDesign load-text icon (the paragraph icon); click an existing text frame into which you want to flow the index, or click anywhere else in a document to have InDesign create the text frame for you and flow the index text into it.

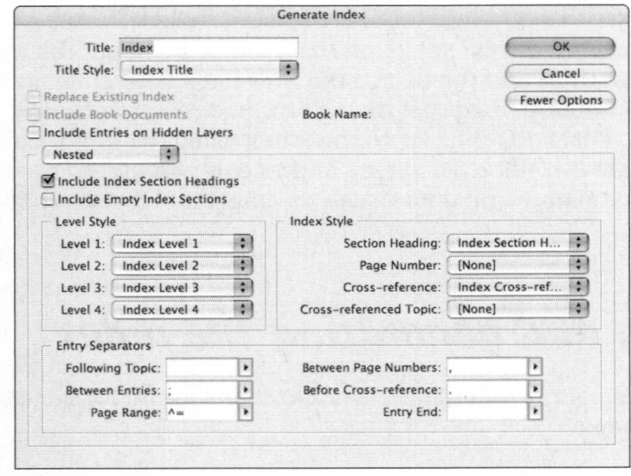

Figure 9-6: The Generate Index dialog box, with all options displayed.

Adding Footnotes

Many books, including academic and technical documents, use footnotes. InDesign lets you add footnotes to your book with very little fuss.

You can import footnotes from Microsoft Word files, or you can add footnotes directly in InDesign. With the text-insertion pointer in your text where you want the footnote marker to appear, choose Type➪Insert Footnote to add a footnote to the bottom of the column that contains the footnote marker, as Figure 9-7 shows. You need to manually enter the text that will go with each numbered footnote, but InDesign updates the footnote numbering as you add and delete footnotes.

You cannot insert footnotes into tables. But you can simulate footnotes by adding a superscripted footnote character in the table text and typing your footnote text below the table — note this "footnote" is not linked to the text, will not renumber automatically as a real footnote would, and cannot be formatted with InDesign's footnote formatting controls.

You can control much of the appearance of footnotes by choosing Type➪Document Footnote Options to open the Footnote Options dialog box, shown in Figure 9-8.

Figure 9-7: Inserting a footnote.

The Numbering and Formatting pane controls the formatting of the footnote text and footnote character in the current InDesign document. The Layout pane controls the placement of the footnote relative to the rest of the document.

To change these settings for future documents, open the dialog box while no document is open and set your new defaults.

Figure 9-8: The Footnote Options dialog box contains two panes: Numbering and Formatting, and Layout.

Part III
Object Essentials

"Oh, that's Jack's area for his paper crafts. He's made some wonderful US Treasury Bonds, Certificates of Deposit, $20's, $50's, $100's, that sort of thing."

In this part . . .

The rubber really hits the road when you've got your basic layout structure in place. Now you can focus on the meat of your documents: the objects that contain your text and graphics. It's amazing all the things you can do to objects, such as rotate them, color them, and apply special effects like drop shadows. And you can even save a lot of these settings so you can apply them consistently to other objects later — a real timesaver that also ensures quality results. You'll learn all that and more in this part.

Note that you can apply most of these effects to objects whether or not they already contain their graphics and text — so if you're a really structured kind of person, you'll probably create your basic object containers first and apply your effects to them, then bring in the text and graphics. But if you're more free-form in your approach, you'll likely bring in all your text and graphics, then start arranging the objects that contain them to produce your final layout. That's fine; you'd just apply the techniques here while doing so.

Chapter 10

Adding Frames, Lines, and Colors

In This Chapter

- Using frames and shapes
- Creating lines
- Creating and applying colors, tints, and gradients

The fundamental components of any layout are its *objects.* An object is a container that can (but doesn't have to) hold text or graphics, as well as display attributes such as color, strokes, and gradients. This chapter explains how to create these building blocks — frames, shapes, and lines — as well as the colors, gradients, and tints you can apply to them.

Creating Frames and Shapes

When an object contains an imported graphic or text, or if an object is created as a placeholder for a graphic or text, it's referred to as a *frame.* Otherwise, it is called a *shape.*

Designing pages in InDesign is largely a matter of creating and modifying frames and shapes, as well as modifying the text and graphics the frames contain.

As Figure 10-1 shows, the Tools palette contains several tools for creating both shapes and frames:

- The Rectangle, Ellipse, and Polygon shape tools (the Ellipse and Polygon tools are available through the pop-up menu that appears if you click and hold on the Rectangle tool).
- The Rectangle, Ellipse, and Polygon frame tools (the Ellipse and Polygon frame tools are available through the pop-up menu that appears if you click and hold on the Rectangle frame tool).
- The Type tool (which can create rectangular text frames).

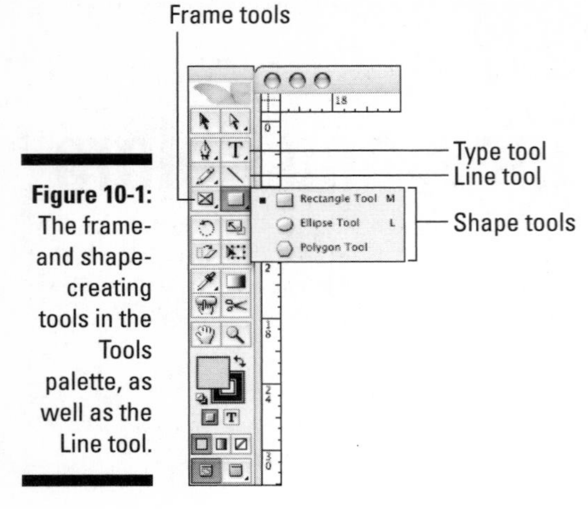

Figure 10-1: The frame- and shape-creating tools in the Tools palette, as well as the Line tool.

Here's how to create a frame (or shape):

1. **Select the desired tool from the Tools palette.**

   For the Polygon and Polygon Frame tools, you can set the shape and number of sides by double-clicking the tool and then using the dialog box that appears. Figure 10-2 shows that dialog box.

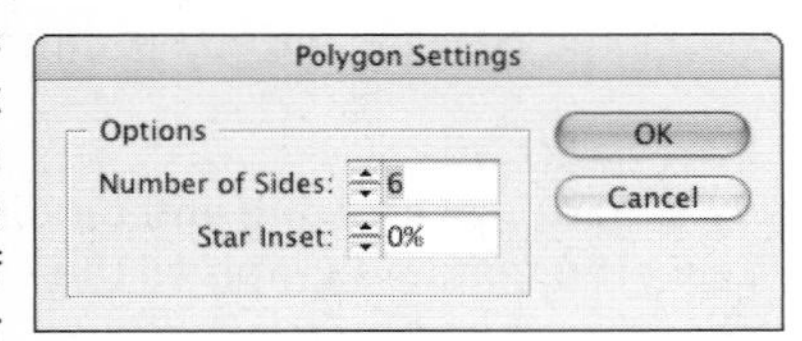

Figure 10-2: The Polygon Settings dialog box lets you specify the number of sides your polygons will have.

2. **Move the mouse pointer anywhere within the currently displayed page or on the pasteboard.**
3. **Click and drag in any direction.**

   As you drag, a crosshair pointer appears in the corner opposite your starting point; a colored rectangle indicates the boundary of the frame. (The color will be blue for objects on the default layer; objects on other layers will have that layer's color. See Chapter 7 for more on layers.) You can look at the width and height values displayed in the Control palette

Frames versus shapes: No real difference

InDesign has tools that let you create both shapes and frames. But there's really no difference between shapes and frames other than how they appear onscreen — frames have an X through them, while shapes don't. (That *X* in frames doesn't print, of course, it's just a visual indicator of a frame.) Both frames and shapes can contain text or graphics, and you can apply colors and other effects to both frames and shapes.

So don't worry about whether you create frames or shapes; in the end, they do the same things. So if we tell you to use the Ellipse Frame tool and you choose the Ellipse tool, for example, don't worry. Both tools do the same thing. And anything we say relating to frames also applies to shapes — unless, of course, we say otherwise.

or the Transform pane as you drag to help you get the size you want. Holding down the Shift key as you drag limits the tool to creating a frame or shape within a square bounding box.

4. **When the frame is the size and shape you want, release the mouse button.**

Pretty easy, huh? At this point, you can begin typing in the frame, paste text or a graphic into it, or import a text or a graphics file, as Chapters 14 and 19 explain.

If you create a text frame with the Type tool, be sure not to click in an existing text frame when your intention is to create a new one. If you click within an existing frame when the Type tool is selected, the flashing cursor appears, and InDesign thinks you want to type text.

When any of the frame-creation tools is selected, you can create as many new frames as you want. Simply keep clicking, dragging, and releasing. After you create a graphics frame, you can modify it (without changing tools) by adding a border or a colored background or by applying any of the effects — such as rotation, shear, and scale — in the Control palette or Transform pane. You can also move or resize a graphics frame, but you have to switch to the Selection tool or the Direct Selection tool to do so. Chapter 12 explains how to resize, move, delete, and otherwise manipulate frames and other objects.

Drawing a Straight Line

Although they're not as flashy or versatile as shapes and frames, lines can serve many useful purposes in well-designed pages. For example, you can use plain ol' vertical rules to separate columns of text in a multicolumn page or the rows and columns of data in a table. Dashed lines are useful for indicating folds and cut lines on brochures and coupons. And lines with arrowheads are handy if you have to create a map or a technical illustration.

InDesign lets you create straight lines with the Line tool and zigzag lines, curved lines, and free-form shapes with the Pen tool. In this chapter, we keep things simple and limit the discussion to the Line tool. See Chapter 21 for the fancy stuff.

Follow these steps to draw a straight line:

1. **Select the Line tool.** (Figure 10-1 shows the Line tool.)
2. **Move the pointer anywhere within the currently displayed page or on the pasteboard.**
3. **Click and drag the mouse in any direction.**

   As you drag, a thin, blue line appears from the point where you first clicked to the current position of the cross-hair pointer. Holding down the Shift key as you drag constrains the line to a horizontal, vertical, or 45-degree diagonal line.
4. **When the line is the length and angle you want, release the mouse button.**

   Don't worry too much about being precise when you create a line. You can always go back later and fine-tune it.

When you release the mouse button after creating a line, the line is active. As illustrated in Figure 10-3, if the Selection tool was previously selected, the line appears within a rectangular bounding box, which contains eight resizing handles. If the Direct Selection tool was previously selected, moveable anchor points appear at the ends of the line. In either case, you have to choose the right tool if you want to change the shape or size of the bounding box or the line:

- The Selection tool lets you change the shape of the line's bounding box (which also changes the angle and length of the line) by dragging any of the resizing handles.
- The Direct Selection tool lets you change the length and angle of the line itself by moving anchor points on the frame.

When you create a line, it takes on the characteristics specified in the Stroke pane (Window⇨Stroke or F10). When you first open a document, the default line width is 1 point. If you want to change the appearance of your lines, double-click the Line tool and adjust the Weight setting in the Stroke pane that appears. If you make this adjustment when no document is open, all new documents will use the new line settings.

As long as the Line tool is selected, you can create as many new lines as you want. Simply keep clicking, dragging, and releasing. After you create a line, you can modify it (without changing tools) by changing any of the attributes — including weight, style, and start/end shapes — in the Stroke pane. Chapter 12 covers strokes in more detail.

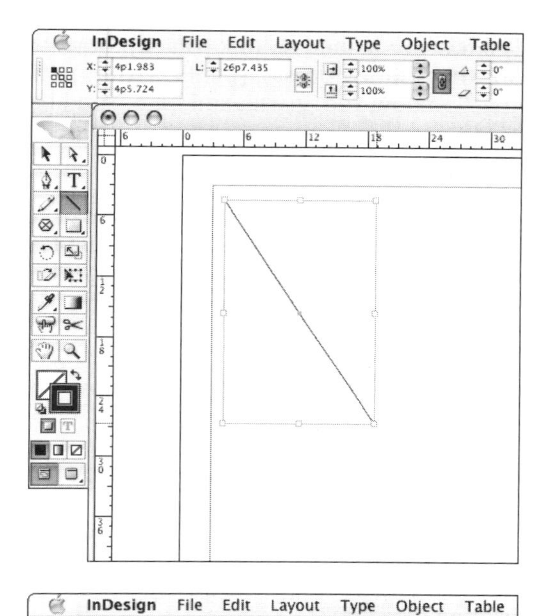

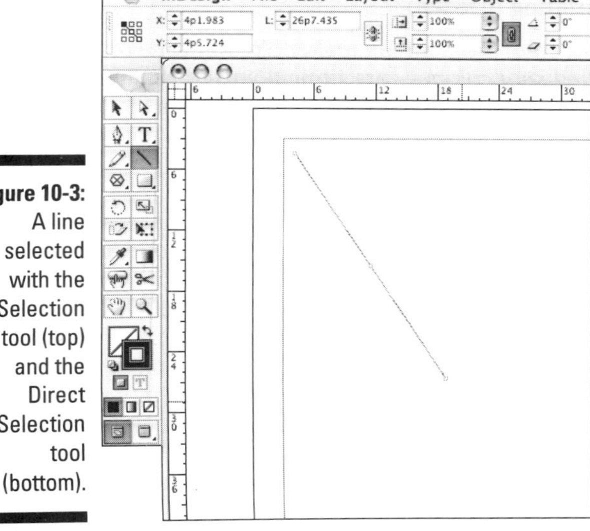

Figure 10-3: A line selected with the Selection tool (top) and the Direct Selection tool (bottom).

2. **In the Color Type pop-up menu, choose from Process or Spot.**

   The difference between process colors and spot colors is discussed later in this chapter; leave the color type at Process if you're not sure.

3. **In the Color Mode pop-up menu, choose the mixing system or swatch library (both are considered to be *color models*) you will use:**

   - **CMYK:** Cyan, magenta, yellow, and black are the colors used in professional printing presses and many color printers.
   - **RGB:** Red, green, and blue are the colors used on a computer monitor, for CD-based or Web-based documents, and for some color printers.
   - **LAB:** Luminosity, *A* axis, *B* axis, is a way of defining colors created by the international standards group Commission Internationale de l'Éclairage (the CIE, which translates to *International Commission on Illumination* in English).
   - **A swatch-based model:** Sets of premixed colors from various vendors, including ANPA, DIC, Focoltone, HKS, Pantone, Toyo Ink, and Trumatch for print documents, as well as a Web-specific set and sets specific to Windows and the Mac OS for on-screen documents.
   - **Other Library:** InDesign also has the Other Library from which you can select any swatch library file in Adobe Illustrator format.

4. **For the CMYK, RGB, and LAB models, use the sliders to create your new color. (A preview appears in the box on the left.) For the swatch-based models, scroll through the lists of colors and select one.**

5. **If you want to create multiple colors, click Add after each color definition and then click Done when you're finished.** To create just one color, click OK instead of Add. You can also click Cancel to abort the cur rent color definition.

The most popular swatch libraries used by North American professional pu lishers are those from Pantone, whose Pantone Matching System (PMS) is t de facto standard for most publishers in specifying spot-color inks. The Pantone swatch libraries come in several variations, of which InDesign includes the following four:

- **Pantone Process Coated:** Use this library when you color-separate Pantone colors and your printer uses the standard Pantone-brand process-color inks. (These colors will reproduce reliably when colo separated, while the other Pantone swatch libraries' colors often wil
- **Pantone Solid Coated:** Use this library when your printer will use Pantone inks (as spot colors) when printing to coated paper stock
- **Pantone Solid Matte:** Use this library when your printer will use ac Pantone inks (as spot colors) when printing to matte-finished pape
- **Pantone Solid Uncoated:** Use this library when your printer will us Pantone inks (as spot colors) when printing to uncoated paper sto

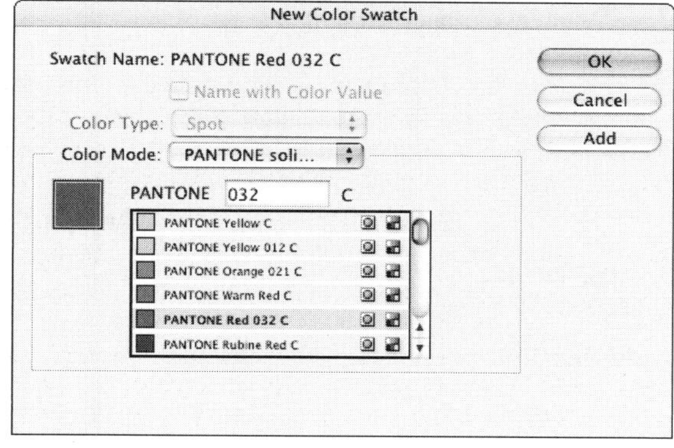

Figure 10-5: The New Color Swatch dialog box lets you define colors.

Color swatches based on the CMYK colors — such as Focoltone, Pantone Process, and Trumatch — will accurately color-separate and, thus, print accurately on a printing press because a printing press uses the CMYK colors. Other swatches' colors often do not color-separate accurately because they are supposed to represent special inks that may have added elements like metals and clays designed to give metallic or pastel appearances that simply can't be replicated by combining cyan, magenta, yellow, and black. Similarly, some colors (like several hues of orange and green) can't be accurately created using the CMYK colors.

Creating tints

A *tint* is a shade of a color. InDesign lets you create such tints as separate color swatches, so they're easy to use for multiple items. The process is easy:

1. **In the Swatches pane, select a color from which you want to create a tint.**
2. **Using the Swatches pane's palette menu, select New Tint Swatch.**

   The New Tint Swatch dialog box, shown in Figure 10-6, appears.

The bad way to create colors

Many people try to use the Color pane (Window⇨Color or F6) to define colors, which can be a mistake. At first, you might not realize that you can create colors from the Color pane. It shows a gradation of the last color used and lets you change the tint for that color on the current object. But if you go to the palette menu and choose a color model (RGB, CMYK, or LAB), you get a set of mixing controls.

So what's the problem? Colors created through the Color pane won't appear in your Swatches pane, so they can't be used for other objects. Called *unnamed colors* because they don't appear anywhere, these can be dangerous for publishers. (Adobe added them to InDesign to be consistent with how Illustrator defines colors — a foolish consistency.)

Fortunately, there is a way to prevent unnamed colors: If you go to the Color pane and modify a color without thinking about it, choose Add to Swatches from the palette menu to add the modified color to the Swatches pane. Of course, if you forget to do this, you have an unnamed color, so it's best to think *Swatches pane* when you think about adding or editing colors instead of the more obvious *Color pane.* If you do forget, you can use the Add Unnamed Colors menu item in the Swatches pane's palette menu to add the colors to the Swatches pane.

Similarly, don't use this new InDesign CS2 feature: the ability to create colors by double-clicking the Stroke and Fill buttons on the Tools palette, using a Photoshop-style color picker. As with colors created in the Color pane, you can rectify this sin by adding any colors created this way to the Swatches pane by using the Add Unnamed Colors menu item. Otherwise, you run the same risk as creating colors through the Color pane.

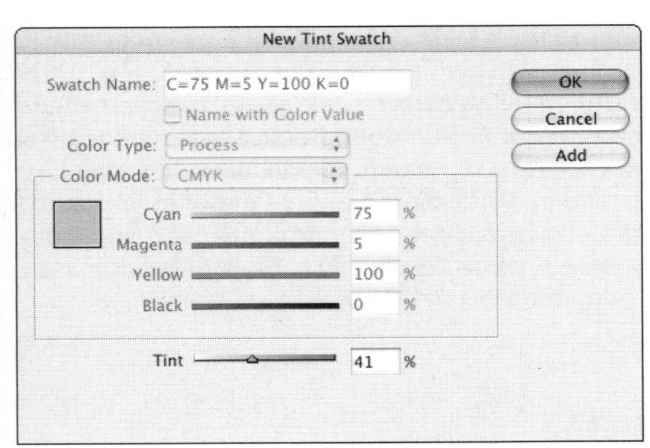

Figure 10-6: The New Tint Swatch dialog box lets you define colors; a nearly identical dialog box named Swatch Options lets you edit them.

3. **Click and drag the slider to adjust the tint, or type a value in a field on the right.**

4. **Click Add to create another tint from the same base color, and then click OK when you're finished. (If you're adding a single tint, there's no need to click Add; just click OK when done.)**

   Click Cancel if you change your mind about the current tint. Any new tint will have the same name as the original color and the percentage of shading, such as Sky Blue 66%.

   You can create a tint from a tint, which can be confusing. Fortunately, InDesign goes back to the original color when letting you create the new tint. Thus, if you select Sky Blue 66% and move the slider to 33%, you get a 33 percent tint of the original Sky Blue, not a 33 percent tint of the Sky Blue 66% (which would be equivalent to a 22 percent tint of the original Sky Blue).

Creating mixed colors

InDesign offers another type of color: mixed-ink color. Essentially, a mixed-ink color combines a spot color with the default process colors (cyan, magenta, yellow, and black) to create new color swatches. For example, you can combine 38 percent black with 100 percent Pantone 130C to get a darker version of Pantone 130C (called a *duotone,* though InDesign doesn't limit you to mixing spot colors with just black, as traditional duotones do).

To create a mixed-ink swatch, follow these steps:

1. **Select the spot color you want to begin with and then choose New Mixed Ink Swatch from the Swatches pane's palette menu. Note that you cannot use process colors.**

   The New Mixed Ink Swatch dialog box appears, as shown in Figure 10-7.

2. **Select the percentages of the spot color and any or all of the default process colors you want to mix and give the new color a name.**

3. **Click Add to add another mixed-ink swatch based on the current spot color.**

   If you're creating just one color, click OK instead of Add. You can click Cancel to abort the current mixed-ink color definition.

4. **Click OK when you're finished.**

Working with gradients

A technique that has increased in popularity is the gradient (also called *blends* and *graduated fills*), which blends two or more colors in a sequence, going smoothly from, say, green to blue to yellow to orange. InDesign has a powerful gradient-creation feature that lets you define and apply gradients to pretty much any object in InDesign, including text, lines, frames, shapes, and their outlines (strokes).

In the Swatches pane, where you define colors and tints, you can also define gradients. Just select the New Gradient Swatch option in the palette menu. You get the dialog box shown in Figure 10-8. The first two options are straightforward:

- Type a name for the gradient in the Swatch Name field. Picking a name is a bit more difficult than for a color, but use something like "Blue to Red" or "Bright Multihue" or "Logo Gradient" that has a meaning specific to the colors used or to its role in your document.
- In the Type pop-up menu, choose Linear or Radial. A linear blend goes in one direction, while a radial blend radiates out in a circle from a central point.

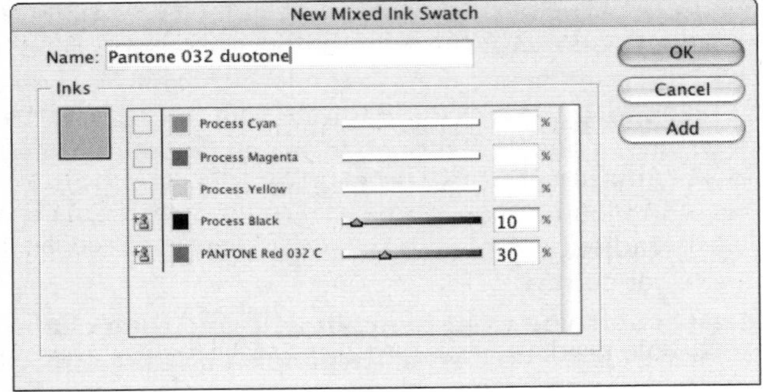

Figure 10-7: The New Mixed Ink Swatch dialog box lets you mix a selected spot color with any or all of the default process colors to create new shades and variations.

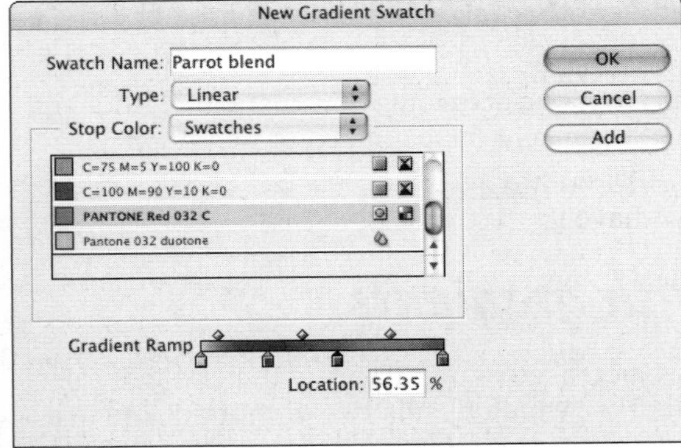

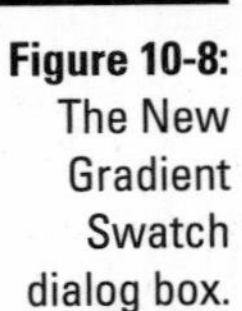

Figure 10-8: The New Gradient Swatch dialog box.

Now it gets a little tricky. Follow these steps:

1. **Select a stop point — one of the squares at the bottom of the dialog box on either end of the gradient ramp that shows the gradient as you define it.**

   The stop points essentially define the start color (the stop point on the left) and the end color (the stop point on the right). With a stop point selected, you can now define its color.

2. **Choose what color model you want to use — select from CMYK, RGB, LAB, and Swatches in the Stop Color pop-up menu.**

   The area directly beneath the pop-up menu changes accordingly, displaying sliders for CMYK, RGB, or LAB, or a list of all colors from the Swatches pane for Swatches, depending on which model you choose.

3. **Create or select the color you want for that stop point.**

   You can select the [Paper] white swatch as a stop point in a gradient. You can also click and drag swatches from the Swatches pane to the gradient ramp.

4. **Repeat Steps 1 to 3 for the other stop point.**

   Note that the color models for the two stop points don't have to be the same — you can blend from a Pantone spot color to a CMYK color, for example. (If a gradient mixes spot colors and process colors, InDesign converts the spot colors to process colors.)

You now have a simple gradient. But you don't have to stop there. Here are your other options:

- You can change the rate at which the colors transition by sliding the diamond icons at the top of the gradient ramp.
- You can create additional stop points by clicking right below the gradient ramp. By having several stop points, you can have multiple color transitions in a gradient. (Think of them like tab stops in text — you can define as many as you need.) You delete unwanted stop points by clicking and dragging them to the bottom of the dialog box.

Notice that there's a diamond icon between each pair of stop points — that means each pair can have its own transition rate.

When you create a new gradient, InDesign uses the settings from the last one you created. If you want to create a gradient similar to an existing one, click that existing gradient before selecting New Gradient Swatch from the palette menu. InDesign copies the selected gradient's settings to the new one, which you can then edit. One reason to use this is to create, say, a radial version of an existing linear gradient.

The Swatches pane shows the actual gradient next to its name. The pattern also appears in the Fill button or Stroke button in the Tools palette if that gradient is currently selected as a fill or stroke, as well as in the Gradient button in that palette, whether or not it's currently applied as a fill or stroke.

Editing a gradient is as simple as double-clicking its name in the Swatches pane or selecting it and choosing Edit Gradient Swatch from the palette menu. You get the Gradient Options dialog box, which is nearly identical to the New Gradient Swatch dialog box in Figure 10-8. What's different in the Gradient Options dialog box is the Preview option, which lets you see a gradient change in a selected object (if it's visible on-screen, of course) as you make changes in the Gradient Options dialog box.

Just as it does with colors, InDesign lets you create *unnamed gradients* — gradients that have no swatches. Unlike unnamed colors, you can use these to your heart's content, since all colors in a gradient are converted to process colors and/or use defined spot-color swatches — so there are no unnamed colors in their output. The process is pretty much the same as creating a gradient swatch, except that you select an object and then open the Gradient pane (Window⇨Gradient). In that pane, you select a stop point and then choose a color to apply to it by clicking a color in the Swatches pane or in the Color pane. You create and adjust stop points here just as you do when defining a gradient swatch.

The Gradient pane can also manipulate gradient swatches: After you apply a linear gradient — whether via a gradient swatch or as an unnamed gradient — you can change the angle of the gradient, rotating the gradient within the object. Just type the desired degree of rotation in the Angle field to rotate the gradient's direction by the value. Negative values rotate counterclockwise, while positive values rotate clockwise.

Note that you can't rotate a radial gradient because it's circular and, thus, any rotation has no effect. That's why InDesign grays out the Angle field for radial gradients. But you can still adjust the location of a radial gradient — as well as that of a linear gradient — by using the Gradient tool in the Tools palette. After applying a gradient to an object, select the Gradient tool and draw a line in the object, as shown in Figure 10-9:

- For a linear gradient, the start point of your line corresponds to where you want the first stop point of the gradient to be; the end point of the line corresponds to the last stop point. This lets you stretch or compress the gradient, as well as offset the gradient within the object. Also, the angle at which you draw the line becomes the angle for the gradient.
- For a radial gradient, the line becomes the start and end point for the gradient, in effect offsetting it.

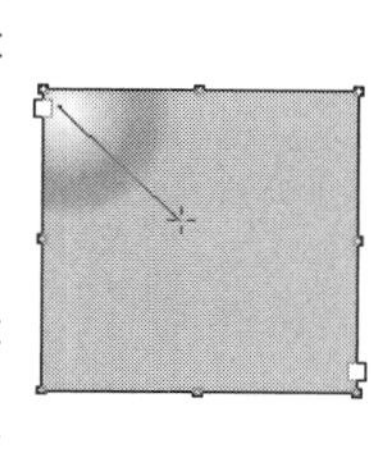

Figure 10-9: The Gradient tool lets you set the offset and adjust the gradient length and (for gradient blends) angle.

Deleting and copying swatches

When you create colors, tints, and gradients, it's easy to go overboard and make too many. You'll also find that different documents have different colors, each created by different people, and you'll likely want to move colors from one document to another. InDesign provides basic tools for managing colors in and across documents.

When selecting swatches for deletion or duplication, you can ⌘+click or Ctrl+click multiple swatches to work on all of them at once. Note that Shift+clicking selects all swatches between the first swatch clicked and the swatch that you Shift+click, whereas ⌘+click or Ctrl+click lets you select specific swatches in any order and in any location in the pane.

InDesign makes deleting swatches easy: Just select the color, tint, or gradient in the Swatches pane. Then choose Delete Swatch from the palette menu, or click the Delete Swatch button at the bottom of the Swatches pane.

Well, that's not quite it. You then get the dialog box shown in Figure 10-10, which lets you either assign a new color to anything using the deleted swatch (the Defined Swatch option) or leave the color on any object that is using it but delete the swatch from the Swatches pane (the Unnamed Swatch option). (As explained earlier in this chapter, unnamed colors should be avoided, so if your document uses a color, keep its swatch.)

If you delete a tint and replace it with another color, any object using that tint gets the full-strength version of the new color, not a tint of it. Likewise, if you delete a color swatch that you've based one or more tints on, those tints are also deleted if you replace the deleted swatch with an unnamed swatch.

However, if you delete a color swatch and replace it with a defined swatch, any tints of that deleted swatch retain their tint percentages of the replacement-defined swatch.

Figure 10-10: The Delete Swatch dialog box lets you replace a deleted color with a new one or leave the color applied to objects using it.

InDesign offers a nice option to quickly find all unused colors in the Swatches pane — the palette menu's Select All Unused option. With this option, you can delete all the unused colors in one fell swoop. Note that you don't get the option to assign each deleted color separately to another color in the Delete Swatch dialog box — they all are replaced with the color you select or are made into unnamed colors. Because no object uses these colors, choosing Unnamed Swatch in essence is the same as *not* replacing them with a color using the Defined Swatch option.

If you delete a swatch and replace it with an unnamed swatch, you can recapture that deleted swatch later by choosing the Add Unnamed Colors menu item in the Swatches pane's palette menu.

To duplicate a swatch, so you can create a new one based on it, use the Duplicate Swatch option in the Swatches pane. The word *copy* will be added to the name of the new swatch. You edit it — including its name — as you would any swatch.

Importing swatches

A quick way to import specific colors from another InDesign document or template is to click and drag the colors from that other file's Swatches pane into your current document or template.

You can import colors from other InDesign, Illustrator, and Illustrator EPS files by choosing Load Swatches from the Swatches pane's palette menu. Plus, you can now also import colors from Adobe Swatch Exchange library files this way. From the resulting dialog box, navigate to the file that contains the colors you want to import, select that file, and click Open.

When you import color swatches from other documents or Adobe Swatch Exchange files, InDesign brings in all the colors. You cannot choose specific colors to import.

Also, when you import a graphic file in PDF or EPS format, any named colors (swatches) in that file are automatically added to the Swatches pane.

Finally, InDesign CS2 lets you save swatches into color library files for use by other Creative Suite 2 users. Just select the colors you want to save and then choose Save Swatches from the Swatches pane's palette menu. You are asked to give the resulting Adobe Swatch Exchange file a name before you save it.

Applying Colors

Applying colors, tints, and gradients to objects in InDesign is easy. Select the object, click the Formatting Affects Text button or Formatting Affects Container button in the Swatches or Gradient pane as appropriate for what you want to apply the color to, and then click the appropriate swatch.

Another way to apply colors, tints, and gradients is by selecting the object and using the Formatting Affects Text, Formatting Affects Content, Fill, or Stroke buttons in the Tools palette to define what part of the object you want to color. You can use the Swatches or Gradients panes to select a swatch, or pick the last-used color and gradient from the Apply Color and Apply Gradient buttons on the Tools palette, shown in Figure 10-11.

For tints, you can use a tint swatch, or you can simply apply a color from the Swatches pane and enter a tint value in the pane's Tint field. Use a swatch for tints you want to use repeatedly in your layout (such as for the background tint in sidebar boxes) to ensure consistency. Use the Tint field for a tint you are applying on the fly, typically for one-time use.

You can also apply colors and tints to gaps in strokes by using the Stroke pane's palette options menu (select Show Options and select a gap color). Open the Stroke pane by choosing Window⇨Stroke or by pressing F10.

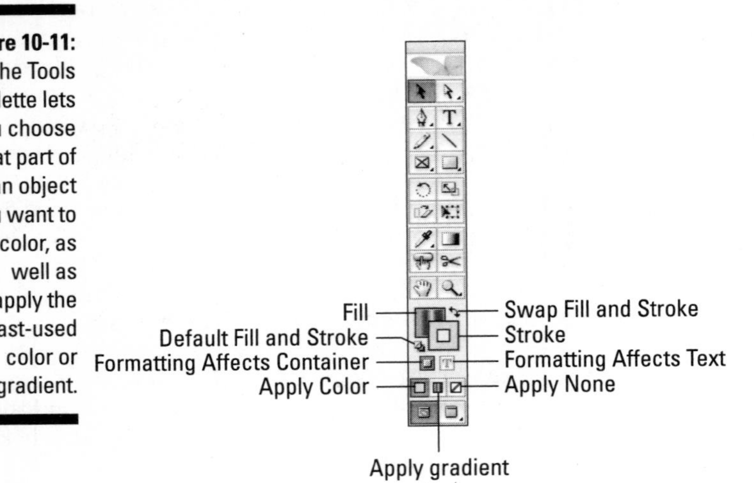

Figure 10-11: The Tools palette lets you choose what part of an object you want to color, as well as apply the last-used color or gradient.

Chapter 11

Aligning Objects with Grids and Guidelines

In This Chapter

- Using exact coordinates
- Working with document grids and guidelines
- Aligning text with baseline grids

When you draw objects like frames or lines, they appear where you draw them. That's what you expect, right? But sometimes you want them to appear where you meant to draw them, not where you actually did. Working with the mouse is inexact, but you can overcome that.

This chapter shows you how to use InDesign's grids and guidelines feature to ensure that your objects and text line up where you want them to, so your layouts are all neat and tidy. You can also use precise positioning — whether or not use you grids and guidelines — to specify the exact placement and size of your objects.

Precise Positioning with Coordinates

The most precise way to position objects is by entering the object's desired coordinates in the X: and Y: fields of the Control palette or the Transform pane. (You can also precisely change the object's size by entering values in the W: and H: fields.) The Control palette is visible by default at the top of the document window. Access the Control palette by choosing Window➪Control or by pressing Option+⌘+6 or Ctrl+Alt+6. The Control palette is more powerful than the Transform pane, which is a holdover from older versions of InDesign, but if you want to use the Transform pane, choose Window➪Object & Layout➪Transform or press F9. Figure 11-1 shows both the Control palette and Transform pane and a selected frame.

But be careful: InDesign has these funny things called *control points* that is easily overlooked. See those nine squares at the upper left of the Control palette and Transform pane? They let you select what part of the object those coordinates position: one of the four corners, one of the midpoints of the sides, or the object center. The black one is the current control point, and all coordinates are based on that. You usually want to enter coordinates based on the upper-left corner, so be sure that the upper-left control point is black (just click it if it is not).

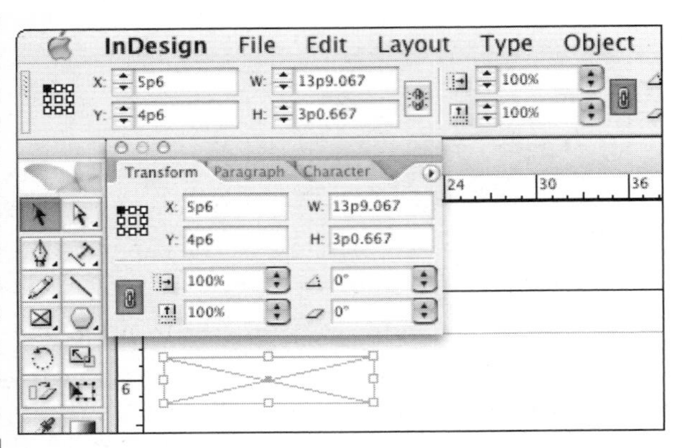

Figure 11-1: The Control palette (top) and Transform pane let you enter precise coordinates for an object's position.

Lining Up Objects with Guidelines and Grids

If you've ever seen a carpenter use a chalked string to snap a temporary line as an aid for aligning objects, you understand the concept behind ruler guidelines and grids. They're not structurally necessary and they don't appear in the final product, yet they still make your work easier.

InDesign provides several types of grids and guidelines:

- **Ruler guides** are moveable guidelines that are helpful for placing objects precisely and for aligning multiple items.
- A **baseline grid** is a series of horizontal lines that help in aligning lines of text and objects across a multicolumn page. When a document is open and it has a baseline grid showing, the page looks like a sheet of lined paper.
- A **document grid** is a set of horizontal and vertical lines that help you place and align objects.
- A **frame-based grid** is similar to a baseline grid except that it is just for a specific text frame.

You won't need all the grids and guidelines at once. You'll most likely use a combination of guides and grids, but using all four at once is more complicated than necessary.

Using ruler guides

InDesign lets you create individual ruler guides manually. You can also set ruler guides automatically with the Create Guides command (Layout➪Create Guides).

Manually creating ruler guides

To create ruler guides on an as-needed basis, follow these steps:

1. **Go to the page or spread onto which you want to place ruler guides.**
2. **If the rulers are not displayed at the top and left of the document window, choose View➪Show Rulers or press ⌘+R or Ctrl+R.**
3. **Drag the pointer (and a guideline along with it) from the horizontal ruler or vertical ruler onto a page or the pasteboard.**
4. **When the guideline is positioned where you want it, release the mouse button.**

   If you release the mouse when the pointer is over a page, the ruler guide extends from one edge of the page to the other (but not across a spread). If you release the mouse button when the pointer is over the pasteboard, the ruler guide extends across both pages of a spread and the pasteboard. If you want a guide to extend across a spread and the pasteboard, you can also hold down the ⌘ or Ctrl key as you drag and release the mouse when the pointer is over a page.

Place both a horizontal and vertical guide at the same time by pressing ⌘ or Ctrl and dragging the *ruler intersection point* (where the two rulers meet) onto a page.

Ruler guides are cyan in color (unless you change the color by choosing Layout➪Ruler Guides) and are associated with the layer onto which they're placed. You can show and hide ruler guides by showing and hiding the layers that contain them. You can even create layers that contain nothing but ruler guides and then show and hide them as you wish. (See Chapter 7 for more information about layers.)

To create ruler guides for several document pages, create a master page, add the ruler guides to the master page, and then apply the master to the appropriate document pages.

Automatically creating ruler guides

Here's how to create a set of ruler guides automatically:

1. **If the documents contain multiple layers, display the Layers pane (Window➪Layers or F7) and click the name of the layer to which you want to add guides.**
2. **Choose Layout➪Create Guides to display the Create Guides dialog box, shown in Figure 11-2. (To see the guides on the page while you create them, check Preview.)**

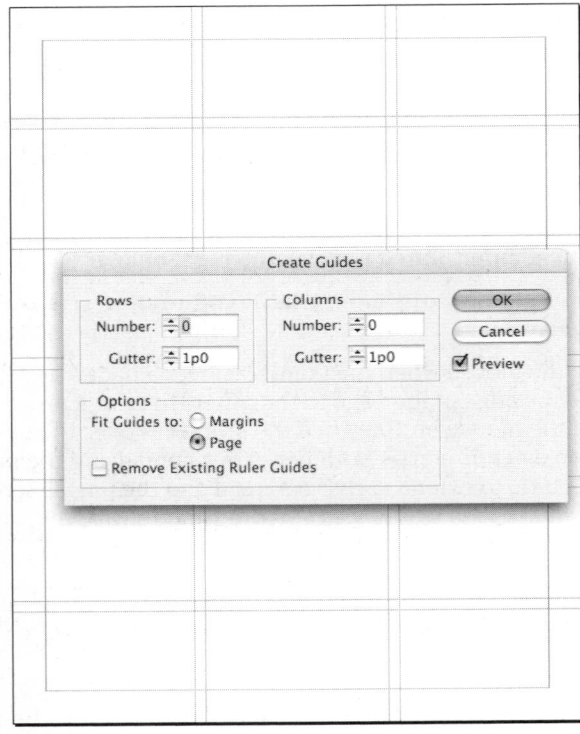

Figure 11-2: The Create Guides dialog box and the guides it created.

3. **In the Rows and Columns areas, specify the number of guides you want to add in the Number fields and, optionally, specify a Gutter width between horizontal (Rows) and vertical (Columns) guides. Enter** 0 **(zero) in the Gutter fields if you don't want gutters between guides.**
4. **In the Options area, click Margins to fit the guides in the margin boundaries; click Page to fit the guides within the page boundary.**
5. **Remove any previously placed ruler guides by checking Remove Existing Ruler Guides.**

6. **When you finish specifying the attributes of the ruler guides, click OK to close the dialog box.**

Working with ruler guides

You can show and hide, lock and unlock, select and move, copy and paste, and delete ruler guides. In InDesign CS2, many options related to grids and guides have been moved from the main View menu to the new Grids & Guides submenu. Here are a few pointers for working with ruler guides:

- **Display or hide ruler guides** by choosing View➪Grids & Guides➪Show/Hide Guides or by pressing ⌘+; (semicolon) or Ctrl+; (semicolon).
- **Lock or unlock all ruler guides** by choosing View➪Grids & Guides➪Lock Guides or by pressing Option+⌘+; (semicolon) or Ctrl+Alt+; (semicolon). Ruler guides are locked when Lock Guides is checked.
- **Select a ruler guide** by clicking it with a selection tool. To select multiple guides, hold down the Shift key and click them. The color of a guide changes from cyan to the color of its layer when it is selected. To select all ruler guides on a page or spread, press Option+⌘+G or Ctrl+Alt+G.
- **Move a guide** by clicking and dragging it as you would any object. To move multiple guides, select them and then drag them. To move guides to another page, select them, choose Edit➪Cut or press ⌘+X or Ctrl+X (or choose Edit➪Copy or press ⌘+C or Ctrl+C), display the target page, and then choose Edit➪Paste or press ⌘+V or Ctrl+V. If the target page has the same dimensions as the source page, the guides are placed in their original positions.
- **Delete ruler guides** by selecting them and then pressing Delete or Backspace.
- **Change the color of the ruler guides and the view percentage above which they're displayed** by choosing Layout➪Ruler Guides. The Ruler Guides dialog box, shown in Figure 11-3, appears. Modify the View Threshold value, choose a different color from the Color pop-up menu, and then click OK. If you change the settings in the Ruler Guides dialog box when no documents are open, the new settings become defaults and are applied to all subsequently created documents.
- **Display ruler guides behind — instead of in front of — objects** by choosing InDesign➪Preferences➪Guides & Pasteboard on the Mac or Edit➪Preferences➪Guides & Pasteboard in Windows, or by pressing ⌘+K or Ctrl+K. Then select the Guides in Back option in the Guide Options section of the dialog box.
- **Make object edges snap (align) to ruler guides when you drag them into the snap zone** by selecting the Snap to Guides option (View➪Grids & Guides➪Snap to Guides, or press Shift+⌘+; [semicolon] or Ctrl+Shift+; [semicolon]). To specify the snap zone (the distance — in pixels — at

which an object will snap to a guide), choose InDesign⇨Preferences⇨Guides & Pasteboard on the Mac or Edit⇨Preferences⇨Guides & Pasteboard in Windows, or press ⌘+K or Ctrl+K, and enter a value in the Snap to Zone field in the Guide Options section of the dialog box.

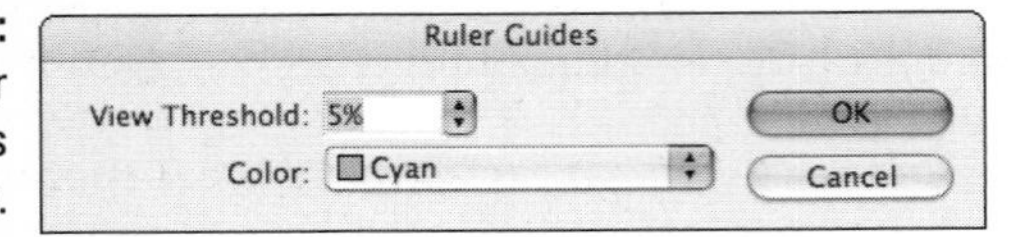

Figure 11-3: The Ruler Guides dialog box.

Using document grids

A document grid is like the grid paper you used in school, a visual crutch to help ensure that the objects you draw and reposition are placed at desired increments. Using a grid can help ensure that objects align and are sized consistently.

If you plan to use a grid, set it up before you start working in the document. Because documents tend to have different grid settings based on individual contents, you probably want to set Grids preferences with a specific document open so that the grid will apply only to that document. The Grids pane of the Preferences dialog box (InDesign⇨Preferences or ⌘+K on the Mac, or Edit⇨Preferences or Ctrl+K in Windows) is shown in Figure 11-4.

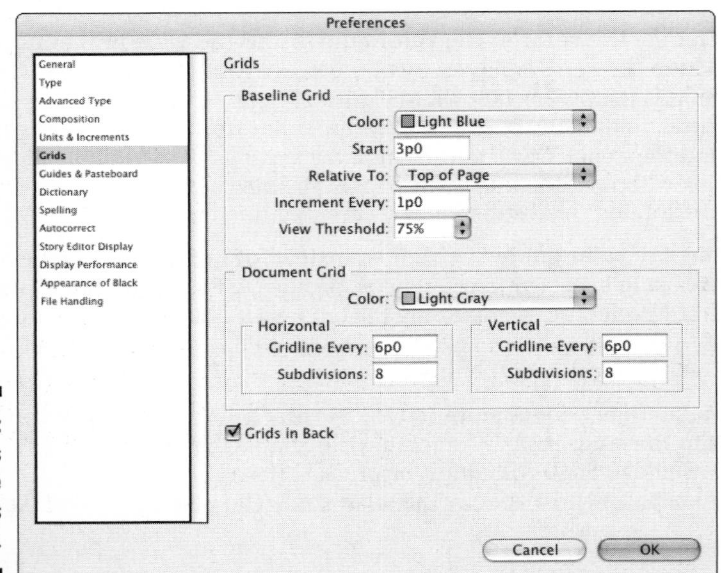

Figure 11-4: The Grids pane of the Preferences dialog box.

You have the following options:

- **Color:** The default color of the document grid is Light Gray. You can choose a different color from the Color pop-up menu or choose Other to create your own.
- **Gridline Every:** The major gridlines, which are slightly darker, are positioned according to this value. The default value is 6p0; in general, you want to specify a value within the measurement system you're using. For example, if you work in inches, you might enter **1 inch** in the Gridline Every field. You set the horizontal and vertical settings separately.
- **Subdivisions:** The major gridlines established in the Gridline Every field are subdivided according to the value you enter here. For example, if you enter **1 inch** in the Gridline Every field and **4** in the Subdivisions field, you get a gridline at each quarter-inch. The default number of subdivisions is 8. You set the horizontal and vertical settings separately.

By default, the document grid appears on every spread behind all objects. You can have grids display in front by deselecting the Grids in Back check box.

To make object edges snap (align) to the grid when you drag them into the snap zone, select the Snap to Document Grid option (View➪Grids & Guides➪Snap to Document Grid, or press Shift+⌘+' [apostrophe] or Ctrl+Shift+' [apostrophe]). To specify the snap zone (the distance — in pixels — at which an object will snap to a gridline), InDesign will use whatever settings you specified for guidelines, as explained earlier in this chapter.

To display the document grid, choose View➪Grids & Guides➪Show Document Grid or press ⌘+' (apostrophe) or Ctrl+' (apostrophe).

Using baseline grids

You may not already know this, but each and every new document you create includes a baseline grid. A baseline grid can be helpful for aligning text baselines across columns and for ensuring that object edges align with text baselines.

But chances are that the default settings for the baseline grid won't match the baselines (leading) for the majority of your text. The default baseline grid begins ½ inch from the top of a document page; the default gridlines are light blue, are spaced 1 pica apart, and appear at view percentages above 75 percent. If you change any of these settings when no documents are open, the changes are applied to all subsequently created documents; if a document is open, changes apply only to that document.

So here's how to modify the baseline grid:

1. **Choose InDesign➪Preferences➪Grids (Mac) or Edit➪Preferences➪Grids (Windows) or press ⌘+K or Ctrl+K and choose the Grids pane.**

   The Grids pane, shown in Figure 11-4, appears.

2. **Pick a color for the baseline from the Color pop-up menu in the Baseline Grid area.**

3. **In the Start field, enter the distance between the top of the page and the first gridline.**

   If you enter **0**, the Increment Every value determines the distance between the top of the page and the first gridline.

4. **In the Increment Every field, enter the distance between gridlines.**

   If you're not sure what value to use, enter the leading value for the publication's body text.

5. **Choose a View Threshold percentage from the pop-up menu or enter a value in the field.**

   You probably don't want to display the baseline grid at reduced view percentages because gridlines become tightly spaced.

6. **Click OK to close the dialog box and return to the document.**

The Show/Hide Baseline Grid command (View➪Grids & Guides➪Show/Hide Baseline Grid, or Option+⌘+' [apostrophe] or Ctrl+Alt+' [apostrophe]) lets you display and hide a document's baseline grid.

When you set a baseline grid, it applies to the entire document. Gridlines are displayed behind all objects, layers, and ruler guides. To get text to line up to the baseline grid, you need to ensure that the Align to Grid pop-up menu is set to either First Line Only or All Lines in your paragraph style or that the Align to Baseline Grid check box is selected in the Paragraph pane or in the Control palette. Chapter 17 covers such paragraph formatting in detail.

A document-wide baseline grid is all fine and dandy, but often it's not enough. The document-wide baseline grid is basically useful for your body text and often your headline text, assuming that the baseline grid's increments match the leading for that text. But what if you have other elements, like sidebars, that have different leading?

The answer is to use text frame–specific baseline grids. You set the grid as part of text frame options by choosing Object➪Text Frame Options or by pressing ⌘+B or Ctrl+B and then going to the Baseline Options pane. Its options are almost identical to those in the Grids pane of the Preferences dialog box. A baseline grid established for a text frame affects only the text in that frame.

Chapter 12

Manipulating Objects

In This Chapter

- Selecting objects
- Resizing, moving, and deleting objects
- Keeping objects from printing
- Rotating, shearing, and flipping objects
- Adding effects such as strokes and fills

Frames, shapes, and lines are the building blocks of your layout. But as anyone who ever played with Legos or Tinkertoys knows, it's how you manipulate the building blocks that results in a unique creation, whether it be a Lego house, a Tinkertoys crane, or an InDesign layout.

InDesign provides a lot of control over layout objects so that you can create really interesting, dynamic publications suited to any purpose. In this chapter, we discuss the controls that apply to all objects.

Chapter 12 covers various effects for graphics frames, while Chapter 15 covers effects for text frames. Chapter 10 explains how to add frames, shapes, and lines in the first place. Chapter 11 explains how to align objects and precisely position them.

Selecting Objects

Before you can manipulate an object, you have to select it so that InDesign knows what you want to work on. To select an object (rather than its contents), use the Selection tool. Selected items will display their item boundary (a rectangle that encompasses the object) as well as eight small resizing handles (one at each of the four corners and one midway between each side of the item boundary). Figure 12-1 shows an example.

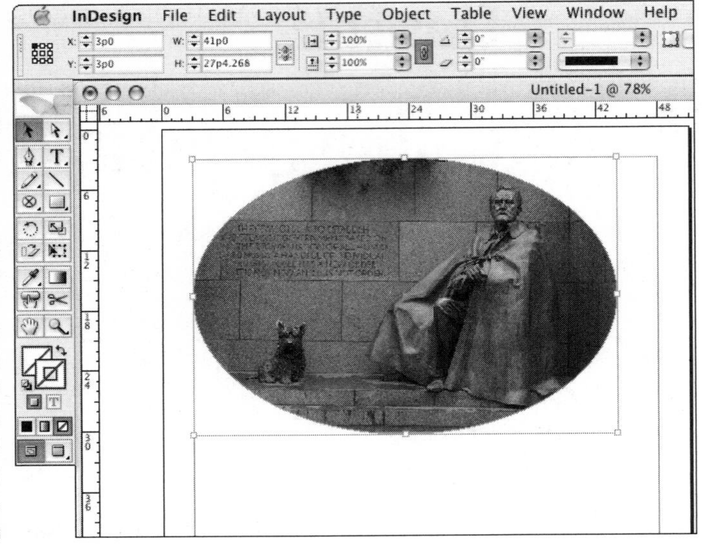

Figure 12-1: When you select a frame with the Selection tool, the bounding box is displayed with eight resizing handles.

To select an individual object, just click it with the Selection tool. To select multiple objects, you have several options:

- Click the first object and Shift+click each additional object.
- Click and drag the mouse to create a selection rectangle (called a *marquee*) that encompasses at least part of each desired object. When you release the mouse, all objects that this marquee touches are selected.
- Choose Edit⇨Select All or press ⌘+A or Ctrl+A to select all objects on the current spread.

If an object is on a master page and you're working on a document page, you must Shift+⌘+click or Ctrl+Shift+click the object to select it. How do you know whether an object is on a master page? Easy: If you try to select it by clicking and it doesn't become selected, it must be on a master page.

Choose View⇨Show Frame Edges or press ⌘+H or Ctrl+H to see object edges if they aren't already visible.

These options are pretty easy, but it can get tricky when you want to select objects that overlap or are obscured by other objects. So how do you select them? By using the Select submenu option in the Object menu.

The first four options in the Select submenu let you select another object relative to the currently selected object:

- First Object Above (Option+Shift+⌘+] or Ctrl+Alt+Shift+]) selects the topmost object.

- Next Object Above (Option+⌘+] or Ctrl+Alt+]) selects the object immediately on top of the current object.
- Next Object Below (Option+⌘+[or Ctrl+Alt+[) selects the object immediately under the current object.
- Last Object Below (Option+Shift+⌘+[or Ctrl+Alt+Shift+[) selects the bottommost object.

If no objects are selected, InDesign bases its selection on the order in which the objects were created, the topmost object being the one that was most recently created.

You can also access these four selection options by Control+clicking or right-clicking an object and choosing the Select menu from the contextual menu that appears.

The Select submenu has four other options:

- If you select an object's content (text or graphic), choose Object⇨Select⇨Container to choose the frame. Using this option is the same as selecting the object with the Selection tool.
- If an object has content (text or graphic) and you select its frame, choose Object⇨Select⇨Content to choose the content within the object. This is basically the same as selecting the frame with the Direct Selection tool (which we discuss later in this chapter).
- If you select an object in a group of objects by using the Direct Selection tool, choose Object⇨Select⇨Previous Object in Group to navigate to the previous object in the group.
- Similarly, if you select an object in a group of objects by using the Direct Selection tool, choose Object⇨Select⇨Next Object in Group to navigate to the next object in the group.

Object creation order determines what is "previous" or "next" in a group.

The Control palette also provides buttons to select the next or previous object, as well as to select the content or container (frame). These last two buttons appear only if you have selected a group. The buttons for selecting the next or previous object appear only if you are using the Direct Selection tool, while the buttons for selecting the content or container appear whether you are using the Selection or Direct Selection tool. (Yes, this is very confusing!) Figure 12-2 shows the buttons.

To deselect objects, just click another object, an empty part of your page, or the pasteboard. To deselect individual objects after you have selected multiple objects, Shift+click those you want to deselect.

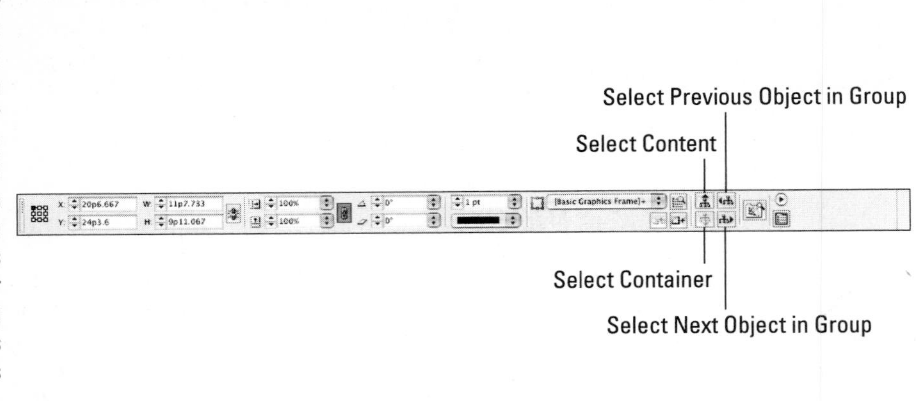

Figure 12-2: The Control palette buttons for selecting the next and previous objects in a group, as well as for selecting contents versus containers.

The Direct Selection tool lets you select any of the individual anchor points (and direction handles of freeform shapes and curved lines) on an object. If you use the Direct Selection tool to click an object that has a bounding box, the shape within is selected, and the bounding box is deselected. You use this tool to work on the contents independently of its container frame. You can also move a graphic within its frame by clicking within the object (see Chapter 20).

Moving, Resizing, and Deleting Objects

The most common tasks you'll do with objects is rearranging them — both moving them and changing their dimensions — plus deleting the ones you don't want or no longer need. In any case, you must first select the object with the Selection tool.

Moving objects

The easiest way to move an object is by using the mouse. With the Selection tool, click an object and drag it to a new location. When you release the mouse, the object will be deposited in the new location.

If you want to more precisely move an object, you can enter specific X: and Y: coordinates in the Control palette or Transform pane, as explained in Chapter 12.

Be sure to select the correct control point when entering coordinates. The little squares at the top left of the Control palette and Transform pane represent the object's control points (corners, side midpoints, and center). Click a control point to make it active (it will turn black); all coordinates are now based on this point.

Resizing objects

You resize objects in pretty much the same way you move them: by using the mouse for inexact sizes or the Control palette or Transform pane for precise sizes.

To resize an object with the mouse, click and drag one of the frame's handles. (Hold the Shift key as you drag to maintain the proportions of the frame.) Drag a corner handle to resize both the width and height or a side handle to resize just the height or width.

You can also enter new value in the W: and H: fields (for *width* and *height*) of the Control palette or Transform pane. Remember those control points for positioning an object? They come into play for resizing objects as well. Basically, the object will grow or shrink starting from the selected control point. So if the upper-left control point is selected and you enter greater W: and H: values, the object will add the extra width to the right and the extra height below. But if you choose the center control point, it will grow on both sides as well as on the top and bottom, spreading the extra size evenly.

Another way to resize a graphic is to enter percentage values in the Scale X Percentage and Scale Y Percentage fields of the Control palette or Transform pane. This is a handy technique for empty frames and shapes, but there are some issues that affect graphics and text that you need to understand fully. (In a nutshell, these Scale fields usually resize the contents of the frame, not just the frame itself.) Chapter 20 covers the use of the Scale X Percentage and Scale Y Percentage fields.

Deleting objects

Alas, not all the objects you create will survive all the way to the final version of your publication. Some will wind up on the cutting room floor. You can always move an object to the pasteboard if you're not sure whether you want to get rid of it altogether (objects on the pasteboard don't print). But when it's time to ax an object, oblivion is just a keystroke or two away.

If you delete a text or graphics frame, the contents are removed as well as the frame.

Here's how to delete objects: Using either selection tool, select the object or objects you want to delete and then press the Delete key or Backspace key. You can also delete a selected item by choosing Edit➪Clear.

Choosing Edit➪Cut or pressing ⌘+X or Ctrl+X also removes a selected object. However, in this case a copy of the object is saved to the Clipboard and can be pasted elsewhere (by choosing Edit➪Paste or by pressing ⌘+V or Ctrl+V) until you cut or copy something else or you shut down your computer.

Preventing Objects from Printing

InDesign lets you prevent an object from printing. To do so, select the object with the Selection or Direct Selection tool, open the Attributes pane (Window➪Attributes), and then select the Nonprinting check box. (The other settings in this pane duplicate stroke settings covered later in this chapter.)

You use this feature for comments and other elements that should not print but that the designer needs to have visible on-screen. Another approach to nonprinting objects is to place them all on a layer and make the entire layer nonprinting.

Transforming Objects

InDesign offers several tools and methods for transforming objects. We discuss resizing and moving earlier in this chapter, but there are several other useful transformation tools, including rotating, shearing (skewing), and flipping.

Rotating is just spinning an object around. Shearing is a little more complicated: Shearing skews an object (slanting it in one direction) while also rotating the other axis at the same time. Regardless of whether you use the mouse or numeric controls to apply rotation and/or shearing to graphics, you first need to follow these steps:

1. **Select the Selection tool.**
2. **Click the object you want to modify.**
3. **If you want, change the object's control point (by default it's the upper-left corner of a frame or shape).**

   You can change the control point by clicking one of the little black boxes in the upper-left corner of the Control palette or Transform pane.
4. **Choose the appropriate tool — Rotate, Shear, or Free Transform — or use the Flip menu options.**

   Figure 12-3 shows the Tools palette icons for all but the flip controls.

If you hold down the Option or Alt key while using a transformation tool, the modification will be performed on a copy of the selected object, rather than on the object itself.

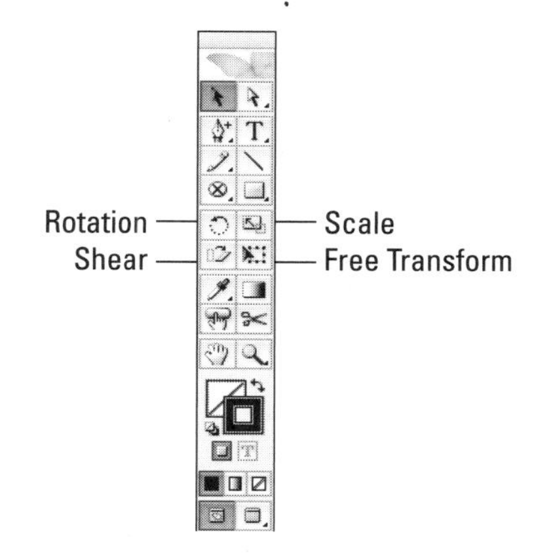

Figure 12-3: The icons for the Rotation, Scale, Shear, and Free Transform tools in the Tools palette.

Rotating objects

After you have selected the Rotate tool, click and drag a selected object to rotate it — the object will rotate following your mouse movement. (Holding down the Shift key while dragging limits rotation increments to multiples of 45 degrees.)

For more precise rotation, use the Control palette or Transform pane. You can change the angle of a selected object by entering a value in the Rotation field. If you choose to enter a value in the Rotation field, positive values rotate the selected item counterclockwise; negative values rotate it clockwise.

Or you can choose one of the predefined angles from the Rotation field's pop-up menu, or choose any of the three rotation options — Rotate 180°, Rotate 90° CW, and Rotate 90° CCW — in the Control palette's or Transform pane's palette menu.

If you choose one of these palette menu options, the current angle of the selected object is added to the applied angle. For example, if you choose Rotate 90° CCW (counterclockwise), an object that's currently rotated 12 degrees will end up with a rotation angle of 102 degrees.

No matter what method you choose to rotate an object, the center of rotation will be whatever control point is selected in the Control palette or Transform pane.

To "unrotate" an object, enter a Rotation value of **0**.

Shearing objects

After you have selected the Shear tool, click and drag a selected object to shear it. (Holding down the Shift key constrains the selected object's rotation value to increments of 45 degrees.) If you drag the mouse in a straight line parallel with one set of edges (such as the top and bottom), you skew the graphic (just slant it in one direction). But if you move the mouse in any other direction, you slant the object's edges closest to the direction that you move the mouse the furthest and rotate the rest of the graphic. Give it a few tries to see what happens.

As with other functions, you can also use the Control palette or Transform pane for more precise control. Just enter a Shear X value in the Control palette or Transform pane or choose a predefined value from the field's pop-up menu. Positive shear values slant an object to the right (that is, the top edge of the object is moved to the right), while negative values slant an object to the left (the bottom edge is moved to the right). You can enter shear values between 1 and 89 (although values above 70 cause considerable distortion).

Note that when you use the Shear tool, you change the selected object's angle of rotation *and* skew angle simultaneously. If you use the mouse, you can in effect get different skew and rotation angles based on how you move the mouse, but if you use the Control palette or Transform pane, both the skew and rotation will have the same angles applied.

To "unshear" an object, enter a Shear X value of **0**.

Flipping objects

The three flipping commands — Flip Horizontal, Flip Vertical, and Flip Both — are available in the Control palette's and Transform pane's palette menus. They let you make a mirror image of a selected object and its contents. If you choose Flip Horizontal, the graphic is flipped along a vertical axis (that is, the

Using the Free Transform tool

Advanced users will like the Free Transform tool. When you select this tool, InDesign lets you scale, rotate, and resize — but not shear — selected objects. If you click within the frame, you can move the object by dragging it. If you select a frame handle (whether corner or midpoint), you can resize the object by dragging. Finally, if you move the mouse very close to a frame handle, you will see a curved arrow, which indicates that you can rotate the object around that object's center point. Having a tool that does more than one thing can be confusing, but once you get the hang of it, it sure beats constantly changing tools!

right edge and left edge exchange places); if you choose Flip Vertical, the object is flipped upside down; and if you choose Flip Both, the object is flipped horizontally and vertically to produce an upside-down and backward version of the original. (You're not making a flipped copy of the select object, but actually flipping the selected object.)

As with other tools, the invisible line over which an object is flipped is based on what control point is currently active for that object.

Repeating transformations

Whatever transformations you use, you can apply them repeatedly. InDesign CS2 remembers the effects that you apply to frames via the Control palette, Transform pane, and transform tools. Choose Object➪Transform Again➪Transform Again (Option+⌘+3 or Ctrl+Alt+3) to repeat the last transformation on the selected object (it can be a different object than you last applied a transformation to).

Or choose Object➪Transform Again➪Transform Sequence Again (Option+⌘+4 or Ctrl+Alt+4) to apply all recent transformations to a selected object. That sequence of transactions stays in memory until you perform a new transformation, which then starts a new sequence, so you can apply the same transformation to multiple objects.

Two other transform-again options are available through the Object➪Transform Again menu option's submenu: Transform Again Individually and Transform Sequence Again Individually. You use these on groups; they work like the regular Transform Again and Transform Sequence Again options but apply any effects to each object individually within the group. For example, choosing Transform Again to a group might rotate the entire group as if it were one unit, but choosing Transform Again Individually would rotate each object in the group separately, not the group as a unit. Try it and see exactly what it does!

Adding Strokes, Fills, and Other Effects

InDesign lets you change an object's appearance in several ways:

- Add a border, or *stroke,* around an object's perimeter and apply a solid color, a tint, or a gradient to the stroke.
- Add a solid color, a tint, or a gradient to the frame's background.
- Apply any of several corner effects.
- Apply transparency, drop-shadow, and feathering effects to objects.

Adding strokes

All objects have a stroke with a width of 0 built in, so you never really have to add strokes. But to use them, you need to modify them so they have some thickness onto which you can apply attributes such as colors and gradients.

Setting stroke appearance

The Stroke pane is where you give the stroke its width, as well as apply the type of stroke and other attributes:

1. **Select either of the selection tools and click the object whose stroke you want to modify.**
2. **If the Stroke pane is not displayed, show it by choosing Window➪Stroke or by pressing F10.** Figure 12-4 shows the pane.

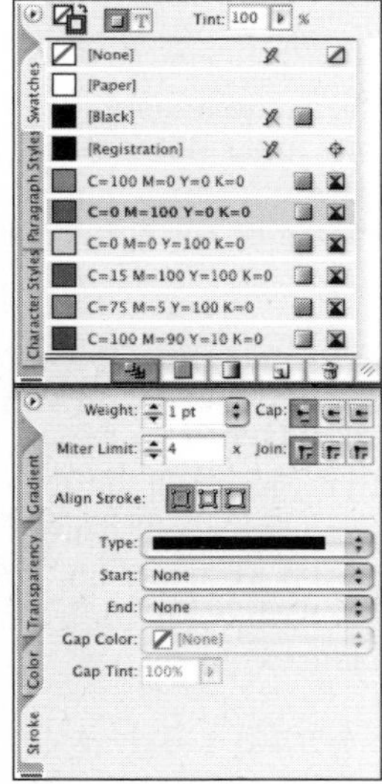

Figure 12-4: The Stroke pane (bottom) and the Swatches pane that is often used at the same time (top).

3. **To change the width of the stroke, enter a new value in the Weight field.** You can also change the Weight value by choosing a new value from the field's pop-up menu or by clicking the up and down arrows. (Each click increases or decreases the stroke by 1 point.)
4. **Set the Miter Limit.** The default of 4 is fine for almost all frames. You rarely need to use this feature, so don't worry about it.
5. **Click any of the three Cap buttons to specify how dashes will look if you create a dashed stroke (covered in Step 9).** Experiment with them in your objects to see which looks best for your situation.

6. **Click any of the three Join buttons to specify how corners are handled.** Again, experiment with these to see what works best for you.
7. **Choose an Align Stroke option.** The default is the first button, Align Stroke to Center, which has the stroke straddle the frame. You can also choose Align Stroke to Inside, which places the entire thickness inside the frame boundary, or Align Stroke to Outside, which places the entire thickness outside the frame boundary.
8. **You can also choose end points for your strokes (this only affects lines, not rectangles, ellipses, and other closed-loop shapes) by using the Start and End pop-up menus.** Figure 12-5 shows the options.

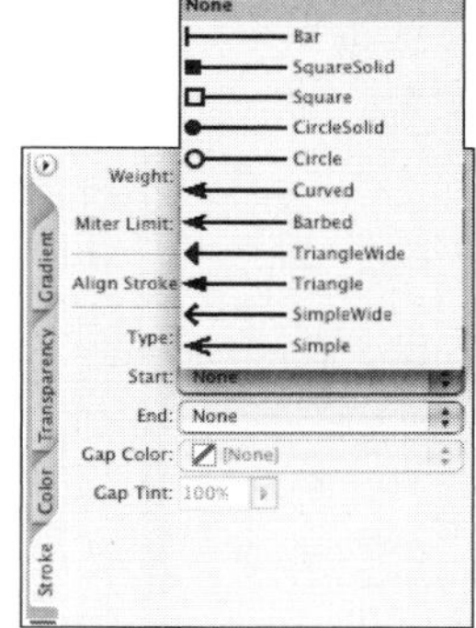

Figure 12-5: The Start options in the Stroke pane. (The End options are identical.)

9. **To create a dashed line instead of a solid line, choose an option from the Type pop-up menu.** (These are also available from the Control palette.) Choose from 16 types of predefined dashes and stripes. The Gap Color and Gap Tint fields at the bottom of the Stroke pane become active as well, to let you choose a specific color and tint for the gaps in dashes and stripes.

Now that you have a visible stroke, you want to color it. Here's how:

1. **Select either of the selection tools and click the frame to which you want to add a stroke.**
2. **Click the Stroke button in the Swatches pane or Tools palette.**
3. **You now can click a color, tint, or gradient from the Swatches pane, or click one of the three boxes at the bottom of the Tools palette, which let you use (from left to right) the last-selected color, last-selected gradient, or None (this removes the stroke's color, tint, or gradient).**

For information about adding colors to the Swatches pane and applying colors to objects, see Chapter 10.

Creating stroke styles

InDesign lets you create custom strokes, known as stroke styles, in any of three types: dashed, dotted, and striped. To create custom dashes or stripes, choose the Stroke Styles option in the Stroke pane's palette menu. In the resulting Stroke Styles dialog box, you can create new strokes, edit or delete existing ones, and import strokes from a stroke styles file, which you create by saving a document's strokes as a separate file for import into other documents. Stroke style files have the filename extension `.inst`.

Note that you cannot edit or delete the seven default stripe patterns shown in the Stroke Styles dialog box, nor can you edit or delete the default dash patterns — they're not even available in the dialog box. When you edit or create a stroke pattern, you get the New Stroke Style dialog box, shown in Figure 12-6. In the Name field, enter a name for your stroke. In the Type pop-up menu, you can choose to create (or convert a stripe you are editing to) a dashed, dotted, or striped stroke.

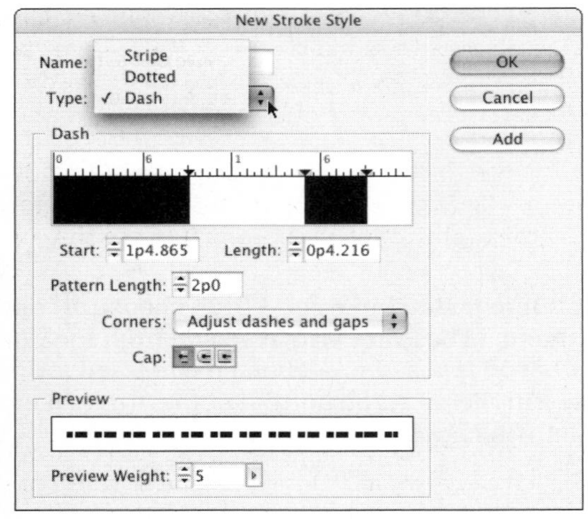

Figure 12-6: The dashes version of the New Stroke Style dialog box.

For dashes, you can resize the dash component by dragging the down-pointing triangle at the end of the dash in the ruler section. You can add dash segments by simply clicking the ruler and dragging a segment to the desired width. Or you can use the Start and Length fields to manually specify them. The Pattern Length field is where you indicate the length of the segment that will be repeated to create a dashed line.

In the Corners pop-up menu, you tell InDesign whether to adjust how the dashes and gaps are handled at corners; the default is Adjust Dashes and Gaps, a setting you should keep — it will make sure your corners have dash segments that extend along both sides of the corner, which looks neater.

(Your other options are Adjust Dashes, Adjust Gaps, and None.) You can also choose a cap style and the stroke weight. The preview section of the pane lets you see your dash as you create or edit it.

For dots, you get a similar dialog box as for dashes. The Start and Length fields disappear, replaced with the Center field that determines where any added dots are placed on the ruler. (The initial dot, shown as a half-circle, starts at 0 and cannot be moved or deleted.) The Caps field is also gone.

To delete a dash or dot segment, just drag it to the left, off the ruler.

For stripes, you also get a similar dialog box. The principle is the same as for dashes: You create segments (in this case vertical, not horizontal) for the stripes by dragging on the ruler. However, the stripes version of the dialog box expresses its values in percentages because the actual thickness of each stripe is determined by the stroke weight — the thicker the stroke, the thicker each stripe is in the overall stroke.

In all three versions of the New Stroke Style dialog box, you click Add to add the stroke to your document, and then you can create a new stroke. When you're done creating strokes, click OK. (When editing a stroke, the Add button won't be available.)

Be sure to use the Preview Weight slider shown in Figure 12-6. This is available in all three versions of the New Stroke Style dialog box. It lets you increase or decrease the preview size so you can better see thin or small elements in your stroke.

Adding fills

The option to add a stroke to any shape becomes even more powerful when combined with the option to fill any shape with a color or tint. For example, adding a fill to a text frame is an effective way to draw attention to a sidebar. Adding a fill to a shape is much like adding a stroke, and the options available for specifying color and tint are identical. The only difference is that you click the Fill button in the Tools palette or Swatches pane rather than the Stroke button.

Adding special effects to corners

Anytime you're working on an object that has any sharp corners, you have the option to add a little pizzazz to those corners via InDesign's Corner Effects feature (Object⇨Corner Effects). Five built-in corner styles, shown in Figure 12-7, are available. Note that if the shape contains only smooth points, any corner effect you apply won't be noticeable.

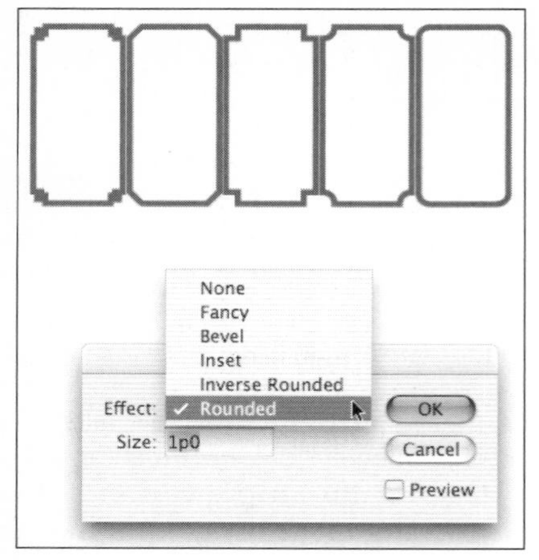

Figure 12-7: The Corner Effects dialog box lets you apply any of five effects to frame corners.

To add a corner effect:

1. **Select either of the selection tools and click the object to which you want to add a corner effect.**
2. **Choose Object⇨Corner Effects to display the Corner Effects dialog box.** (Select the Preview check box to view changes as you make them.)
3. **Choose an option from the Effect pop-up menu.**
4. **Enter a distance in the Size field.**

   The Size value determines the length that the effect extends from the corner.
5. **Click OK to close the dialog box and apply your changes.**

If you can't see a corner effect after applying one, make sure that a color is applied to the stroke or try making the object's stroke thicker. Increasing the Size value in the Corner Effects dialog box can also make a corner effect more visible.

Using transparency

One of InDesign's most sophisticated tools is its set of transparency options, which let you make objects partially transparent. You apply transparency with the Transparency pane (Window⇨Transparency or Shift+F10). Figure 12-8 shows the pane as well as a text title that uses transparency as it overprints a background photo. Notice how the semi-transparent text fades away toward the top and is brighter toward the bottom.

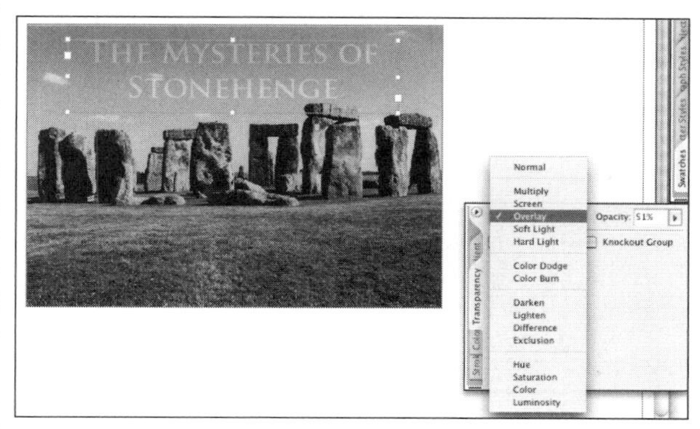

Figure 12-8: The Transparency pane and its palette menu, as well as a semi-transparent object overprinting a photograph.

You cannot apply transparency to text selections or to layers, nor can you apply different transparency settings to an object's fill and stroke. Also, if you remove an object from a group that had transparency applied (via cut and paste or copy and paste), that pasted object will not retain the group's transparency settings.

There are 16 different transparency types — called *blending modes* — as shown in Figure 12-8 (Photoshop and Illustrator users will recognize these options.) The differences among them can be subtle or extreme, depending on a variety of issues. You should experiment with them to see what effect works best in each case.

The Difference, Exclusion, Hue, Saturation, Color, and Luminosity modes do not blend spot colors — only process colors.

You have two other options in the Transparency pane:

- **Isolate Blending** restricts the blending modes to the objects in a group, instead of also applying them to objects beneath the group. This can prevent unintended changes to those underlying objects.
- **Knockout Group** obscures any objects below the selected group. But those objects are still affected by any blend mode settings applied to the group, unless Isolate Blending is also checked.

Using drop shadows

To apply a drop shadow to an object, you first select it with a selection tool. Then open the Drop Shadow dialog box, shown in Figure 12-9, by choosing Object➪Drop Shadow or by pressing Option+⌘+M or Ctrl+Alt+M. In the dialog box, you set the following options:

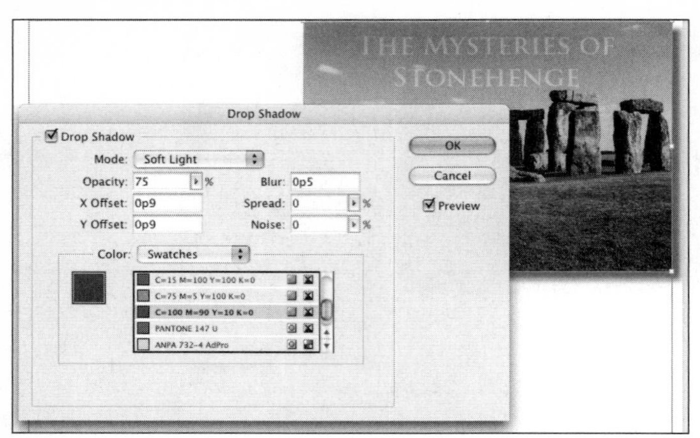

Figure 12-9: The Drop Shadow dialog box and an example drop shadow.

- Select the Drop Shadow option to turn on the drop shadow function.
- Select a lighting type (technically, a *blend mode*) by choosing one of the 16 options in the Mode pop-up menu. (These are the same blending modes used in transparencies.)
- Specify the opacity by entering a value in the Opacity field — 0% is invisible, while 100% is completely solid.
- Specify the shadow's position relative to the object by using the X Offset and Y Offset fields. A positive X Offset moves the shadow to the right; a positive Y Offset moves the shadow down. Negative values go in the other direction.
- Specify the shadow's size by entering a value in the Blur field — this blurs a copy of the text used in the drop shadow to make it look like it was created by shining light on solid letters.
- Choose a color source — Swatches, RGB, CMYK, or LAB — from the Color pop-up menu and then select a color from the sliders or swatches below that menu. You get sliders for RGB, CMYK, and LAB colors, or a set of previously defined color swatches if you selected Swatches in the Color pop-up menu.
- To see the effects of your various setting adjustments in the actual layout, check the Preview option.

Using feathering

A similar option to drop shadows is feathering, which essentially softens the edges of objects. Like drop shadows, feathering can be applied only to objects, not to individual text, paths, or strokes. To feather an object, first select it and then choose Object⇨Feather. You get the dialog box shown in Figure 12-10.

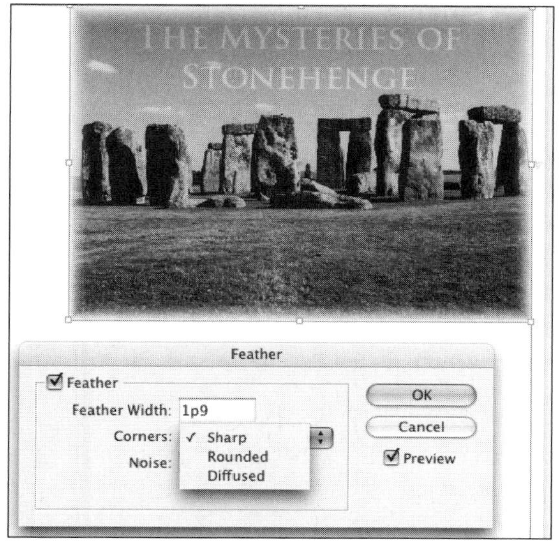

Figure 12-10: The Feather dialog box and a sample feathering effect.

To apply feathering, select the Feather option. You then enter a value for the degree of feathering — smaller numbers have the least effect, larger numbers have the most effect. The feathering area starts at the outside edge of the object and "eats into" the object, making it a wispier version of itself. The Corners pop-up menu gives you three options: Sharp, Rounded, and Diffused. The Sharp option retains the original shape as much as possible. The Rounded option rounds the corners of the object; it can distort the shape dramatically at larger Feather Width settings. The Diffused option creates a soft, almost smoky effect by making the feathered part of the object more translucent.

Chapter 13

Organizing Objects

In This Chapter

- Creating object styles
- Anchoring objects to text
- Grouping and ungrouping objects
- Locking and unlocking objects
- Changing objects' stacking order
- Moving objects to other documents

You use objects throughout your layout: lines, text frames, graphics frames, shapes, and so forth. A big part of working with them involves organizing them — deciding when to group them together, when to lock them in location, when to associate them with other objects, and so on. That's where this chapter comes in.

But first, you'll learn about a powerful new feature called *object styles* that lets you save object attributes and apply them to other objects for consistent, easy formatting.

Working with Object Styles

For many years, desktop publishing programs have let designers save textual styles for easy reuse and application throughout a document. Yet only in 2005 did someone get the brilliant idea that this capability would work well for objects, too. (Well, actually, someone had that idea about 15 years ago, in a program that didn't survive the early years of desktop publishing, but it's still fantastic that a mainstream publishing tool has picked up the idea.)

InDesign now lets you create object styles, so you can assure that multiple objects have the same attributes and that any changes to the style are made to all the objects using that style.

Designers will find the process of creating and applying object styles very familiar because the concept is the same as creating other types of styles, such as paragraph, character, and stroke styles.

Creating object styles

You create object styles by using the Object Styles pane (Window➪Object Styles or ⌘+F7 or Ctrl+F7), shown in Figure 13-1. You can also click the New Object Style button at the bottom of the pane.

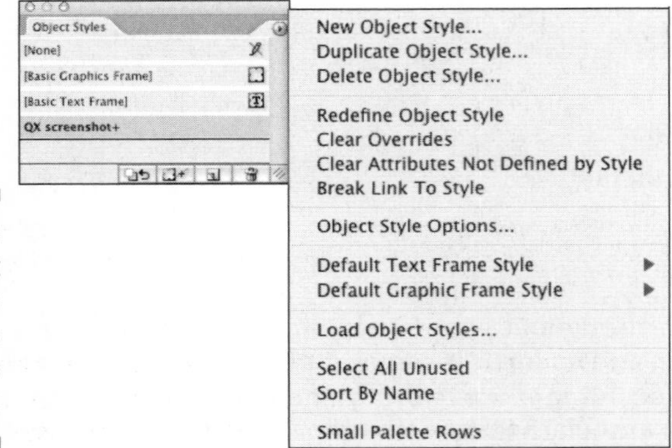

Figure 13-1: The Object Styles pane and its palette menu.

The simplest way to create an object style is to select an already-formatted object with the Selection or Direct Selection tool, then choose New Object Style from the Object Style pane's palette menu. InDesign records all the settings automatically from the selected object, so they're in place for the new object style.

Whether you start with an existing object or create a new object style completely from scratch, you use the New Object Style menu option that opens the New Object Style dialog box shown in Figure 13-2.

At the left side of the dialog box is a list of types of attributes that are or can be set. The checked items are in use for this style — you can uncheck an item so InDesign doesn't apply its settings to objects using the style. For example, if Fill is unchecked, the object style won't apply any Fill settings to objects using that style (and won't change any fill settings that have been applied to that object locally).

To switch from one type of attribute to another, simply click the item name for the type of attribute that you want to adjust, such as Stroke or Transparency.

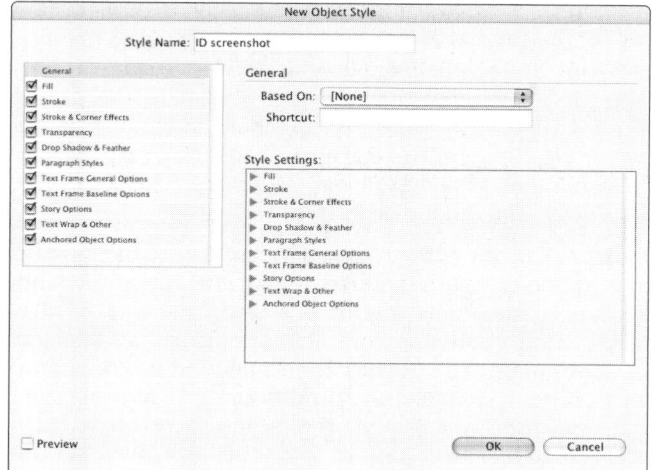

Figure 13-2: The New Object Style dialog box and its General pane.

Be sure to select the Preview option to see the results of object styles on the currently selected object. Of course, you need to make sure that the object is visible on-screen to see those effects.

When you open the New Object Style dialog box, you see the General pane, which lets you create a new style based on an existing object style (by using the Based On pop-up menu), and which lets you assign a keyboard shortcut for fast application of this style (by using the Shortcuts field).

You can use the Based On feature to create families of object styles. For example, you can create a style called *Photo-Standard* for the bulk of your placed photographs, and then create variations such as *Photo-Sidebar* and *Photo-Author.* The Photo-Standard style might specify a hairline black stroke around the photo, while Photo-Sidebar might change that to a white stroke. But if you later decide you want the stroke to be 1 point and change it in Photo-Standard, Photo-Sidebar automatically gets the 1-point stroke while retaining the white color.

The General pane also lets you see the current style settings. Click any of the arrows in the Style Settings section to get more details on how they are set for this object style.

The other panes in the New Object Styles dialog box provide the same capabilities that you find elsewhere in InDesign, brought into one convenient place so you can use them in styles. These panes are:

- **The Fill pane** lets you set colors for fills using whatever colors are defined in the Swatches pane. You can also set the tint and, if you select a gradient fill, the angle for that gradient. Finally, you can choose to have the fill overprint the contents of the frame by selecting the Overprint Fill option.

- **The Stroke pane** is identical to the Fill pane except that options specific to fills are grayed out, and options available to strokes are made available. The color, tint, and gradient angle options are the same as for the Fill pane. You can also choose the type of stroke (solid line, dashed line, or dotted line) by using the Type pop-up menu, and adjust the thickness by filling in the Weight field. You can also choose to overprint the stroke over underlying content, plus determine — if your stroke is a dotted or dashed line — the color, tint, and overprint for the gap.
- **The Stroke & Corner Effects pane** lets you set stroke position and how corners and line ends are handled. It also lets you apply fancy corners to frames. The Stroke Effects section is where you align the strokes to the frame edges, determine how lines join at corners, and decide what line endings are applied. The Corner Effects section is where you select from five fancy corners, such as Bevel and Rounded, by using the Effect pop-up menu, and where you specify the radius, or reach, of the corner by using the Size field. (See Chapter 12 for the low-down on stroke and corner effects.)
- **The Transparency pane** controls an object's opacity, with 0 percent being invisible and 100 percent being completely solid. The Mode pop-up menu lets you select the transparency effect. The Isolate Blending and Knockout Group options affect how transparency affects other objects in specific cases. (See Chapter 12 for details.)
- **The Drop Shadow & Feather pane** controls two types of lighting effects for objects: drop shadows and feathering, which are discussed in Chapter 12.
- **The Paragraph Styles pane** controls what paragraph style, if any, is applied to text in the frame. Chances are you won't use this setting except for frames that contain only consistent, very simple text, such as pull-quotes or bios. (See Chapter 17 for details.)
- **The Text Frame General Options pane** controls how text is handled within a frame. This essentially replicates the controls in the General pane of the Text Box Options dialog box (Object⇨Text Frame Options or ⌘+B or Ctrl+B), including number of columns, column width, gutter settings, inset spacing (how far from the frame edge text is placed), vertical justification (how text is aligned vertically in the frame), and whether text wrap settings are ignored when this frame overlaps other frames. (See Chapter 15 for details.)
- **The Text Frame Baseline Options pane** controls how text is handled within a frame. This essentially replicates the controls in the Baseline Options pane of the Text Box Options dialog box (Object⇨Text Frame Options or ⌘+B or Ctrl+B), including how the text baseline is calculated for the frame and whether the text frame gets its own baseline grid. (See Chapter 11 for details.)

- **The Story Options pane** enables optical margin alignment — its controls are the same as the Story pane (Window➪Type & Tables➪Story), discussed in Chapter 18. Optical margin alignment adjusts the placement of text along the left side of a frame so the text alignment is more visually pleasing.
- **The Text Wrap & Other pane** lets you set text wrap, mirroring the features of the Text Wrap pane (Window➪Text Wrap or Option+⌘+W or Ctrl+Alt+W, discussed in Chapter 18), as well as make an object nonprinting (normally handled through the Attributes pane by choosing Window➪Attributes).
- **The Anchored Object Options pane** lets you set the attributes for inline and anchored frames, mirroring the controls in the Anchored Object Options dialog box (Object➪Anchored Object➪Options), which is covered later in this chapter.

Managing object styles

The Object Styles pane's palette menu (refer to Figure 13-1) has several options for managing object styles:

- **Duplicate Object Style:** Click an object style's name and then choose this menu option to create an exact copy. If you want to create an object style that's similar to one you already created, you might want to choose New Object Style rather than Duplicate Object Style, and then use the Based On option to create a child of the original. If you choose Duplicate Object Style, the copy is identical to, but not based on, the original; if you modify the original, the copy is not affected.
- **Delete Object Style:** Choose this to delete selected object styles. To select multiple styles, press and hold ⌘ or Ctrl as you click their names. To select a range of styles, click the first one, and then press and hold Shift and click the last one. You can also delete styles by selecting them in the pane and then clicking the Delete Selected Styles (trashcan icon) at the bottom of the pane.
- **Redefine Object Style:** To modify an existing object style, first make changes to an object that already has an object style defined for it, and then select Redefine Object Style. The newly applied formats are applied to the object style.
- **Object Style Options:** This option lets you modify an existing object style. When a style is highlighted in the Object Styles pane, choosing Object Style Options displays the Object Style Options dialog box, which is identical to the New Object Style dialog box covered earlier.

- **Load Object Styles:** Choose this option if you want to import object styles from another InDesign document. After selecting the document from which to import the styles, you will get a dialog box listing the styles in the chosen document, so you can decide which ones to import. Note the Incoming Style Definitions window at the bottom of the dialog box; it lists the style definitions to help you decide which to import, as well as which to overwrite or rename.
- **Select All Unused:** Select this option to highlight the names of all object styles that have not been applied to any objects in the current document. This is a handy way of identifying unused styles in preparation for deleting them (by choosing the Delete Object Style menu option).
- **Sort by Name:** This option alphabetizes your object styles for easier access. (InDesign adds styles to the Object Styles pane in the order in which they were created.)
- **Small Palette Rows:** Select this option to reduce the text size in the Object Styles pane. Although harder to read, a pane with this option selected lets you access more styles without having to scroll. To return the pane to its normal text size, deselect this option.

InDesign comes with three predefined object styles — [Normal Text Frame], [Normal Graphics Frame], and [Normal Grid] — that you can modify as desired.

Applying object styles

After you create an object style, applying it is easy. Just click an object and then click the object style name in the Object Styles pane or press its keyboard shortcut. (Windows users must make sure Num Lock is on when using shortcuts for styles.)

The Quick Apply option

Another way to apply object styles is by using the new Quick Apply palette. Quick Apply is a consolidated list of styles that you access by choosing Edit⇨Quick Apply or by pressing ⌘+Return or Ctrl+Enter. If you select an object, the Quick Apply palette presents all available paragraph, character, and object styles in an alphabetical list. You can scroll down to the one you want or type the first few letters of the style name in the text field at the top to jump to styles beginning with those letters, then navigate to the one you want and press Return or Enter, which brings you back to where you were working with your object and closes the Quick Apply palette.

This feature is handy if you're working on layouts from your keyboard — perhaps you're a layout artist working on a notebook while commuting. You can switch to the Quick Apply palette, apply the style, and return to your object or text, all without touching the mouse.

You can set which object styles are automatically used for new text and graphics frames: In the Object Styles pane's palette menu, choose Default Text Frame Style and select the desired style from the submenu to set a default text frame; choose Default Graphics Frame Style and select the desired style from the submenu to set a default graphics frame. To no longer have object styles automatically applied to new objects, choose [None] in the Default Text Frame and/or Default Graphics Frame submenus.

How existing formatting is handled

When you apply an object style to selected objects, all local formats are retained. All other formats are replaced by those of the applied style — that is, unless you do one of the following:

- If you press and hold Option or Alt when clicking a name in the Object Styles pane, any local formatting that has been applied to the objects is removed. You can achieve the same effect by choosing Clear Attributes Not Defined by Style from the Object Styles pane's palette menu or by clicking the Clear Attributes Not Defined by Style button at the bottom of the Object Styles pane.
- If you want to override any local changes with the settings in the object style, choose Clear Overrides in the palette menu or click the Clear Overrides button at the bottom of the Object Styles pane. The difference is that Clear Attributes Not Defined by Style removes all attributes for which the object style contains no settings, while Clear Overrides imposes the object style's settings over conflicting attributes that you set manually.

If a plus sign (+) appears to the right of an object style's name, it means that the object has local formats that differ from those of the applied object style. This can occur if you apply an object style to object text to which you've done some manual formatting, or if you modify formatting for an object after applying an object style to it. (For example, you may have changed the fill color; that is a local change to the object style and will cause the + to appear.)

Removing an object style from an object

To remove a style from an object, choose Break Link to Style from the Object Styles pane's palette menu. The object's current formatting won't be affected, but it will no longer be updated when the object style is changed.

Creating Inline and Anchored Frames

In most cases, you want the frames you place on your pages to remain precisely where you put them. But sometimes, you want to place frames relative to related text in such a way that the frames move when the text is edited. For example, if you're creating a product catalog that's essentially a continuous list of product descriptions and you want to include a graphic with each description, you can paste graphics within the text to create inline graphics frames.

A close cousin to the inline frame is the anchored frame, in which a frame follows a point in the text, but that frame is not actually in the text. For example, you might have a "For More Information" sidebar that you want to appear to the left of the text that first mentions a term. By using an anchored frame, you can have that sidebar move with the text so it always appears to its left, perhaps in an adjacent column or in the page margins.

Figure 13-3 shows examples of both an inline frame and an anchored frame.

Note that the process of creating inline and anchored frames — especially anchored frames — can appear overwhelming. It does require thinking through the frame's placement and visualizing that placement so you pick the right options in the various dialog boxes. But relax: You can experiment until you get the hang of it. That's why InDesign lets you undo your work.

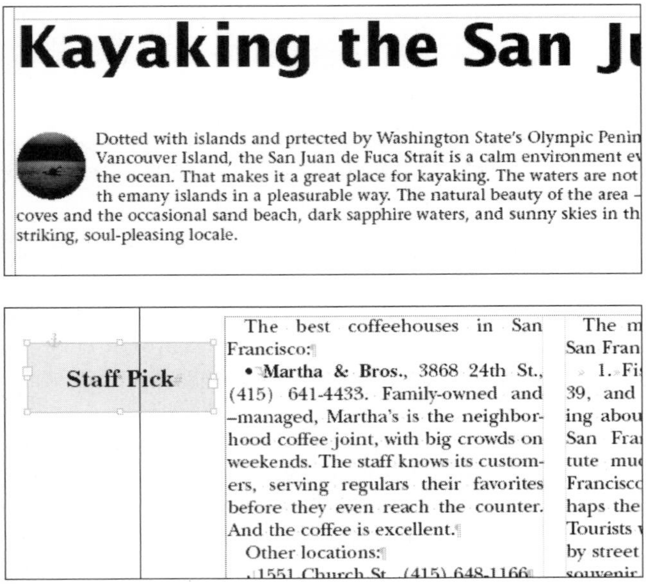

Figure 13-3: An inline frame (at top) and an anchored frame (the "Staff Pick" box is anchored to the word "Martha").

Working with inline frames

An inline frame is treated like a single character. If you insert or delete text that precedes an inline frame, the frame moves forward or backward along with the rest of the text that follows the inserted or deleted text. Although inline frames usually contain graphics, they can just as easily contain text or nothing at all.

Inline frames may interfere with line spacing in paragraphs that have automatic leading. If the inline frame is larger than the point size in use, the automatic leading value for that line is calculated from the inline frame. This leads to inconsistent line spacing in the paragraph. To work around this, you can apply a fixed amount of leading to all characters in the paragraph, adjust the size of inline frames, place inline frames at the beginning of a paragraph, or place inline frames in their own paragraphs.

There are three ways to create inline frames: pasting the frame into text, placing the frame into text, and using the new Anchored Object menu option. The first two are the simplest, but the third gives you more control over the inline frame when you create it. The third way also lets you create anchored frames, which are covered later in this chapter.

Using the Paste command

If you want to create an inline frame from an object you already created, all you have to do is copy or cut the object and then paste it into text as you would a piece of highlighted text. Here's how:

1. **Use the Selection tool to select the object you want to paste within text.**

   Any type of object can be used: a line, an empty shape, a text or picture frame, even a group of objects.

2. **Choose Edit➪Copy or press ⌘+C or Ctrl+C.**

   If you don't need the original item, you can use the Cut command (Edit➪Cut or ⌘+X or Ctrl+X) instead of the Copy command.

3. **Select the Type tool and then click within the text where you want to place the copied object.**

   Make sure the cursor is flashing where you intend to place the inline frame.

4. **Choose Edit➪Paste or press ⌘+V or Ctrl+V.**

Inline frames often work best when placed at the beginning of a paragraph. If you place an inline frame within text to which automatic leading has been applied, the resulting line spacing can be inconsistent. To fix this problem, you can resize the inline frame.

Using the Place command

You can also use the Place command to create an inline graphics frame from an external picture file. (You can't use this technique for inline text frames.) Here's how:

1. **Select the Type tool and then click within a text frame to establish the insertion point.**

2. **Choose File➪Place or press ⌘+D or Ctrl+D.**

3. **Locate and select the graphics file you want to place within the text; then click Choose or Open.**

To delete an inline frame, you can select it and then choose Edit⇨Clear or Edit⇨Cut, or you can position the cursor next to it and press Delete or Backspace.

Adjusting inline frames

After you create an inline frame, you can adjust its position vertically or horizontally. Again, there are several methods.

Two quick-and-dirty methods to move an inline frame vertically are as follows:

- Use the Type tool to highlight the inline frame as you would highlight an individual text character. In the Character pane or Control palette, type a positive value in the Baseline Shift field to move the inline frame up; type a negative value to move the frame down.
- Use the Selection tool or Direct Selection tool to select the inline frame; then drag the frame up or down.

A quick way to move an inline frame horizontally is to follow these steps:

1. **With the Type tool selected, click between the inline frame and the character that precedes it.**
2. **Use the kerning controls in the Character pane or Control palette to enlarge or reduce the space between the inline frame and the preceding character.**

You can more precisely control the position of inline frames by using the Anchored Object Options dialog box, covered in the next section.

Of course, you can also adjust its other attributes as needed, such as strokes, fills, dimensions, rotation, and skew, by using the Tools palette, Control palette, and other panes.

Working with anchored frames

Anchored frames give you a whole new way of organizing objects. Essentially, they follow the relevant text within the parameters you specify, such as staying to the left of the text or staying at the top of the page that contains the text.

Note that an inline frame is a type of anchored frame, one where the frame stays within the text it is linked to. For simplicity, we're using the term *anchored frame* to mean only those frames that are outside the text frame but remain linked to a specific point in the text.

Anchored frames are new to InDesign CS2. Not only can you create them, but InDesign CS2 now retains anchored frames set up in Microsoft Word documents. It also preserves anchored frames when exporting as Rich Text Format.

To create anchored frames, do the following:

1. **Select the Type tool and then click within a text frame to establish the insertion point.**
2. **Choose Object⇨Anchored Object⇨Insert.**

   The Insert Anchored Object dialog box appears.
3. **In the Object Options section of the dialog box, specify the anchored frame's settings.**

   You can choose the type of frame (text, graphics, or unassigned) with the Content pop-up menu, apply an object style by using the Object Style pop-up menu, apply a paragraph style via the Paragraph Style pop-up menu, and set the anchored frame's dimensions in the Height and Width fields. Note that the Paragraph Style you choose, if any, applies to the anchored frame, not to the paragraph in which the anchored frame is linked. InDesign lets you apply a paragraph style to the anchored frame even if it contains no text.
4. **In the Position pop-up menu, choose what kind of frame you are creating: Inline or Above Line (both are inline frames) or Custom (an anchored frame).**

   The dialog box will show different options based on that choice, as Figure 13-4 shows.

   Anchored frames added by choosing Object⇨Anchored Object⇨Insert do not have text automatically wrapped around them. Use the Text Wrap pane (Window⇨Text Wrap or Option+⌘+W or Ctrl+Alt+W) to open this pane and set text wrap. But anchored frames created by pasting a graphic into text *do* automatically have text wrap around them.

   Selecting the Prevent Manual Positioning option ensures that the positions of individual anchored frames can't be adjusted by using InDesign's other text and frame controls (such as Baseline Shift). This forces users to use this dialog box to change the anchored frame's position, reducing the chances of accidental change.
5. **Decide whether to select the Relative to Spine option.**

   If this option is *not* selected, the anchored frame is placed on the same side of the text frame on all pages, whether those pages are left-facing or right-facing. If the Relative to Spine option is selected, InDesign places the text frame on the outside of both pages or inside of both pages, depending on how the anchored position is set.

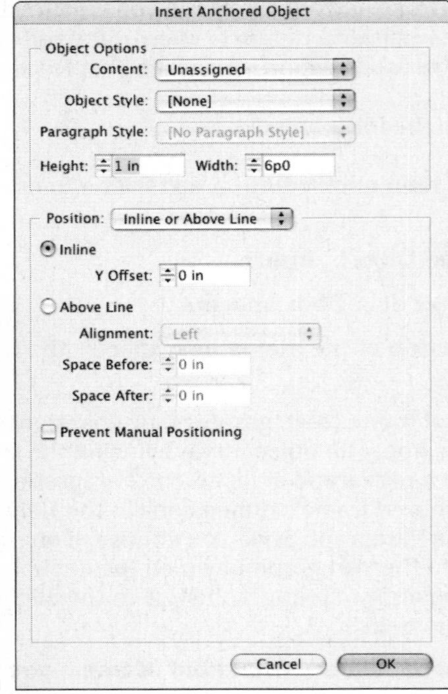

Figure 13-4: The Insert Anchored Object dialog box for inline frames (left) and anchored frames (right).

6. **In the Anchored Object section of the dialog box, click one of the positioning squares to set up the text frame's relative position.**

   Note that you need to think about both the horizontal and vertical position you desire. For example, if you want the anchored frame to appear to the right of the text reference, click one of the right-hand squares. (Remember that selecting the Relative to Spine option overrides this, making the right-hand pages' positions mirror that of the left-hand pages, rather than be identical to them.) If you choose the topmost right-hand square, the anchored frame is placed to the right of the text reference and vertically appears at or below that text reference. But if you choose the bottommost right-hand square, you're telling InDesign you want the anchored frame to appear vertically above the text reference. Experiment with your layout to see what works best in each case.

7. **In the Anchored Position section of the dialog box, click one of the positioning squares to set up the text reference's relative position.**

   Although there are nine squares shown, the only three that matter are those in the middle row. Typically, you place the text reference on the opposite side of the anchored frame — if you want the anchored frame to be to the left, you would indicate that the text reference is to the right. (If you set the text reference on the same side as the anchored frame, InDesign places the anchored frame over the text.) The reason there are three squares (left, middle, and right) is to accommodate layouts in which you want some anchored frames to appear to the left of the text and some to the right; in that case, choose the middle position here and select the right- or left-hand position in the Anchored Object section as appropriate to that object.

8. **There are three options in the Anchored Position section that give InDesign more precise instructions on how to place the anchored frames:**
   - **The X Relative To pop-up menu** tells InDesign from where the horizontal location is calculated, using the following options: Anchor Marker, Column Edge, Text Frame, Page Margin, and Page Edge. The right option depends both on where you want the anchored frames placed and whether you have multicolumn text boxes (in which case Text Frame and Column Edge result in different placement, while in a single-column text frame they do not). You can also specify a specific amount of space to place between the chosen X Relative To point and the anchored frame by typing a value in the X Offset field.
   - **The Y Relative To pop-up menu** tells InDesign from where the vertical location is calculated, using the following options: Line (Baseline), Line (Cap-height), Line (Top of Leading), Column Edge, Text Frame, Page Margin, and Page Edge. As you expect, you can also indicate a specific amount of space to place between the chosen Y Relative To point and the anchored frame by typing a value in the Y Offset field.
   - **The Keep Within Top/Bottom Column boundaries check box** does exactly what it says.
9. **Click OK to insert the anchored frame.**

You can create inline frames using the same basic process as above, choosing Inline or Above Line in Step 4. You'll get most of the same controls as for anchored objects, such as the frame size and type, but of course there are no controls for the relative position, since an inline frame goes at the text-insertion point. But it's easier to use the techniques described in the previous section for creating inline frames: copying or placing a frame into text.

Converting existing frames to anchored frames

After you get the hang of when and how to use anchored frames, you'll likely want to convert some frames in existing documents into anchored frames. There's no direct way to do that in InDesign, but there is a somewhat circuitous path you can take:

1. **Use the Selection or Direct Selection tool to cut the existing frame that you want to make into an anchored frame by choosing Edit⇨Cut or by pressing ⌘+X or Ctrl+X.**

   You can also copy an existing frame by choosing Edit⇨Copy or by pressing ⌘+C or Ctrl+C.

2. **Switch to the Type tool and click in a text frame at the desired location to insert the text reference to the anchored frame.**
3. **Paste the cut or copied frame into that insertion point by choosing Edit⇨Paste or by pressing ⌘+V or Ctrl+V.**

   You now have an inline frame.
4. **Select the frame with the Selection tool, then choose Object⇨Anchored Object⇨Options to display the Anchored Object Options dialog box.**

   This dialog box looks like the Insert Anchored Options dialog box, shown in Figure 13-4, except that it doesn't include the top Object Options section.
5. **Choose Custom from the Position pop-up menu.**

   This converts the frame from an inline frame to an anchored frame.
6. **Adjust the position for the newly minted anchored frame as described in the previous section.**
7. **Click OK when you're done.**

Anchoring caveats

There are several caveats to consider when creating anchored frames:

- Because an anchored frame follows its text as it flows throughout a document, you need to ensure that your layout retains clear paths for those anchored objects to follow. Otherwise, anchored frames could overlap other frames as they move.
- Anchored frames should generally be small items and/or used sparingly. The more items you have anchored to text, the greater the chance that they will interfere with each other's placement. Likewise, large items can be moved only so far within a page, so the benefit of keeping them close to their related text disappears.
- Items such as pull-quotes are obvious candidates for use as anchored frames. But in many layouts, you want the pull-quotes to stay in specific locations on the page for good visual appearance. The InDesign anchored-frame function can accommodate that need for specific positioning on a page, but you need to be careful as you add or delete text so that you do not end up with some pages that have no pull-quotes at all because there is so much text between the pull-quotes' anchor points. Conversely, you need to make sure you don't have too many pull-quotes anchored close to each other, which could result in overlapping.

Typically, you use anchored frames for small graphics or icons that you want to keep next to a specific paragraph (such as the Tip and Warning icons used in this book). Another good use would be for cross-reference ("For More Information") text frames.

Adjusting anchored frames

After you create an anchored frame, you can adjust its position.

A quick-and-dirty method is simply to click and drag anchored frames or use the Control palette or Transform pane to adjust their position. If the text the frame is anchored to moves, however, InDesign overrides those changes. (You can't manually move an anchored frame if the Prevent Manual Positioning option is selected in the Insert Anchored Object dialog box or Anchored Object Options dialog box. This option is deselected by default.)

For the most control of an anchored frame's position, choose Object➪Anchored Object➪Options. The resulting Anchored Object Options dialog box is identical to the Insert Anchored Object dialog box (covered previously in this section and shown in Figure 13-4) but without the Object Options section.

And, of course, you can adjust the frame's other attributes as needed, such as strokes, fills, dimensions, rotation, and skew.

Releasing and deleting anchored frames

If you no longer want an anchored frame to be anchored to a text location, you can release the anchor. To do so, select the anchored frame with the Selection or Direct Selection tool and then choose Object➪Anchored Object➪Release.

It's also easy to delete an anchored frame: Select the frame with the Selection or Direct Selection tool and then choose Edit➪Clear or press Delete or Backspace. If you want to remove the object but keep it on the Clipboard for pasting elsewhere, choose Edit➪Cut or press ⌘+X or Ctrl+X.

Combining Objects into a Group

InDesign lets you combine several objects into a group. A group of objects behaves like a single object, which means that you can cut, copy, move, or modify all the objects in a group in a single operation.

To create a group, select all the objects (which can include other groups) that you want to include in your group and then choose Object➪Group or press ⌘+G or Ctrl+G.

Groups have many uses. For example, you might create a group to:

- Combine several objects that make up an illustration so that you can move, modify, copy, or scale all objects in a single operation.

- Keep a graphics frame and its accompanying caption (text) frame together so that, if you change your mind about their placement, you can reposition both objects at once.
- Combine several vertical lines that are used to separate the columns of a table so that you can quickly change the stroke, color, length, and position of all lines.

If you want to manipulate a group, choose the Selection tool and then click any object in the group. The group's bounding box appears. Any transformation you perform is applied to all objects in the group. If you want to manipulate a specific object in a group, use the Direct Selection tool. (See Chapter 12 for more details on selecting objects within groups.)

If you create a group from objects on different layers, all objects are moved to the top layer and stacked in succession beneath the topmost object.

You cannot create a group if some of the selected objects are locked and some are not locked. All selected objects must be locked or unlocked before you can group them. (Locking and unlocking objects are covered in the following section.)

After creating a group, you may eventually decide that you want to return the objects to their original, ungrouped state. To do so, simply click any object in the group with the Selection tool and then choose Object⇨Ungroup or press Shift+⌘+G or Ctrl+Shift+G. If you ungroup a group that contains a group, the contained group is not affected. To ungroup this group, you must select it and choose Ungroup again.

Locking Objects

If you're certain that you want a particular object to remain exactly where it is, you can select Object⇨Lock Position or press ⌘+L or Ctrl+L to prevent the object from being moved. Generally, you want to lock repeating elements such as headers, footers, folios, and page numbers so that they're not accidentally moved. (Such repeating elements are usually placed on a master page; you can lock objects on master pages, too.)

A locked object can't be moved whether you click and drag it with the mouse or change the values in the X: and Y: fields in the Control palette or Transform pane. Not only can you *not* move a locked object, you can't delete it, either. However, you can change other attributes of a locked object, including its stroke and fill.

To unlock a selected object, choose Object⇨Unlock Position or press Option+⌘+L or Ctrl+Alt+L.

You can also lock entire layers, as described in Chapter 7.

Stacking Objects

Each time you begin work on a new page, you start with a clean slate (unless the page is based on a master page, in which case the master objects act as the page's background; see Chapter 8 for more on master pages). Every time you add an object to a page — either by using any of InDesign's object-creation tools or with the Place command (File⇨Place or ⌘+D or Ctrl+D) — the new object occupies a unique place in the page's object hierarchy, or *stacking order.*

The first object you place on a page is automatically positioned at the bottom of the stacking order; the next object is positioned one level higher than the first object (that is, in front of the backmost object); the next object is stacked one level higher; and so on for every object you add to the page. (It's not uncommon for a page to have several dozen or even several hundred layers.)

Although each object occupies its own level, if the objects on a page don't overlap, then the stacking order is not an issue. But some of the most interesting graphic effects you can achieve with InDesign involve arranging several overlapping objects, so it's important to be aware of the three-dimensional nature of a page's stacking order.

You may change your mind about what you want to achieve in your layout after you've already placed objects in it. To change an object's position in a page's stacking order, use the Arrange command (Object⇨Arrange), which offers four choices:

- **Bring to Front** (Shift+⌘+] or Ctrl+Shift+])
- **Bring Forward** (⌘+] or Ctrl+])
- **Send Backward** (⌘+[or Ctrl+[)
- **Send to Back** (Shift+⌘+[or Ctrl+Shift+[)

To select an object that's hidden behind one or more other objects, press and hold ⌘ or Ctrl and then click anywhere within the area of the hidden object. The first click selects the topmost object; each successive click selects the next lowest object in the stacking order. When the bottom object is selected, the next click selects the top object. If you don't know where a hidden object is, you can simply click the object or objects in front of it, then send the object(s) to the back.

Sharing Objects among Documents

Often, you want to use an object from one InDesign layout in another InDesign document. It's really easy to do. Choose from any of these methods, all of which preserve the object's attributes, including styles:

- The simplest method is to select an object with the Selection tool and drag it into another document. This copies the object to the target document. You need to have both documents open and to have at least some portion of each document visible so that there's a place to drag the object to.
- You can use copy and paste or cut and paste to copy or move an object.
- You can place objects in a library for use in other documents. (See Chapter 8 for more on libraries.)

- You can drag an object onto the desktop or onto any folder, which creates a snippet file that you can then drag into another InDesign document. This is sort of like having a one-item library.

Part IV
Text Essentials

"THAT'S A LOVELY SCANNED IMAGE OF YOUR SISTER'S PORTRAIT. NOW TAKE IT OFF THE BODY OF THAT PIT VIPER BEFORE SHE COMES IN THE ROOM."

In this part . . .

Getting words on the page is an important part of what you do with InDesign. After you have the words in place, you want to tweak the letters and lines, and the space between them, to make your pages sparkle. This part shows you how to arrange words on the page. You find out how to set text in columns, and how to add bullets and numbers to that text. You also find out how to stretch, squeeze, rotate, and add color to text. Additionally, you see how to become skilled at using character and paragraph styles to make your life easier and to speed up your publishing workflow.

Chapter 14

The Ins and Outs of Text

In This Chapter

- Importing text into your InDesign document
- Copying and dragging in text
- Editing text
- Searching and replacing words and formats
- Checking spelling as you type or all at once
- Customizing the spelling and hyphenation dictionaries

For most publications, text conveys the essential messages to the readers. Often, that text will be imported from another program, so this chapter explains how to work with imported text and its formatting to achieve the smoothest import process possible.

Whether you import text or type it into text frames directly in InDesign, you'll appreciate the tools that let you search and replace, spell-check, hyphenate, and edit your text. You'll learn all about these capabilities here, too.

InDesign works with text inside *frames* — containers for the copy, as described in Chapter 10. You can create a text frame in advance or let InDesign create it for you when you import text.

Importing Text

You can import text from a word processor file (Word 97/98 or later, RTF, ASCII [text-only], or InDesign Tagged Text files) into an InDesign text frame using the Place dialog box (File⇨Place, or ⌘+D or Ctrl+D). Many of the text's original styles will remain intact, although you will want to review the imported text carefully to see if any adjustments need to be made.

Follow these steps to place imported text:

1. **Choose File⇨Place, or press ⌘+D or Ctrl+D to open the Place dialog box.**

2. **Locate the text file you want to import.**
3. **To specify how to handle current formatting in the file, check the Show Import Options check box.**

   This opens the appropriate Import Options dialog box for the text file's format. (Note that there are no import options for ASCII text.) Then click OK to return to the Place dialog box.
4. **Click the Open button to import the text.**
5. **If you selected an empty frame with the Type tool, InDesign will flow the text into that frame. If you selected a text frame with the Type tool, InDesign will flow the text at the text-insertion point in that frame, inserting the new text within the existing text.**

   If you hadn't already selected a frame before starting to import the text, specify where to place it by clicking and dragging the loaded-text icon to create a rectangular text frame, clicking in an existing frame, or clicking in any empty frame.

You can't click on a master text frame — a text frame that is placed on the page by the master page in use — and simply start typing. To select a master text frame and add text to it, Shift+⌘+click or Ctrl+Shift+click it. (For more on master pages, see Chapter 8.)

Import options for Microsoft Word and RTF files

InDesign offers a comprehensive set of import options for Word and RTF files. With these options, you can control how these files will import into an InDesign. To save time on future imports, you can save your import preferences as a preset file for repeat use.

Figure 14-1 shows the Microsoft Word Import Options dialog box. The import options for RTF files are identical.

The Preset pop-up menu, at the top of the page, lets you select from saved sets of import options. You can save the current settings by clicking the Save Preset button. And you can set a preset as the default import behavior by clicking the Save as Default button; these settings will be used for all Word file imports unless you choose a new default or make changes in this dialog box. This lets you avoid using the Import Options dialog box for your routine imports.

The ability to save import presets is new to InDesign CS2, and is available only for Word and RTF import.

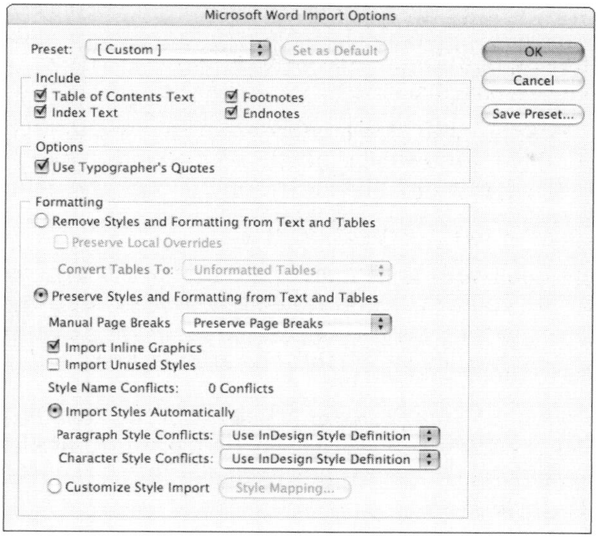

Figure 14-1: The Import Options dialog box for a Word file.

The Include section of the Import Options dialog box is where you decide whether to strip out specific types of text (Table of Contents Text, Index text, Footnotes, and Endnotes) from the Word file. If you check items, their corresponding text will be imported. You probably won't want to import table-of-contents or index text because you can create much nicer-looking tables of contents and indexes in InDesign.

The third section, Options, has just one option: Use Typographer's Quotes. If this box is checked, InDesign converts keyboard quotes from your source file (' and ") to “curly” typographic quotes (‘, ’, “, and ”).

The fourth section, Formatting, is fairly complex, so you'll want to leave it alone unless you know what you're doing.

To remove text formatting during import so that you can do the formatting in InDesign, select the Remove Styles and Formatting from Text and Tables option. You have two additional controls for this option:

- Preserve Local Overrides, which will retain local formatting such as italics and boldface while ignoring the paragraph style attributes. You'd usually want this option checked so that meaning-related formatting is retained.
- You also can choose how tables are “unformatted” during import via the Convert Tables To pop-up menu. Unformatted Tables retains the table's cell structure but ignores text and cell formatting, while Unformatted Tabbed Text converts the table to tabbed text (with a tab separating what used to be cells and a paragraph return separating what used to be rows) and strips out any formatting. If you intend to keep tables as tables but format them in InDesign, choose Unformatted Tables.

The two controls for handling "unformatting" are new to InDesign CS2.

To retain text formatting during import, so that the InDesign document at least starts out using the settings used in Word, choose the Preserve Styles and Formatting from Text and Tables option. This option includes several controls and bits of information (all of these options are new to InDesign CS2 except for the Manual Breaks pop-up menu):

- The Manual Page Breaks pop-up menu lets you retain any page breaks entered in Word, convert them to column breaks, or strip them out.
- Checking the Import Inline Graphics check box will enable the import of any graphics in the Word text.
- Checking the Import Unused Styles check box means that all Word style sheets will transfer into InDesign, rather than just the ones you actually applied to text in the file. Unless you want all those extra Word styles, keep this box unchecked.
- If InDesign detects that the Word file has a style with the same name as your InDesign document, it will note how many to the right of the Style Name Conflicts label. You have choices in how to handle these conflicts:
    - Use InDesign Style Definition preserves the current InDesign style sheets and applies them to any text in Word that uses a style sheet of the same name. Redefine InDesign Style causes the Word style sheet's formatting to permanently replace that of InDesign's corresponding style sheet. Auto Rename renames the Word file's style sheet adds it to the Paragraph Styles or Character Styles pane. This preserves your existing InDesign styles while also preserving those imported from the Word file.
    - Customize Style Import lets you decide which specific InDesign styles override same-name Word styles sheet, which Word styles sheet override same-name InDesign styles, and which Word styles sheet are renamed during import to prevent any overriding.

Import options for Microsoft Excel files

When importing Excel spreadsheets, you have several options, as Figure 14-2 shows.

In the Options section, you can control the following settings:

- The Sheet pop-up menu lets you choose which sheet in an Excel workbook to import. The default is the first sheet, which is usually named Sheet1 unless you renamed it in Excel. (If you want to import several sheets, you'll need to import the same spreadsheet several times, choosing a different sheet each time.)

- The View pop-up menu lets you import custom views that are defined in Excel for that spreadsheet. If the spreadsheet has no custom views, this pop-up menu is grayed out. You can also ignore any custom views by choosing [Ignore View] from the pop-up menu.
- In the Cell Range pop-up menu, you specify a range of cells using standard Excel notation *Sx:Ey,* where *S* is the first row, *x* the first column, *E* the last row, and *y* the last column, such as A1:G35. You can enter a range directly in the pop-up menu, which also acts as a text-entry field, or choose a previously entered range from the pop-up menu.
- Checking the Import Hidden Cells Not Saved in View check box will import hidden cells. Be careful when doing so, because these cells are usually hidden for a reason (typically, they show interim calculations and the like).

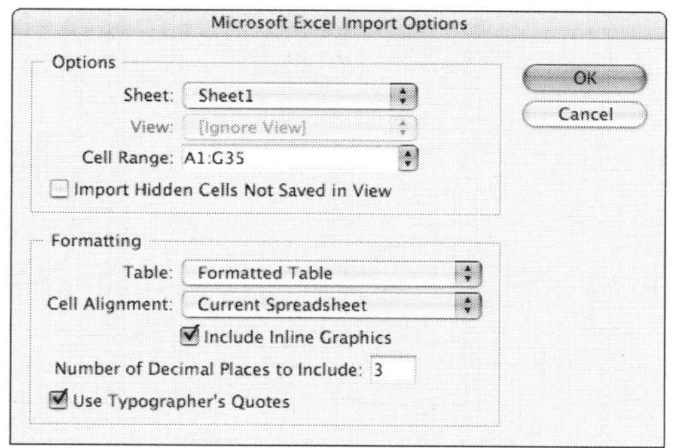

Figure 14-2: The Import Options dialog box for an Excel file.

In the Formatting section, you can control the following settings:

- In the Table pop-up menu, you choose from Formatted Table, which imports the spreadsheet as a table and retains text and cell formatting, Unformatted Table, which imports the spreadsheet as a table but does not preserve formatting, and Unformatted Tabbed Text, which imports the spreadsheet as tabbed text (tabs separate cells and paragraph returns separate rows) with no formatting retained.
- In the Cell Alignment pop-up menu, you tell InDesign how to align the text in cells. You can retain the spreadsheet's current alignment settings by choosing Current Spreadsheet, or override them by choosing Left, Right, or Center.
- Checking the Include Inline Graphics check box imports any graphics placed in the Excel cells.
- The Number of Decimal Places to Include field is where you enter how many decimal places to retain for numbers.
- Check the Use Typographer's Quotes check box to convert keyboard quotes (' and ") to the "curly" typographic quotes (‘, ’, “, and ”). It's a good idea to keep this box checked.

Keep characters to a minimum

When you're working with text in a professional publishing application, such as InDesign, you need to keep in mind some differences between the professional method and traditional way of typing:

- Remember that you don't need to type two spaces after a period or colon; books, newspapers, magazines, and other professional documents all use just one space after such punctuation.
- Don't enter extra paragraph returns for space between paragraphs and don't enter tabs to indent paragraphs — instead, set up this formatting using InDesign's paragraph attributes (Type⇨Paragraph, or Option+⌘+T or Ctrl+Alt+T).
- To align text in columns, don't enter extra tabs; place the same number of tabs between each column, and then align the tabs (Type⇨Tabs, or Shift+⌘+T or Ctrl+Shift+T).

To see where your InDesign document has tabs, paragraph breaks, spaces, and other such invisible characters, use the command Option+⌘+I or Ctrl+Alt+I, or choose Type⇨Show Hidden Characters.

Pasting text into an InDesign document

As you probably already know, you can hold text on the Mac or Windows Clipboard by cutting it or copying it from its original location. After you've captured some text on the Clipboard, you can paste it into an InDesign document at the location of the cursor. You can also replace highlighted text with the text that's on the Clipboard. If no text frame is active when you do the pasting, InDesign creates a new text frame to contain the pasted text.

InDesign uses standard menu commands and keyboard commands for cutting/copying text to the Clipboard, and for pasting text. On the Mac, press ⌘+X to cut, ⌘+C to copy, and ⌘+V to paste. In Windows, press Ctrl+X to cut, Ctrl+C to copy, and Ctrl+V to paste.

Text that is cut or copied from InDesign normally retains its formatting, while text pasted from other programs loses its formatting. Text pasted from other programs always retains its special characters such as curly quotes, em dashes, and accented characters.

In InDesign CS2, you can specify whether pasted text from other programs always retains its formatting. Go to the Type pane in the Preferences dialog box (choose InDesign⇨Preferences on the Mac or Edit⇨Preferences in Windows, or press ⌘+K or Ctrl+K) and select the All Information option in the When Pasting Text and Tables from Other Applications section. If you select this option, you can tell InDesign to *not* preserve the formatting by choosing Edit⇨Paste without Formatting (Shift+⌘+V or Ctrl+Shift+V) for those times you want the text to use InDesign's local formatting instead of the original formatting.

Dragging and dropping text

You can drag highlighted text from other programs — or even text files from the desktop or a folder — into an InDesign document. Text that you drag and drop is inserted at the location of the cursor, replaces highlighted text, or is placed in a new rectangular text frame.

When you drag and drop a text selection, its original formatting is lost However, when you drag and drop a text file, the process is more like a text import: The text retains its formatting and styles. Unlike the Place command (File⇨Place, or ⌘+D or Ctrl+D) that imports text, drag and drop does not give you the option to specify how some of the formatting and styles in the imported text file are handled.

Editing Text

InDesign offers basic editing capabilities, not unlike those found in a word processor: cutting and pasting, deleting and inserting text, searching and replacing of text and text attributes, and spell checking. (Cutting, pasting, inserting, and deleting text works just like it does for any standard Mac or Windows program, so we won't repeat those details for you here.)

To do anything with text, you need to use the Type tool. When the Type tool is selected, you can click in any empty frame with the Type tool. (If it's not already a text frame, it will become one automatically when you click it with the Type tool.) Or you can click and drag to create a new text frame. You can even click in an existing block of text. From this point, start typing to enter text.

Controlling text view

In many layout views, the text is too small to work with. Generally, you'll zoom in around the block of text using the Zoom tool. Select the tool, then click to zoom in. To zoom out, hold the Option or Alt key when clicking.

Another way to zoom in is to use the keyboard shortcut ⌘+= or Ctrl+=. Each time you use it, the magnification increases. (Zoom out via ⌘+– [hyphen] or Ctrl+– [hyphen].)

In addition to seeing the text larger, zooming in also helps you see the spaces, tabs, and paragraph returns that exist in the text. Choose Type⇨Show Hidden Characters or press Option+⌘+I or Ctrl+Alt+I to have the nonprinting indicators for those characters display.

Navigating through text

To work at a different text location in your InDesign document, click in a different text frame or another location in the current text frame. You can also use the four arrow (cursor) keys on the keyboard to move one character to the right, one character to the left, one line up, or one line down. Add ⌘ or Ctrl to the arrow keys to jump one word to the right or left, or one paragraph up or down. The Home and End keys let you jump to the beginning or end of a line; add ⌘ or Ctrl to jump to the beginning or end of a story. (A *story* is text within a text frame or that is linked across several text frames.)

Highlighting text

To highlight (or select) text, you can click and drag. Or you can use some keyboard options. For example, Shift+⌘+right arrow or Ctrl+Shift+right arrow highlights the next word to the right. Likewise, Shift+⌘+End or Ctrl+Shift+End highlights all the text to the end of the story.

To highlight a word, double-click (this will not select its punctuation) and triple-click to select the entire paragraph. If you're highlighting a word and also want to include the punctuation that follows the word, double-click, then press Shift+⌘+right arrow or Ctrl+Shift+right arrow to extend the selection.

To select an entire story, choose Edit⇨Select All, or press ⌘+A or Ctrl+A.

To deselect text, choose Edit⇨Deselect All or press Shift+⌘+A or Ctrl+Shift+A. An even easier way to deselect text is simply to select another tool or click another area of the page.

Undoing text edits

It's nice to know that InDesign makes it easy for you to change your mind about text edits. Choose Edit⇨Undo and Edit⇨Redo any time you change your mind about edits. The Undo and Redo keyboard commands are definitely worth remembering: ⌘+Z and Shift+⌘+Z or Ctrl+Z and Ctrl+Shift+Z.

Using the Story Editor

The Story Editor is a window that lets you see your text without the distractions of your layout. In it, you see your text without line breaks or other nonessential formatting — you just see attributes like boldface and italics, as well as the names of the paragraph styles applied in a separate pane to the left (see Figure 14-3). After clicking in a text frame, you open the Story Editor by choosing Edit➪Edit in Story Editor or by pressing ⌘+Y or Ctrl+Y.

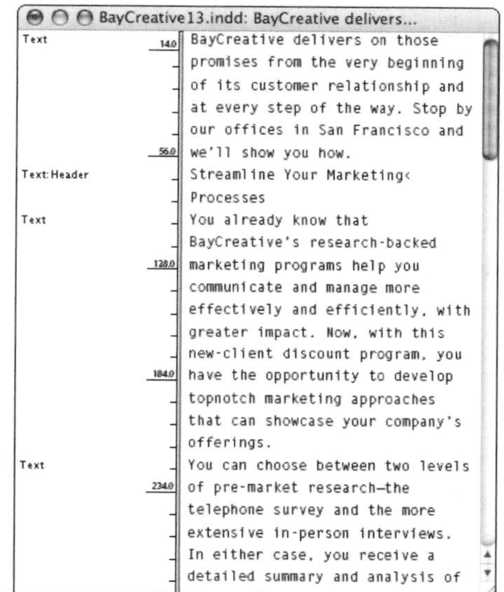

Figure 14-3: The Story Editor.

In the Story Editor, you use the same tools for selection, deletion, copying, pasting, and search and replace as you would in your layout. The Story Editor is not a separate word processor; it's simply a way to look at your text in a less distracting environment for those times when your mental focus is on the meaning and words, not the text appearance.

The Story Editor also shows you the column depth for text, using a ruler along the left side of the text, just to the right of the list of currently applied paragraph styles. Overset text (text that goes beyond the text frame, or beyond the final text frame in a threaded story) is indicated by a depth measurement of *OV* and is furthermore noted with a red line to the right of the text.

The display of column depth for text and the highlighting of overset text in the Story Editor are new to InDesign CS2.

Searching and Replacing Text

InDesign has a handy Find/Change feature (Edit➪Find/Change, or ⌘+F or Ctrl+F) that is similar to the search-and-replace features with which you may already be familiar if you've used any word processor or page-layout application.

With the Find/Change dialog box, you can find and change text or you can extend the search to include attributes. Before starting a Find/Change operation, determine the scope of your search:

- To search within a text selection, highlight the selection.
- To search from one point in a story to its end, click the cursor at that beginning location.
- To search an entire story, select any frame or click at any point in a frame containing the story.
- To search an entire document, simply have that document open.
- To search multiple documents, open all of them (and close any that you don't want to search).

Figure 14-4 shows the Find/Change dialog box.

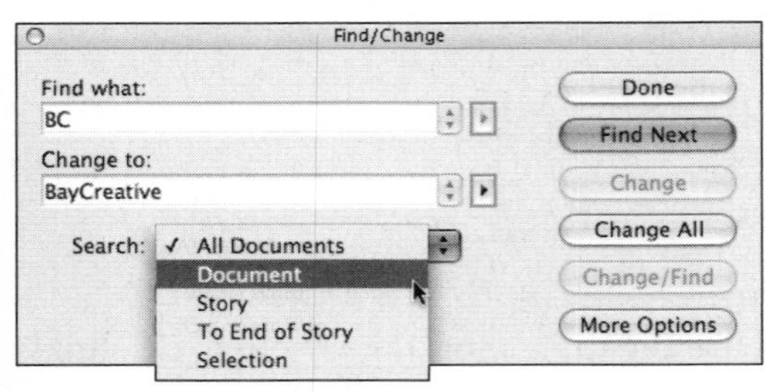

Figure 14-4: The Find/Change dialog box.

Replacing text

To search for text, follow these steps:

1. **Determine the scope of your search and open the appropriate documents and insert the text cursor at the appropriate location.**
2. **Choose Edit➪Find/Change or press ⌘+F or Ctrl+F.**
3. **Use the Search pop-up menu, as shown in Figure 14-5 to specify the scope of your search by choosing All Documents, Document, Story, End of Story, or Selection.**

   Which options are available will be based on your current text selection in InDesign. Unavailable options are grayed out.
4. **Type or paste the text you want to find in the Find What field.**
5. **Type or paste the replacement text into the Change To field.**

To use special characters, use the pop-up list (the right-facing arrow icon) to select from a menu of special characters (see Figure 14-5).

6. **Specify whether to find the word within other words (for example, *rest* within *restaurant*, or just *rest*) by checking or unchecking the Whole Word check box.**

   (If Whole Word is checked, Find/Change will only locate standalone instances of the Find What text.)

7. **Specify whether to consider capitalization patterns in the Find/Change operation by checking or unchecking the Case Sensitive check box.**

   When checked, Find/Change follows the capitalization of the text in the Find What and Change To fields exactly.

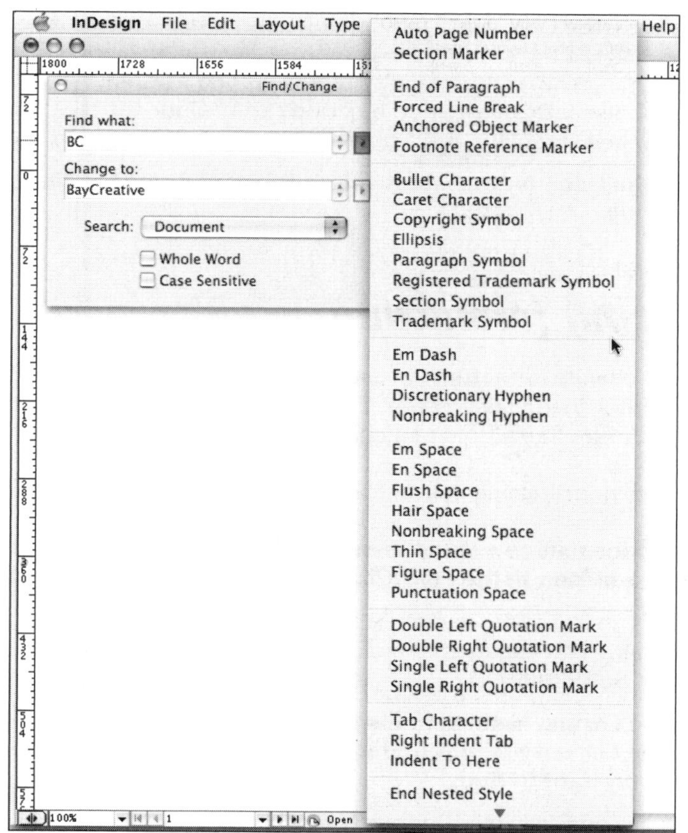

Figure 14-5: The special characters pop-up list in the Find/Change dialog box.

8. **To search for or replace with specific formatting, use the Format buttons.**

   These buttons are available only if you had clicked the More Options button.

9. **Click the Find Next button to start the search.**

   When the search has begun, click the Find Next button to skip instances of the Find What text, and click the Change, Change All, or Change/Find buttons as appropriate. (Clicking the Change button simply changes the found text, clicking the Change All button changes every instance of that found text in your selection or story, and clicking the Change/Find button changes the current found text and moves on to the next occurrence of it — it basically does in one click the actions of clicking Change and then Find Next.)

   If you use the Change All feature, InDesign reports how many changes were made. If the number looks extraordinarily high and you suspect the Find/Change operation wasn't quite what you wanted, remember that you can use InDesign's undo function (Edit⇨Undo, or ⌘+Z or Ctrl+Z) to cancel the search and replace, and then try a different replace strategy.

10. **Click the Done button when you're finished doing the finding and replacing.**

Replacing formatting

To find and change formatting or text with specific formatting, use the expanded Find/Change dialog box. For example, you might find all the words in 14-point Futura Extra Bold and change them to 12-point Bodoni.

To replace text formatting, follow these steps:

1. **To add formats to a Find/Change operation for text, click the More Options button in the Find/Change dialog box (if it was not clicked earlier).**

   The dialog box expands to include the Find Format Settings and Change Format Settings areas.

2. **Use the Format buttons to display the Find Format Settings and Change Format Settings dialog boxes, which let you specify the formats you want to find.**

   Your options are Style Options (paragraph and character styles), Basic Character Formats, Advanced Character Formats, Indents and Spacing, Keep Options, Character Color, OpenType Features, Underline Options,

Strikethrough Options, and Drop Caps and Other. You can change multiple attributes at once by making selections from as many panes as needed.

Open one of these dialog boxes, select the desired formatting to search or replace, then click OK when done. Now open the other dialog box to select its formatting, then click OK when done.

3. **Click Find Next and then Change to change the next occurrence, or click Change All to change all occurrences. Click Done when you are finished with the search and replace.**

To search and replace formatting only — regardless of the text to which it is applied — leave the Find What and Change To fields blank.

Checking Spelling

The Check Spelling feature not only helps you eradicate spelling errors, it also catches repeated words, as well as words with odd capitalization such as the internal capitalization (called *intercaps*). InDesign also flags words not found in the spelling dictionary. You can customize the spelling dictionary, and you can purchase additional spelling dictionaries.

Checking spelling as you type

You can have InDesign check your spelling as you type by simply choosing Edit⇨Spelling⇨Dynamic Spelling. If that menu option is checked, your spelling will be checked as you type, as will the spelling of any text already in the document. Suspected errors are highlighted with red squiggle underlining, so that you can correct them as needed. If you want InDesign to suggest proper spelling, you'll need to use the Check Spelling dialog box, covered in the next section.

The dynamic spelling feature is new to InDesign CS2.

Correcting mistakes on the fly

If you use a word processor, chances are it is one that corrects mistakes as you type. Microsoft Word, for example, has a feature called AutoCorrect that lets you specify corrections to be made as you type, whether those be common typos you make or the expansion of abbreviations to their full words (such as having Word replace *tq* with *thank you*). Automatic correction is also a handy way to convert two hyphens to an em dash or a keyboard sequence like *(R)* to the ® symbol.

InDesign offers the same functionality, which it calls *Autocorrect.* Note that Autocorrect works only for text entered in InDesign after Autocorrect is turned on; it will not correct imported or previously typed text.

The Autocorrect feature is new to InDesign CS2.

You enable Autocorrect in the Autocorrect pane of the Preferences dialog box (InDesign➪Preferences on the Mac or Edit➪Preferences in Windows, or ⌘+K or Ctrl+K). If you want InDesign to automatically fix capitalization errors, check the Autocorrect Capitalization Errors check box. Typically, this finds typos involving capitalizing the second letter of a word in addition to the first. For example, InDesign would replace *FOrmat* with *Format.*

To add your own custom corrections, click the Add button. This opens the Add to Autocorrect List dialog box, where you can enter the typo text or code that you want InDesign to be alert for in the Misspelled Word field, as well as the corrected or expanded text you want InDesign to substitute in the Correction field.

Using the Check Spelling dialog box

The Check Spelling dialog box not only lets you choose what part of the document to spell check, it also provides suggestions on correct spelling. Plus, you can use the dialog box to add correctly spelled words to InDesign's spelling dictionary. Even if you use the new dynamic spell-checking feature, you'll still want to do a final spell-checking pass with the Check Spelling dialog box.

Specifying the text to check is a two-step process: First set up the spell check's scope in the document, and then specify the scope in the Search menu.

To set up the scope for the spell check, highlight text, click in a story to check from the cursor forward, select a frame containing a story, or open multiple documents.

Next, open the Check Spelling dialog box (Edit➪Spelling➪Check Spelling, or ⌘+I or Ctrl+I) and choose an option from the Search pop-up menu: Document, All Documents, Story, To End of Story, and Selection. Figure 14-6 shows the dialog box. You may not see all the options in the Search pop-up menu; the list of options depends on how you set up the scope. For example, if you didn't highlight text, the Selection option will not be available. However, you can change the scope setup in the document while the Check Spelling dialog box is open — for example, you can open additional documents to check.

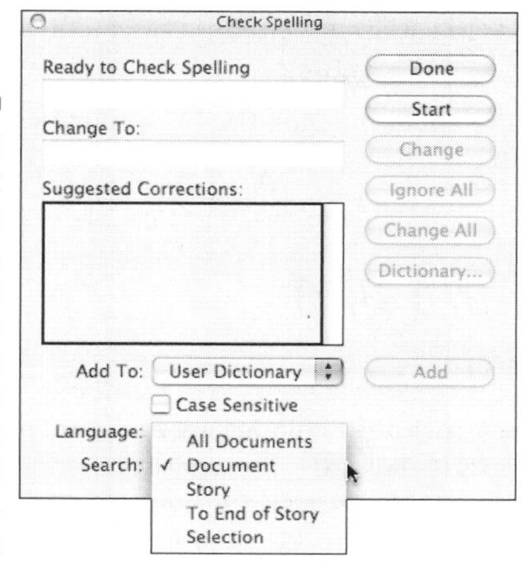

Figure 14-6: In the Check Spelling dialog box, use the Search pop-up menu to specify which text to spell check.

When you first open the Check Spelling dialog box, it displays "Ready to Check Spelling" at the top. To begin checking the text scope you specified in the Search pop-up menu, click Start. When the spell checker encounters a word without a match in the dictionary or a possible capitalization problem, the dialog box displays "Not in Dictionary" at the top and shows the word. When the spell checker encounters a duplicate word, such as *of of,* the dialog box displays "Duplicate Word" and shows which word is duplicated. Use the buttons along the right side of the dialog box to handle flagged words as follows:

- Click the Ignore button to leave the current instance of a Not in Dictionary word or Duplicate Word unchanged. To leave all instances of the same problem unchanged, click the Ignore All button.
- To change the spelling of a Not in Dictionary word, click a word in the Suggested Corrections list or edit the spelling or capitalization in the Change To field. To make the change, click the Change button.
- To correct an instance of a Duplicate Word, edit the text in the Change To field, and then click the Change button.
- To change all occurrences of a Not in Dictionary word or a Duplicate Word to the information in the Change To field, click the Change All button.
- To add a word flagged as incorrect — but that you know is correct — to InDesign's spelling dictionary, click the Add button.
- To add a word flagged as incorrect to a specific dictionary, click the Dictionary button. A Dictionary dialog box appears, which enables you to choose the dictionary to which you want to add the word, as well as what language to associate it with.

The Dictionary button in the Check Spelling dialog box is new to InDesign CS2.

- After you've finished checking spelling, click the Done button to close the Check Spelling dialog box.

Changing the spelling and hyphenation dictionaries

The spelling dictionary that comes with InDesign is pretty extensive, but it's very likely that you will need to add words to it. For example, your company might use words that are company-specific terms. Or you might use some product or individuals' names that would not typically be found in the dictionary. Additionally, you might have some words that you prefer not to hyphenate, others that you want to hyphenate in a specific manner. To address these issues, you can customize InDesign's spelling and hyphenation dictionaries. InDesign handles both spelling and hyphenation in one dictionary for each language, so you use the same controls to modify both spelling and hyphenation.

Changes made to a dictionary file are saved only in the dictionary file, not with an open document. So if you add words to the English: USA. dictionary, the modified dictionary is used for spell checking and hyphenating all text in documents that uses the English: U.S.A. dictionary.

If you're in a workgroup, be sure to share the edited dictionary file so that everyone is using the same spelling and hyphenation settings. (The file is located in the Dictionaries folder inside the Plug-ins folder inside your InDesign folder.) You can copy it for other users, who must then restart InDesign or press Option+⌘+/ or Ctrl+Alt+/ to reflow the text according to the new dictionary's hyphenation.

Customizing the spelling dictionary

When you add a word to the spelling dictionary, this word will no longer be flagged when you check spelling, and you can be sure that when it's used, it is spelled as it is in the dictionary.

While adding words to the dictionary, you can specify their capitalization. For example, InDesign's dictionary prefers *E-mail.* You can add *e-mail* if you prefer a lowercase *e* or *email* if you prefer to skip the hyphen. To add words to the dictionary, follow these steps:

1. **Choose Edit⇨Spelling⇨Dictionary.**

   The Dictionary dialog box, shown in Figure 14-7, appears.

2. **Choose whether the addition to the dictionary affects just this document or all documents.**

   The Target pop-up menu lists the current document name as well as the name of the user dictionary.

3. **Choose the dictionary that you want to edit from the Language pop-up menu.**

4. **Type or paste a word in the Word field.**

   The word can have capital letters if appropriate, and it can include special characters such as accents and hyphens.

5. **To have the added word accepted as being spelled correctly only with the capitalization specified in the Word field, check the Case Sensitive check box.**

   This new feature lets you add proper names, for example, but have them still flagged when entered in all lowercase or with extra capital letters.

6. **To edit the hyphenation of the word, click the Hyphenate button.**

   We cover hyphenation in the next section.

7. **Click the Add button.**

8. **To import a word list or export one for other users to import into their copies of InDesign, click the Import or Export button.**

   You will then navigate to a folder and choose a filename in a dialog box. Note that when you click the Export button, InDesign will export all selected words from the list. If no words are selected, it will export all the words in the list.

9. **When you're finished adding words, click the Done button.**

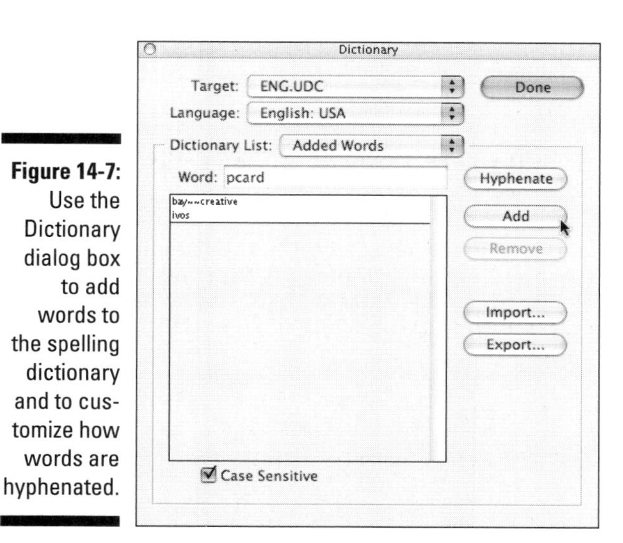

Figure 14-7: Use the Dictionary dialog box to add words to the spelling dictionary and to customize how words are hyphenated.

To delete a word that you added to the dictionary, select it in the list and click the Remove button. To change the spelling of a word you added, delete it then re-add it with the correct spelling. You can see all deleted words — just those deleted since you opened the dialog box — by selecting Removed Words from the Dictionary List pop-up menu, so you can add back any deleted by error.

Customizing hyphenation points

People can be particular about how to hyphenate words. Fortunately, InDesign lets you modify the hyphenation dictionary by specifying new, hierarchical hyphenation points.

Follow these steps to specify hyphenation points:

1. **Choose Edit⇨Spelling⇨Dictionary.**
2. **In the Language pop-up menu, pick the dictionary that you want to edit.**
3. **Type or paste the word in the Word field; you can also double-click a word in the list.**
4. **To see InDesign's suggestions for hyphenating the word, click the Hyphenate button.**

   If you want to change the hyphenation, continue on to Step 5.
5. **Type a tilde (~, obtained by pressing Shift+`, the open single keyboard quote at the upper left of the keyboard) at your first preference for a hyphenation point in the word.**

   If you don't want the word to hyphenate at all, type a tilde in front of it.
6. **To indicate an order of preference, use two tildes for your second choice, three tildes for your third choice, and so on.** InDesign will first try to hyphenate your top preferences (single tildes), then it will try your second choices if the first ones don't work out, and so on.
7. **Click the Add button.**
8. **Continue to add words until you're finished, and then click the Done button.**

To revert a word to the default hyphenation, select it in the list and click the Remove button. To change the hyphenation, double-click a word in the list to enter it in the Word field, change the tildes, and then click the Add button. When you're adding variations of words, you can double-click a word in the list to place it in the Word field as a starting place.

Chapter 15

The Text Frame Tango

In This Chapter

- Creating text frames
- Threading text from frame to frame
- Working with text columns
- Creating form letters

Text is more than words — it's also a layout element that flows through your pages in the locations that you need. Much of the work you do in InDesign will be controlling that flow and working with the text as blocks that need to have the right arrangement to fit your layout's goals.

This chapter can help you manage that flow and arrangement, showing you how to deftly maneuver the text through your layout, just as you would move your way through the dance floor.

Working with Text Frames

When you're creating a simple layout, such as a single-page flyer or a magazine advertisement, you will probably create text frames as you need them. But if you're working on a book or a magazine, you'll want your text frames placed on master pages so your text will be consistently framed automatically when it appears on document pages. And you'll still have individual text frames you create for specific elements like sidebars.

Chapter 10 shows you how to create frames (including text frames), while Chapter 8 shows you how to create master pages. Here, we bring those two concepts together to show you how to work with text frames, both those in master pages and those you create in your document pages.

Creating master text frames

Master pages — predesigned pages that you can apply to other pages to automate layout and ensure consistency — can contain several types of text frames:

- Text frames containing standing text, such as page numbers or page headers.
- Text frames containing placeholder text for elements such as figure captions or headlines.
- One master text frame (an automatically placed text frame for flowing text throughout pages), which you create in the New Document dialog box (File⇨New⇨Document, or ⌘+N or Ctrl+N).

Think of a master text frame as an empty text frame on the default master page that lets you automatically flow text through a document. When you create a new document, you can create a master text frame at the same time. Here's how it works:

1. **Choose File⇨New⇨Document or press ⌘+N or Ctrl+N.**
2. **Check the Master Text Frame check box at the top of the New Document dialog box.**
3. **Specify the size and placement of the master text frame by entering values in the Margins area for Top, Bottom, Inside, and Outside (or Left and Right if Facing Pages is unchecked) fields.**

   InDesign places guides according to these values and places a text frame within the guides. The text frame fits within the boundaries of these values and those of the guides on the master page.
4. **To specify the number of columns in the master text frame, enter a value in the Number field in the Columns area.**

   You can also specify the amount of space between the columns by entering a value in the Gutter field.
5. **Establish any other needed settings as described in Chapter 5.**

   Check the Facing Pages check box if your pages will have different inside and outside margins (for example, a book might have different inside and outside margins for left-hand and right-hand pages).
6. **Click OK to create a new document containing a master text frame.**

After you create a document with a master text frame, you'll see guides on the first document page that indicate the placement of the frame.

Creating individual text frames

While the master text frame is helpful for containing body text that flows through a document, there's a good chance you'll need additional text frames, on both master pages and document pages. Generally, these are smaller text frames that hold text such as headlines or captions.

To add text frames to a master page for repeating elements such as headers and footers, first display the master page. Choose Window⇨Pages or press F12 to display the Pages pane. Then double-click the A-Master icon in the upper portion of the pane, as shown in Figure 15-1. That displays the A-Master master page. (If you have multiple master pages in your document, you can follow these instructions to add text frames to any of them. Just choose the desired master page.)

To add text frames to a document page, first go to the page. You can use any of the techniques described in Chapter 6 to move among pages.

Now draw the desired frame using any of the frame or shape tools, or the Type tool, as described in Chapter 10. Modify them with the Control palette or Transform pane, or by using the mouse, also as described in that chapter.

Text frames you add to a master page will show up on any document pages based on that master page.

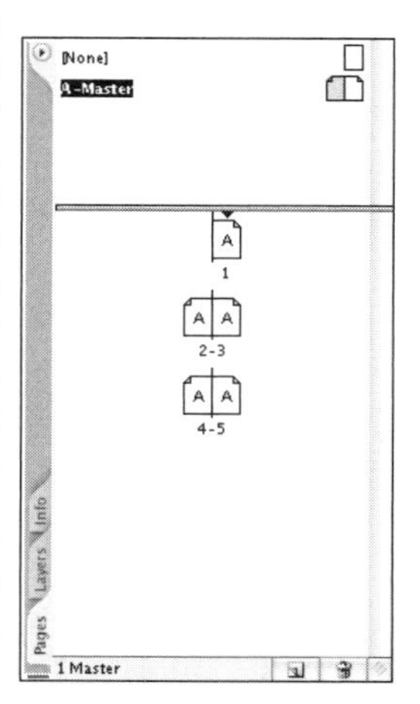

Figure 15-1: To access a master page so you can add or modify text frames and other objects, double-click the master-page icon in the upper portion of the Pages pane.

If you're working on a document page and want to type inside a text frame placed on the page by a master page, select the Type tool and then Shift+⌘+click or Ctrl+Shift+click the frame.

Making changes to text frames

You're not confined to the settings you originally established when you set up a master text frame or an individual text frame — you may need to change the size, shape, and/or number of columns in the text frame. Use the Selection tool to click the desired text frame and then modify it with the following options (the first six are covered in detail in Chapter 10):

- Change the placement of a selected master text frame by using the X: and Y: fields in the Control palette or Transform pane.
- Change the size of the master text frame by using the W: and H: fields.
- Change the angle by using the Rotation field.
- Change the skew by using the Shear X field.
- Enter values in the Scale fields to increase or decrease, by percentage amounts, the width and height of the text frame.
- To change the shape of the text frame, use the Direct Selection tool, which lets you drag anchor points on the frame to other positions.
- Use the General pane of the Text Frame Options dialog box (Object➪Text Frame Options, or ⌘+B or Ctrl+B, shown in Figure 15-2) to make further modifications:
    - Change the number of columns and the space between them.
    - Specify how far text is inset from each side of the frame.
    - Align text vertically within the frame.
    - Control the placement of the first baseline.
- Use the Baseline Options of the Text Frame Options dialog box to set a baseline grid, if desired, for the text to align to. Chapter 11 describes this feature in more detail.

  If you don't want the text inside this text frame to wrap around any items in front of it, check Ignore Text Wrap at the bottom of the dialog box.

  If you open the Text Frame Options dialog box with no document open, any changes you make will become the default for all new documents.
- Specify character styles, paragraph styles, object styles, Story pane settings, text-wrap settings, and other text attributes to apply in the text frame to the document text you flow into that frame. (You can always override those attributes by applying other styles or formatting to the text later.) Chapters 13, 17, and 18 cover these other settings.

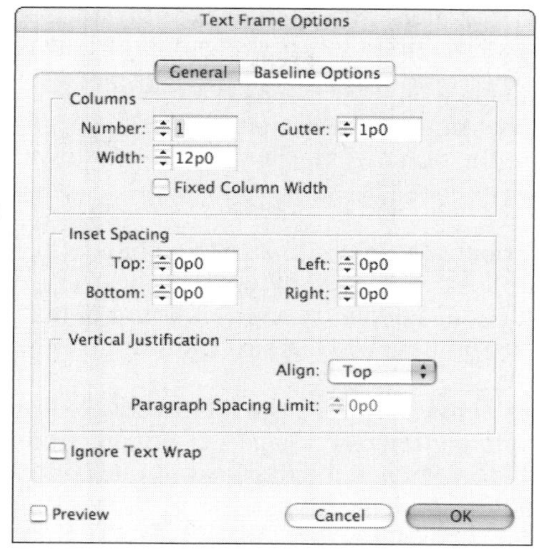

Figure 15-2: Change the properties of a text frame using the Text Frame Options dialog box.

Threading Text Frames

The text that flows through a series of frames is what InDesign considers a *story,* and the connections among those frames are called *threads.* When you edit text in a threaded story, the text reflows throughout the text frames. You can also spell-check and do a find/change operation for an entire story, even though you have just one of the story's text frames active on-screen.

When you have threaded text frames, you'll see visual indicators on your text frame, assuming you choose View➪Show Text Threads (Option+⌘+Y or Ctrl+Alt+Y) and have selected the frame with one of the selection tools. At the lower right of the text frame is a small square, called the *out port,* that indicates the outflow status:

- If the square is empty, that means there is no text flowing to another frame, and not enough text to flow to another frame.
- If the square is red and has a plus sign in it, that means there is more text than fits in the selected frame but that it is *not* flowing to another frame. This is called *overset text.*
- If the square has a triangle icon, that means the text that it is flowing to another frame. That doesn't mean that text *is* flowing, just that if there is more text than the current frame can hold, it *will* flow.

Similarly, there's an *in port* at the upper left of a text frame that indicates whether text is flowing from another frame into the current frame:

- If the square is empty, that means there is no text flowing from another frame, making this frame the first (and perhaps only) frame in a story.
- If the square has a triangle icon, that means the text that it is flowing from another frame. That doesn't mean that text *is* flowing, just that if there is more text than the other frame can hold, it *will* flow into this frame.

So how do you thread the frames in the first place? You have three options in InDesign: manual, semi-autoflow, and autoflow. Each of these options has its own icon. The method you choose depends on the amount of text you're dealing with and the size and number of your text frames:

- To link two text frames across several pages (for example, for an article that starts on page 2 and continues on page 24), you might use the manual method, in which you click the first text frame's out port and then on the second text frame.

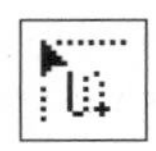

- To link a succession of text frames, you might want to use the semi-autoflow method, which allows you to click a series of text frames to flow text from one frame to the next.

- To import text that is intended for long documents (such as a book chapter or brochure), you might want to use the autoflow method to add text frames and pages that accommodate the text you're importing.

For a quick glance at your text threads while you're threading text across pages, simply change the document view briefly to 20 percent or so.

Text flows in the order in which you select frames. If you move a frame, its order in the text flow remains unchanged. If you're not careful, you could, for example, accidentally have text flow from a frame at the top of the page to a frame at the bottom of a page and then to one in the middle of a page.

Threading frames manually

To thread text frames manually, you simply use a selection tool to link out ports to in ports. You can pre-thread existing text frames by linking empty text frames, and add text later, or you can create threads from a text frame that contains text.

Always switch to a selection tool when you're threading frames. Oddly, you cannot thread frames while the Type tool is selected. Oh well.

To thread text frames, follow these steps:

1. **Create a series of text frames that will hold the text you import.**

   These text frames do not need to be on the same page.

2. **Click either the Selection tool or the Direction Selection tool.**
3. **Click the out port of the first text frame in the thread.**

   The pointer becomes the loaded-text icon.
4. **Click the in port of the second text frame in the thread.**

   You can also click any empty frame or click and drag to draw a new text frame. How text flow behaves depends on the text frame's status:

   - If the first frame held no text, then any text placed or typed in later will flow into the second frame if it doesn't all fit in the first text frame.
   - If the first frame held text but was not already linked to another text frame, any overset text will flow into the existing text frame.
   - If the first text frame was already linked to another text frame, the text will now be redirected to the text frame you just selected.
5. **Use the Pages pane to add or switch pages while you continue clicking out ports and in ports until your chain of threaded text frames is complete.**
6. **When you're finished threading text frames, select another object on the page or select another tool.**

   A story imported into any text frame in this chain will start in the upper-right corner of the first frame and flow through the frames in the same order as the threads.

Threading frames with the semi-autoflow method

InDesign includes a *semi-autoflow* method of threading text frames, which incorporates a few automatic shortcuts but varies only slightly from the manual method. Follow the same steps for threading text frames manually, except hold down the Option or Alt key each time you click in the next text frame. Doing so lets you bypass the in ports and out ports and simply click from text frame to text frame to establish links.

If you want to begin a semi-autoflow process when you place a word-processing file for the first time, you can Option+click or Alt+click in the first text frame that will hold the placed text.

As you're threading frames, Option+click or Alt+click each text frame, or you'll revert to manual threading.

Threading frames and automatically adding pages

You can flow a lengthy story quickly through a document using the autoflow method for threading frames. You can either autoflow text into the master text frame or into automatically created text frames that fit within the column guides. InDesign flows the text into any existing pages, and then adds new pages based on the current master page. You can initiate autoflow before or after placing a word processing file.

Placing text while autoflowing

If you haven't imported text yet, you can place a file and have it automatically flow through the document. This method works well for flowing text into pages that are all formatted the same way (as in a book). Here's how it works:

1. **Before you begin, check your master page.**

   Make sure that the master page you're using includes a master text frame or appropriate column guides.

2. **With no text frames selected, choose File⇨Place or press ⌘+D or Ctrl+D.**
3. **Locate and select the word-processing file you want to import, and then click Open.**
4. **When you see the loaded-text icon, Shift+click in the first column that will contain the text.**

   InDesign adds all the necessary text frames and pages, and flows in the entire story.

Autoflowing after placing text

Even if you've already placed a text file into a single text frame or a threaded chain of text frames, you can still autoflow text from the last text frame. To do this, click the out port, then Shift+click any page to indicate where to start the autoflow.

You might use this method if you're placing the introduction to an article in an elaborately designed opener page. Then you can flow the rest of the article into standard pages.

Breaking and rerouting threads

Once text frames are threaded, you have three options for changing the threads: You can break threads to stop text from flowing, insert a text frame into an existing chain of threaded text frames, and remove text frames from a thread. Here are the techniques in a nutshell:

- Break the link between two text frames by double-clicking either an out port or an in port. The thread between the two text frames is removed, and all text that had flowed from that point is sucked out of the subsequent text frames and stored as overset text.
- Insert a text frame after a specific text frame in a chain by clicking its out port. Then, click and drag the loaded-text icon to create a new text frame. That new frame is automatically threaded to both the previous and the next text frames.
- Reroute text threads — for example to drop the middle text frame from a chain of three — by clicking the text frame with the Selection tool and then pressing Delete or Backspace. This deletes the text frame and reroutes the threads. You can also Shift+click to multiple-select text frames to remove. Note that you cannot reroute text threads without removing the text frames.

Working with Columns

Where you place columns on the page — and the amount of space you allow between columns — has a big impact on readability. Used with a little know-how, column width works with type size and leading to make text easier to read. Columns help you keep from getting lost from one line to the next, and from getting a headache as you're trying to read the words on the page.

Generally, as columns get wider, the type size and leading increase. For example, you might see 9-point text and 15-point leading in 2½-inch columns, while 15-point text and 13-point leading might work better in 3½-inch columns.

InDesign lets you place columns on the page automatically, create any number of columns within a text frame, and change columns at any time.

Specifying columns in master frames

You can specify the number of columns at the same time you create a *master text frame* — a text frame placed automatically within the margin guides.

In the Columns area in the New Document dialog box, use the Number field to specify how many columns, and the Gutter field to specify how much space to place between the columns. (The gutter is the space between columns.) Whether or not you check Master Text Frame (which makes the frame appear on all pages), guides for these columns will still be placed on the page and can be used for placing text frames and other objects.

Changing columns in text frames

You can change the number of columns in a text frame (whether an individual text frame or a master text frame), even after you've flown text into the frame — and doing so isn't difficult. First, select the text frame with a selection tool or the Type tool (or Shift+click to select multiple text frames and change all their columns at once). Then choose Object⇨Text Frame Options, or press ⌘+B or Ctrl+B, and set the desired Number and Gutter values in the General pane of the Text Frame Options dialog box, shown in Figure 15-2. You can also use the Control palette to quickly change the number of columns.

Some designers like to draw each column as a separate frame. We recommend against this practice; it's too easy to create columns of slightly different widths and slightly different positions, so text doesn't align properly. Instead, specify columns in your text frames so you won't have to worry about sloppy layouts.

Note that the options in the Columns area of the Text Frame Options dialog box works differently depending on whether Fixed Column Width is checked or unchecked:

- If Fixed Column Width is unchecked, InDesign subtracts from the text frame the space specified for the gutters, and then divides the remaining width by the number of columns to figure out how wide the columns can be. For example, if you specify a 10-inch-wide text frame with three columns and a gutter of ½ inch, you end up with three 3-inch columns and two ½-inch gutters. The math is $(10–2 \times 0.5) \div 3$.
- If Fixed Column Width is checked, InDesign resizes the text frame to fit the number of columns you selected at the indicated size, as well as the gutters between them. For example, suppose you're using a 10.5-inch-wide text frame with a column width of 5 inches and a gutter of ½ inch, and you choose three columns: You end up with a 16-inch-wide text frame containing three 5-inch columns and two ½-inch gutters. The math is $(5 \times 3) + (2 \times 0.5)$.

Check Preview to see the effects of your changes before finalizing them.

Adding ruling lines between columns

Let's face it: A crowded page can be hard to read. If you have columns separated by relatively narrow gutters, you might want to consider using vertical *rules* (thin lines) between the columns. These lines are also called *intercolumn rules,* and offer an effective way to separate columns with small gutters. Intercolumn rules can also add visual interest to a document and even a sense of old-fashioned authority (as they were for newspapers a century ago — and you can still find them in *The Wall Street Journal*).

But InDesign lacks an automatic method for creating intercolumn rules — if you want them, you draw lines on the page (in the center of each gutter), using the Line tool. Because you might resize text frames or change the number of columns while designing a document, you should add the vertical rules at the end of the process. In a document with a standard layout (such as a newspaper or magazine), you can place the rules between columns in text frames on the master page so they're automatically placed on every page. As always with such objects, you can modify them on individual document pages as needed (just be sure to Shift+⌘+click or Ctrl+Shift+click to select them when working in your document pages).

Use rulers to precisely position the lines when you are drawing rules between columns. After you've drawn the lines, Shift+click to select all the lines and the text frames, then choose Object⇨Group, or ⌘+G or Ctrl+G. If the lines are grouped so that they are attached to the text frame, you can move the lines and text frame as one unit. This also prevents someone from accidentally moving a vertical rule later.

Intercolumn rules should be thin: usually a hairline (¼ point) or ½ point. Any intercolumn rules larger than that are usually too thick; they're too easily confused with the border of a sidebar or other boxed element.

Working with Merged Data

Mass mailings are a ton of work (but you knew that). Fortunately, word processors like Microsoft Word have long let you create forms with mail merge so you can send a standard letter to hordes of people — personalizing each copy by letting Word insert each individual name, address, and so forth (Word even prints each copy automatically). InDesign CS2 incorporates a data merge — originally part of the $49 PageMaker Plug-In Pack for InDesign CS, but now a built-in feature. (At last!) Merged data is new to InDesign CS2, although it based on an optional plug-in for InDesign CS. Merged-data documents include:

- Form letters, where one layout is printed multiple times, with each copy having personalized information.
- Labels, where layout components are repeated several times in the same layout, but with different information. Usually just one copy is printed.

Setting up a form letter or a label

InDesign uses the same procedure for setting up form letters and labels. Just follow these steps:

1. **Create a text file, using either tabs or commas to separate the data.**

   Either/or is the best approach here: Use either one but don't mix the two.

2. **Start a new record by pressing Enter or Return (a new paragraph).**
3. **Make sure the first row contains the names of the fields.**

   For example, for a local guidebook listing coffee shops, your data might look like this (the → characters here indicate the tabs you should actually type):

```
name→address→phone
Jolt Coffee House→38 4th St.→(415) 799-1213
→51 C St.→(415) 608-9066
→2800 California St.→(415) 931-2281
Shaking Grounds→75 Irwin St.→(415) 827-9003
Pop's Coffeehouse→13 Ninth St.→(415) 712-9445
```

   Voilà — a simple file with three fields per entry: the café name, its address, and its phone number. (The file uses tabs as the separator.)

Merging data into a new document

A data-merge operation (which creates a new document) is also pretty straightforward. Just follow these steps:

1. **With the source file ready, create (or go to) the text frame into which you want to flow your data.**
2. **Use the Type tool to select the insertion point for your data.**
3. **Open the Data Merge pane by choosing Window⇨Automation⇨Data Merge.**
4. **Choose Select Data Source from the Data Merge pane's palette menu (shown in Figure 15-3).**

   A dialog box opens.

5. **Use the dialog box to navigate to the desired file, and then click Open.**

   Your chosen file opens. The Data Merge pane shows the name of the data file and lists the fields it contains.

   - If your data file has changed since you last accessed it, you can import its most current version by choosing Update Data Source from the Data Merge pane's palette menu.
   - Choose Remove Data Source to remove a data file from the pane.

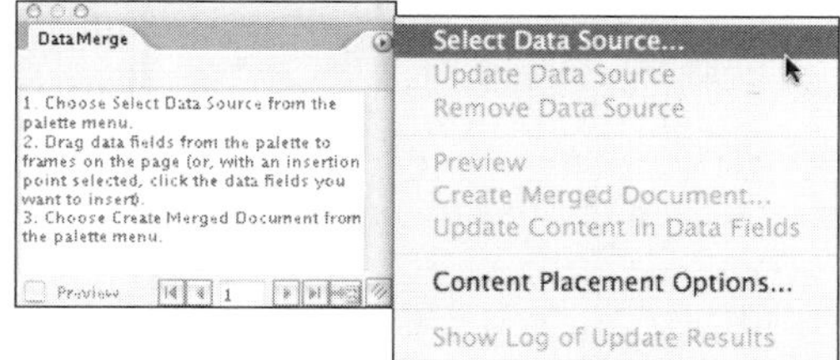

Figure 15-3: The Data Merge pane and its palette menu.

6. **Drag the fields to the appropriate spots in your layout (or double-click a field name to insert it at the current text-insertion point).**

   For example, in a form letter, you might drag the Name field to right after the text `Dear` and before the comma in the salutation. The field names will be enclosed in guillemets, the French quotation marks («»). Here's what this would look like in your layout:

   ```
   Dear «Name»,
   ```

   You can use a field more than once in the layout. Then the pane shows the page numbers for all pages that use the field (to the right of the field name).

7. **Format the fields as desired.**

8. **Click the Create Merged Document icon at the bottom right of the pane or choose Create Merged Document from the palette menu.**

   Doing so imports the entire data file's contents into your layout. A Create Merged Document dialog box opens, showing the Records pane with the following options:

   - In the Records to Merge section, choose which record(s) to import. You can choose all, a specific record, or a range.
   - In the Records per Document Page pop-up menu, choose Single Record if you want a new page output per record (as in a form letter) or Multiple Records if you want to print multiple copies of the same record on a page (as for address labels).

9. **Go to the Options pane and verify the import options work for your document.**

   These options are as follows:

   - In the Image Placement section, choose how to fit any imported graphics by choosing an option in the Fitting pop-up menu. The usual choice is the default, Fit Images Proportionally.
   - In the lower section of the pane, you can remove blank lines created by empty field by checking the Remove Blank Lines for Empty Fields check box. You can also limit the number of pages in the merged document by checking Page Limit per Document and entering a value in its field.

10. **Click OK.**

    InDesign creates a new document based on the original layout and merged data.

Chapter 16

Handling Character Details

In This Chapter

- Working with character formats
- Changing font families, styles, and sizes
- Applying other character formats
- Controlling horizontal and vertical spacing
- Creating character styles

When you create documents, you have lots of opportunities to make decisions about how the text appears. With its comprehensive set of character-formatting tools, InDesign lets you change the look of type so it can precisely match the communication needs of your publications. You can control not just the font and size of type, but also many other variations.

Decisions about type matter. A document relies on good typography to allow others to easily read and understand it. The appearance of type supports the message you're conveying, and doing a good job of character formatting is worth your time.

Specifying Character Formats

InDesign lets you modify the appearance of highlighted characters or selected paragraphs with the following options:

- **Character pane:** Highlight the text and open the Character pane (Type⇨Character, or ⌘+T or Ctrl+T), which is shown in Figure 16-1. Be sure Show Options is visible in the palette menu in order to see all the possible options.

  The Character pane provides access to most of InDesign's character formatting options. Three of the options — Font Family, Type Style, and Font Size — are also available on the Type menu, and several options have keyboard shortcuts.

- **Paragraph pane:** Select a paragraph and open the Paragraph pane (Type➪Paragraph, or Option+⌘+T, or Ctrl+Alt+T or Ctrl+M).

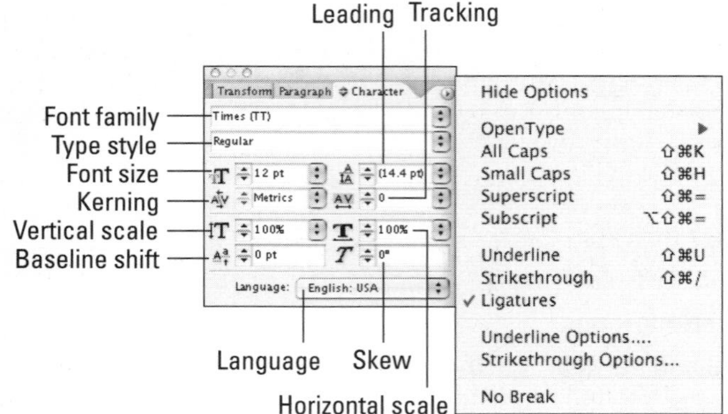

Figure 16-1: The Character pane and its palette menu with all options shown.

- **Control palette:** The Control palette offers all the formatting options of the Character pane plus others, as shown in Figure 16-2. (If the Control palette doesn't show all the character formatting options, select the text and then click the A icon on the palette.)

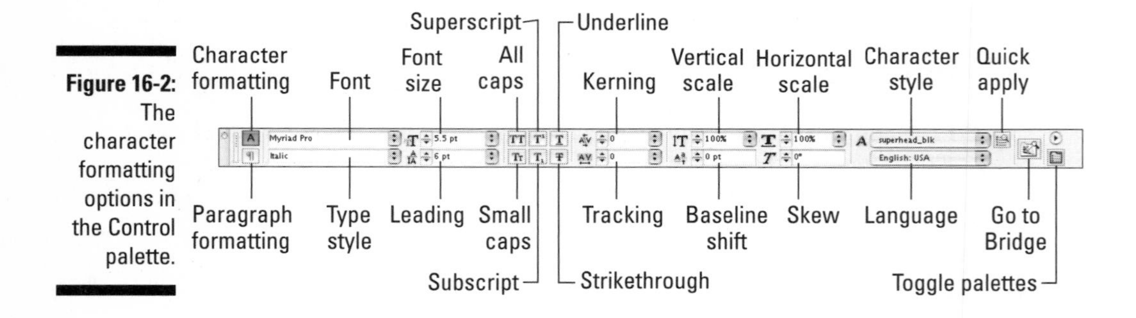

Figure 16-2: The character formatting options in the Control palette.

To change the default character formats — the settings that InDesign will use when you type text into an empty frame — make changes in the Character pane or Control palette when no text is selected or when the text-insertion cursor isn't flashing. That'll save you the hassle of having to reformat new text.

You can choose to apply character formats to highlighted text in two ways:

- Create and apply character styles. Character styles offer an important advantage: A character style's settings are stored, so you can apply the exact same settings easily to other text. When you change a character style's settings, any text based on that style is automatically changed to reflect the new settings.

- Use the local controls in the Character pane, the Control palette, the Type menu, or their keyboard shortcuts, which we discuss in the upcoming sections.

  Even if you do use character styles, you'll probably also do some local formatting from time to time. For example, you would probably use the Character pane to format the type on the opening spread of a feature magazine article, and then use character styles to quickly format the remainder of the article.

Modifying Font, Type Style, and Size

Many people use typographic terms — *font, face, typeface, font family,* and *type style* — inconsistently. Which terms you use doesn't matter as long as you make yourself understood, but we recommend becoming familiar with the font-related terms in InDesign's menus and panes:

- **Font or typeface:** A collection of characters — including letters, numbers, and special characters — that share the same overall appearance, including stroke width, weight, angle, and style.

  For example, Helvetica Regular and Adobe Garamond Semibold Italic are well-known fonts.

- **Font family:** A collection of several fonts that share the same general appearance but differ in stroke width, weight, and/or stroke angle.

  For example, Helvetica and Adobe Garamond are font families.

- **Type style:** Each of the fonts that make up a font family. When you choose a font family from the Character pane's Font Family menu, InDesign displays the family's type style variations in the accompanying Type Styles pop-up menu.

  For example, Regular and Semibold Italic are examples of type styles.

Changing font family and type style

When you change from one font to another in InDesign, you can choose a new font family and type style independently in the Character pane. For example, changing from Arial Bold to Times Bold or from Arial Regular to Berthold Baskerville Regular is a simple change of font family (Arial to Berthold Baskerville). However, if you switch from, say, Bookman Light to Century Schoolbook Bold Italic, you're changing both family and type style (Bookman to Century, then Light to Bold Italic).

InDesign CS2 can display previews of fonts when you select fonts via the Control palette, various text-oriented panes, and the Type menu. You turn on this capability in the Type pane of the Preferences dialog box (choose InDesign➪Preferences➪Type on the Mac or Edit➪Preferences➪Type in Windows, or press ⌘+K or Ctrl+K). But doing so makes your menus huge, often so much that they are unwieldy to use. While it can help you get familiar with your fonts, its unwieldy nature may not be worth that benefit. Only you can decide, but if you do use it, we recommend keeping the preview size small to limit its size.

Whether you use the Control palette or Character pane, you can choose between two methods for changing the font family:

- Choose the Font Family menu, and then select a name from the list of available font families.
- Place the cursor in front of or highlight the font name displayed in the Font Family field, type the first few letters of the font family you want to apply, and then press Return or Enter. For example, entering **Cas** selects Caslon (if it's available on your computer).

If you choose only a font family when type styles are available in an accompanying submenu, no changes are applied to the selected text. So be sure to select a type style from the submenu.

Changing type size

You can be very precise with type sizes (what InDesign calls *font size*). InDesign supports sizes from 0.1 point to 1,296 points (108 inches) in increments as fine as 0.001 point. Of course, you want to use good judgment when choosing type sizes. For example, headlines should be larger than subheads, which in turn are larger than body text, which is larger than photo credits, and so on.

Change the type size of highlighted text with the following methods:

- Choose Type➪Size, and then choose one of the predefined sizes listed in the Size submenu. If you choose Other from the submenu, the Font Size field is highlighted in the Character pane. Enter a custom size, and then press Return or Enter.
- Use the Character pane or Control palette:
    - Choose one of the predefined sizes from the Font Size menu.
    - Highlight the currently applied type size displayed in the accompanying editable field, enter a new size, and then press Return or Enter.

- Make sure the Font Size field is selected, then use the up and down arrow keys to increase or decrease the size in 1-point increments. Pressing Shift multiplies the increment to 10.

- Control+click or right-click a text selection, and then choose a size from the Size submenu. If you choose Other from the submenu, the Font Size field is highlighted in the Character pane. Enter a custom size, and then press Return or Enter.

If text is highlighted and the Font Size field is empty, more than one type size is used in the selected text.

Using Other Character Formats

In the Control palette, you can adjust other character formats, including all caps, small caps, superscript, subscript, underline, strikethrough, kerning, tracking, horizontal and vertical scale, baseline shift, skew, character style, and language. Through the palette menu, you can also set ligatures, modify underline and strikethrough settings, control whether text may break (be hyphenated), and select OpenType features. (OpenType fonts can have a dozen kinds of special formatting. These are expert features, so we don't get into the details here, but feel free to explore the options for any OpenType fonts you have.)

In the Character pane, you can adjust kerning, tracking, horizontal and vertical scale, baseline shift, skew, and language. Through its palette menu (refer to Figure 16-1), you can also set all caps, small caps, superscript, subscript, underline, strikethrough, ligatures, and underline and strikethrough settings, as well as control whether text may break (be hyphenated) and select OpenType features. (InDesign also lets you create custom underlines and strikethroughs, as described in Chapter 18.)

You must choose Show Options from the Character pane's pop-up menu to display the Vertical Scale, Horizontal Scale, Baseline Shift, Skew, and Language options in the pane.

The Control palette has the same functions as the Character pane, except the all caps, small caps, superscript, subscript, underline, and strikethrough options are in the palette rather than in its palette menu.

Figure 16-3 shows the various effects in action. In its top row, *Some* has been scaled vertically, and *special* horizontally, while *effects* has each of the last three letters baseline shifted by a different amount. In its middle row, the word *with* has been skewed, while the word *this* is in real italics. Note the use of superscript and subscript after the word *text.*

Some special effects
with this text$^{1}_{b}$
in InDesign.

Figure 16-3: Various character formatting options applied to text.

Horizontal and Vertical Scale options

InDesign's Horizontal Scale option lets you condense and expand type by squeezing or stretching characters. Similarly, the Vertical Scale option lets you shrink or stretch type vertically.

Typographers tend to agree that excessive scaling should be avoided. If you need to make text bigger or smaller, your best bet is to adjust font size; if you need to squeeze or stretch a range of text a bit, use InDesign's kerning and tracking controls (covered later in this chapter) because the letter forms aren't modified — only the space between letters changes when you kern or track text.

Unscaled text has a horizontal and vertical scale value of 100 percent. You can apply scaling values between 1 percent and 1,000 percent. If you apply equal horizontal and vertical scale values, you're making the original text proportionally larger or smaller. In this case, changing font size is a simpler solution.

To change the scale of highlighted text, enter new values in the Horizontal and/or Vertical Scale fields in the Character pane or Control palette. If a value is highlighted in the Horizontal Scale or Vertical Scale field, you can also use the up and down arrow keys to increase and decrease the scaling in 1-percent increments; press Shift to increase or decrease in 10-percent increments.

Baseline shift

The *baseline* is an invisible horizontal line on which a line of characters rests. The bottom of each letter sits on the baseline (except descenders, such as in *y, p, q, j,* and *g*). When you perform a *baseline shift,* you move highlighted text above or below its baseline. This feature is useful for carefully placing such characters as trademark and copyright symbols and for creating custom fractions.

To baseline-shift highlighted text, enter new values in the Baseline Shift field in the Character pane or Control palette. You can also use the up and down arrow keys to increase the baseline shift in 1-point increments, or press Shift with the arrow keys to increase or decrease it in 10-point increments.

Skew (false italic)

For fonts that don't have an italic type style, InDesign provides the option to skew, or slant, text to create an artificial italic variation of any font. Like horizontal and vertical text scaling, skewing is a clunky way of creating italic-looking text. Use this feature to create special typographic effects, as shown in Figure 16-4, or in situations where a true italic style is not available. Skewing works better for sans-serif typefaces than for serif typefaces, because the characters are simpler and have fewer embellishments that can get oddly distorted when skewed.

To skew highlighted text, you have three options:

- Enter an angle value between –85 and 85 in the Skew field in the Character pane or Control palette. Positive values slant text to the left; negative values slant text to the right.
- Press the accompanying up/down arrow keys when the cursor is in the Skew field to skew text in 1-degree increments. Pressing the Shift key with an arrow key changes the increment 4 degrees.
- You can also skew all the text in a text frame using the Shear tool or by changing the value in the Shear X Angle field in the Transform pane or Control palette after selecting the frame. Slanting text by shearing a text frame does not affect the skew angle of the text. You can specify a skew angle for highlighted text independently from the frame's shear angle.

Skewed text can look like this.

Figure 16-4: Characters in skewed text can slant forward, like italics, or backward, as in this example.

All Caps and Small Caps

When you choose All Caps, the uppercase version of all highlighted characters is used: Lowercase letters are converted to uppercase, and uppercase letters remain unchanged.

Similarly, the Small Caps option affects just lowercase letters. When you choose Small Caps, InDesign automatically uses the Small Caps type style if one is available for the font family (few font families include this style). If a Small Caps type style is not available, InDesign generates small caps from uppercase letters using the scale percentage specified in the Advanced Type pane of the Preferences dialog box (choose InDesign➪Preferences➪Advanced Type on the Mac or Edit➪Preferences➪Advanced Type in Windows, or press ⌘+K or Ctrl+K). The default scale value used to generate small caps text is 70% (of uppercase letters).

Superscript and Subscript

When you apply the Superscript and Subscript character formats to highlighted text, InDesign applies a baseline shift to the characters, lifting them above (for superscript) or lowering them below (for subscript) their baseline, and reduces their size.

The amount of baseline shift and scaling that's used for the Superscript and Subscript formats is determined by the Position and Size fields in the Advanced Type pane of the Preferences dialog box (choose InDesign➪Preferences➪Advanced Type on the Mac or Edit➪Preferences➪Advanced Type in Windows, or press ⌘+K or Ctrl+K). The default Position value for both formats is 33.3%, which means that characters are moved up or down by one-third of the applied leading value. The default Superscript and Subscript Size value is 58.3%, which means that superscripted and subscripted characters are reduced to 58.3% of the applied font size. The Advanced Type pane lets you specify separate default settings for Superscript and Subscript.

To apply the Superscript or Subscript format to highlighted text, choose the appropriate option from the Character pane's pop-up menu. Figure 16-3 shows examples of characters to which the default Superscript and Subscript settings have been applied.

Underline and Strikethrough

Underline and Strikethrough formats are typographically considered to be unacceptable for indicating emphasis in text, which is better accomplished by using bold and/or italic type styles.

Underlines can be useful in kickers and other text above a headline, as well as in documents formatted to look as if they are typewritten. Strikethrough can be used in cases where you want to indicate incorrect answers, eliminated choices, or deleted text.

If you use underlines and strikethrough, InDesign lets you specify exactly how they look through the Underline Options and Strikethrough Options dialog boxes available in the palette menus of the Character pane and Control palette.

InDesign lets you create your own underlines and strikethroughs, in addition to using the standard ones, as Chapter 18 explains.

Ligatures

A *ligature* is a special character that combines two letters. Most fonts include just two ligatures — ﬁ and ﬂ. When you choose the Ligature option, InDesign automatically displays and prints a font's built-in ligatures — instead of the two component letters — if the font includes ligatures.

One nice thing about the Ligature option is that, even though a ligature looks like a single character on-screen, it's still fully editable. That is, you can click between the two-letter shapes and insert text if necessary. Also, a ligature created with the Ligatures option doesn't cause InDesign's spell checker to flag the word that contains it.

To use ligatures within highlighted text, choose Ligatures from the Character pane's or Control palette's palette menu (Ligatures is set to On by default). Figure 16-5 shows an example of text with a ligature.

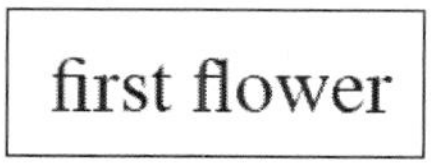

Figure 16-5: Ligatures are used between the *fi* and *fl* letter pairs in the two words.

ﬁrst ﬂower

For most Mac fonts that include ligatures, pressing Option+Shift+5 inserts the ﬁ ligature, while Option+Shift+6 inserts the ﬂ ligature. In Windows, you have to use a program such as Character Map that comes with Windows (usually available by choosing Start⇨Accessories⇨System Tools⇨Character Map) to access the ligature characters in fonts that support them. Either way, if you enter ligatures yourself, InDesign's spell checker flags any words that contain them. For this reason, you may want to let the program handle the task of inserting ligatures.

Turning off hyphenation

You can prevent individual words from being hyphenated or a string of words from being broken at the end of a line. For example, you may decide that you don't want to hyphenate company names, such as *BayCreative.* The Hyphenate option was created for situations such as these.

To prevent a word or a text string from being broken, highlight it, and then uncheck Hyphenate from the Paragraph pane or the Control palette. You can also prevent a word from being hyphenated by placing a discretionary hyphen (Shift+⌘+– [hyphen] or Ctrl+Shift+– [hyphen]) in front of the first letter.

Controlling Space between Characters and Lines

The legibility of a block of text depends as much on the space around it — called *white space* — as it does on the readability of the font. InDesign offers two ways to adjust the space between characters:

- *Kerning* is the adjustment of space between a pair of characters. Most fonts include built-in kerning tables that control the space between character pairs, such as *LA, Yo,* and *WA,* that otherwise could appear to have a space between them even when there isn't one. For large font sizes — for example, a magazine headline — you may want to manually adjust the space between certain character pairs to achieve consistent spacing.
- *Tracking* is the process of adding or removing space among all letters in a range of text.

You can apply kerning and/or tracking to highlighted text in 1⁄1,000-em increments, called units. An em is as wide as the height of the current font size (that is, an em for 12-point text is 12 points wide), which means that kerning and tracking increments are relative to the applied font size.

Leading (rhymes with sledding) controls the vertical space between lines of type. It's traditionally an attribute of paragraphs, but InDesign lets you apply leading on a character-by-character basis. To override the character-oriented approach, ensuring that leading changes affect entire paragraphs, check the

Apply Leading to Entire Paragraphs option in the Type pane of the Preferences dialog box (choose InDesign➪Preferences➪Type on the Mac or Edit➪Preferences➪Type in Windows, or press ⌘+K or Ctrl+K).

Kerning

The Kerning controls in the Character pane and Control palette provide three options for kerning letter pairs:

- **Metrics:** Controls the space between character pairs in the highlighted text using a font's built-in kerning pairs.
- **Optical:** Evaluates each letter pair in highlighted text and adds or removes space between the letters based on the shapes of the characters.
- **Manual:** Adds or removes space between a specific letter pair in user-specified amounts.

When the flashing text cursor is between a pair of characters, the Kerning field displays the pair's kerning value. If Metrics or Optical kerning is applied, the kerning value is displayed in parentheses.

To apply Metrics or Optical kerning to highlighted text, choose the appropriate option from the Kerning pop-up menu. To apply manual kerning, click between a pair of letters, and then enter a value in the Kerning field or choose one of the predefined values. Negative values tighten; positive values loosen.

When letter shapes start to collide, you've tightened too far.

Tracking

Tracking is uniform kerning applied to a range of text. You might use tracking to tighten character spacing for a font that you think is too spacey or loosen spacing for a font that's too tight. Or you could track a paragraph tighter or looser to eliminate a short last line or a *widow* (the last line of a paragraph that falls at the top of a page or column).

To apply tracking to highlighted text, enter a value in the Character pane's Tracking field or choose one of the predefined values. Negative values tighten; positive values loosen (in 0.001-em increments).

You might wonder how tracking is different than kerning. They're essentially the same thing, with this difference: Tracking applies to a selection of three or more characters, while kerning is meant to adjust the spacing between just two characters. You use tracking to change the overall tightness of character spacing, while you use kerning to improve the spacing between letters that just don't quite look right compared to the rest of the text.

Leading

Leading refers to the vertical space between lines of type as measured from baseline to baseline. Leading in InDesign is a character-level format, which means that you can apply different leading values within a single paragraph. InDesign looks at each line of text in a paragraph and uses the largest applied leading value within a line to determine the leading for that line.

By default, InDesign applies Auto Leading to text, which is equal to 120 percent of the type size. As long as you don't change fonts or type sizes in a paragraph, Auto Leading works pretty well. But if you do change fonts or sizes, Auto Leading can result in inconsistent spacing between lines. For this reason, specifying an actual leading value is safer.

In most cases, using a leading value that is slightly larger than the type size is a good idea. When the leading value equals the type size, text is said to be set *solid.* That's about as tight as you ever want to set leading, unless you're trying to achieve a special typographic effect or working with very large text sizes in ad-copy headlines. As is the case with kerning and tracking, when tight leading causes letters to collide — ascenders and descenders are the first to overlap — you've gone too far.

You can change InDesign's preset Auto Leading value of 120%. To do so, choose Type➪Paragraph, or press Option+⌘+T or Ctrl+Alt+T, to display the Paragraph pane. Choose Justification in the palette menu, enter a new value in the Auto Leading field, and then click OK. (What Auto Leading has to do with Justification is a mystery.)

To modify the leading value applied to selected text, choose one of the predefined options from the Leading pop-up menu in the Character pane or Control palette, or enter a leading value in the field. You can enter values from 0 to 5,000 points in 0.001-point increments. You can also use the up and down arrow keys to change leading in 1-point increments.

Creating and Applying Character Styles

A character style is a set of character formats you can apply to a range of highlighted text in a single step. For example, you could use a character style to do any of the following:

- Create a style variation, such as small caps as a lead-in for a paragraph. With a character style, you can switch the font style to small caps, but also change the size, color, and font family applied to that selection of text.
- Apply different formatting to such text elements as Web site, e-mail, and ftp addresses within body text.
- Create other body text variations book and movie titles, or product and company names.

Using character styles is much the same as using paragraph styles, which we cover in Chapter 16. First you create the styles; then you apply them. And you use the Character Styles pane (Type⇨Character Styles or Shift+F11), shown in Figure 16-6, to do both.

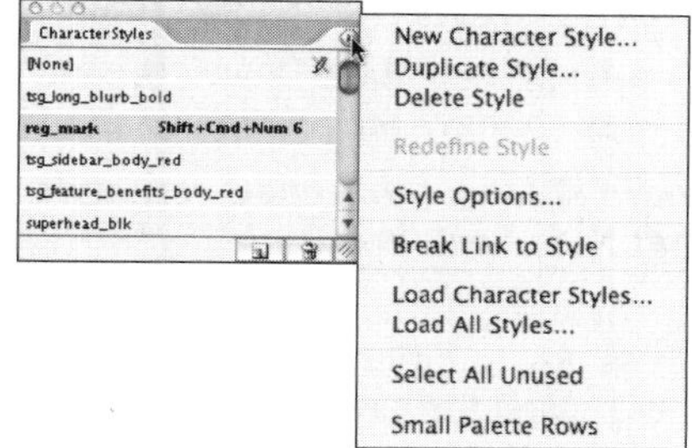

Figure 16-6: The Character Styles pane and its palette menu.

To create a character style, follow these steps:

1. **Show the Character Styles pane by choosing Type⇨Character Styles or pressing Shift+F11.**
2. **Choose New Character Style from the Character Styles pane's pop-up menu.**

   The New Character Style dialog box, shown in Figure 16-7, appears.

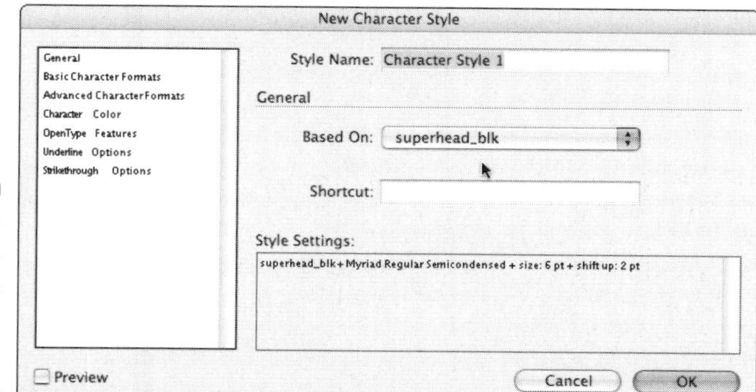

Figure 16-7: The New Character Style dialog box.

3. **Enter a name for the character style in the Style Name field.**

4. **To change any character-level formats, choose the appropriate option from the scroll list to the left of the Style Name field.**

   The scroll list displays seven options: General, Basic Character Formats, Advanced Character Formats, Character Color, OpenType Features, Underline Options, and Strikethrough Options.

5. **Modify the settings as desired in the seven panes listed in the scroll list.**

6. **Create a set of related styles with the Based On pop-up menu, which displays the names of other character styles.**

   For example, you can create a style called Body Copy/Base Character that uses the same character attributes as your base Body Copy paragraph style and then create variations such as Body Text/Emphasis, Body Text/URLs, and so on. If you used the Based On pop-up menu to base each of the variations on Body Text/Base Character and you then modified this "parent" style, your changes are applied to all the variations.

7. **If you want, assign a keyboard shortcut to a character style (Windows users need to make sure that Num Lock is on).**

   In the Shortcut field, hold down any combination of ⌘, Option, and Shift, or Ctrl, Alt, and Shift, and press any number on the keypad. (Letters and non-keypad numbers cannot be used for keyboard shortcuts.)

8. **When you finish specifying the attributes of your character style, click OK.**

   To apply character styles, select the text that you want styled, then click the appropriate character style name in the Character Styles pane. That's all there is to it! (See Chapter 17 for details on overriding and removing styles from text.)

Chapter 17

Handling Paragraph Details

In This Chapter

- Understanding paragraph fundamentals
- Changing basic and advanced paragraph formats
- Applying bullets and numbering
- Working with hyphenation and justification
- Modifying other paragraph formats
- Using paragraph styles

Paragraphs are more than lines of text; they are chunks of information that help convey meaning by organizing that information into related bits. Various types of paragraph formatting let you both make those chunks clearly distinguishable from each other and highlight some chunks, such as lists or long quotes, from others.

This chapter explains what you need to know about formatting paragraphs, from setting indents and alignment — the two most commonly used paragraph attributes — to applying styles to multiple paragraphs for consistency throughout your document.

Applying Paragraph Formats

InDesign provides three ways to apply paragraph formats:

- Use the controls in the Paragraph pane, shown in Figure 17-1, or their keyboard shortcuts. This method is great for working on individual paragraphs, though it's not the best method when working with lots of paragraphs you want to have the same formatting.
- Use the controls in the Control palette (be sure that the Type tool is active and that the ¶ button is selected in the palette to display

paragraph-oriented functions). These controls mirror those in the Paragraph pane, and using them instead of the Paragraph pane can reduce screen clutter.

- Create and apply paragraph styles, as covered later in this chapter. Paragraph styles let you apply consistent formatting — and easily change it to all affected paragraphs — throughout your document.

Whichever method you use — and you'll use them all — the types of formatting available to you is the same.

The Paragraph pane and Control palette provide access to most of InDesign's paragraph-formatting options. Also, several of the options have keyboard shortcuts, as shown in the menus. But to set tabs, you must open the Tabs pane by choosing Windows⇨Type & Tables⇨Tabs or by pressing Shift+⌘+T or Ctrl+Shift+T, as covered in Chapter 18.

Figure 17-1 shows the Paragraph pane. If you choose Hide Options from the pop-up menu, the Space Before/After, Drop Cap, and Hyphenate controls are not displayed. You can also use the Control palette's paragraph formatting options.

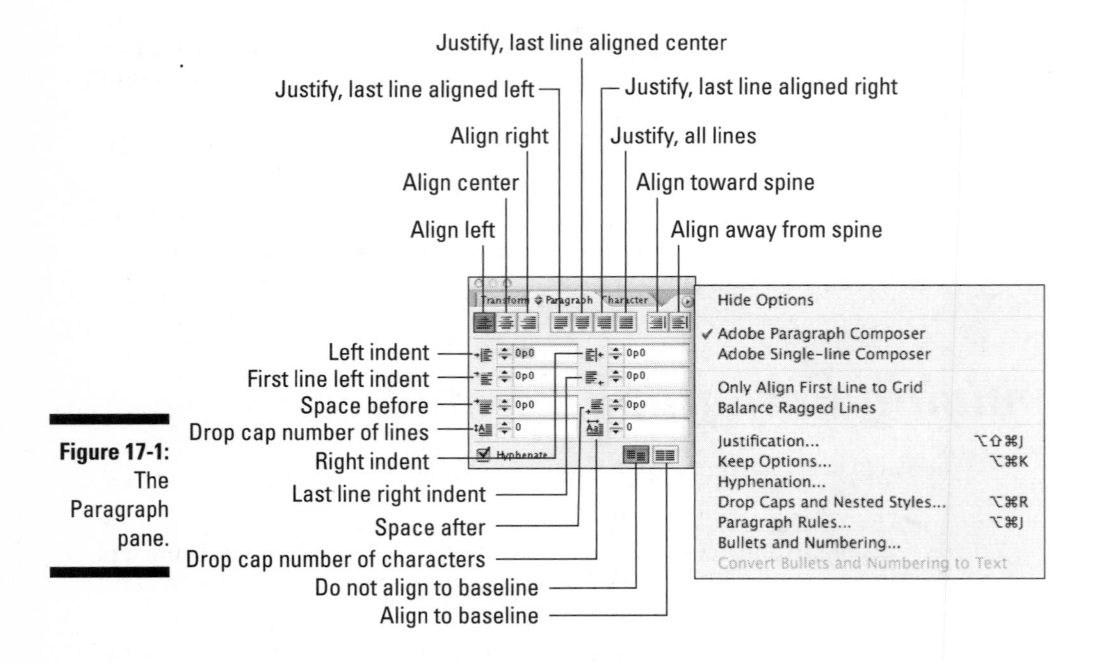

Figure 17-1: The Paragraph pane.

Specifying Alignment and Indents

Alignment and indents give paragraphs their fundamental appearance. Indentation helps readers visually separate paragraphs — the indent acts as the separator, like the blank lines used to separate paragraphs in typewritten documents — while alignment provides visual texture.

Controlling alignment

The alignment buttons at the top of the Paragraph pane control how a selected paragraph begins and ends relative to the left and right margins. To apply a paragraph alignment to selected paragraphs, click one of the buttons. You can also use the keyboard shortcuts described in the following list. Here's a description of each alignment option (the icons themselves illustrate what they do):

- **Align Left** (Shift+⌘+L or Ctrl+Shift+L): This alignment places the left edge of every line at the left margin (the margin can be the frame edge, frame inset, left indent, or column edge) and fits as many words (or syllables, if the hyphenation is turned on) on the line as possible. In left-aligned paragraphs, the right margin is said to be *ragged* because the leftover space at the right end of each line differs from line to line and produces a ragged edge.
- **Align Center** (Shift+⌘+C or Ctrl+Shift+C): This alignment makes both the left and right edges of the paragraphs equally ragged.
- **Align Right** (Shift+⌘+R or Ctrl+Shift+R): This is a mirror opposite of Align Left. The right edge is straight; the left edge is ragged.
- **Justify, Last Line Aligned Left** (Shift+⌘+J or Ctrl+Shift+J): In justified text, the left and right ends of each line are flush with the margins. (There's more about justification later in this chapter.) Justified text is nearly always hyphenated — if you don't hyphenate justified text, spacing between letters and words is very inconsistent. Aligning the last line flush left is the traditional way of ending a paragraph.
- **Justify, Last Line Aligned Center:** This produces justified text with the last line centered.
- **Justify, Last Line Aligned Right:** This produces justified text with the last line aligned to the right.
- **Justify All Lines** (Shift+⌘+F or Ctrl+Shift+F): This produces justified text with the last line forcibly justified. This option can produce last lines

that are very widely spaced. The fewer the number of characters on the last line, the greater the spacing.

The previous three alignment options are rarely used, and for good reason. People expect justified text to have the last line aligned left; the space at the end of the line marks the end of the paragraph. By changing the position of that last line, you can confuse your reader.

- **Align Toward Spine:** Essentially, this option automatically creates right-aligned text on left-hand pages and left-aligned text on right-hand pages. InDesign chooses a left or right alignment based on the location of the spine in a facing-pages document.

- **Align Away from Spine:** This option is the same as Align toward spine except that the alignment is reversed: Text aligns to the left on left-hand pages and to the right on right-hand pages.

Adjusting indent controls

The indent controls in the Paragraph pane let you both move the edges of paragraphs away from the left and/or right margins and indent the first line.

Your options are as follows:

- **Left Indent:** Moves the left edge of selected paragraphs away from the left margin by the amount you specify in the field. You can also click the up and down arrows. Each click increases the value by 1 point; holding down the Shift while clicking increases the increment to 1 pica.
- **Right Indent:** Moves the right edge of selected paragraphs away from the right margin by the amount you specify in the field. You can also use the up and down arrows.
- **First-Line Left Indent:** Moves the left edge of the first line of selected paragraphs away from the left margin by the amount you specify in the field. You can also click the up and down arrows to adjust the indentation. The value in the First-Line Left Indent field is added to any Left Indent value. Using a tab or spaces to indent the first line of a paragraph, which is what was done in the age of typewriters, is usually *not* a good idea. You're better off specifying a First-Line Left Indent.

- **Last-Line Right Indent:** Moves the right edge of the last line of selected paragraphs away from the right margin by the amount you specify in the field. You can also click the up and down arrows.

Inserting space between paragraphs

To format a lengthy chunk of text with multiple paragraphs, you can indicate a new paragraph by indenting the paragraph's first line (by specifying a First-Line Left Indent value, as covered earlier). Or you can insert some extra space between the new paragraph and the preceding one. While no rule states that you can't use both spacing methods, it's a good idea to use one or the other — not both.

What you don't want to do is insert extra paragraph returns between paragraphs. Doing so makes it harder to ensure that columns begin with text (as opposed to blank lines).

- To insert space before selected paragraphs, enter a value in the Space Before field in the Paragraph pane or Control palette. You can also use the up and down arrow buttons; each click increases the value by 1 point and holding down Shift key increases the increment to 1 pica.
- The Space After field works the same as the Space Before field but inserts space below selected paragraphs. If you use Space Before to space paragraphs, you won't need to use Space After, and vice versa; combining both can be confusing.

Controlling space between lines

Leading (pronounced "ledding") is the space between lines of text *within* a paragraph. Even though leading is traditionally an attribute of the paragraph, InDesign treats it as a character format, which you specify by using the Leading control in the Character pane or Control palette.

To change this character-oriented approach to affect entire paragraphs, select the Apply Leading to Entire Paragraphs option in the Type pane of the Preferences dialog box (choose InDesign➪Preferences on the Mac or Edit➪Preferences in Windows, or press ⌘+K or Ctrl+K).

Another way to control space between lines of text is to use baseline grids, as described in Chapter 11. Essentially, a baseline grid overrides the leading specified for paragraphs — you choose whether it overrides the spacing of every line in the paragraph or just the first line. To align to baseline grids, you must click the Align to Baseline button in the Paragraph pane (the rightmost button on the bottom of the pane) for the selected paragraphs. To prevent such locking to the baseline, click the Do Not Align to Baseline button to its immediate left. These same buttons also exist on the right side of the Control palette.

Controlling where paragraphs break

InDesign's Keep Options feature lets you prevent widows and orphans; it also lets you keep paragraphs together when they would otherwise be broken at the bottom of a column. A *widow* is the last line of a paragraph that falls at the top of a column. (The poor thing has been cut off from the rest of the family, the last survivor.) An orphan is the first line of a paragraph that falls at the bottom of a column. (It, too, has become separated from its family, the only survivor.)

When you choose Keep Options from the Paragraph pane's palette menu, the Keep Options dialog box, shown in Figure 17-2, is displayed.

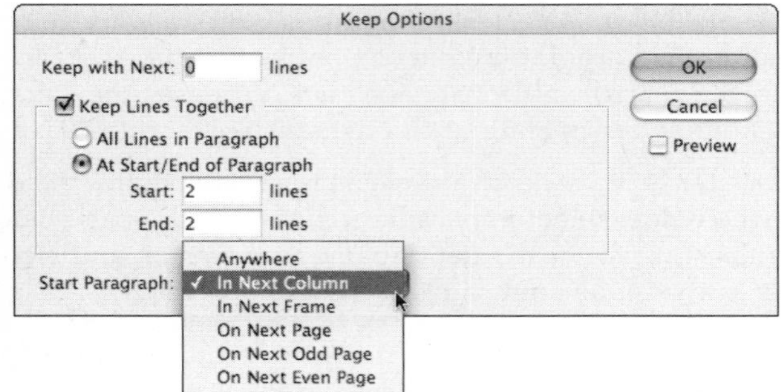

Figure 17-2: The Keep Options dialog box.

The Keep Options dialog box holds several options for how paragraphs are managed as text breaks across columns and pages:

- **Keep with Next__Lines:** This option applies to two consecutive paragraphs and controls the number of lines of the second paragraph that must stay with the first paragraph if a column or page break occurs within the second paragraph.
- **Keep Lines Together:** If you click this check box, it will prevent paragraphs from breaking. When this box is checked, the two radio buttons below it become available. The radio buttons present an either/or choice. One must be selected; At Start/End of Paragraph is selected by default.
- **All Lines in Paragraph:** This option prevents a paragraph from being broken at the end of a column or page. When a column or page break occurs within a paragraph to which this setting has been applied, the entire paragraph moves to the next column or page.
- **At Start/End of Paragraph:** Select this check box to control widows and orphans. When this button is selected, the two fields below it become available:
  - **Start lines:** This field controls orphans. The value you enter is the minimum number of lines at the beginning of a paragraph that must be placed at the bottom of a column when a paragraph is split by a column ending.
  - **End lines:** This field controls widows. The value you enter is the minimum number of lines at the end of a paragraph that must be

placed at the top of a column when a paragraph is split by a column ending.

- **Start Paragraph:** From this pop-up menu, choose Anywhere to let the paragraph begin where it would fall naturally in the sequence of text (no forced break). Choose In Next Column to force a paragraph to begin in the next column or frame; choose On Next Page to force a paragraph to begin on the next page (such as for chapter headings). Your other choices are similar: On Next Odd Page and On Next Even Page.

Adding Drop Caps

Drop caps are enlarged capital letters that are often used to embellish paragraphs (usually the first paragraph of a chapter or story) and to draw attention to paragraphs. In the Paragraph pane or Control palette, InDesign lets you specify the number of letters you want to include in a drop cap and the number of lines you want to drop them down into.

To add one or more drop caps to selected paragraphs, enter a number in the Drop Cap Number of Characters field in the Paragraph pane or Control palette. The number you enter determines how many characters in a selected paragraph will be made into drop caps. To specify the number of lines a drop cap will extend into a paragraph (and therefore the height of the drop cap), enter a number in the Drop Cap Number of Lines field.

After you create a drop cap, you can modify it by highlighting it and changing any of its character formats — font, size, color, and so on — by using the Character pane or Control palette as well as other panes, such as Stroke and Swatches. Figure 17-3 shows two examples of drop caps.

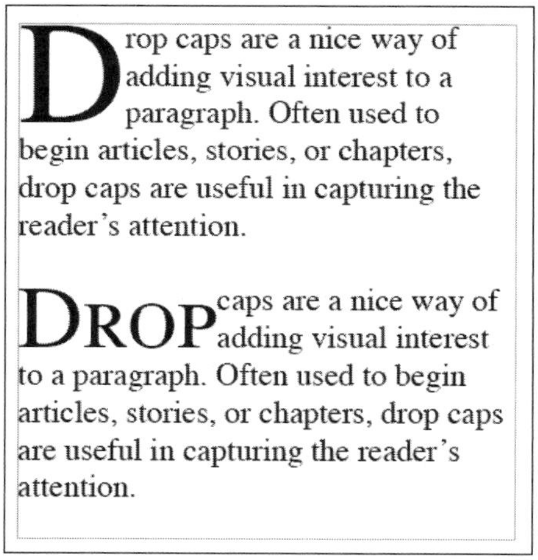

Drop caps are a nice way of adding visual interest to a paragraph. Often used to begin articles, stories, or chapters, drop caps are useful in capturing the reader's attention.

DROP caps are a nice way of adding visual interest to a paragraph. Often used to begin articles, stories, or chapters, drop caps are useful in capturing the reader's attention.

Figure 17-3: A one-character drop cap three lines deep, and a two-line, four-character drop cap with the first word set in small caps.

Controlling Hyphenation and Justification

Hyphenation is the placement of hyphens between syllables in words that won't fit at the end of a line of text. A hyphen is a signal to the reader that the word continues on the next line. InDesign gives you the option to turn paragraph hyphenation on or off. If you choose to hyphenate, you can customize the settings that determine when and where hyphens are inserted.

Justification is the addition or removal of space between words and/or letters that produces the flush-left/flush-right appearance of justified paragraphs. InDesign's justification controls let you specify how space is added or removed when paragraphs are justified. If you justify paragraphs, you almost certainly want to hyphenate them, too. If you opt for left-aligned paragraphs, whether to hyphenate is a personal choice.

InDesign offers both manual and automatic hyphenation.

Manual hyphenation

To break a particular word in a specific place, you can place a *discretionary hyphen* in the word. If the word won't entirely fit at the end of a line in a hyphenated paragraph, InDesign will use the discretionary hyphen to split the word if the part of the word before the hyphen fits on the line. To insert a discretionary hyphen, use the shortcut Shift+⌘+– (hyphen) or Ctrl+Shift+– (hyphen) in the text where you want the hyphen to appear.

If a word has a discretionary hyphen, and hyphenation is necessary, InDesign breaks the word *only* at that point. But you can place multiple discretionary hyphens within a single word. If a word needs to be hyphenated, InDesign will use the hyphenation point that produces the best results.

You can prevent a particular word from being hyphenated either by placing a discretionary hyphen in front of the first letter or by highlighting the word and choosing No Break from the palette menu of the Control palette or from the palette menu of the Character pane.

Automatic hyphenation

To have InDesign automatically hyphenate selected paragraphs, all you have to do is check the Hyphenate check box in the Paragraph pane or Control palette. (The Hyphenate check box is displayed only if you choose Show Options from the palette menu.)

You can control how InDesign actually performs the hyphenation via the Hyphenation option in the palette menu. When you choose Hyphenation, the Hyphenation Settings dialog box, shown in Figure 17-4, appears.

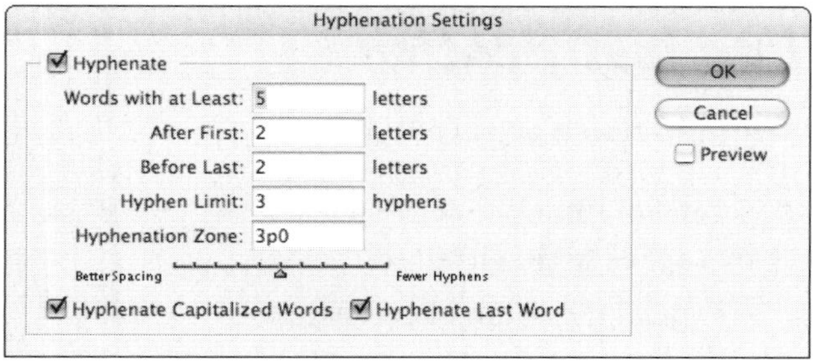

Figure 17-4: The Hyphenation Settings dialog box.

The options in the Hyphenation Settings dialog box include:

- **Hyphenate check box:** This is a duplicate of the Hyphenate check box in the Paragraph pane and Control palette. If you didn't check it before opening the Hyphenation Settings dialog box, you can check it here.
- **Words with at Least__Letters:** This is where you specify the number of letters in the shortest word you want to hyphenate.
- **After First__Letters:** In this field, enter the minimum number of characters that can precede a hyphen.
- **Before Last__Letters:** The number entered in this field determines the minimum number of characters that can follow a hyphen.
- **Hyphenation Limit:** In this field, you specify the number of consecutive lines that can be hyphenated. Several consecutive hyphens produce an awkward, ladder-like look, so consider entering a small number, such as **2** or **3**, in this field.
- **Hyphenation Zone:** The entry in this field applies only to nonjustified text and only when the Adobe Single-Line Composer option is selected (in the Paragraph pane's palette menu). A hyphenation point must fall within the distance specified in this field in relation to the right margin in order to be used. Acceptable hyphenation points that do not fall within the specified hyphenation zone are ignored. You can also use the Better Spacing/Fewer Hyphens slider below the field to pick a value rather than entering a value in the Hyphenation Zone field.
- **Hyphenate Capitalized Words:** If you check this box, InDesign will hyphenate, when necessary, capitalized words. If you don't check this

box, a capitalized word that would otherwise be hyphenated will get bumped to the next line, which may cause excessive spacing in the previous line.

- **Hyphenate Last Word:** Check this box to allow InDesign to break the last word in a paragraph. Otherwise, InDesign will move the entire word to the last line and space the preceding text as necessary.

Controlling justification

To control how justification is achieved, you can:

- Condense or expand the width of spaces between words.
- Add or remove space between letters.
- Condense or expand the width of characters.

The options in the Justification dialog box, shown in Figure 17-5, let you specify the degree to which InDesign will adjust normal word spaces, character spacing, and character width to achieve justification. Access this dialog box via the palette menu in the Control palette or in the Paragraph pane, or by pressing Option+Shift+⌘+J or Ctrl+Alt+Shift+J. When specifying values in the Justification dialog box, Minimum values must be smaller than Desired values, which in turn must be smaller than Maximum values.

Figure 17-5: The Justification dialog box.

The Justification dialog box lets you specify the following options:

- **Word Spacing:** Enter the percentage of a character that you want to use whenever possible in the Desired field. (The default value is 100%, which uses a font's built-in width.) Enter the minimum acceptable percentage in the Minimum field; enter the maximum acceptable percentage in the Maximum field. The smallest value you can enter is 0%; the largest is 1,000%.
- **Letter Spacing:** The default value of 0% in this field uses a font's built-in letter spacing. In the Desired field, enter a positive value to add space (in increments of 1% of an en space) between all letter pairs; enter a

negative value to remove space. Enter the minimum acceptable percentage in the Minimum field; enter the maximum acceptable percentage in the Maximum field.

- **Glyph Scaling:** The default value of 100% uses a character's normal width. In the Desired field, enter a positive value to expand all character widths; enter a negative value to condense character widths. Enter the minimum acceptable percentage in the Minimum field and the maximum acceptable percentage in the Maximum field. If you do apply glyph scaling, it's best to keep it to a range of 97 to 103 percent at most.

If you use the Adobe Paragraph Composer option (explained in the following sections) for justified paragraphs, specifying a narrow range between minimum and maximum Word Spacing, Letter Spacing, and Glyph Scaling will generally produce good-looking results. However, if you choose the Adobe Single-Line Composer option, a broader range between Minimum and Maximum gives the composer more leeway in spacing words and letters and hyphenating words and can produce better-looking results. The best way to find out what values work best is to experiment with several settings. Print out hard copies and let your eyes decide which values produce the best results.

Composing text

The Paragraph pane's palette menu offers two options for implementing the hyphenation and justification settings you establish: the Adobe Single-Line Composer and the Adobe Paragraph Composer. (These options are also available in the Justification dialog box, covered in the previous section.)

Adobe Single-Line Composer

In single-line composition, hyphenation, and justification settings are applied to each line in a paragraph, one line at a time. The effect of modifying the spacing of one line on the lines above and below it is not considered in single-line composition, so it can cause poor spacing.

Adobe Paragraph Composer

InDesign's Adobe Paragraph Composer is selected by default. It takes a broader approach to composition than the Adobe Single-Line Composer by looking at the entire paragraph at once. If a poorly spaced line can be fixed by adjusting the spacing of a previous line, the Adobe Paragraph Composer will reflow the previous line.

The Adobe Paragraph Composer is more sophisticated than the Single-Line Composer, offering better overall spacing because it will sacrifice optimal spacing a bit on one line to prevent really bad spacing on another, something the single-line method does not do.

Ruling Your Paragraphs

If you want to place a horizontal line within text so that the line moves with the text when editing causes the text to reflow — an often effective highlighting device — you need to create a paragraph rule. A paragraph rule looks much like a line created with the line tool but behaves like a text character. Here's how to create paragraph rules:

1. **Select the paragraph(s) to which you want to apply a rule above and/or a rule below and then choose Paragraph Rules from the Paragraph pane's or Control palette's palette menu or use the shortcut Option+⌘+J or Ctrl+Alt+J.**

   You can also specify rules as part of a paragraph style. The Paragraph Rules dialog box, shown in Figure 17-6, is displayed.

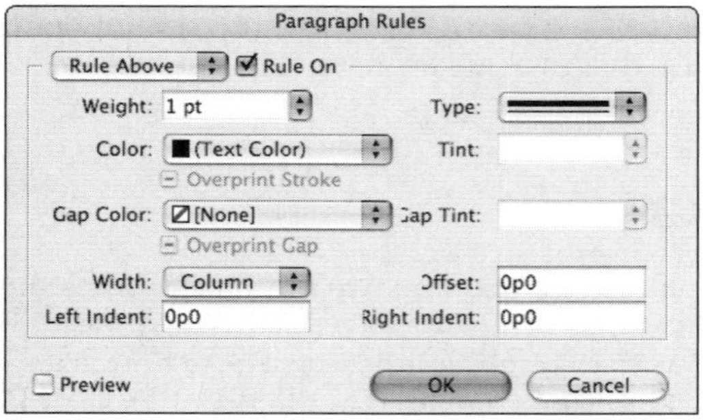

Figure 17-6: The Paragraph Rules dialog box.

2. **Choose Rule Above or Rule Below and then click Rule On.**

   To add rules both above and below, click Rule On for both options and specify their settings separately. To see the rule while you create it, select the Preview option.

3. **Choose a predefined thickness from the Weight pop-up menu or enter a value in the Weight field.**
4. **Choose a rule type from the Type pop-up menu.** You can choose from 17 types, including dashed, striped, dotted, and wavy lines.
5. **Choose a color for the rule from the Color pop-up menu.** This menu lists the colors displayed in the Swatches pane (Window⇨Swatches or F5).
6. **From the Width pop-up menu, choose Column to have the rule extend from the left edge of the column to the right edge of the column; choose Text to have the rule extend from the left edge of the frame or column to the right.**

7. **To indent the rule from the left and/or right edges, enter values in the Left Indent and/or Right Indent fields.**
8. **Control the vertical position of the rule by entering a value in the Offset field.** For a rule above, the offset value is measured upward from the baseline of the first line in a paragraph to the bottom of the rule; for a rule below, the offset is measured downward from the baseline of the last line in a paragraph to the top of the rule.
9. **Check the Overprint Stroke box if you want to print a rule on top of any underlying colors.** This ensures that any misregistration during printing will not result in white areas around the rule where the paper shows through. There's a similar Overprint Gap check box for lines that have a Gap Color.
10. **Click OK to close the dialog box, implement your changes, and return to the document.**

To remove a paragraph rule, click in the paragraph to which the rule is applied, choose Paragraph Rules from the Paragraph pane's pop-up menu, uncheck the Rule On box, and then click OK.

Paragraph Styles

If you're laying out pages and formatting text, creating styles for repetitive text elements is a great idea: Doing so ensures consistent formatting, and it lets you change all paragraphs at the same time just by updating the style applied to them. The Paragraph Styles pane (select Type⇨Paragraph Styles or press F11) is where you both create and apply styles.

Creating paragraph styles

InDesign comes with a predefined default paragraph style, called [Basic Paragraph], that text in a new frame automatically has applied to it. You can edit [Basic Paragraph] like any other style.

Here's how you create a paragraph style:

1. **If it's not displayed, show the Paragraph Styles pane by choosing Type⇨Paragraph Styles or by pressing F11.**

   The New Paragraph Style dialog box is displayed.

2. **Enter a name for the style in the Style Name field.** Be descriptive with your style names. For example, for body copy, use a style name along the lines of **Body Copy**.
3. **To change any character or paragraph formats, choose the appropriate category from the list on the left side of the dialog box, shown in Figure 17-7, and make your changes.**

In the General pane of the New Paragraph Style dialog box, the Based On pop-up menu displays the names of other paragraph styles. You use this feature to create families of styles. Thus, if you change a style that other styles are based on, all those styles are updated with the new settings.

When you enter text, the paragraph formats of the preceding paragraph are automatically used for the subsequent paragraph unless you create paragraph styles that automatically change paragraph formats from one paragraph to another. To have InDesign automatically apply a different style to the next paragraph when you type in text, choose a style name from the Next Style pop-up menu while defining a style. For example, when you define a style named Headline, you might choose Byline as the next style, so after you type in a headline, the next paragraph will be formatted for a byline. Obviously, you need to have the Byline style available.

4. **When you finish specifying the attributes of the paragraph style, click OK.**

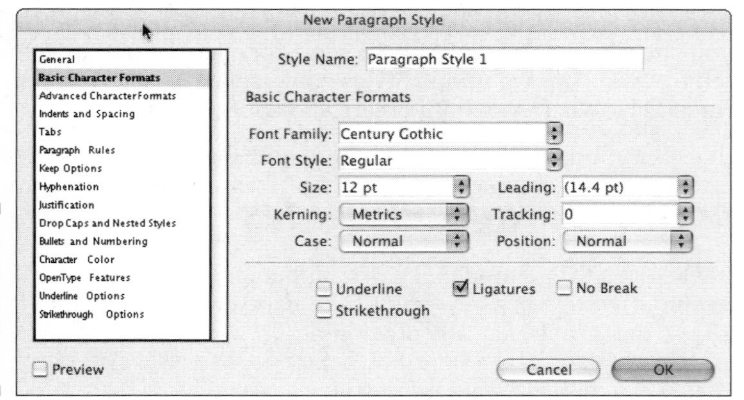

Figure 17-7: The New Paragraph Style dialog box.

The easiest way to create a paragraph style is to manually apply character and paragraph formats to a sample paragraph and then — with the sample paragraph selected — follow the steps below. If no text is selected when you create a style, you have to specify all the desired character and paragraph formats as you create the style, which is more difficult than formatting a paragraph in advance.

Applying paragraph styles

To apply a paragraph style, just click within a paragraph or highlight text in a range of paragraphs and then click the style name in the Paragraph Styles pane or press its keyboard shortcut. (Windows users must make sure Num Lock is on when using shortcuts for styles.)

If your group of selected paragraphs uses more than one paragraph style, the Paragraph Styles pane will display the text (Mixed) at the lower left.

When you apply a style to selected paragraphs, all local formats and applied character styles are retained. All other formats are replaced by those of the applied style. If you want to override those attributes, choose Clear Overrides from the Paragraph Styles pane's palette menu. If you want to remove a style from a paragraph, so it's not changed if the style is later changed, choose Break Link to Style from the palette menu.

Another way to apply paragraph (and character) styles is by using the Quick Apply feature in InDesign CS2. Quick Apply is a consolidated list of styles that you access by choosing Edit⇨Quick Apply or by pressing ⌘+Return or Ctrl+Enter. If you have selected text or have the text-insertion point active, the Quick Apply palette presents all paragraph, character, and object styles available. You can scroll down to the one you want, or you can type the first few letters of the style name in the text field at the top to jump to styles beginning with those letters and then navigate to the one you want. Then press Return or Enter, which brings you back to where you were working with your text. Pressing ⌘+Return or Ctrl+Enter again closes the Quick Apply palette.

For users who are working on layouts from their keyboards — perhaps a layout artist who's working on a notebook while commuting — Quick Apply can be handy because you can switch to it, apply the style, and return to your text without touching the mouse.

Chapter 18

Tricks with Text

In This Chapter

- Adding bullets and formatting lists
- Creating reverse type
- Specifying hanging punctuation
- Rotating and scaling text
- Using tabs and tables

With the myriad of text-formatting techniques available in InDesign, you can create some snazzy and sophisticated effects. You can stretch, skew, rotate, and color text. You can use a wide range of characters for bullets. You can add shadows and feathering effects to give words a dramatic flair. As with all good things, moderation in your use of text effects will keep your documents looking professional. This chapter shows you some InDesign features that can produce typographic special effects and gives some suggestions on when to use them. (Chapters 16 and 17 cover more prosaic formatting controls.)

Using Bulleted and Numbered Lists

Automatic bullets and numbering are available as a paragraph format in InDesign. You access these options (after selecting the paragraphs you want to make into automatic lists, of course) by choosing Bullets and Numbering Options from the Paragraph pane's or Control palette's palette menus. Doing so displays the Bullets and Numbering dialog box shown in Figure 18-1.

Bulleted and numbered lists are new to InDesign CS2, although a less capable version was available for InDesign CS as part of the $49 PageMaker Plug-in Pack.

Figure 18-1: The Bullets and Numbering dialog box.

To set bullets or numbered lists in the Bullets and Numbering dialog box, first select either Bullets or Numbers from the List Type pop-up menu, and then follow these steps (select the Preview check box to see the results of your choices before you finalize them):

1. **For bullets, choose a bullet character from the Bullet Character area.** The area will show bullet characters available for the current font; you can change the selection by changing the selected font or by clicking the Add button.

   For numbered lists, choose a numbering style from the Style pop-up menu and a separator character from the Separator pop-up menu and type a starting number in the Start At field. In the Start At field, note that if multiple paragraphs are selected, the starting number will apply just to the first paragraph, and the others will be numbered consecutively from that start value.

2. **Adjust the font settings for the bullets or numbers by using the Font Family, Type Style, Size, and Color pop-up menus.** The default settings match the formatting that is currently applied to the selected paragraphs.

   InDesign sometimes refers to *Type Style* as *Font Style* in its user interface and documentation. They're the same thing.

3. **In the Bullet or Number Position section of the dialog box, set the indentation for the list.** Using the Position pop-up menu, choose Hanging to have a hanging indent (the bullet or number extends to the left of the text that follows, like the numbered list you're reading right

now) or Flush Left to have the bullet or number and the following text all align to the paragraph's left margin.

4. **When you finish formatting the bulleted or numbered list, click OK.**

It's possible that the bulleted or numbered list you're working with was first created in a word processor and then placed in InDesign. Perhaps the writer simply used an asterisk followed by a space to indicate a bullet, or used the word processor's automatic bullet or numbering feature. You can deal with imported bulleted and numbered lists as follows:

- If the document imported into InDesign was formatted with an automatic bullet or numbering feature, the numbers and their punctuation arrive in InDesign intact. However, these won't use the InDesign bullets and numbering feature, so new bullets and list numbers won't be automatically added or adjusted when you edit the copy in InDesign. Your best bet is to override these imported paragraphs with an InDesign paragraph style that uses InDesign's bullets and numbering formatting capabilities. You need to delete the word-processor-generated bullets and numbers from such imported text and then apply InDesign's automatic bullets or numbering. You might be able to use the Find/Change dialog box (Edit⇨Find/Change or ⌘+F or Ctrl+F) to get rid of the now extraneous bullet characters imported from the word processor.
- InDesign sometimes converts a word processor's automatic bullets to characters in the current font; they will need to be changed to bullets. Or, rather than using automatic bullets, the writer might have typed asterisks, hyphens, or another character to indicate bullets. After you determine what characters indicate bullets in your text, use Find/Change to change them to the bullet character you want.

For the bullets in a list, you're not limited to using the small round bullet (•) included in most typefaces. You can use any character in the body text font, or you can switch to a symbol or pi font and choose a more decorative character. Zapf Dingbats and Wingdings are the most common symbol fonts, offering an array of boxes, arrows, crosses, stars, and checkmarks.

Labeling Paragraphs

Along with using drop caps, which we cover in Chapter 16, changing the formatting of the first few words in a paragraph as a *label* can serve as a visual indicator that the reader has arrived at the beginning of a story, chapter, or new topic. To experiment with label formatting, use the attributes available via the Character pane or Control palette and their palette menus, such as font changes, horizontal scale, or small caps. After you decide on the formatting for labels, you can apply it by using character styles after paragraph styles are applied — and after the text is final. You might also be able to use the nested styles feature if the label text follows a specific pattern, such as a specific number of words or characters or an entire sentence.

The following descriptions show frequently used label formatting:

- **Boldface:** Bold type is often used for titles and subheads in magazines, newspapers, and reports. To apply boldface in InDesign, select the bold version of the typeface from the Type Style pop-up menu in the Character pane.
- *Italics:* Italic text is a good choice for emphasizing specific words and for applying to tertiary heads. To apply italics in InDesign, select the oblique version of the typeface from the Type Style pop-up menu on the Character pane.
- Underlines: Underlined text isn't used as frequently as it once was, simply because page-layout programs such as InDesign offer more sophisticated options for labeling text. Still, you might have occasion to use underlines, such as to emphasize a label. Use the Underline command in the menu on the Character pane. Note that you have no control over the style, thickness, or placement of the underline if you use this option; for custom underlines, use the controls described later in this chapter.
- SMALL CAPS: Small caps offer a subtle, classic look that blends well with the rest of the document. You have two choices for applying small caps from the Character pane: Choose a small-caps variation of a typeface from the Type Style pop-up menu or choose the Small Caps command from the palette menu.
- **Typeface change:** Rather than relying on different variations of a font, you can use a different font altogether, such as Futura Medium, for a label. To contrast with serif body text, you might choose a sans-serif typeface that complements the look of your publication. To apply a different typeface, use the Font Family pop-up menu in the Character pane or Control palette.
- Scaled text: Scaling text horizontally — up 10 or 20 percent — is a subtle effect that makes the section of text visually distinct. Scaling text vertically, however, can be *too* subtle unless combined with boldface or another style. Use the Horizontal Scale and Vertical Scale fields in the Character pane or Control palette to scale text.
- Size change: Bumping the size of a label up a point or two is another subtle design choice. To change the size of type, use the Font Size field in the Character pane or Control palette.

Adding Special Type Treatments

Skilled graphic designers make decisions based on what best serves the content. In doing so, they often rely on special typographic techniques. For example, the use of reverse type helps to break up pages and to organize text, while careful formatting of fractions and hanging punctuation add a professional touch.

Reversing type out of its background

Reversed type is white type on a black background rather than black type on a white background. Of course, reversed type doesn't have to be white on black; it can be any lighter color on a darker color. You often find reversed type in table headings, kickers (explanatory blurbs following headlines), and decorative layout elements.

To lighten the text, highlight it with the Type tool, click the Fill button on the Tools palette, and choose a light color from the Swatches pane (Window➪Swatches or F5). For the dark background, you have three options: filling the text frame with a darker color, making the text frame transparent and placing it on top of darker objects, or placing a thick, dark ruling line behind the text.

For the first two options, select the text frame with the Selection tool or the Direct Selection tool and then click the Fill button on the Tools palette.

- To fill the text frame with a darker color, click a color from the Swatches pane.
- To make the text frame transparent, click the Apply None button on the Tools palette. Then place the text frame in front of a darker object or graphic.

To create reversed type that is not in its own text frame, use a ruling line of the appropriate width (at least a couple points larger than the text size). If you use a Ruling Line Above, move the line down behind the text; if you use a Ruling Line Below, move it up. Figure 18-2 shows reversed type used as a heading, as well as the Paragraph Rules dialog box and the settings used to create the effect. (To access this dialog box, choose Paragraph Rules from the palette menu of the Control palette or Paragraph pane, or press Option+⌘+J or Ctrl+Alt+J.)

We explain how to create and adjust ruling lines in greater detail in Chapter 17.

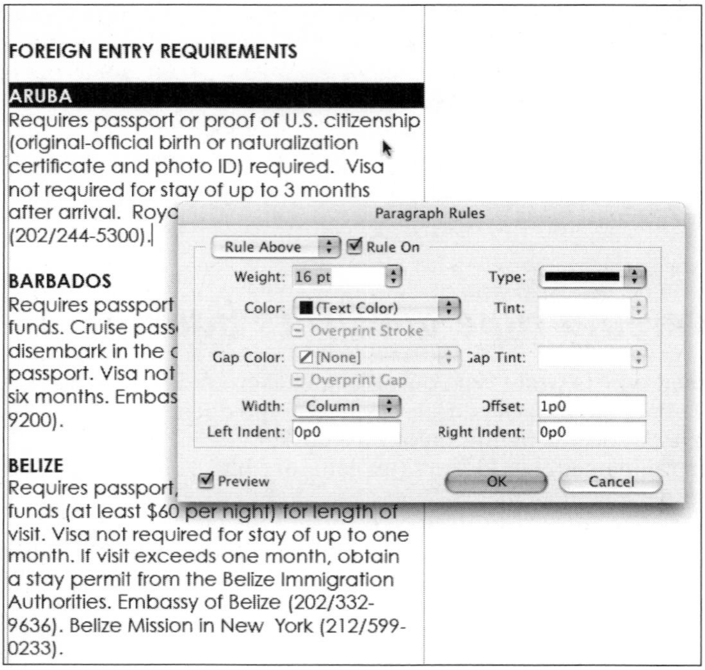

Figure 18-2: This travel guide uses reversed-out text, created via ruling lines, for its subtitles.

Creating sidebars and pull-quotes

A *sidebar* is supplemental text that is often formatted differently from the rest of the document and placed within a shaded or outlined box. Sidebars help break up text-heavy pages and call attention to information that is often interesting but not essential to the main story.

Particularly in text-heavy publications, pulling in-depth information or related text into sidebars can help provide visual relief. To create a sidebar, you usually place the text in its own frame, then stroke the frame and optionally fill it with a tint. To inset the text from the edges of the frame, use the Text Frame Options dialog box (Object⇨Text Frame Options or ⌘+B or Ctrl+B).

A *pull-quote* is a catchy one- or two-line excerpt from a publication that is enlarged and reformatted to achieve both editorial and design objectives. Pull quotes draw readers into articles with excerpts that do everything from summarize the content to provide shock value. From the design perspective, pull-quotes break up static columns and offer opportunities for typographic treatment that emphasizes the content, such as colors and typefaces that support the mood of an article.

To create a pull-quote, copy and paste the relevant text into its own text frame and then reformat the text and frame as you wish. Use the Text Wrap pane (Window➪Text Wrap or Option+⌘+W or Ctrl+Alt+W) to control how text in columns wraps around the pull-quote.

Formatting fractions

Creating fractions that are formatted correctly can be handy. Compare the top line in Figure 18-3, which is not formatted appropriately for a fraction, to the bottom line, which is correctly formatted. Although InDesign doesn't provide an automatic fraction maker, you can use expert typefaces or character formats to achieve professional-looking fractions.

Applying a fraction typeface

Some expert typefaces include a variation, appropriately called Fractions, that includes a number of common fractions, such as ½, ⅓, ¼, and ¾. Adobe has Expert Collection variants for many of its popular fonts; these collections include true small caps, true fractions, and other typographic characters. Many OpenType formats include these characters as well. You can also use a symbol font, though the numerals may not exactly match the appearance of numerals in the rest of your text because symbol fonts typically use plain fonts like Helvetica as their basis.

To use a true fraction from an Expert Collection or OpenType font, choose Type➪Glyph, select the font and face from the pop-up menus at the bottom of the dialog box shown in Figure 18-3, and then select the fraction you want to use.

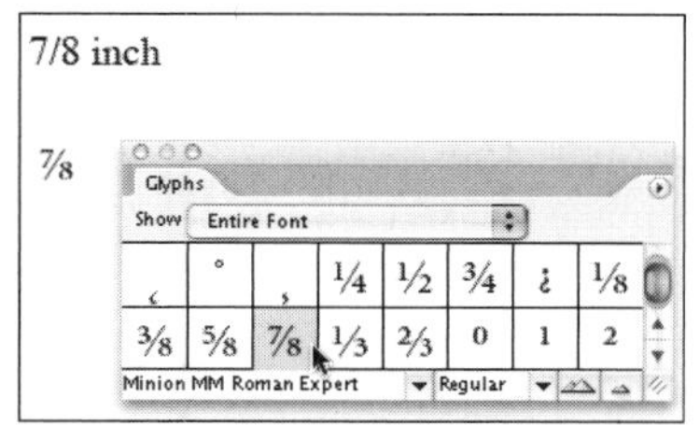

Figure 18-3: In the second line of text, the "7/8" text is formatted correctly with an expert font.

Formatting fractions manually

If you're dealing with a wide range of fractions in something like a cookbook, you probably won't find all the fractions you need in your Expert Collection or OpenType font. Because it would be difficult to format fractions such as 3⁄16 exactly the same as an expert font's ¼, you might opt for formatting all the fractions manually.

Expert fractions are approximately the same size as a single character in that font, and this is your eventual goal in formatting a fraction manually. Usually, you achieve this by decreasing the size of the two numerals, raising the numerator (the first, or top, number in the fraction), and kerning on either side of the slash as necessary.

Macintosh fonts provide another option for refining fractions: a special kind of slash called a *virgule,* which is smaller and at more of an angle than a regular slash. Press Option+Shift+1 to enter a virgule, then kern around it as you would a slash.

Unless you rarely use fractions, by all means save your formatting as character styles. You can apply the formats with a keystroke or use Find/Change (Edit⇨Find/Change or ⌘+F or Ctrl+F) to locate numbers and selectively apply the appropriate character style.

Hanging punctuation

When display type, such as a pull-quote or headline type in ads, is left-aligned or justified, the edges can look uneven due to the gaps above, below, or next to quotation marks, other punctuation, and some capital letters. Notice the text frame on the left in Figure 18-4, which does not have hanging punctuation. To correct the unevenness, you can use a technique called *hanging punctuation,* or *Optical Margin Alignment,* which extends the punctuation slightly beyond the edges of the rest of the text, as shown in the text frame on the right in Figure 18-4.

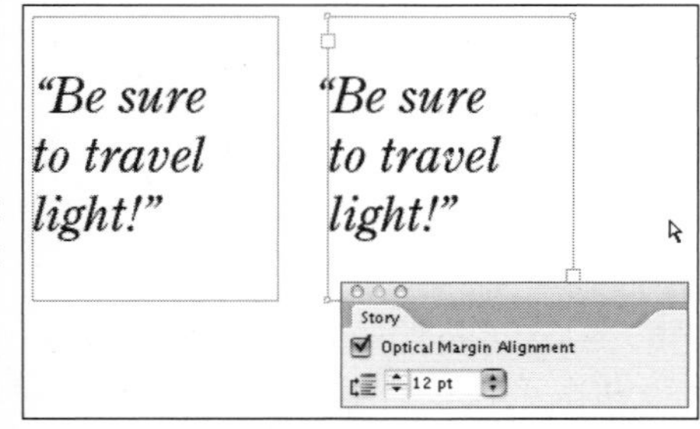

Figure 18-4: Notice the difference between the standard alignment on the left and the hanging punctuation on the right.

The "edge" of text is defined by the edges of the text frame or any Inset Spacing specified in the Text Frame Options dialog box (Object➪Text Frame Options or ⌘+B or Ctrl+B).

The Optical Margin Alignment feature automates hanging punctuation, extending punctuation and the edges of some glyphs (such as a capital *T*) slightly outside the edges of the text. Unfortunately, you can't control how much the characters "hang" outside the text boundaries — InDesign decides that for you. And Optical Margin Alignment applies to all the text frames in a story, rather than to highlighted text. Therefore, you need to isolate into its own story any text for which you want hanging punctuation.

To specify Optical Margin Alignment, select any text frame in a story and choose Window➪Type & Tables➪Story. Check the Optical Margin Alignment option, as shown in Figure 18-4.

Optical Margin Alignment usually improves the look of display type. However, Optical Margin Alignment will actually cause columns of body text to look uneven (because they are).

Adding Color to Text

Adding color to text is another way to add visual interest. But just because you're printing on a four-color printing press or a color printer doesn't mean you should get carried away with coloring text. Keep your content legible and unified, but feel free to explore extending beyond all black ink on white paper. Using color in headlines, banners, subheads, and pull-quotes is common these days. However, you rarely see color applied to body text.

In general, the smaller the type, the darker its color should be — with pastels reserved for large text, bright colors for bold text, and dark colors for body text. InDesign lets you make an entire character one color, or make the fill (inside) and stroke (outlines) of a character two different colors. You can even apply gradients to fills and strokes.

To color text, follow these steps:

1. **Click the Type tool in the Tools palette.**
2. **Highlight the text you want to color.**
3. **Click the Fill button or the Stroke button on the Tools palette to specify whether you're coloring the character or its outline.**

4. **If necessary, open the Swatches pane by choosing Window➪Swatches or by pressing F5.**
5. **Click a color, tint, or gradient swatch to apply it to the stroke or fill.**
6. **To specify the thickness of the stroke, use the Stroke pane (Window➪Stroke or F10); to apply a custom gradient not available as a swatch to the stroke or fill, use the Gradient pane (Window➪Gradient).**

Rotating Text

No doubt you've seen publications with rotated text. Perhaps you saw a magazine with section titles listed vertically in the outside margin of the page, a newsletter with nameplates running horizontally down the first page, or a catalog with sale prices splashed diagonally across pages.

In InDesign, you rotate text by placing the text you want to rotate in its own frame and then rotating the entire frame. You can rotate any object from 180 degrees to –180 degrees — basically, full circle. You can rotate in increments as small as 0.01 degree by using the Rotate tool or as small as 0.001 degree by using the Rotation Angle field on the Transform pane or Control palette. (Figure 18-5 shows the rotation settings in the Control palette.)

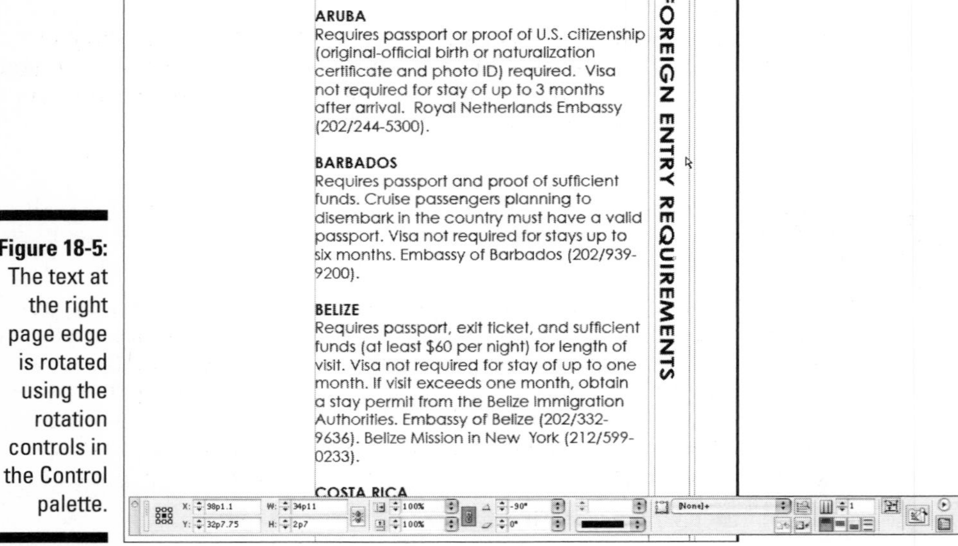

Figure 18-5: The text at the right page edge is rotated using the rotation controls in the Control palette.

Using the Rotation Angle field

Use the Rotation Angle field on Control palette or the Transform pane if you know the angle you need. For example, to run text along the right side of the page, like in the travel guide shown in Figure 18-5, you rotate the frame –90 degrees. To use the Rotation Angle field, select the object with the Selection tool. Then choose an option from the pop-up menu, which offers 30-degree increments, or enter a value in the field. Press Return or Enter to rotate the object.

When entering rotation angles, a positive number rotates the frame clockwise, and a negative number rotates the frame counterclockwise.

Using the Rotate tool

If you want to experiment with rotating text to different angles while you design your pages, use the Rotate tool. To rotate items freehand, select the Rotate tool by clicking it in the Tools palette.

If the object you want to rotate isn't selected, ⌘+click it or Ctrl+click it. Drag in any direction to rotate the object, releasing the mouse button as necessary to check the placement and any text wrap. To restrict the rotation to 45-degree increments, hold the Shift key while you drag.

You can also double-click the Rotate tool to get a dialog box in which you enter a precise rotation value. Not only can you set the rotation amount, you can control whether the content rotates with the frame or whether the rotation applies to a copy of the item.

Scaling Text

While you're figuring out the design specifications for a layout, you'll probably find yourself changing type sizes, object placement, and colors as you go. Changing the size of text can become a bit tedious — especially if the text is tucked into its own frame. You have to select the Type tool, highlight the text, enter a new size, and then often switch to the Selection tool to resize the frame so the text doesn't overflow. For a more interactive method of resizing text, you can use the Scale tool to resize the text and its frame at the same time.

To use the Scale tool, click it in the Tools palette. If the text frame is not already selected it, you need to ⌘+click or Ctrl+click it. Then simply drag any frame edge or handle in any direction. To scale proportionally so the text is not distorted, press the Shift key while you drag. The amount of scaling is reported in the Scale X Percentage and Scale Y Percentage fields in the Control palette or in the Transform pane.

Be careful when you scale text frames and the text within them. If you modify multiple text frames that contain similar items (such as headlines), you could end up with inconsistent text formatting for items that should be similar, and this design error will not give your document the professional look you desire. Scale text only when the text is used as a unique element, such as a headline in an ad.

Custom Underline and Strikethrough Options

You can use InDesign to create text with custom underlines and strikethroughs. Although you should use these effects sparingly, they can be effective for signs and other design-oriented text presentations, such as the examples shown in Figure 18-6.

Scratch these rules.

Sign up here!

Figure 18-6: Examples of custom underlines and strikethroughs.

You can find both the Underline Options and Strikethrough Options menu items in the Character pane's and Control palette's palette menus, and you can use these menu options to get just the look you're interested in. (Note that you must have the character variant of the Control palette selected to access these options; click the A button to display it.) The process for setting both Underline Options and Strikethrough Options is similar:

1. **Highlight the text to which you want the custom underline or strikethrough.**
2. **Specify the thickness, type, color, and other settings for the line that makes up the underline or the strikethrough line.**

If you choose an underline or strikethrough line type that has gaps — such as dashed, dotted, or striped lines — you can also choose a gap color. Figure 18-7 shows the Underline Options dialog box.

Figure 18-7: The Underline Options dialog box. At right is the list of line types available for underlines.

3. **Apply the underline style via the Control palette, Character pane, or keyboard shortcut (Shift+⌘+U or Ctrl+Shift+U). Apply the strikethrough style via the Control palette, Character pane, or keyboard shortcut (Shift+⌘+/ or Ctrl+Shift+/).**

Note that a custom underline or strikethrough created and applied this way is in effect only for the first text to which an underline or strikethrough is applied. InDesign reverts to the standard settings the next time you apply an underline or strikethrough. If you want to use a custom underline or strikethrough setting repeatedly, you should define the setting as part of a character style.

Working with Tabs and Tables

Tabs and tables in InDesign work somewhat like the same functions in Microsoft Word, so if you're familiar with Word's tabs and tables, it'll be a quick adjustment to InDesign's, at least for the basic capabilities.

Setting tabs

To set tabs in InDesign you use the Tabs pane, which floats above your text so that you can keep it open until you're finished experimenting with tabs. To open the Tabs pane, choose Window➪Type & Tables➪Tabs or press Shift+⌘+T or Ctrl+Shift+T. Figure 18-8 shows the Tabs pane along with a simple table created using one tab stop.

Four buttons — Left, Center, Right, and Align On — on the Tabs pane let you control how the text aligns with the tab you're creating. The Align On option is usually used for decimal tabs, which means that a period in the text aligns on the tab stop. But you can align on any character, not just periods — simply specify the align-on character in the Align On field. (If you enter nothing in the Align On field, InDesign assumes you want to align to periods.)

The X field of the Tabs pane lets you specify a position for a new tab stop. You can type a value in this field in 0.01-point increments, and then press Shift+Enter or Shift+Return to create a tab. InDesign positions tabs relative to the left edge of the text frame or column. Or you can just click the mouse on the ruler where you want the tab to be, as described later.

Rather than typing values in the X field, you can position tabs by clicking on the ruler at the bottom of the Tabs pane. You can also drag tab stops within the ruler.

If you need a tab flush with the right margin, for example, to position a dingbat at the end of the story, press Shift+Tab — there's no need to use the Tabs pane.

Bereaved Families of Ontario	905-318-0070
Big Brothers of Halton	905-637-9911
Big Sister of Oakville	905-338-0238
Child Support Guidelines	1-800-980-4962
Children's Aid	905-333-4441
Children's Information	905-815-2045
Halton Child & Youth Services	905-339-3525
Halton Autism Resource Team	905-339-3522
Halton Child Care Registry	905-875-0235
Halton Consumer Credit Counseling	905-842-1459
Halton Family Services.	905-845-3811
Halton Preschool Speech & Language Program.	905-815-1551
Halton Region	905-825-6000
Halton Trauma Centre	905-825-3242
Halton Women's Place (24-hour Crisis Line).	905-878-8555
Healthy Babies Healthy Children	905-693-4242
Kids Help Phone	416-586-0100

Figure 18-8: The Tabs pane and a table created using tab settings.

InDesign lets you specify up to eight characters, including special characters that will repeat to fill any white space. This is called a *leader.* When you set a leader for a tab stop, the leaders actually fill any space prior to that tab stop (between the previous text and the tab location). To spread out the leader characters, type spaces between the characters you enter. Don't enter spaces before and after a single character though, as that will result in two spaces between the characters when the pattern repeats (unless that's the look you're going for).

In addition to setting tabs in the Tabs pane, InDesign provides two additional options through the palette menu: Clear All and Repeat Tab.

- The Clear All command deletes any tabs you've created, and any text positioned with tabs reverts to the position of the default tab stops. (You can delete an individual tab stop by dragging its icon off the ruler.)
- The Repeat Tab command lets you create a string of tabs across the ruler that are all the same distance apart. When you select a tab on the ruler and choose this command, InDesign measures the distance between the selected tab and the previous tab (or, if it's the first tab on the ruler, the distance between the selected tab and the left indent/text inset). The program then uses this distance to place new tabs, with the same alignment, all the way across the ruler. InDesign repeats tabs only to the right of the selected tab, but it inserts tabs between other tab stops.

Setting up tables

You can create tables using tabs. But the more complex the table, the more work that requires. So make your life easier and use InDesign's table editor, which lets you specify almost any attribute imaginable in a table through the Table pane and the Table menu.

InDesign lets you import tables from Microsoft Word, RTF, and Microsoft Excel files, including some of their cell formatting. Likewise, you can convert their tables to tabbed text by using the options in the Import Options dialog box that is accessible when you place a file through the Place dialog box (File⇨Place, or ⌘+D or Ctrl+D), as covered in Chapter 14.

To create a table in InDesign, you first create or select a text frame with the Type tool and then choose Table⇨Insert Table or press Option+Shift+⌘+T or Ctrl+Alt+Shift+T. That produces the Insert Table dialog box, where you type the number of body rows and columns and the number of header and footer rows. Click OK to have InDesign create the basic table, which will be set as wide as the text frame. The depth will be based on the number of rows, with each row defaulting to the height that will hold 12-point text.

With the basic table in place, you now format it using the Table pane and the Table menu. The pane contains cell formatting tools: You can increase or decrease the number of rows and columns, set the row and column height, set the text's vertical alignment within selected cells (top, middle, bottom, and justified), choose one of four text-rotation angles, and set the text margin within a cell separately for the top, bottom, left, and right. Note that all the Table pane's options affect only the currently selected cell(s), except for the Number of Rows and Number of Columns fields. Figure 18-9 shows the Table pane with its icons defined.

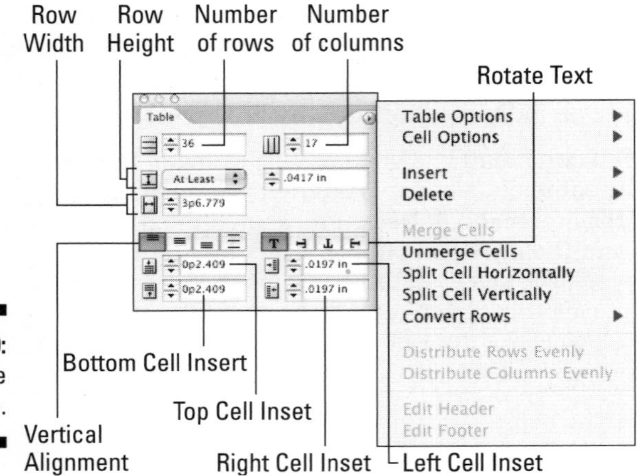

Figure 18-9: The Table pane.

You set cell text's horizontal alignment using the paragraph formatting controls covered in Chapter 17. You can apply character formatting to cell text as described in Chapters 16. You can also apply tabs within cells using the Tabs pane covered earlier in this chapter.

To add items to a table, you can type text in any cell, paste text or graphics into a cell, or place text or graphics into a cell by choosing File⇨Place or pressing ⌘+D or Ctrl+D.

For more sophisticated table attributes, use the Table Options dialog box and its five panes. These are expert features, so they're not covered in this book.

Converting tabs to tables

Often, you'll have a table done using tabs — whether imported from a word processor or originally created in InDesign with tabs — that you want to convert to a real InDesign table. That's easy. Select the tabbed text you want to covert and choose Table➪Convert Text to Table.

In the Convert Text to Table dialog box, you can choose a Column Separator (Tab, Comma, Paragraph, or a text string you type in the field) or a Row Separator (same options). Although most textual data uses tabs to separate columns and paragraphs to separate rows, you may encounter other data that uses something else. For example, spreadsheets and databases often save data so that commas separate columns rather than tabs. That's why InDesign lets you choose the separator characters before conversion.

During the conversion, InDesign formats the table using the standard settings, using the current text formatting and the default cell insets and stroke types. You can then adjust the table using the tools covered earlier in this chapter. Note that the conversion treats all rows as body rows.

You can also convert a table to text by selecting multiple cells or an entire table, as described earlier, and choosing Table➪Convert Table to Text. InDesign presents the same options as it does in the Convert Text to Table dialog box, so you can determine how the converted data appears.

Part V
Graphics Essentials

"Of course graphics are important to your project, Eddy, but I think it would've been better to scan a picture of your worm collection."

In this part . . .

They say a picture is worth a thousand words. Well, a lot of them are. Graphics make layouts come alive, providing a visceral connection that text by itself just cannot. So it should be no surprise that InDesign has tons of features to work and even create graphics. This part shows you how to work with imported graphics files, cropping them and applying effects to them. You'll also learn how to draw your own shapes and edit them as you refine your layout. And you'll discover how to convert text to graphics, giving you a whole new creative arrow in your design quiver.

Chapter 19

Importing Pictures

In This Chapter

- Preparing pictures for use in InDesign
- Importing and placing pictures
- Working with layered images
- Managing links to source files

What is a layout without pictures? Boring, that's what. And that's why InDesign lets you import a wide variety of picture types, so you have a lot of choices and flexibility in the images you use.

And through the Mac and Windows Clipboards (copy and paste), you can import file formats — to a limited degree — that are not directly supported by InDesign.

The terms *picture* and *graphic* are interchangeable, referring to any type of graphic. An *image* is a bitmapped graphic, such as that produced by an image editor, digital camera, or scanner, while an *illustration* or *drawing* is a vector file produced by an illustration program.

Preparing Graphics Files

InDesign offers support for many major formats of graphics files. Some formats are more appropriate than others for certain kinds of tasks. The basic rules for creating your graphics files are as follows:

- Save line art (drawings) in a format such as EPS, PDF, Adobe Illustrator, Windows Metafile (WMF), Enhanced Metafile (EMF), or PICT. (These object-oriented formats are called *vector* formats. Vector files are composed of instructions on how to draw various shapes.) InDesign works best with EPS, PDF, and Illustrator files.

- Save bitmaps (photos and scans) in a format such as TIFF, Adobe Photoshop, PNG, JPEG, PCX, Windows Bitmap (BMP), GIF, Scitex Continuous Tone (SCT), or PICT. (These pixel-oriented formats are called *raster* formats. Raster files are composed of a series of dots, or pixels, that make up the image.) InDesign works best with TIFF and Photoshop files.

Make EPS and TIFF formats your standards, because these have become the standard graphics formats in publishing. If you and your service bureau are working almost exclusively with Adobe software, you can add the PDF, Illustrator, and Photoshop formats to this mix. (The Illustrator and PDF formats are variants of EPS.) If you use transparency in your graphics, it's best to save them in Photoshop, Illustrator, or PDF formats, because other formats (particularly EPS and TIFF) remove much of the transparency layering data that will help an imagesetter optimally reproduce those transparent files.

The graphic file formats that InDesign imports include (the text in monofont is the PC filename extension for the format):

- **BMP:** The native Windows bitmap format. `.bmp`, `.dib`
- **EPS:** The Encapsulated PostScript vector format favored by professional publishers. `.eps`
- **GIF:** The Graphics Interchange Format common in Web documents. `.gif`
- **JPEG:** The Joint Photographic Experts Group compressed bitmap format often used on the Web. `.jpg`
- **Illustrator:** The native format in Adobe Illustrator 5.5 through CS2. This file format is similar to EPS. `.ai`
- **PCX:** The PC Paintbrush format that was very popular in DOS programs and early version of Windows; it has now been largely supplanted by other formats. `.pcx`, `.rle`
- **PDF:** The Portable Document Format that is a variant of EPS and is used for Web-, network-, and CD-based documents. InDesign CS2 supports PDF versions 1.3 through 1.6 (the formats used in Acrobat 4 through 7). `.pdf`
- **Photoshop:** The native format in Adobe Photoshop 5.0 through CS2. `.psd`
- **PICT:** Short for *Picture,* the Mac's native graphics format until Mac OS X (it can be bitmap or vector) that is little used in professional documents and is becoming less common even for inexpensive clip art. `.pct`
- **PNG:** The Portable Network Graphics format that Adobe introduced several years ago as a more capable alternative to GIF. `.png`
- **QuickTime movie:** For use in interactive documents, InDesign supports this Apple-created, cross-platform format. `.mov`

- **Scitex CT:** The continuous-tone bitmap format used on Scitex prepress systems. `.ct`
- **TIFF:** The Tagged Image File Format that is the bitmap standard for professional image editors and publishers. `.tif`, `.tiff`
- **Windows Metafile:** The format native to Windows but little used in professional documents. Since Office 2000, Microsoft applications create a new version called Enhanced Metafile, also supported by InDesign. `.wmf`, `.emf`

Spot colors (called spot inks in Photoshop) are imported into InDesign when you place Photoshop, Illustrator, and PDF images into InDesign. They appear in the Swatches pane, which is covered in Chapter 10.

Importing and Placing Pictures

It's important to understand that when you import a graphic into a document, InDesign establishes a link between the graphics file and the document file and then sends the original graphics file to the printer when the document is output.

InDesign links to graphics because a graphics file, particularly a high-resolution scanned graphic, can be very large. If the entire graphics file is included in an InDesign document when you import it, InDesign documents would quickly become prohibitively large. Instead, InDesign saves a low-resolution preview of an imported graphics file with the document, and it's this file that you see displayed on-screen. InDesign remembers the location of the original file and uses this information when printing.

The Place command (File⇨Place, or ⌘+D or Ctrl+D) is the method you typically use to bring pictures into your InDesign layout. Here's how to use the Place command to import a graphic:

1. **Choose File⇨Place or press ⌘+D or Ctrl+D.**

   If you want to import a graphic into an *existing frame,* select the target frame using either of the selection tools (either before you choose File⇨Place or afterwards). If you want InDesign to create a *new frame* when you import the graphic, make sure no object is selected when you choose Place. Either way, the Place dialog box appears, as shown in Figure 19-1.

   You can import a graphic into any kind of frame or shape (including a curved line created with the Pen tool) except a straight line. Be carefu
   If the Type tool is selected when you use the Place command to imp
   graphic into a selected text frame, you'll create an inline graphic at
   text cursor's location.

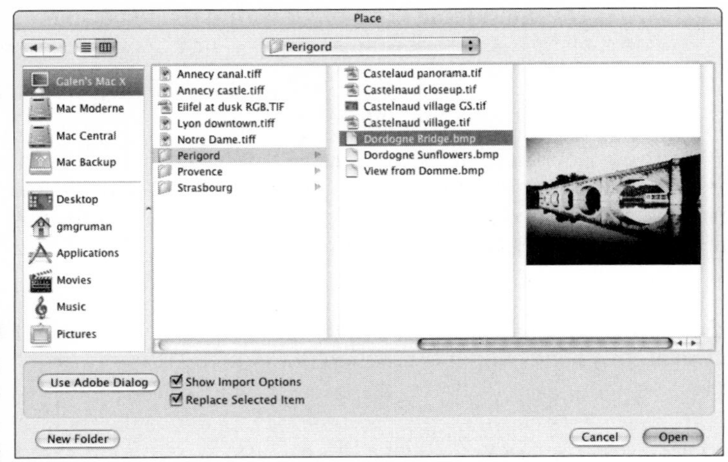

Figure 19-1: The Place dialog box.

2. **Use the controls in the Place dialog box to locate and select the graphics file you want to import.**

   If you want to display import options that let you control how the selected graphics file is imported, either select Show Import Options, and then click Open; or hold down the Shift key and double-click on the filename or Shift+click Open. If you choose to Show Import Options, the EPS Import Options, Place PDF, or Image Import Options dialog box, depending on what kind of graphic you are importing, is displayed.

3. **Specify the desired import options, if any are applicable, and then click OK.**

   These options are covered later in this chapter.

4. **You can place the graphic in an existing frame or in a new frame, as follows:**

   - If an empty frame is selected, the graphic is automatically placed in the frame. The upper-left corner of the graphic is placed in the upper-left corner of the frame, and the frame acts as the cropping shape for the graphic.
   - If a frame already holding a graphic is selected, InDesign will replace the existing graphic with the new one if you've selected the Replace Selected Item check box in the Place dialog box. Otherwise, InDesign will assume you want to put the new graphic in a new frame.
   - To place the graphic into a new frame, click the loaded-graphic icon on an empty portion of a page or on the pasteboard. The point where you click establishes the upper-left corner of the resulting graphics frame, which is the same size as the imported graphic and which acts as the graphic's cropping shape.

- To place the graphic in an existing, unselected frame, click in the frame with the loaded-graphic icon. The upper-left corner of the graphic is placed in the upper-left corner of the frame, and the frame acts as a cropping shape.

After you place a graphic, it's displayed in the frame that contains it, and the frame is selected. If the Selection tool is selected, the eight handles of its bounding box are displayed; if the Direct Selection tool is selected, handles are displayed only in the corners. At this point, you can modify either the frame or the graphic within, or you can move on to another task.

When importing JPEG files, InDesign CS2 now automatically scales the image to fit in the page. This feature helps deal with digital-camera graphics that tend to be very large in dimension, so when imported end up taking much more than the width of a page. While you'll likely still need to scale the image to fit your layout, you can at least see the whole image before doing so.

Specifying Import Options

If you've ever used a graphics application — for example, an image-editing program like Adobe Photoshop or an illustration program like Adobe Illustrator or Macromedia FreeHand — you're probably aware that when you save a graphics file, you have several options that control such things as file format, image size, color depth, preview quality, and so on. When you save a graphics file, the settings you specify are determined by the way in which the image will be used. For example, you could use Photoshop to save a high-resolution TIFF version of a scanned graphic for use in a slick, four-color annual report or a low-resolution GIF version of the same graphic for use on the company's Web page. Or you could use Illustrator or FreeHand to create a corporate logo that you'll use in various sizes in many of your printed publications.

If you choose to specify custom import settings when you import a graphics file, the choices you make will depend on the nature of the publication. For example, if it's bound for the Web, there's no need to work with or save graphics using resolutions that exceed a computer monitor's 72-dpi resolution. Along the same lines, if the publication will be printed, the image import settings you specify for a newspaper that will be printed on newsprint on a SWOP (Specification for Web-Offset Printing) press will be different than those you specify for a four-color magazine printed on coated paper using a sheet-fed press.

If you select Show Import Options when you place a graphic, the options d' played in the resulting dialog boxes depend on the file format of the selec' graphic. When you set options for a particular file, the options you specify remain in effect for that file format until you change them. If you don't select the Show Import Options check box when you place a graphic, the most recent settings for the file format of the selected graphic are used.

Import options for bitmap graphics

InDesign gives you two sets of import options for the following types of bitmap images: TIFF, GIF, JPEG, Scitex CT, BMP, and PCX. You get three options for PNG files, and a different set of three for Photoshop files. No import options are available for PICT or QuickTime movie files. Figure 19-2 shows three of the four possible panes for bitmap images: The Image and Color panes are for most bitmap formats; PNG files have a third pane, PNG Settings, and Photoshop files also have a third pane, Layers, covered later in this chapter.

The Image pane lets you apply any embedded clipping path and/or alpha channel to the image in order to mask, or cut out, part of the image. Check the Apply Photoshop Clipping Path option to import the clipping path along with the image; select an alpha channel from the Alpha Channel pop-up menu to import the alpha channel along with the image. (Chapter 20 covers clipping paths in more detail.)

Color pane

In the Color pane, you can turn on color management for the image and control how the image is displayed. Check the Enable Color Management option to enable color management.

Using the Profile pop-up menu, choose a color-source profile that matches the device (scanner, digital camera, and so on) or software used to create the file. InDesign will try to translate the colors in the file to the colors that the output device is capable of producing. (These profiles are installed in your operating system by other applications, not by InDesign.)

Use the Rendering Intent pop-up menu to determine how InDesign translates the color in the selected graphics file with the gamut of the output device. If the graphic is a scanned photograph, choose Perceptual (Images). The other options — Saturation (Graphics), Relative Colorimetric, and Absolute Colorimetric — are appropriate for images that contain mostly areas of solid color, such as Illustrator EPS files that have been opened in Photoshop and saved as TIFFs.

PNG Settings pane

Use the PNG Settings pane — available only if you place a PNG file — to use the transparency information in a PNG file, assuming it has a transparent background. You have two choices for controlling transparency handling: White Background and File-Defined Background. The former forces the transparent portion to display as white in InDesign; the latter uses whatever background color is specified in the PNG file itself.

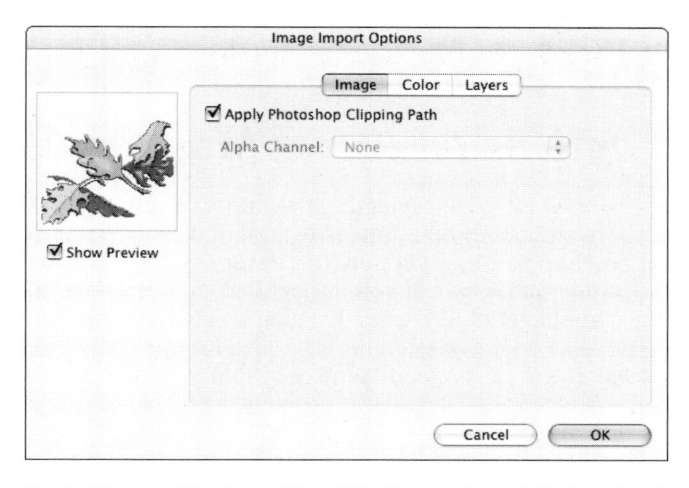

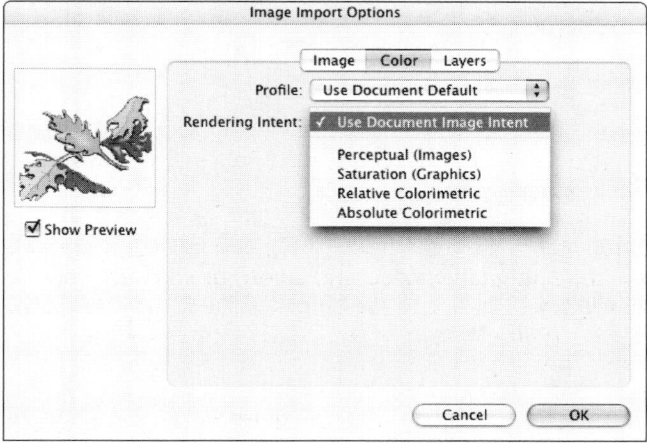

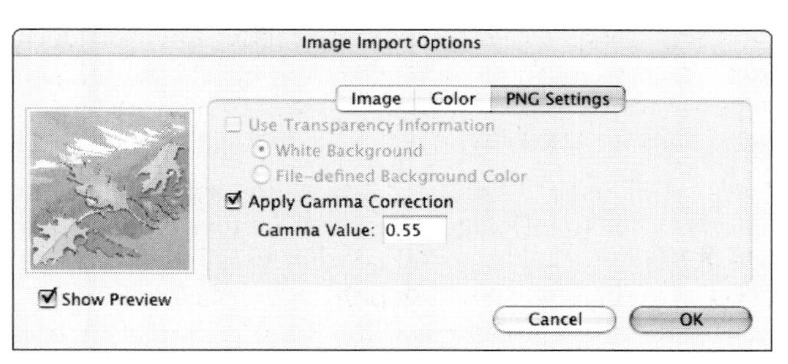

Figure 19-2: The Image, Color, and PNG Settings panes in the Image Import Options dialog box.

This pane also lets you adjust the gamma value during import — the gamma is a setting that describes the color temperature of a device, and to ensure most accurate reproduction, you'd want the gamma setting for the PNG file to be the same as that of your output device (a printer or monitor). It is meant to correct for the file being created on a specific type of monitor. However, to use this feature, you need to know the gamma setting for the final output device. If you don't, leave it alone.

Import options for vector file formats

If you're importing vector files, selecting the Import Options check box will result in one of two dialog boxes appearing, depending on what the vector file type is. If you import older-version Illustrator or EPS files, you'll get the EPS Import Options dialog box; if you import PDF and newer-version Illustrator files, you'll get the Place PDF dialog box, which has two panes. (Both dialog boxes are shown in Figure 19-3.) No import options are available for Windows Metafile or Enhanced Metafile graphics.

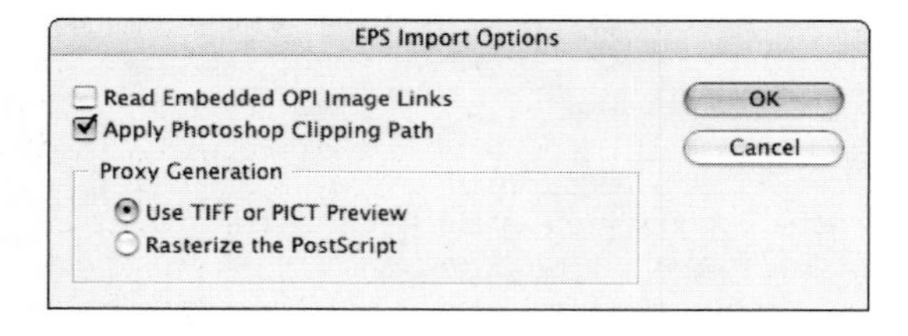

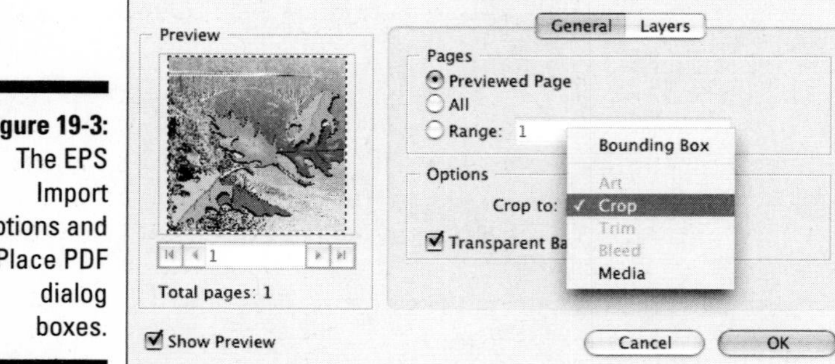

Figure 19-3: The EPS Import Options and Place PDF dialog boxes.

Illustrator CS and CS2 use PDF as their native file format, even though the filename extension is `.ai`, so InDesign detects these files as PDF files and provides the PDF options during import. In earlier versions of Illustrator, the native format was actually a variant of EPS.

EPS Import Options dialog box

Use this dialog box to import any clipping paths embedded in images that are in the EPS file. Check the Apply Photoshop Clipping Path option to enable this option.

Also, use this pane to control how the EPS file appears on-screen in InDesign. If you select the Use TIFF or PICT Preview option, InDesign will use the low-resolution proxy image embedded in the EPS file for display on-screen and print the graphic using the embedded high-resolution PostScript instructions. If you select the Rasterize the PostScript option, InDesign will convert the PostScript file into a bitmap image during import. There's rarely a reason to rasterize an imported EPS file — it just takes up some of your valuable time.

Place PDF dialog box

When you use the Place command to import a PDF file and you select the Show Import Options check box, the Place PDF file dialog box, shown in Figure 19-4, is displayed. It provides several controls for specifying how the file is imported. The General pane provides the following options:

- In the Pages section, select Previewed Page, All, or Range to determine which page(s) you want to import. You can change the previewed page by using the arrow buttons under the preview image at left or entering a specific page number in the field below the preview image. If you want to import a range, use commas to separate pages and a hyphen to indicate range; for example, **3, 5-9, 13** will import pages 3, 5 through 9, and 13.

  When you place the PDF in InDesign, you'll get a separate loaded-graphic icon for each page, so as you place each page, a new loaded-graphic icon will appear for the next page, until there are no more to place. You can tell you're placing multiple pages because the loaded-graphics icon will have a plus sign in it.

- In the Options section, select one of the cropping options from the Crop To pop-up menu. If you choose Content, the page's bounding box or a rectangle that encloses all items, including page marks, is used to build the graphics frame. Choosing Art places the area defined by the file's creator, if any, as placeable artwork. For example, the person who created the file might have designated a particular graphic as placeable artwork. Choosing Crop places the area displayed and printed by Adobe Acrobat. Choosing Trim places the graphic in an area equal to the final, trimmed piece. Choosing Bleed places the page area plus any specified bleed area. Choosing Media places an area defined by the paper size specified for the PDF document, including page marks.
- Also in the Options section, select the Transparent Background check box if you want the white areas of the PDF page to be transparent. Uncheck this option if you want to preserve the page's opaque white background.

The ability to import multiple pages from a PDF file is new to InDesign CS2.

Working with image layers

InDesign CS2 now lets you work with individual layers in some imported graphics. What that means is that you have more control over what displays because you can turn on or off individual layers. Of course, to use this capability, the source graphic must be constructed with multiple layers.

Use the Layers pane in the Image Import Options dialog box or the Place PDF dialog box to select which layer(s) you want visible in InDesign. (The Layers pane is available only if you place an Illustrator, PDF, or Photoshop graphic.) You will see a list of image layers. Any that have the Eye icon will display in InDesign, and you can select or deselect layers by clicking the box to the right of the layer name to make the Eye icon appear or disappear. (You cannot change their order — you'd need to go back to Photoshop or Illustrator and change the layer order there.) Figure 19-4 shows the Layers pane.

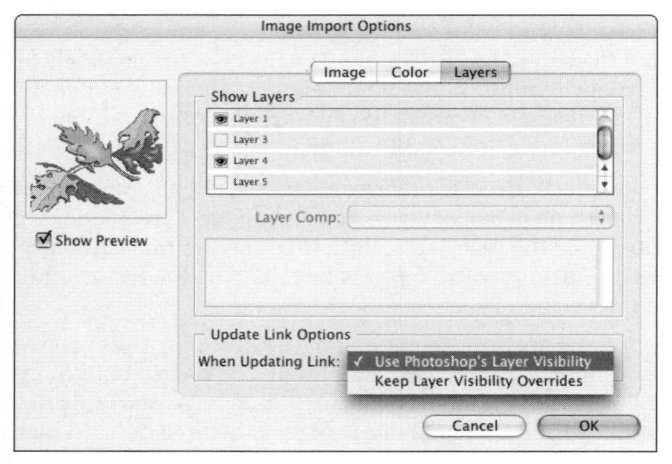

Figure 19-4: The Layers pane of the EPS Import Options and Place PDF dialog boxes.

Although you can save an image file in the TIFF format and preserve any layers, InDesign CS2 does not give you the ability to manage which layers you import from a TIFF file into InDesign.

There's also an option, in the When Updating Link pop-up menu, to control how changes to the file are handled in terms of layer management: If you choose Use Photoshop's Layer Visibility or Use Illustrator's Layer Visibility, InDesign will make all layers that are visible in Photoshop or Illustrator visible when you update the link to the graphic from InDesign. If you choose

Keep Layer Visibility Overrides in the When Updating Link pop-up menu, InDesign will import only the layers chosen in this dialog box if you later update the graphic in Photoshop or Illustrator.

Using Other Ways to Import Graphics

If you want to specify custom import options for an imported graphics file, you must use the Place command. However, if you don't need this level of control, InDesign offers three other options for importing graphics:

- You can use your computer's Copy (File⇨Copy, or ⌘+C or Ctrl+C) and Paste (File⇨Paste, or ⌘+V or Ctrl+V) commands to move a graphics file between two InDesign documents or from a document created with another program into an InDesign document. If you copy an object in an InDesign document and then paste it into a different InDesign document, the copy retains all the attributes of the original, as well as the link to the original graphics file. Otherwise, a link between the original graphics file and the InDesign document is *not* established; the graphic becomes part of the InDesign document, as though you created it using InDesign tools.
- You can drag and drop graphics file icons from your computer's desktop into InDesign documents. A link between the original graphics file and the document is established, just as it would be if you had used the Place command.
- For Illustrator files, you can drag objects directly from Illustrator into InDesign. Each object becomes a separate, editable InDesign object, as though you had created it in InDesign. (And no links are established to the source file.)

If you use these methods to add a graphic to an InDesign document, some of the attributes of the original graphic may not survive the trip. The operating system, the file format, and the capabilities of the originating application all play roles in determining which attributes are preserved. If you want to be safe, use the Place command.

Managing Links and Versions

The Links pane (Window⇨Links, or Shift+⌘+D or Ctrl+Shift+D) is a handy place to manage the links to your graphics, particularly when you need to update them. (Figure 19-5 shows the Links pane.) The first eight commands in the Links pane's palette menu let you reestablish links to missing and modified graphics files, display an imported graphic in the document window, open the program used to create a graphic file, and work on copies and versions of the source graphics:

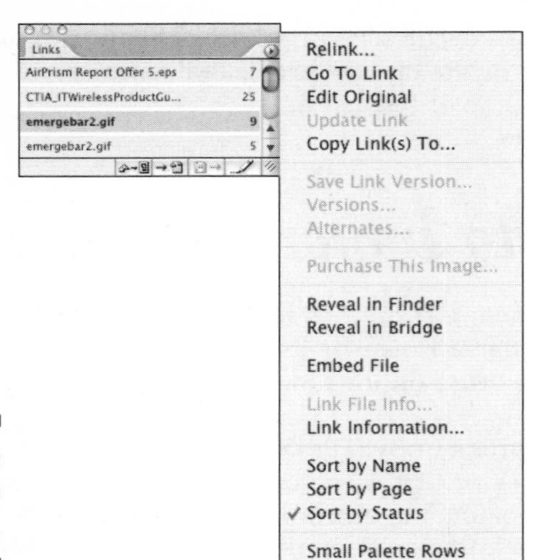

Figure 19-5: The Links pane.

- **Relink:** This command, and the Relink button (the leftmost at the bottom of the pane), lets you reestablish a missing link or replace the original file you imported with a different file. When you choose Relink or click the button, the Relink dialog box is displayed and shows the original path name and filename. You can enter a new path name and filename in the Location field, but it's easier to click Browse, which opens a standard Open a File dialog box. Use the controls to locate and select the original file or a different file, and then click OK. (You can also drag and drop a file icon from the Mac OS Finder or Windows Explorer directly into the Relink dialog box.) If you want to restore broken links to multiple files, highlight their filenames in the scroll list, and then choose Relink or click the Update Link button.
- **Go To Link:** Choose this option, or click the Go to Link button (second from left) to display the highlighted graphics file in the document window. InDesign will, if necessary, navigate to the correct page and center the image in the document window. You can also display a particular graphic by double-clicking its name in the scroll list while holding down the Option or Alt key.
- **Edit Original:** If you want to modify an imported graphic, choose Edit Original from the palette menu or click the Edit Original button (far right). InDesign will try to locate and open the program used to create the file. This may or may not be possible, depending on the original program, the file format, and the programs available on your computer.
- **Update Link:** Choose this option or click the Update Link button (third from the left) to update the link to a modified graphic. Highlight multiple filenames, and then choose Update Link or click the Update Link button to update all links at once.

To update multiple links at once, select all the links you want to modify in the Links pane (Shift+click to select a range; ⌘+click or Ctrl+click to select noncontiguous files), and then choose Update Link from the palette menu.

When you update missing and modified graphics, any transformations — rotation, shear, scale, and so on — that you've applied to the graphics or their frames are maintained.

- **Copy Link To:** Choose this option to copy the source graphic to a new location and update the link so that it refers to this new copy.

The Copy Link To, Versions, and Alternates menu options are new to InDesign CS2. (The Versions and Alternates options are expert Version Cue features and thus not covered in this book.)

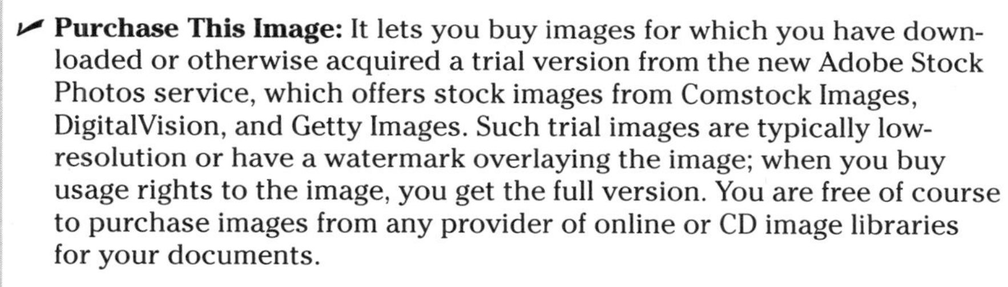

- **Purchase This Image:** It lets you buy images for which you have downloaded or otherwise acquired a trial version from the new Adobe Stock Photos service, which offers stock images from Comstock Images, DigitalVision, and Getty Images. Such trial images are typically low-resolution or have a watermark overlaying the image; when you buy usage rights to the image, you get the full version. You are free of course to purchase images from any provider of online or CD image libraries for your documents.

- **Reveal in Finder (Macintosh) and Reveal in Explorer (Windows):** This menu option will open a window displaying the contents of the folder that contains the source file, so you can perhaps move, copy, or rename it. (The Reveal in Bridge option is a similar feature for the expert Version Cue capability not covered in this book.)
- **Embed:** This option lets you embed the complete file of any imported graphic. (InDesign normally imports only a low-resolution screen preview when you place a graphic that is 48K or larger.) If you want to ensure that the graphics file will forever remain with a document, you can choose to embed it — however, by embedding graphics, you'll be producing larger document files, which means it will take you longer to open and save them. To embed a graphic, click on its name in the scroll list, and then choose Embed from the Links pane's palette menu. An alert is displayed and informs you about the increased document size that will result. Click Yes to embed the file.
- **Link Information:** This option displays the Link Information dialog box, which actually doesn't let you do much. (The Previous and Next buttons let you display information about the previous and next files in the list, but that's about it.) But it does display 11 sometimes-useful bits of information about the highlighted graphics file, including its name, status, creation date, file type, and location.

- **Sort by Status:** This option lists files with missing links first, followed by files that have been modified, and finally files whose status is okay.
- **Sort by Name:** This option lists all files in alphabetical order.
- **Sort by Page:** This option lists imported files on page 1 first, followed by imported files on page 2, and so on.
- **Small Palette Rows:** This option lets you reduce the size of text in the pane and decrease the space between entries so that you can see more entries at once. Of course, the reduced rows are also harder to read. To go back to the normal display size, simply select this option again.

Chapter 20

Special Effects with Graphics

In This Chapter

- Cropping and resizing graphics
- Rotating, shearing, and flipping graphics
- Applying color to bitmapped graphics
- Working with graphics in irregular shapes
- Using the Scissors tool

After you import a graphic into an InDesign document, you can modify either the graphic or the frame that contains it. The most common actions you'll take are cropping and resizing. *Cropping* is a fancy term for deciding what part of the picture to show. *Resizing* is, of course, making the picture bigger or smaller. But you'll also apply other effects — at least some of the time — such as rotating, shearing, flipping, and colorizing. And if you want to get really fancy, you might work with clipping paths to create "masks" around picture portions or even cut the graphic into pieces.

In almost every case, you select graphics with the Direct Selection tool to apply effects to the graphic, rather to the frame. If you use the Selection tool, the work you do will apply to the frame, as Chapter 12 explains.

Cropping and Resizing

Remember, when you import a graphic using the Place command (File⇨Place, or ⌘+D or Ctrl+D) or by dragging a graphics file into a document window, that the graphic is contained in a graphics frame — either the frame that was selected when you placed the graphic or the frame that was automatically created if a frame wasn't selected. The upper-left corner of an imported graphic is automatically placed in the upper-left corner of its frame.

Cropping graphics

The easiest way to crop a graphic is to resize the frame that contains it. To resize the frame, go to Chapter 12. Note that resizing the frame does *not* resize the graphic.

You can also click on a graphic with the Direct Selection tool, and then drag the graphic within its frame to reveal and conceal different parts of the graphic. For example, you could crop the top and left edges of a graphic by dragging the graphic above and to the left of its original position (in the upper-left corner of the frame).

Of course, you could accomplish the same thing by selecting the frame with the Selection tool and dragging the upper-left corner down and to the right. The advantage of moving the image within the frame is that you don't have to move the frame from its desired position in the layout.

You can also use the Control palette (Window⇨Control, or Option+⌘+6 or Ctrl+Alt+6), shown in Figure 20-1, to crop a graphic. (You can also use the Transform pane [Window⇨Object & Layout⇨Transform or F9], also shown in Figure 20-1.) Select the graphic with the Direct Selection tool and crop it by changing the values in the X+ and/or Y+ fields.

If you want to *mask out* (hide) portions of an imported graphic, you have the option of using an irregular shape as the frame, a graphic's built-in clipping path (if it has one), or a clipping path you generated in InDesign (by choosing Object⇨Clipping Path or pressing Option+Shift+⌘+K or Ctrl+Alt+Shift+K). Clipping paths are covered later in this chapter.

Resizing graphics

To resize a graphic, be sure to choose the Direct Selection tool, then enter new Scale X and Scale Y Percentage values in the Control palette or Transform pane.

If you select the graphic with the Selection tool, you are actually changing the frame's size, while if you select the graphic with the Direct Selection tool, you are actually changing the graphic's size. What's more confusing is that if you choose a graphic whose frame size is 0 points, resizing it with the Selection tool actually resizes the graphic — but the Control palette and Transform pane show you a new size of 100% if the Selection tool is active and an accurate new size if you then switch to the Direct Selection tool. So always use the Direct Selection tool to resize.

If you make a graphic larger by resizing it using the Direct Selection tool, the frame dimensions don't change, which thus causes you to crop out part of the graphic.

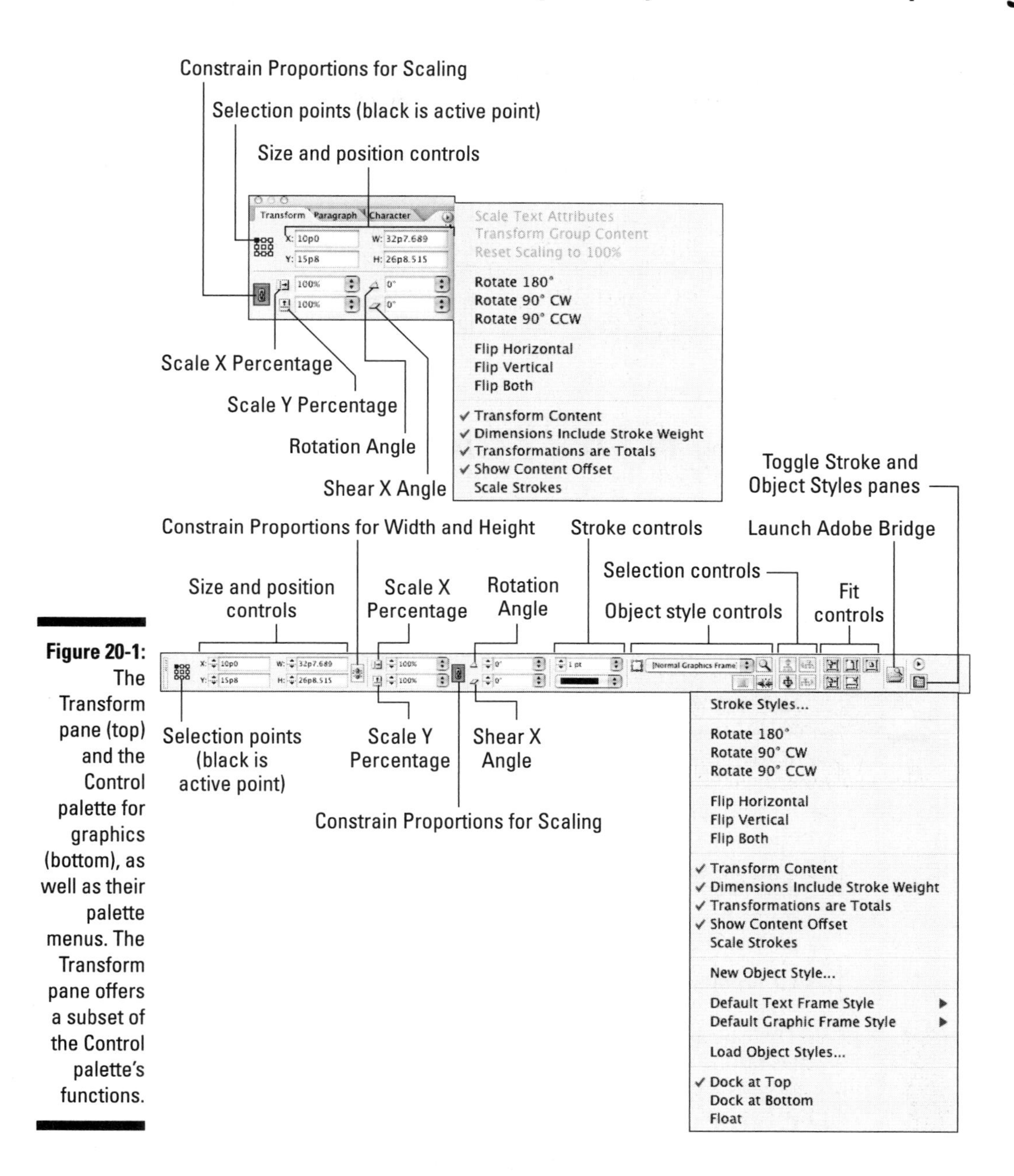

Figure 20-1: The Transform pane (top) and the Control palette for graphics (bottom), as well as their palette menus. The Transform pane offers a subset of the Control palette's functions.

You can enter size values between 1% and 10,000%. If you want to maintain a graphic's original proportions, make sure the values in the Horizontal Scale and Vertical Scale fields are the same. If you want to return a graphic to the size it was when you first imported it, specify Horizontal Scale and Vertical Scale values of 100%.

You can use math when scaling. For example, if you want the scale to be 30 percent larger, you could enter **+30%** rather than **130%**. Or you could enter **/6** to make the object one-sixth of its current size. Other legitimate actions include subtraction (for example, enter **–29%**) and multiplication (for example, type ***7**).

In addition to specifying a value in the Horizontal Scale or Vertical Scale field, you can choose one of the predefined values from the fields' pop-up menus, or you can highlight a value and press the up or down arrow keys on the keyboard. Each press of an arrow key changes the value by 1 percent. If you hold down the Shift key while clicking an arrow, the increment of change is 10 percent.

Figuring out the fitting commands

If you've placed a graphic in a frame that's either larger or smaller than the graphic, you can use the Fitting options (available by choosing Object⇨Fitting or by using the appropriate buttons in the Control palette) to scale the graphic to fit the frame proportionately or disproportionately or to scale the frame to fit the graphic. Another option lets you center the graphic in the frame. These are very handy, and a *lot* easier than trying to resize a graphic to fit using the mouse or the Control palette or Transform pane.

Keep in mind that the fitting commands for graphics are available only if you've used the Selection tool to select a graphic's frame. Here's a description of each of the five options:

- **Fit Content to Frame:** To resize a graphic to fill the selected frame, choose Object⇨Fitting⇨Fit Content to Frame or press Option+⌘+E or Ctrl+Alt+E. If the frame is larger than the graphic, the graphic is enlarged; if the frame is smaller, the graphic is reduced. If the graphic and the frame have different proportions, the graphic's proportions are changed so that the image completely fills the frame.
- **Fit Frame to Content:** To resize a frame so that it wraps snugly around a graphic, choose Fit Frame to Content or press Option+⌘+C or Ctrl+Alt+C. The frame will be enlarged or reduced depending on the size of the graphic, and the frame's proportions will be changed to match the proportions of the graphic.
- **Center Content:** To center a graphic in its frame, choose Center Content or press Shift+⌘+E or Ctrl+Shift+E. Neither the frame nor the graphic are resized when you center a graphic.
- **Fit Content Proportionally:** To resize a graphic to fit in the selected frame while maintaining the graphic's current proportions, choose Object⇨Fitting⇨Fit Content Proportionally or press Option+Shift+⌘+E or Ctrl+Alt+Shift+E. If the frame is larger than the graphic, the graphic is

enlarged; if the frame is smaller, the graphic is reduced. If the graphic and the frame have different proportions, a portion of the frame background will show above and below or to the left and right of the graphic. If you want, you can drag frame edges to make the frame shorter or narrower and eliminate any portions of the background that are visible.

- **Fill Frame Proportionally:** To resize a frame to fit the selected graphic, choose Object➪Fitting➪Fill Frame Proportionally or press Option+Shift+⌘+C or Ctrl+Alt+Shift+C. This guarantees that there will be no space between the graphic and the frame. (The Fit Frame to Content option can result in such space at the bottom and/or right sides of a graphic.)

The Fill Frame Proportionally option is new to InDesign CS2.

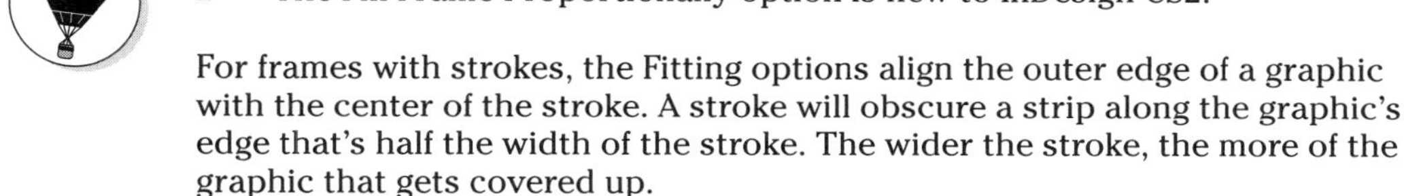

For frames with strokes, the Fitting options align the outer edge of a graphic with the center of the stroke. A stroke will obscure a strip along the graphic's edge that's half the width of the stroke. The wider the stroke, the more of the graphic that gets covered up.

Rotating, Shearing, and Flipping

Rotating, shearing, or flipping a graphic *within* its frame — leaving the frame unaffected — is essentially the same process as rotating or shearing an object (see Chapter 12). The key differences are:

- You need to use the Control palette or Transform pane to work on the contents (graphic or text), rather than on its frame. The Rotation, Shear, and Free Transform tools (described in Chapter 12) work on the frames and the content simultaneously.
- You need to select the frame with the Direct Selection tool — *not* the Selection tool — to ensure that the effects are applied to the contents, rather than to the frame itself.

Coloring Bitmapped Graphics

When it comes to performing graphic modifications in InDesign, the only difference between bitmap graphics and vector-based graphics is that you can apply color and, optionally, tint to grayscale and black-and-white bitmapped images, such as those in the TIFF and Photoshop formats. These options are not available for vector-based images and color bitmapped images. To apply color to an image, follow these steps:

1. **Click the Direct Selection tool.**
2. **Click in the graphic's frame to select the graphic.**

3. **Make sure that the Fill button is active in the Tools palette to color the image's background.**
4. **If it's not displayed, show the Swatches pane by choosing Windows➪Swatches or pressing F5.**
5. **Click a color in the Swatches pane's scroll list, or drag a swatch from the pane onto the graphic.**

Applying a *color tint* — that is, a shade or a percentage of the applied color — to a graphic is the same process as applying a color swatch. There's just one additional step: Enter a value in the Tint field in the Swatches pane. You can also use a tint swatch instead, ensuring the same tint is applied to multiple objects (see Chapter 10 for information about defining colors and tints).

Working with Graphics in Irregular Shapes

While most graphics you use will be placed in rectangular frames, InDesign does give you other choices:

- You can select any type of frame — oval or polygonal, not just rectangular — to place or copy your graphic into.
- You can draw your own shape using the Pencil or Pen tool and then place or copy your graphic into it. When you create the free-form shape, make sure that the default color for the Pen tool is set to None so that the shape you create is transparent. Otherwise, the colored area in the shape will obscure the graphic behind it.

  The Pen tool lets you create one shape at a time. The Compound Paths command lets you combine multiple shapes to create more complex objects. For example, you can place a small circle on top of a larger circle, and then use the Compound Paths command to create a doughnut-shaped object. (See Chapter 21 for more information about creating complex shapes with the Compound Paths command.)

  If you copy the graphic into a frame or shape, you must use the Paste Into command (Edit➪Paste Into, or Option+⌘+V or Ctrl+Alt+V) to place the copied graphic inside the selected shape, rather than on top of it.
- You can use a clipping path that was defined in the graphic itself when it was created or a clipping path that was created in InDesign.

So what is a clipping path, anyway? A *clipping path* is used to mask certain parts of a graphic and reveal other parts; it's basically an invisible outline placed in the graphic that InDesign can then work with. For example, if you want to create a silhouette around a single person in a crowd, open the file in an image-editing program such as Photoshop, and then create and save a clipping path that isolates the shape of the person. (You can also erase everything except the person you want to silhouette; not only can this be time-consuming, but if you want to reveal other parts of the graphic later, you're out of luck.) TIFF, Photoshop EPS, and Photoshop-native (.PSD) files can have embedded clipping paths.

Regardless of the method you use to clip an imported graphic, you can modify a clipping path by moving, adding, deleting, and changing the direction of anchor points and by moving direction lines.

You can convert a clipping path — whether imported or created in InDesign — to a frame by choosing Convert Clipping Path to Frame for a selected object using the contextual menu (right-click or Control+click the object).

See Chapter 21 for more information about modifying free-form shapes. See the *Photoshop For Dummies* series (Wiley Publishing) for more on creating clipping paths in Photoshop.

Using a graphic's own clipping path

In an ideal world, any graphics that you want to have fit in an irregular shape will come with their own clipping paths. In that wonderful situation, you would first be sure to import the clipping path when you place the graphic and then use InDesign's Text Wrap pane to access that clipping path.

The steps are easy:

1. **Be sure to select the Show Import Options check box in the Place dialog box (File⇨Place, or ⌘+D or Ctrl+D) when you import the image and select the Apply Photoshop Clipping Path option in the Image Import Options dialog box (as described in Chapter 19).**
2. **Open the Text Wrap pane (Window⇨Text Wrap, or Option+⌘+W or Ctrl+Alt+W), as shown in Figure 20-2.**
3. **Select the graphic.**
4. **Click the Wrap Around Object Shape button (the third one from the left) at the top of the Text Wrap pane.**
5. **If you want, adjust the space between the surrounding text and the obstructing shape by typing values in the Top Offset field.**
6. **Now select the clipping source from the Type pop-up menu in the Contour Options section of the Text Wrap pane. Choose from two relevant options:**
    - Alpha Channel uses the image's alpha channel, if any, to create a wrapping boundary. (An *alpha channel* is another type of clipping

path and is also created in the source program such as Photoshop.)

- Photoshop Path uses the image's clipping path, if any, to create a wrapping boundary. Use the Path pop-up menu to select which path to use, if your image has more than one embedded clipping path.

See Chapter 18 for the basics of text wraps.

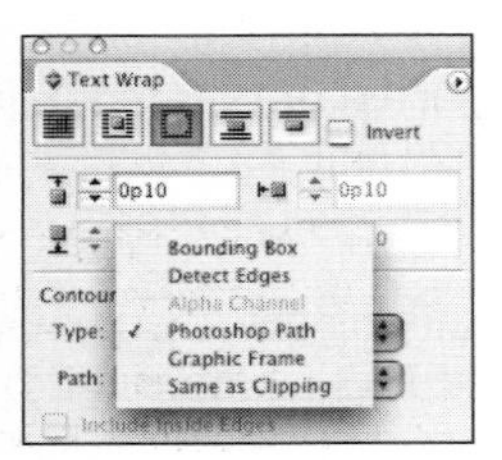

Figure 20-2: The Text Wrap pane and its Type menu.

Creating a clipping path in InDesign

If you import a graphic that doesn't have a clipping path, you have two sets of options to create a clipping path.

The easiest is to use the Text Wrap pane as described in the previous section but to instead choose one of the following options from the Type pop-up menu:

- Detect Edges tries to determine the graphic's outside boundary by ignoring white space — you would use this for bitmapped images that have a transparent or white background.
- Same as Clipping uses the clipping path for the graphic created in InDesign — you would use this when the desired clipping path can't be created through the Detect Edges option. (We cover this method of clipping-path creation shortly.)

You can further modify the clipping path by selecting the graphic with the Direct Selection tool. The text-wrap boundary appears as a blue line — you can make the boundary easier to select by setting offsets in the Text Wrap pane, which moves the boundary away from the frame edge. Now use InDesign's free-form editing tools, as covered in Chapter 21, to edit the text-wrap boundary.

A slightly more difficult way to create a clipping path — but one that gives you more control — is to use the Clipping Path command (Object⇨Clipping Path, or Option+Shift+⌘+K or Ctrl+Alt+Shift+K) to generate one automatically:

1. **Select the graphic to which you want to add a clipping path.**

   It's best to use the Direct Selection tool, so that you can see the clipping path within the frame as you work.

2. **Choose Object⇨Clipping Path, or press Option+Shift+⌘+K or Ctrl+Alt+Shift+K.**

   The Clipping Path dialog box appears, as shown in Figure 20-3.

3. **To have InDesign detect the likely boundary of the image, as opposed to a white or other light background, choose Detect Edges from the Type pop-up menu.**

   You can use the other options to select Alpha Channel or Photoshop Path as the clipping path for graphics that have one or more of these. (InDesign can only use one alpha channel or Photoshop path as the clipping path, so use the Path pop-up menu to choose the one you want.)

4. **Type a value in the Threshold field or click and drag the field's slider to specify the value below which pixels will be placed outside the clipping path shape (that is, pixels that will become transparent).**

   Pixels darker than the Threshold value remain visible and thus are inside the clipping path shape. The lowest possible Threshold value (0) makes only white pixels transparent. As the value gets higher, less of the graphic remains visible. The lightest areas are removed first, then midtones, and so on. (Select the Preview option to see the results of your changes without closing the dialog box.)

5. **Type a value in the Tolerance field.**

   This value determines how closely InDesign looks at variations in adjacent pixels when building a clipping path. Higher values produce a simpler, smoother path than lower values. Lower values create a more complicated, more exact path with more anchor points.

6. **If you want to enlarge or reduce the size of the clipping path produced by the Threshold and Tolerance values, type a value in the Inset Frame field.**

   Negative values enlarge the path; positive values shrink it. (The Inset Frame value is also applied to the path's bounding box.)

7. **Select the Invert option to switch the transparent and visible areas of the clipping path produced by the Threshold and Tolerance values.**

8. **If you want to include light areas in the perimeter shape InDesign generates based on the Threshold and Tolerance values, select the Include Inside Edges option.**

   For example, if you have a graphic of a doughnut and you want to make the hole transparent (as well as the area around the outside of the doughnut), click Include Inside Edges. If you don't click Include Inside Edges, InDesign builds a single shape (in the case of a doughnut, just the outside circle). The portion of the graphic in the shape remains visible; the rest of the graphic becomes transparent.

9. **Select the Restrict to Frame option if you want InDesign to generate a clipping path from just the portion of the graphic visible in the graphic frame, as opposed to the entire graphic (such as if you cropped the graphic).**

10. **Select the Use High Resolution Image option if you want InDesign to use the high-resolution information in the original file instead of using the low-resolution proxy image.**

    Even though using the high-resolution image takes longer, the resulting clipping path is more precise than it would be if you didn't check Use High Resolution Image.

11. **When you've finished specifying clipping path settings, click OK to close the dialog box and apply the settings to the selected graphic.**

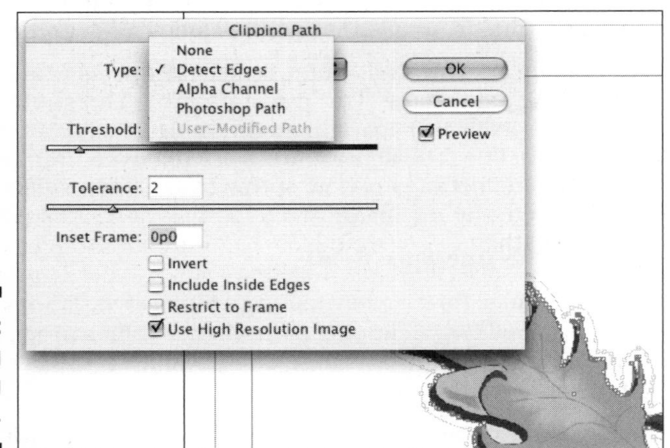

Figure 20-3: The Clipping Path dialog box.

If you use the Clipping Path command to generate a clipping path for a graphic that has a built-in clipping path, the one that InDesign generates replaces the built-in path.

Figure 20-4 shows a graphic before and after a clipping path was applied to it using the Clipping Path command. At left is a graphic of coastal France with a graphic of a glider superimposed. At right is the same set of graphics, but with a clipping path applied to the glider so the outside area is masked out, making it transparent.

The Clipping Path command works very well for images that have a white or light background but no clipping path. It's less useful for graphics with backgrounds that contain a broad range of intermingling values.

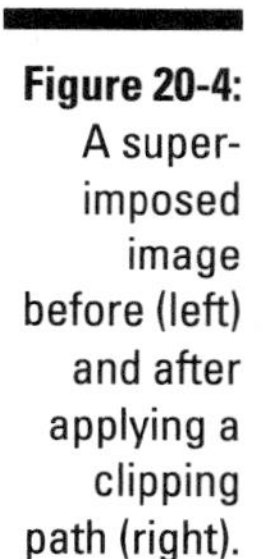

Figure 20-4: A superimposed image before (left) and after applying a clipping path (right).

You can remove a clipping path by choosing None as the Type in the Clipping Path dialog box. You can also select a different path — Detect Edges, Alpha Channel, Photoshop Path, or User-Modified Path — than was selected previously if you decide to change the current clipping path.

Slicing Up Graphics

Not that Freddy Krueger is a role model, but sometimes slicing things up is part of a good layout. InDesign's Scissors tool lets you slice objects into parts. Figure 20-5 shows a graphic that's been cut into halves with the Scissors tool. To slice a graphic, follow these steps:

1. **Select the Scissors tool.**
2. **Position the cross-hair pointer anywhere over a graphics frame, and then click.**
3. **Move the pointer to a different position along the frame edge, and then click again.**

4. **After you've clicked twice on the frame edge, you can switch to either of the selection tools and then click and drag either of the two graphic pieces that your scissors cut created.**

That's it!

If you use the Scissors tool to split a frame to which a stroke has been applied, the resulting edges will not include the stroke.

Figure 20-5: The Scissors tool was used to create the split image (right) from a clone of the original image (left).

Chapter 21

Creating Complex Shapes

In This Chapter

- Understanding path basics
- Drawing your own shapes
- Modifying shapes and paths
- Combining and merging paths
- Applying corner effects to paths
- Converting text into graphics

InDesign's basic drawing tools let you create basic shapes, such as straight lines, rectangles and squares, circles and ellipses, and equilateral polygons. But what about when you need to create shapes that aren't so basic, such as an amoeba or a cursive version of your first name? That's where InDesign's Pen and Pencil tools come in.

In this chapter, you'll find out how to use these tools to create any kind of line or closed shape, called *paths.* And you'll learn how anything you create with these tools can be used as an independent graphic element or as a frame for text or a picture.

Finding Out about Paths

But before we get into how to create paths, it's important that you understand some of the theory behind paths, which will help you create and manipulate them more easily.

Every object you create with InDesign's object-creation tools is a *path.* Regardless of the tool you use to create a path, you can change its appearance by modifying any of four properties that all paths share:

- **Closure:** A path is either open or closed. Straight lines created with the Line tool and curved and zigzag lines created with the Pen tool are examples of open paths. Basic shapes created with the Ellipse, Rectangle, and Polygon tools and free-form shapes created with the Pen and Pencil tools are examples of closed shapes. A closed free-form shape is an uninterrupted path with no endpoints.

- **Stroke:** If you want to make a path visible, you can apply a stroke to it by selecting it with a selection tool, entering a Weight value in the Stroke pane (Window➪Stroke or F10), and selecting a color from the Swatches pane (Window➪Swatches or F5). (An unselected, unstroked path is not visible.) Be sure that the Stroke button is active in the Tools palette or Swatches palette by clicking the Stroke button in either location before applying the color, as described in Chapter 12.
- **Fill:** A color, color tint, or gradient applied to the background of a path is called a *fill.* You apply fills by using the Swatches pane.
- **Contents:** You can place a text file or a graphics file in any path except a straight line. When a path is used to hold text or a picture, the path functions as a frame. Although InDesign can place text in an open path, placing text and pictures in closed paths is far more common than placing them in open paths.

No matter how simple or complicated, all paths are made up of the same components. Figure 21-1 shows the parts that make up a path:

- A path contains one or more straight or curved *segments.*
- An anchor point is located at each end of every segment. The anchor points at the ends of a closed path are called *endpoints.* When you create a path of any kind, anchor points are automatically placed at the end of each segment. After you create a path, you can move, add, delete, and change the direction of corner points.
- InDesign has two kinds of anchor points: *smooth points* and *corner points.* A smooth point connects two adjoining curved segments in a continuous, flowing curve. At a corner point, adjoining segments — straight or curved — meet at an angle. The corners of a rectangular path are the most common corner points.
- A *direction line* runs through each anchor point and has a handle at both ends. You can control the curve that passes through an anchor point by dragging a direction line's handles, as we explain a little later on.

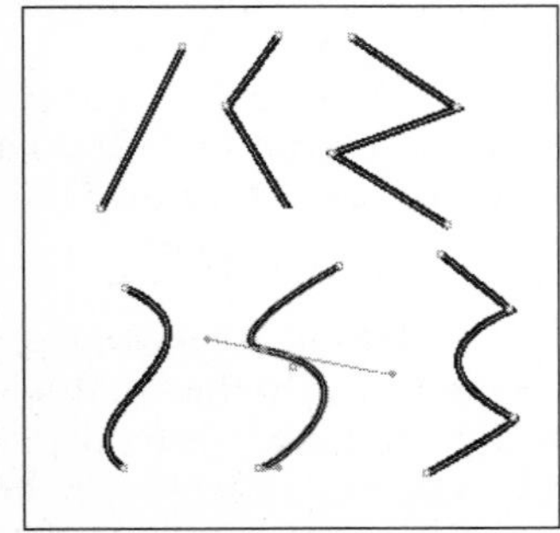

Figure 21-1: Anchor points can be smooth or corner, resulting in curved or angular connections between segments.

Drawing Your Own Shapes

Even if you're an artistic master with a piece of charcoal or a Number 2 pencil, you need to practice with the Pen tool for awhile before your drawing skills kick in. The good news is that once you get comfortable using the Pen tool, you can draw any shape you can imagine. (Of course, if you can't draw very well in the first place, using the Pen tool won't magically transform you into a master illustrator!) If this is new terrain for you, start simply and proceed slowly.

When creating paths, use as few anchor points as possible. As you become more comfortable creating free-form paths, you should find yourself using fewer anchor points to create paths.

For an easy way to draw free-form shapes, use the Pencil tool. This tool simply traces the movement of your mouse (or pen tablet) as you move it, much like a pencil works on paper. Although not as exact as the Pen tool, the Pencil tool creates Bézier curves that you can later edit. Note that the Pencil tool is not meant for creating straight lines — unless you are capable of drawing perfectly straight lines by hand, that is.

Straight and zigzag lines

Follow these steps to draw lines with straight segments, such as a zigzag:

1. **Select the Pen tool.**
2. **Move the Pen pointer to where you want to start your line segment.**
3. **Click and release the mouse button. (Make sure you don't drag before you release the mouse button.)**

   An anchor point will appear; it looks like a small, filled-in square.
4. **Move the Pen pointer to where you want to place the next anchor point.**
5. **Click and release the mouse button.**

   InDesign draws a straight line between the two anchor points. The first anchor point changes to a hollow square, and the second anchor point is filled in, which indicates that it is the active anchor point.
6. **Repeat Steps 4 and 5 for each additional anchor point.**

   To reposition an anchor point after you click the mouse button but before you release it, hold down the spacebar and drag. Otherwise, you need to select it with the Direct Selection tool after you finish drawing the line and then click and drag it to its new location.

How smooth and corner points work

Bézier paths have two kinds of points to join segments: corner and smooth.

The two segments that form a smooth point's direction line work together as a single, straight line. When you move a handle, the line acts like a teeter-totter; the opposite handle moves in the opposite direction. If you shorten one of the segments, the length of the other segment doesn't change. The angle and length of direction lines determine the shape of the segments with which they're associated.

A corner point that connects two curved segments has two direction lines; a corner point that connects two straight segments has no direction lines; and a corner point that connects a straight and curved segment has one direction line. If you drag a corner point's direction line, the other direction line, if there is one, is not affected.

7. **To complete the path, ⌘+click or Ctrl+ click elsewhere on the page or simply choose another tool.**

   If you ⌘+click or Ctrl+click, the Pen tool remains active, so you can continue creating new paths.

Curved lines

Knowing how to draw zigzag lines is fine, but chances are, you want to draw curved shapes as well. The basic process is similar to drawing straight segments, but drawing curved paths (technically called *Bézier paths*) is more complicated and will take you some time to get the hang of.

If you want to draw a continuously curvy path that contains no corner points and no straight segments, you should create only smooth points as you draw. Here's how:

1. **Select the Pen tool.**
2. **Move the Pen pointer to where you want to start the curve segment.**
3. **Click and hold down the mouse button.**

   The arrowhead pointer appears.
4. **Drag the mouse in the direction of the next point you intend to create and then release the mouse button.**

   As you drag, the anchor point, its direction line, and the direction line's two handles are displayed, as shown in Figure 21-2.

   If you hold down the Shift key as you drag, the angle of the direction line is limited to increments of 45 degrees.

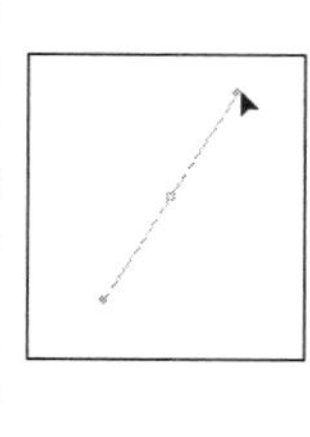

Figure 21-2: To create a smooth point when beginning a path, click and hold the mouse and drag in the direction of the next point.

5. **Move the Pen pointer to where you want to place the next anchor point — and end the first segment — and then drag the mouse.**

   If you drag in roughly the same direction as the direction line of the previous point, you create an S-shaped curve; if you drag in the opposite direction, you create a C-shaped curve.

6. **When the curve between the two anchor points looks how you want it to look, release the mouse button.**

   Alternatively, when you want to connect curved segments to corner points (shown in Figure 21-3), move the Pen pointer to where you want to place the next anchor point — and end the first segment — and then press and hold Option or Alt as you click and drag the mouse. As you drag, the anchor point's handle moves, and the direction line changes from a straight line to two independent segments. The angle of the direction line segment that you create when you drag the handle determines the slope of the next segment.

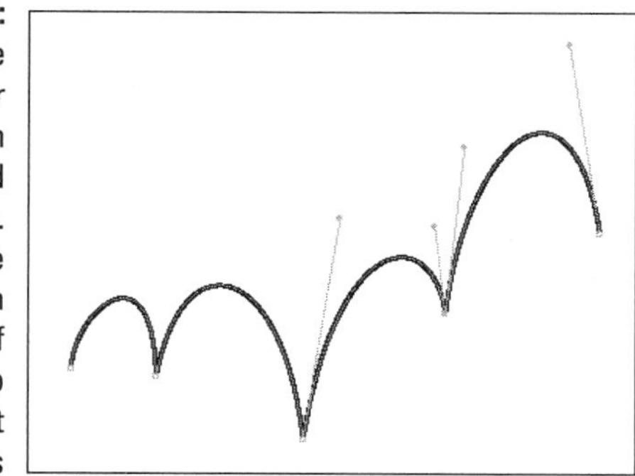

Figure 21-3: Three corner points join four curved segments. The direction handles of the two right-most segments are visible.

7. **Repeat Steps 5 and 6 for each additional desired curved segment.**
8. **To complete the path, ⌘+click or Ctrl+click elsewhere on the page or simply choose another tool.**

   If you ⌘+click or Ctrl+click, the Pen tool remains active, so you can create new paths.

   You can also complete the path by clicking on the first point you created. This creates a closed path.

Closed paths

A *closed path* is simply a path that ends where it began. When it comes to creating closed paths with the Pen tool, the process is exactly the same as for creating open paths, as explained earlier in this section, with one difference at the end:

- To create a straight segment between the endpoint and the last anchor point you created, click and release the mouse button.
- To create a curved segment, click and drag the mouse in the direction of the last anchor point you created, and then release the mouse button.

Just like an open path, a closed path can contain straight and/or curved segments and smooth and/or corner anchor points. All the techniques explained earlier in this chapter for drawing lines with curved and straight segments and smooth and corner points apply when you draw closed paths.

Modifying Your Paths and Shapes

No matter how skillful you become with InDesign's Pen tool, it's difficult to create exactly what you want on your first attempt. For example, after creating a path, you might want to add detail, smooth out a rough spot, or turn a straight segment into a curved one. No problem. In the following sections, we discuss the ways in which InDesign lets you modify the paths you create.

Generally, when you want to manipulate a path, you use one of the three variations of the Pen tool, all of which are displayed in a single pop-up menu in the Tools palette (shown in Figure 21-4).

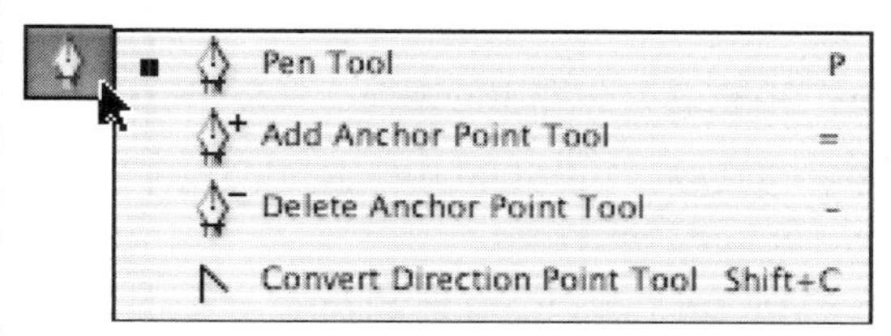

Figure 21-4: The four Pen tool variants in the Tools palette.

Working with anchor points

If you want to add detail to an existing path, you need to add anchor points that give you more precise control over a portion of the path. Perhaps you've drawn the profile of a face and you want to add detail to the nose. Or maybe you've written your name longhand and you need to add a flourish that your original attempt lacks. In both cases, you can add smooth or corner points and then manipulate the curves associated with those points by moving them or manipulating their direction lines.

On the other hand, maybe you've created a path that's more complicated than necessary. Perhaps you drew a hand with six fingers instead of five, or a camel with one too many humps. In these instances, you need to simplify the path by removing anchor points. InDesign lets you add and delete as many anchor points as you want.

Follow these steps to add an anchor point:

1. **Select the path by clicking it with the Direct Selection tool.**

   You can also select multiple paths and then modify them one at a time.

2. **Select the Add Anchor Point tool.**
3. **Move the Pen pointer to the location where you want to add an anchor point and click.**

   A new anchor point is created where you click. If you click a straight segment between two corner points, a corner point is created. If you click a curved segment between two smooth points or between a smooth point and a corner point, a smooth point is created. You can also click, drag, and then release the mouse button if you want to adjust the direction line of the point you create.

   After you add an anchor point, you can hold down the ⌘ or Ctrl key or switch to the Direct Selection tool and drag it or either of its direction handles to adjust the adjoining segments.

Whenever you're working on a path, you can hold down the ⌘ or Ctrl key and then click and drag any element of the path — an anchor point, a direction line, or the entire path.

Here's how you delete an anchor point:

1. **Select the path by clicking it with the Direct Selection tool.**

   You can also select multiple paths and then modify them one at a time.

2. **Select the Delete Anchor Point tool.**
3. **Click the anchor point that you want to delete.**

Pretty easy, huh?

Moving anchor points is also an easy process. When you select a path with the Direct Selection tool, its anchor points are displayed as small, hollow squares. When you click and drag an anchor point, the two adjoining segments change, but the direction handles, if present, are not affected. If you hold down the Shift key as you drag an anchor point, movement is restricted to increments of 45 degrees.

If all you need to do is resize a path — particularly a simple rectangle — rather than change its shape, you should select it with the Selection tool rather than the Direct Selection tool and then click and drag one of its bounding box handles.

Converting anchor points

If you want to change a wavy path that contains only curved segments to a zigzag path that contains only straight segments, you can do so by converting the smooth anchor points of the wavy path into corner points. Similarly, by converting corner points to smooth points, you can smooth out a path that contains straight segments.

To convert an anchor point, follow these steps:

1. **Select the path by clicking it with the Direct Selection tool.**
2. **Choose the Convert Direction Point tool or simply hold down Option+⌘ or Ctrl+Alt when the Direct Selection tool is selected.**
3. **Move the pointer over the anchor point you want to convert.**

   Depending on the point you want to convert, do one of the following:

   - To convert a corner point to a smooth point, click the corner point and then drag (direction lines are created and displayed as you drag).
   - To convert a smooth point to a corner point without direction lines, click and release the mouse.

- To convert a smooth point to a corner point with independent direction lines, click and drag either of the smooth point's direction handles.
- To convert a corner point without direction lines to a corner point with direction lines, click and drag the corner point to create a smooth point and then release the mouse button. Then click and drag either of the direction lines.

Handling handles

In addition to dragging and converting anchor points, you can adjust the shape of a curved segment by dragging any of the handles for direction lines associated with the anchor points at either end of the segment. Figure 21-5 shows how moving direction lines affects a curved segment.

To drag a curved segment's direction handle, use the Direct Selection tool to select the path, then just drag the desired handle. (Press Shift as you drag to constrain movement to multiples of 45 degrees.) As you drag, the handle at the opposite end of the direction line moves in the opposite direction, like a teeter-totter. However, if you lengthen or shorten one side of a direction line, the other side is not affected. Release the mouse button when the shape is as you want it.

Corner points between straight segments don't have direction handles. If you want to modify the segments associated with a corner point, simply click and drag the point.

If you use the Convert Direction Point tool (instead of the Direct Selection tool) to click and drag a smooth point's direction-line handle, the opposite portion of the direction line remains unchanged. This lets you adjust the segment on one side of a smooth point without affecting the segment on the other side.

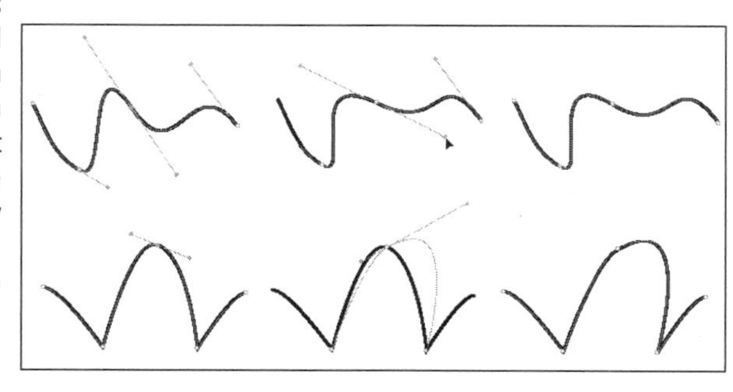

Figure 21-5: The top and bottom shapes on the right were created by dragging a direction line of a smooth point.

Closing an open path

Closing an open path works in much the same way as extending an open path. The only difference is that you *complete* the path — that is, you close it — by clicking the other endpoint. For example, if you slice a graphics frame into two pieces with the Scissors tool (which is explained in Chapter 20), two open paths are created. If you add a stroke to these open frames, a portion of the graphic edge (the nonexistent segment between the endpoints) will not be stroked.

A quick way to close an open path is to select it and then choose Object➪Path➪Close Path. You can also open a closed path by choosing Object➪Path➪Open Path; this will separate the start point into a start point and end point, letting you move either point or the segments attached to them independently.

Converting shapes

Although you can edit a shape with the techniques described earlier in this section, doing so can be a lot of work for what should be a simple operation. InDesign CS2 gives you a new, easy way to convert an object's shape: Choose Object➪Convert Shape and then choose one of the submenu options: Rectangle, Rounded Rectangle, Beveled Rectangle, Inverse Rounded Rectangle, Ellipse, Triangle, Polygon, Line, or Orthogonal Line. You can also use the Pathfinder pane (Window➪Object & Layout➪Pathfinder), shown later in this chapter in Figure 21-7.

Using the Erase tool

Just as it has tools to create paths, InDesign has a tool to delete them: the Erase tool, accessible via the Pencil tool's pop-up menu.

To erase straight lines, drag the tool alongside the path segment to cut — making sure not to cross the path — and then release the mouse. The segment disappears.

But for freeform shapes, the tool takes some experimenting with. As Figure 21-6 shows, using the Erase tool results in a different shape depending on what side of a shape you use it on. At the top is the result of using the Erase tool outside a closed path. At the bottom is the result of using the tool inside the path.

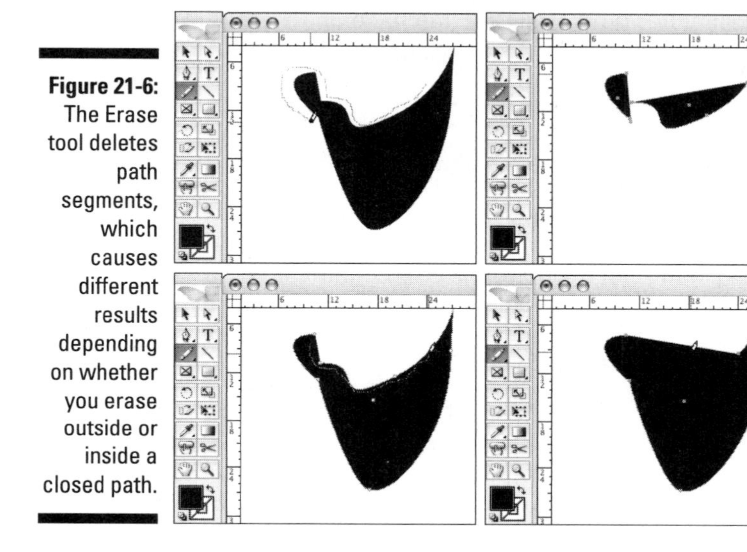

Figure 21-6: The Erase tool deletes path segments, which causes different results depending on whether you erase outside or inside a closed path.

Combining Paths

Sometimes, you want to combine multiple paths to make them into one object. InDesign gives you two basic ways to do so, depending on what you are trying to combine. One case is when you want to join several paths into one object, called a *compound path.* The other is when you want to merge several paths into a new shape.

Working with compound paths

When more than one path is selected, you can use the Make (Compound Path) command (Object➪Compound Paths➪Make or ⌘+8 or Ctrl+8) to convert the paths into a single object. You can use this command to create a complex shape, such as a flower, from multiple individual shapes.

A compound path is similar to a group (see Chapter 13), except that when you create a group out of several objects, each object in the group retains its original attributes, such as stroke color and width, fill color or gradient, and so on. By contrast, when you create a compound path, the attributes of the bottommost path are applied to all the other paths (that is, the attributes of the bottommost path replace the attributes of the other paths).

After you create a compound path, each original path becomes a subpath, so you can still work on its shape. You can change the shape of any of the subpaths by clicking one with the Direct Selection tool and then clicking and dragging any of its anchor points or direction handles. The Pen, Add Anchor Point, Delete Anchor Point, and Change Direction Line tools covered earlier in this chapter work the same for subpaths as for other paths, which means that you can reshape them however you want.

But moving a subpath is a little tricky because you can't drag just that subpath. If you try, all the subpaths move. If you want to move an entire subpath, you must move each of the subpath's anchor points individually. In this case, it's probably easier to release the compound path, as described next, move the path as needed, and then re-create the compound path.

If you want to delete a subpath, you must use the Delete Anchor Point tool to delete all its anchor points. If you delete a single anchor point of a closed subpath, it becomes an open subpath.

If the Selection tool is active, you can't delete anchor points with the Cut command, the Clear command, or the Backspace, Clear or Delete keys. All of these keyboard commands remove the entire path. To work on those individual points, be sure the Direct Selection tool is active instead.

If you decide you want to deconstruct a compound path, you can do so by clicking anywhere within the compound path and then choosing Object⇨Compound Paths⇨Release or pressing Option+⌘+8 or Ctrl+Alt+8. The resulting paths retain the attributes of the compound path (their original attributes won't come back).

Using the Pathfinder tools

The other way to combine paths is to merge them with the Pathfinder tool. After selecting the objects to merge, choose Object⇨Pathfinder. You can also use the Pathfinder pane (Window⇨Object & Layout⇨Pathfinder). You see five options in the Object⇨Pathfinder submenu and in the Pathfinder pane: Add, Subtract, Intersect, Exclude Overlap, and Minus Back. Figure 21-7 shows how they affect a group of paths (two open and one closed).

These effects are hard to explain, so you want to experiment, but at a basic level, here's what they do:

- **Add** adds all objects' shapes together.
- **Subtract** subtracts all objects from the bottommost object in the stack.
- **Intersect** creates an object in which objects overlap — this works only on closed paths.
- **Exclude Overlap** removes overlapping paths and keeps the non-overlapping paths of all objects.
- **Minus Back** subtracts all objects from the top object in the stack.

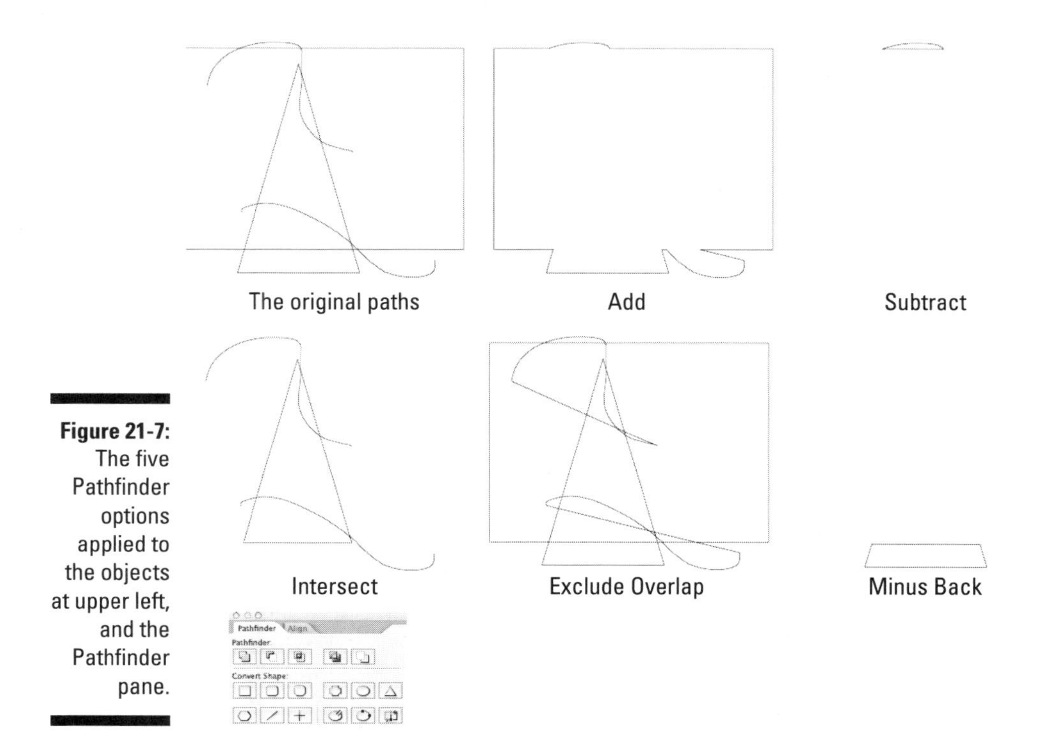

Figure 21-7: The five Pathfinder options applied to the objects at upper left, and the Pathfinder pane.

Special Effects for Graphics

In addition to everything else InDesign lets you do with paths and shapes, it also includes a few fun special effects that you won't use every day, but that can add a neat touch when it's appropriate.

Adding corner effects to paths

When a path is selected, the Corner Effects command (Object⇨Corner Effects) lets you apply any of several graphic embellishments to the path's corner points (if it has any corner points). For example, you can use a corner effect to add pizzazz to the border of a coupon or a certificate. Generally, corner effects work best with rectangular shapes, but they can also produce interesting results when applied to free-form shapes, as shown in Figure 21-8. (Chapter 12 covers the use of corner effects with frames and shapes.)

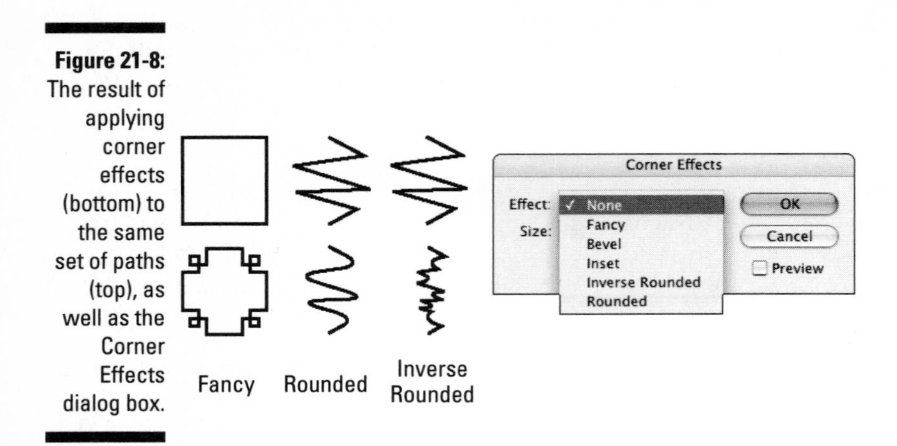

Figure 21-8: The result of applying corner effects (bottom) to the same set of paths (top), as well as the Corner Effects dialog box.

To apply a corner effect to a path:

1. **Use either of the selection tools to select a path.**
2. **Choose Object⇨Corner Effects.**

   The Corner Effects dialog box appears.
3. **Choose a Corner Effect from the Effect pop-up menu.**

   If you want to see the effect while you create it, click Preview and, if necessary, move the dialog box out of the way so you can see the selected path.
4. **In the Size field, type the distance away from the corner point that the effect will extend.**
5. **After you finish specifying the appearance of the corner effect, click OK to close the dialog box.**

InDesign doesn't let you modify the built-in corner effects or add your own to the list of choices. Nor can you use the Direct Selection tool to modify the corner of a path to which a corner effect has been applied (anchor points are not displayed for the additional segments that are added when a corner effect is applied to a corner point). The only control you have over a corner effect is the value you specify in the Radius field of the Corner Effects dialog box.

Converting text into shapes

If you want to use the shape of a letter or the combined shapes of several letters as a frame for text or a graphic, you could test your skill with the Pen tool and create the letter shape(s) yourself. But getting hand-drawn characters to look just the way you want them to can take lots of time. A quicker solution is to use the Create Outlines command to convert text characters into editable outlines. The Create Outlines command is particularly useful if you want to hand-tweak the shapes of characters, particularly at display font sizes, or place text or a graphic within character shapes.

If all you need to do is apply a stroke or fill to characters within text, you don't have to convert the characters into outlines. Instead, simply highlight the characters and use the Stroke pane (Window⇨Stroke or F10) and Swatches pane (Window⇨Swatches or F5) to change their appearance. This way you can still edit the text. (See Chapter 18 for more details.)

When you use the Create Outlines command, you have the choice of creating an inline compound path that replaces the original text or an independent compound path that's placed directly on top of the original letters in its own frame. If you want the text outlines to flow with the surrounding text, create an inline compound path. If you want to use the outlines elsewhere, create an independent compound path.

To convert text into outlines:

1. **Use the Type tool to highlight the characters you want to convert into outlines.**

   Generally, this feature works best with large font sizes.

2. **Choose Type⇨Create Outlines or press Shift+⌘+O or Ctrl+Shift+O (that's the letter *O*, not a zero).**

   If you hold down the Option or Alt key when you choose Create Outlines, or if you press Shift+Option+⌘+O or Ctrl+Alt+Shift+O, a compound path is created and placed in front of the text. In this case, you can use either of the selection tools to move the resulting compound path. If you don't hold down Option or Alt when you choose Create Outlines, an inline compound path is created. This object replaces the original text and flows with the surrounding text.

When you create outlines out of a range of highlighted characters, a compound path is created, and each of the characters becomes a subpath. You can use the Release (Compound Path) command (Object⇨Compound Paths⇨Release or Option+⌘+8 or Ctrl+Alt+8) to turn each of the subpaths into independent paths, as described earlier in this chapter.

After you create text outlines, you can modify the paths the same as you can modify hand-drawn paths — by selecting them with the Direct Selection tool and then adding, deleting, or moving anchor points; clicking and dragging direction handles; and converting smooth points to corner points and vice versa. You can also use the transformation tools, the Control palette (Window➪Control or Option+⌘+6 or Ctrl+Alt+6), and the Transform pane (Window➪Transform or F9) to change the appearance of text outlines. You cannot, however, edit text after converting it to outlines.

Additionally, you can use the Place command (File➪Place or ⌘+D or Ctrl+D) or the Paste Into command (Edit➪Paste Into or Option+⌘+V or Ctrl+Alt+V) to import text or a graphic into the frames created by converting text to graphics.

Part VI
Printing and Output Essentials

"Look into my Web site, Ms. Carruthers. Look deep into its rotating, nicely animated spiral, spinning, spinning, pulling you in, deeper... deeper..."

In this part . . .

Finally, your layout is done. It's beautiful, it's well-written, and you're eager to share it with your readers. This part shows you how to take the final step to print or create a PDF version of your layout so you can distribute it. InDesign gives you a lot of control over output, so you can optimize the results based on what you are printing it to, such as ensuring color fidelity and the best possible image resolution. Then you can start the whole creation, refinement, and output process over again with your next layout!

Chapter 22

Setting Up for Output

In This Chapter

- Setting up printers in your operating system
- Checking your files before you print

You've finished your document and you want to share it with the whole world, or at least your audience. So you reach for your mouse and choose File⇨Print or quickly press ⌘+P or Ctrl+P so you can print.

Stop. Cancel. If this is your first print job with InDesign, you need to make sure that you've properly set up your printer to get the results you need.

You also should do a visual proof of your layout before you print. It's amazing what you don't notice when you're focused on specific elements as you lay out a page. Change your view setting so the entire page or spread fits in the window (choose View⇨Fit Page in Window or View⇨Fit Spread in Window, as desired) and then review your pages.

Properly Setting Up Your Printer

Before you can print or create a PDF file of your document, you first need to make sure your system is set up with the right printer driver and printer description files — without these, your output is not likely to match your needs or expectations.

It's also important to set these up before you use the Preflight tool (covered later in this chapter) to detect possible output problems before you print, because the Preflight tool checks your document against the active printer settings (such as color separations), and you can't have selected printer settings until the printer is set up.

The Mac and Windows platforms handle printing differently, so in this chapter we've divided all system-specific printing information, such as the coverage of drivers, into platform-specific sections.

Setting up Macintosh printers

Although you choose the printer type in the Setup pane of the InDesign Print dialog box, you still need to set up the printer on your Mac before you can use it.

The process varies based on which version of the Mac OS you have:

- In Mac OS X 10.3 (Panther) and later, use the Printer Setup Utility, which you access by choosing ⇨System Preferences⇨Print & Fax and then clicking Set Up Printers in the resulting Print & Fax pane. You get the Printer List dialog box.
- In Mac OS X 10.2 (Jaguar), you use an application called the Print Center, which is in the Utilities folder of the Applications folder.

The Printer List dialog box or the Print Center will list any installed printers. If you see the printer to which you want to print in the Printer List or Print Center, you've already installed your printer.

Otherwise, make sure the printer you want to set up is connected to your Mac (directly or through the network) and turned on. (If you use a network printer, make sure the right network protocols, such as IP and AppleTalk, are turned on through the Network pane in the System Preferences dialog box, which you access by choosing ⇨System Preferences.)

Either way, to install a printer, you typically run a program that comes with the printer. Such programs often add the printer to the Printer List. If not, click Add (in the Printer List) and locate the printer driver for your printer (again, usually found on a CD that accompanies the printer).

Figure 22-1 shows the Printer List that appears when you open the Mac OS X 10.3 Print & Fax pane and click Set Up Printers.

How you configure an installed printer varies based on the software provided with the printer. In some cases, a printer's configuration software is accessible when you add a printer through the Printer List dialog box. (In Mac OS X 10.3, select the printer and click Show Info to get the Printer dialog box, which will have a pop-up menu that lets you move among the various setup panes. In earlier versions of Mac OS X, select the printer and click the Configure button.)

In other cases, you need to run a separate utility that comes with the printer or use controls on the printer itself.

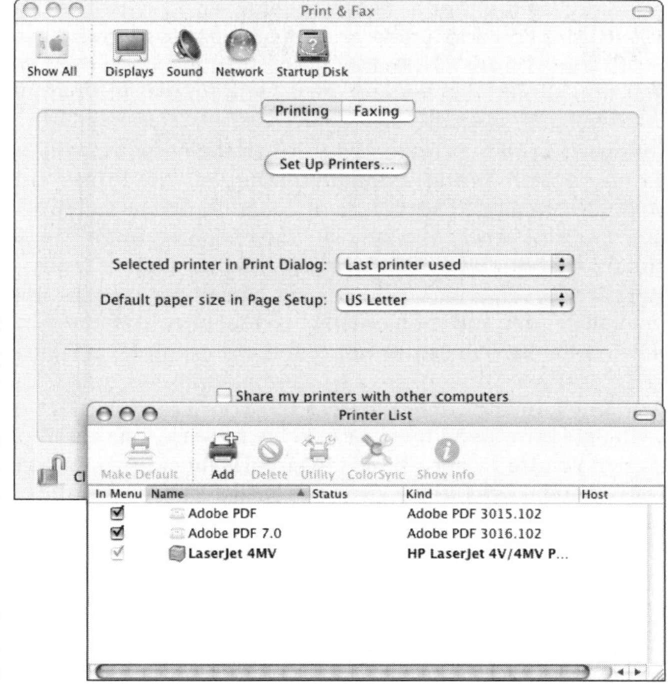

Figure 22-1: The Printer List dialog box shows which printers are installed and lets you add and configure them.

You may need to install a PostScript Printer Description (PPD) file that contains specific details about your printer. This file should come on a disk or CD with your printer and is often installed with the printer's setup program. Otherwise, download it from the printer manufacturer's Web site. These files should reside in the PPD folder in the Mac's `System\Library\Printers` folder. Note that Mac OS X preinstalls some PPDs for you, particularly those for Apple-branded printers and some Hewlett-Packard printers. If you're installing a printer not connected to your computer or network, such as the imagesetter used by your service bureau, you need to install the PPD files so InDesign knows what its settings are; installing the printer software isn't necessary.

Mac OS X supports multiple printers, but it also lets you define the default printer. To change the default printer, open the Printer List dialog box, choose the printer you want to be the default, and then click Make Default.

Setting up Windows printers

To set up a Windows XP printer, choose Start➪Settings➪Printers and Faxes. (Some XP users will have to choose Start➪Control Panel➪Printers and Other Hardware.) In Windows 2000, choose Start➪Settings➪Printers. You see a window with a list of existing printers and an icon labeled Add New Printer. Double-click the printer that you want to set up or double-click Add New

Printer (you likely need either a disk that came with the printer or the Windows CD-ROM if you add a new printer because Windows needs information specific to that printer). Note that some printers have their own setup software that you should use instead of the Add Printer utility in Windows.

If you're setting up a printer connected through the network, you usually select the Local Printer option during installation. The Network Printer option is for printers connected to a print server, as opposed to printers connected to a hub or router. (A print server is a special kind of router, but it's typically used only for printers that don't have networking built in, such as many inkjet printers.) In some cases, even if your printer uses a print server, you still install the printer as a local printer and then create a virtual port that maps to a network address (Hewlett-Packard uses this approach, for example, in Figure 22-2).

If you're installing a printer not connected to your computer or network, such as the imagesetter used by your service bureau, you need to install the PPD (PostScript Printer Description) file so InDesign knows what its settings are. (You don't need to install the printer software.) This file should come on a disk or CD with your printer and is often installed with the printer's setup program. Otherwise, download it from the printer manufacturer's Web site. (Windows places PPD files in the `Windows\System32\spool\drivers\w32x86` folder; note that the first folder may be named `WinNT` or `WinXP` instead of `Windows`.)

After you open an existing printer, choose Printer➪Properties to display the dialog box shown in Figure 22-2. The one pane you most need to pay attention to is the Device Settings pane, which is where you specify all the device settings, from paper trays to memory to how fonts are handled. For PostScript printers, this pane contains several key options, as follows:

- **Font Substitution Table:** This option opens a list of available fonts and lets you select how any TrueType fonts are translated to PostScript. The best (and default) setting is to have the printer translate TrueType fonts such as Arial to PostScript fonts such as Helvetica. (The Windows standards of Arial, Times New Roman, Courier New, and Symbol are set by default to translate to the PostScript fonts Helvetica, Times, Courier, and Symbol. PostScript fonts are set by default to Don't Substitute.)
- **Add Euro Currency Symbol to PostScript Fonts:** Be sure to select this option so the euro symbol (€) is available in all output.

We strongly recommend that you use Adobe's PostScript driver rather than Microsoft's. The Microsoft driver often doesn't send fonts to the printer, and it often prints extra blank pages at the end of a job. The Adobe Universal PostScript driver doesn't have these issues. You can download the Adobe driver from `www.adobe.com/support/downloads/main.html` in the PostScript Printer Drivers section. When you install the driver, it gives you the option of converting your existing PostScript printers to the Adobe driver. You can also run this program again to install new printers using the

Adobe driver — using the Add Printer wizard automatically installs the Microsoft driver for those new printers — or you can use the Drivers pop-up menu in the Advanced pane of the printer's Properties dialog box.

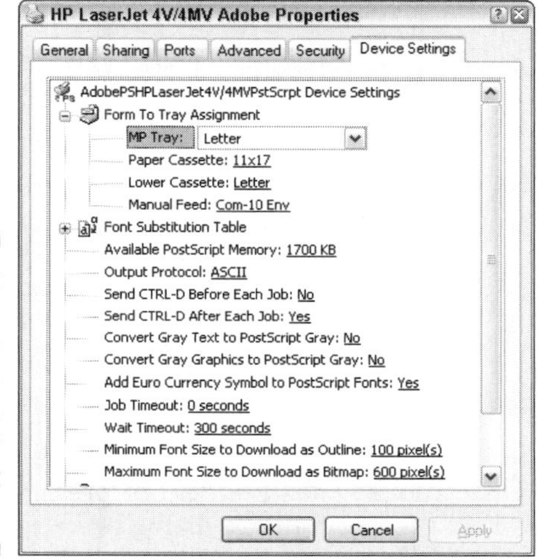

Figure 22-2: The Device Settings pane in Windows setup for PostScript devices.

To set a printer as the default printer, right-click the printer in the Printers window (as described earlier in this section) and select Set Default Printer from the contextual menu that appears.

Checking Your Document before Printing

Now that your printers are set up, you can use InDesign's preprinting checkup tool, called Preflight. The Preflight tool examines your document for any issues of concern and gives you a report on what might need to be fixed.

You may wonder why you need a Preflight tool to check for things such as missing fonts and images when InDesign lists any missing fonts and graphics when you open a document. The answer is that sometimes fonts and graphics files are moved after you open a file, in which case you won't get the alerts from InDesign. This is more likely to happen if you work with files and fonts on a network drive, rather than with local fonts and graphics. Preflight also checks for other problematic issues, such as the use of RGB files and TrueType fonts.

If you're working with the InDesign books feature (see Chapter 9), you can preflight the book's chapters from an open book's pane by using the Preflight Book option in its palette menu. (If one or more documents in the book are selected in the pane, the menu option changes to Preflight Selected Documents.) The options are the same as for preflighting individual documents.

Giving InDesign a preflighting target

Before you run the Preflight tool, you may want to set up your printer output so the tool accurately checks your document's setup in anticipation of, for example, whether you plan to output color separations or spot colors. To do this, choose File⇨Print Presets⇨Define to open the Print Preset dialog box, and then click New. The New Print Preset dialog box will appear, giving you the same options as the Print dialog box (covered in Chapter 23). Click OK when you are finished with your preset, then click OK again to close the Print Presets dialog box and return to your layout. (You can also save settings in the Print dialog box by clicking Save Preset before printing.)

But don't confuse InDesign's print setup with the operating system's printer setup. InDesign's Print dialog box contains a button called Printer (on the Mac) and Setup (in Windows) that lets you change print settings for all applications — it's essentially a shortcut to the operating-system controls described earlier in this section. You should change these operating-system settings only for output controls that InDesign's Print dialog box does not provide.

Running the Preflight tool is easy. Choose File⇨Preflight or press Shift+Option+⌘+F or Ctrl+Alt+Shift+F. In a few seconds, a dialog box appears that shows the status of your document. Here's what the six panes in the Preflight dialog box do:

- **The Summary pane** (shown in Figure 22-3) shows you a summary of alerts. If your document has layers, you can select or deselect the Show Data for Hidden Document Layers option. If selected, layers that won't print are analyzed for font, image, and other issues. Select this option only if the person receiving your document plans on printing hidden layers. For example, in a French-and-English document, you may have hidden the French layer for proofing but still want it checked because the service bureau is instructed to print the document twice — once with the English layer on and the French layer off, and once with the English layer off and the French layer on.
- **The Fonts pane** (shown in Figure 22-4) shows the type of each font (Type 1 PostScript, OpenType, or TrueType) so you can spot any TrueType fonts before they go to your service bureau. (TrueType fonts usually don't print easily on imagesetters, so use a program like Pyrus FontLab to translate them to PostScript instead.) It will also show if any fonts are missing from your system. You can search for missing fonts, as well as replaced unwanted TrueType fonts, by clicking Find Font.
- **The Links and Images pane** shows whether any graphics files are missing or if the original image has been modified since you placed it in your layout. You can click Update to correct any such bad links one at a time, or Repair All to have InDesign prompt you in turn for each missing or modified file. The pane also shows whether a color profile is embedded in your graphics in case files that should have them don't or in case a file that should not have an embedded profile does. (See Chapter 23 for

all the goods on color profiles.) It also alerts you if you use RGB images; although such images will print and color-separate, InDesign provides the warning because it's usually better to convert RGB images to CMYK in an image editor or illustration program so you can control the final appearance, rather than rely on InDesign or the output device to do the translation.

- **The Colors and Inks pane** shows the color of the inks that will be used in the output. (If you are printing color separations, these correspond to the color plates that will eventually be used to print the document on a printing press.) You can't modify anything here — it's simply for informational purposes — but it's a handy way to ensure that you aren't accidentally using a spot color that will print to a separate color plate when you meant to print it as a process color using the standard CMYK plates.

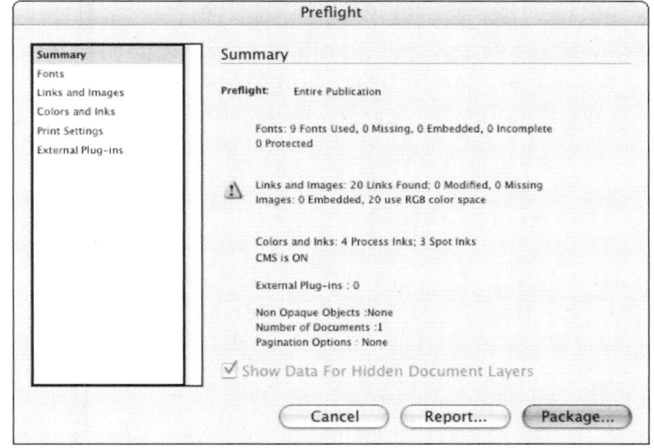

Figure 22-3: The Summary pane of the Preflight dialog box.

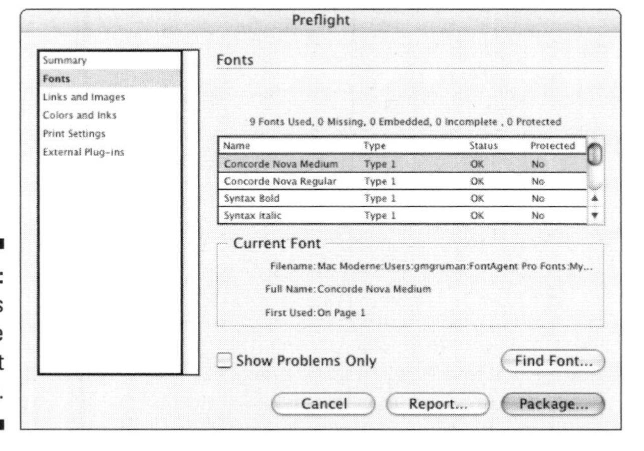

Figure 22-4: The Fonts pane of the Preflight dialog box.

- **The Print Settings pane** shows how the document is configured to print in the Print dialog box. This is why it's key to configure the output settings, as described earlier, before preflighting your document.
- **The External Plug-ins pane** shows any plug-in programs that are required in order to output the file. Amazingly, some third-party plug-ins make changes to the InDesign document that require the same plug-in to be installed at each computer that opens the file. This dialog box alerts you if you have such a dependency.

You can limit the status list in most panes to display only problems by selecting the Show Problems Only option.

By clicking Report, you can generate a text file containing the information from the Preflight dialog box's panes, which you can give to your service bureau to check its settings and files against.

You can also click Package to gather all related fonts and files into one folder for delivery to a service bureau or other outside printing agency. Click Cancel to exit the Preflight dialog box and go back to your document.

Chapter 23

Printing and Other Output Techniques

In This Chapter

- Calibrating colors for accurate reproduction
- Printing your layouts to printers and other devices
- Exporting to PDF files
- Collecting files for service bureaus

Printing is more complex than just choosing File➪Print, or it can be, depending on what you're printing and on what printing device you're using. For example, printing a full-color brochure involves more settings and steps than printing a proof copy to your laser printer or inkjet printer. So as you go through this chapter, keep in mind that many steps aren't relevant every time you print — but understanding the basics of printing ensures that you follow the right steps for each type of project. When you know the steps for printing one document, the process for printing every other document is very easy.

Chapter 22 explains how to set up your Mac or PC for printing in InDesign. Be sure that those settings are in place before you try to print anything.

Calibrating Color

If you're producing color documents for printing on a printing press, you may want to use InDesign's built-in color calibration tools. In a sense, you have to, because color calibration is now always on. But color calibration is something you don't do in a vacuum — you have to do it in your graphics programs as well, so that every piece of software that handles your graphics is working from the same color assumptions.

If you use Adobe Creative Suite 2, you can use a consistent color management system (CMS) in all of the CS2 programs, ensuring consistent color. For scanned images, digital camera photos, and the like, you can also tell InDesign the source device so InDesign knows the color assumptions that the device makes and can use that information to adjust the colors during printing accordingly.

In InDesign CS2, color management is always on, which is a change from previous versions.

Ensuring consistent color

You can set the CMS settings in InDesign by choosing Edit⇨Color Settings to get the dialog box shown in Figure 23-1. Most of Adobe's Creative Suite 2 applications have the same dialog box, although sometimes you access it in different ways:

- **Photoshop CS2:** Choose Photoshop⇨Color Settings on the Mac and Edit⇨Color Settings in Windows, or pressing Shift+⌘+K or Ctrl+Shift+K.
- **Illustrator CS2:** Choose Illustrator⇨Color Settings or press Ctrl+⌘+K on the Mac; choose Edit⇨Color Settings or press Ctrl+Shift+K in Windows.
- **GoLive CS2:** Choose GoLive⇨Color Settings on the Mac and Edit⇨Color Settings in Windows. (No keyboard shortcut is available.)
- **Acrobat 7:** Choose Acrobat⇨Preferences or press ⌘+K on the Mac; choose Edit⇨Preferences or press Ctrl+K in Windows, and then go to the Color Management pane. Note that this pane's appearance differs from the appearance of other Creative Suite 2 applications' color-settings panes.

When you load a bitmapped image into InDesign, the active CMS applies the default settings defined in the Color Settings dialog box (choose Edit⇨Color Settings). If the document has no embedded color profile, a dialog box appears with a list of color profiles, as well as options to apply the default you've set up in InDesign or to apply no profile. (If you choose not to apply a profile, the color won't be adjusted during printing.)

Whether or not there are embedded profiles for the document, you can change the color settings for specific images as follows:

- As you import each file, select Show Import Options in the Place dialog box (choose File⇨Place or press ⌘+D or Ctrl+D) when you place a graphic into InDesign. In the resulting Image Import Options dialog box, go to the Color pane and select the appropriate profile from the Profile menu.
- Any time after you place an image, select it and choose Object⇨Image Color Settings to apply a different profile. (You can also choose Graphics⇨Image Color Settings from the contextual menu.)

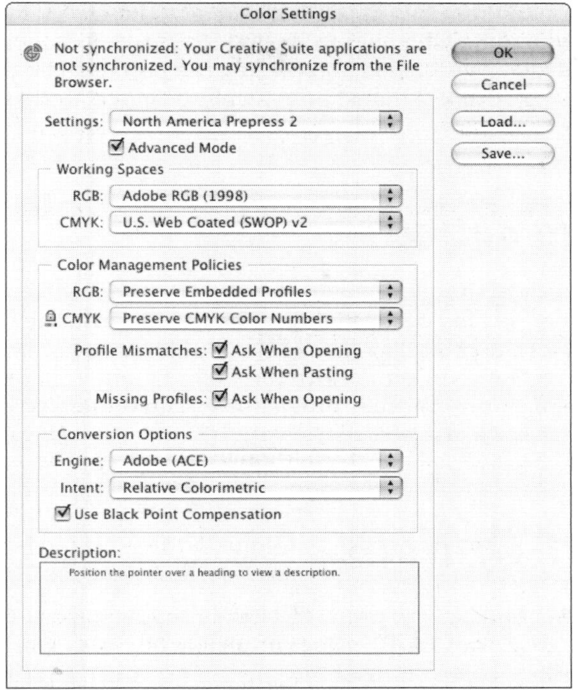

Figure 23-1: The Color Settings dialog box lets you set application color defaults.

Saving color management preferences

You can save and use color management settings in other documents. The process is simple: Click Save in the Color Settings dialog box to save the current dialog box's settings to a file. If you want to use the saved color-settings information in another document, open that document and click Load in the Color Settings dialog box, and then browse for and select the color settings file. That's it! This is a handy way to ensure consistency in a workgroup.

Changing document color settings

If you put together a document with specific color settings, but then decide you want to apply a new profile across your pictures or replace a specific profile globally in your document, you can:

- Choose Edit➪Assign Profiles to replace the color management settings globally.
- Choose Edit➪Convert to Profile to change the document's color workspace. It also lets you change the CMS engine, rendering intent, and black-point compensation settings.

There's real overlap in these two dialog boxes. Using the Assign Profiles dialog box to replace the document profile does the same job as the Convert to Profile dialog box when it comes to replacing the profiles. The only difference is that the Assign Profiles dialog box can also remove profiles from the document.

Calibrating output

When you're ready to output your document to a printer or other device, set the profile and rendering intent for that destination device in the Color Management pane of the Print dialog box (choose File➪Print or press ⌘+P or Ctrl+P), which has a Options section with the Color handling and Printer Profile pop-up menus. Here you select the appropriate option for your output device. (If you don't know, ask an expert.)

Choosing Print Options

When your document is ready to print, go to the Print dialog box (choose File➪Print or press ⌘+P or Ctrl+P). The Print dialog box has eight panes as well as several options common to all the panes. (We cover just the essential ones here.) Change any options and click Print, and InDesign sends your document to the printer. Figure 23-2 shows the dialog box.

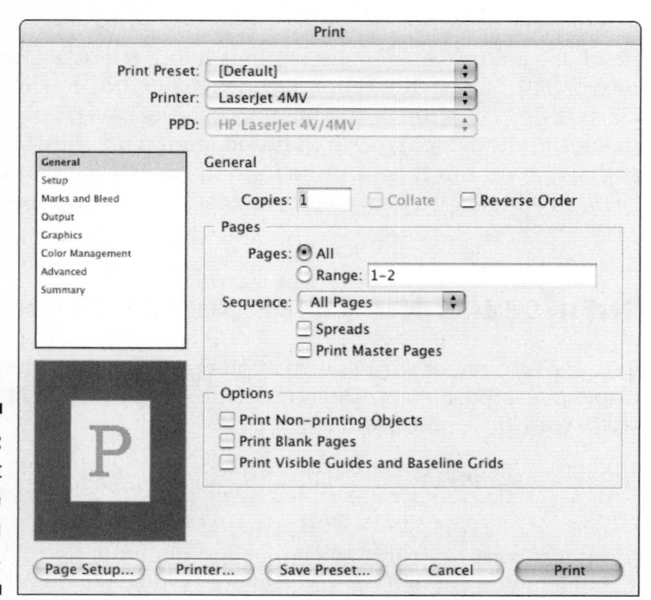

Figure 23-2: The default view for the Print dialog box.

If you're working with the InDesign books feature (see Chapter 9), you can print the book's chapters from an open book's pane by using the Print Book option in its palette menu. (If one or more documents in the book are selected in the pane, the menu option changes to Print Selected Documents.) The setup options are the same as for printing individual documents.

General options

The general options available in the dialog box, no matter what pane is selected, are as follows:

- **Print Preset:** This pop-up menu lets you save a group of printer settings, which makes it easy to switch between, say, a proofing printer and a final output device.
- **Printer:** This pop-up menu lets you select the printer to use.
- **PPD:** This pop-up menu lets you select PostScript Printer Descriptions, which are files that contain configuration and feature information specific to a brand and model of printer. You installed these into your operating system by using software that comes from your printer manufacturer. If InDesign finds no compatible PPDs, it uses generic options. If InDesign finds just one compatible PPD, it uses that automatically; otherwise, it lets you select a PPD.
- **Save Preset:** Clicking this button saves any settings that you change in the Print dialog box and lets you choose a name for those saved settings for reuse. If you change the dialog box's settings but don't save these changes as a print preset, InDesign changes the name of the current settings in the Print Preset pop-up menu to [Custom] to remind you the settings are changed and unsaved.

  You can also create print presets by choosing File⇨Print Presets⇨Define, or edit an existing preset by choosing File⇨Print Presets⇨*Preset Name.* When you click New or Edit in the resulting dialog box, a dialog box identical to the Print dialog box appears, except that the Print button becomes the OK button.
- **Setup (Windows); Page Setup and Printer (Mac):** These buttons give you access to printer-specific controls. You use these dialog boxes to specify options such as printing to file, paper sources, and printer resolution. Note that if you add a printer, you may need to quit InDesign and restart it for it to see the new printer.
- **Cancel:** Clicking this button closes the Print dialog box without printing. Use this if you've clicked Save Preset but don't want to print, as well when you have any reason not to print.
- **Print:** Clicking this button prints the document based on the current settings.

- **Page preview panel:** This panel at lower left shows the current settings graphically. The page is indicated by the blue rectangle, and the direction of the large *P* indicates the printing orientation; in Figure 23-2, shown previously, the *P* is unrotated. The panel shows that the paper itself is the same size as the page (the page is shown in white, and if the paper were larger than the page, you'd see a light gray area around the page indicating the excess paper). This preview changes as you adjust settings in the dialog box.

The General pane

The General pane contains the basic settings for your print job. Most are self-explanatory, but note the following:

- When specifying a range of pages in the Pages option, you can type non-consecutive ranges, such as **1–4, 7, 10–13, 15, 18, 20**. If you want to print from a specific page to the end of the document, just type the hyphen after the initial page number, such as **4–**. InDesign figures out what the last page is. Similarly, to start from the first page and end on a specified page, just start with the hyphen, as in **–11**. InDesign lets you type absolute page numbers in the Range field. For example, typing **+6–+12** would print the document's 6th through 12th pages, no matter what their page numbers are.
- Selecting the Spreads option prints facing pages on the same sheet of paper, such as putting two letter-size pages on one 11-×17-inch sheet. This is handy when showing clients proposed designs, but make sure you have a printer that can handle a large paper size or that you scale the output down to fit (through the Setup pane, which we cover in the following section).

The Setup pane

The Setup pane is where you tell InDesign how to work with the paper (or other media, such as film negatives) to which you're printing. The options are straightforward, so we just highlight a few notes and tips:

- **Custom page size:** Choosing some printer models will in turn let you choose a Custom option in the Page Size pop-up menu, in which case you type the dimensions in the Width and Height fields, as well as position the output through the Offset and Gap fields. These latter two options are usually used when printing to a roll, such as in an imagesetter using photo paper (called *RC paper,* a resin-coated paper that keeps details extremely sharp), so you can make sure there is space between the left edge of the roll and the page boundary (the offset), as well as between pages (the gap). Most printers can't print right to the edge, thus the

Offset setting. You also want a gap between pages for crop and registration marks, as well as to have room to physically cut the pages.

- **Traverse option:** Don't use the Transverse option, which rotates the output 90 degrees, unless your service bureau or production department tells you to. Otherwise, you might have your pages cut off on the final negatives.
- **Tile options:** Use the Tile options to print oversized documents. InDesign breaks the document into separate pages — called *tiles* — that you later can assemble together. To enable tiling, select the Tile option, and then choose the appropriate option from the adjoining pop-up menu:
  - **Manual:** This lets you specify the tiles yourself. To specify a tile, you change the origin point on the document ruler, and the new origin point becomes the upper-left corner of the current tile. (To change the origin point, just drag the upper left corner of the rulers to a new position in your document.) To print multiple tiles this way, you need to adjust the origin point and print, adjust the origin point to the next location and print, and so on, until you're done.
  - **Auto:** This lets InDesign figure out where to divide the pages into tiles. You can change the default amount of overlap between tiles of 1.5 inches by using the Overlap field. The overlap lets you easily align tiles by having enough overlap for you to see where each should be placed relative to the others.
  - **Auto Justified:** This is similar to Auto except that it makes each tile the same size, adjusting the overlap if needed to do that. (The Auto option, by contrast, simply starts at the origin point and then does as much of the page as will fit in the tile, which means the last tile may be a different width than the others. You can see the difference between the two by watching how the page preview window at left changes as you select each option.

The Marks and Bleed pane

The Bleed and Slug area of the Marks and Bleed pane controls how materials print past the page boundary. A bleed is used when you want a picture, color, or text to go right to the edge of the paper. Because there is slight variation on positioning when you print because the paper moves mechanically through rollers and might move slightly during transit, publishers have any to-the-edge materials actually print beyond the edge, so there are never any gaps. It's essentially a safety margin. A normal bleed margin would be 0p9 (⅛ inch), though you can make it larger if you want.

A *slug* is an area beyond the bleed area in which you want printer's marks to appear. The reader never sees this, but the workers at the commercial printer do, and it helps them make sure they have the right pages, colors, and so on. Like the bleed, the slug area is trimmed off when the pages are bound into a magazine, newspaper, or whatever. (The word *slug* is an old newspaper term for this identifying information, based on the lead slug once used for this purpose on old printing presses.) The purpose of the slug is to ensure there is enough room for all the printer's marks to appear between the bleed area and the edges of the page. Otherwise, InDesign will do the best it can.

It's best to define your bleed and slug areas in your document itself when you create the document in the New Document dialog box (choose File⇨New⇨Document or press ⌘+N or Ctrl+N), as covered in Chapter 5. You can also use the Document Setup dialog box (choose File⇨Document Setup or press Option+⌘+P or Ctrl+Alt+P). The two dialog boxes have the same options; if they don't show the Bleed and Slug section, click More Options to see them.

But if you didn't define your bleeds previously, you can do so in the Print dialog box's Marks and Bleed pane. You can also override those New Document or Document Setup document settings here. To use the document settings, select the Use Document Bleed Settings option. Otherwise, type in a bleed area by using the Top, Bottom, Left, and Right fields. If you want the four fields to be the same, click the broken-chain button to the right of the Top field; it becomes a solid chain, indicating that all four fields will have the same value if any is modified. Any bleed area is indicated in red in the preview pane at the bottom left.

If you want to set the slug area, select the Include Slug Area option. InDesign then reserves any slug area defined in the New Document or Document Setup dialog box. You can't set up the slug area in the Print dialog box.

The Output pane

The next pane is the Output pane, which controls the processing of colors and inks on imagesetters, platesetters, and commercial printing equipment. For proof printing, such as to a laser printer or an inkjet printer, the only option that you need to worry about is on the Color pop-up menu, which controls whether the colors print as color or as grayscale.

The options in the Output pane are for experts and should be specified in coordination with your service bureau and commercial printer — they can really mess up your printing if set incorrectly.

One area that you should set is in the Ink Manager dialog box. Accessed by clicking Ink Manager, the Ink Manager dialog box, shown in Figure 23-3, gives you finer controls over how color negatives output. If any colors should have been converted to process color but weren't, you have three choices:

- **Click the spot color icon.** You can override the spot color in the Ink Manager dialog box by clicking this icon (a circle) to the left of the color's name. That converts it to a process color. (Clicking the process color icon, a four-color box, converts a color back to a spot color.) This is the way to go for a quick fix.

- **Make the spot color a process color instead.** Do this by closing the Ink Manager and Print dialog boxes, and editing the color that was incorrectly set as a spot color in the Swatches pane (choose Window⇨Swatches or press F5) as we cover in Chapter 10. This ensures that the color is permanently changed to a process color for future print jobs.
- **Convert all spot colors to CMYK process equivalents.** Do this by selecting the All Spots to Process option. This is the easiest method to make sure you don't accidentally print spot-color plates for a CMYK-only document.

The other Ink Manager options are for experts and should be changed only in consultation with your service bureau, production department, and/or commercial printer.

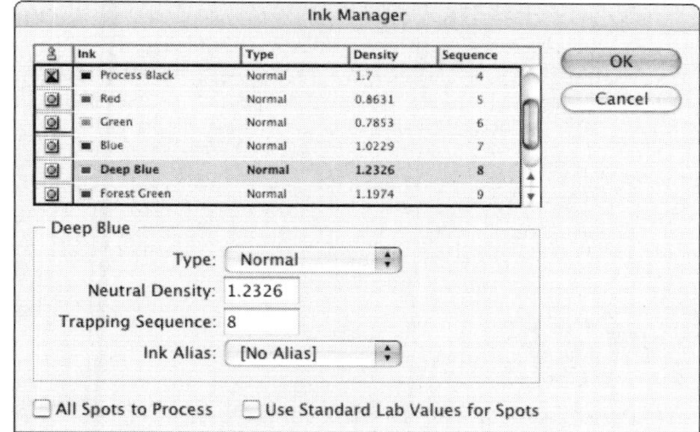

Figure 23-3: The Ink Manager dialog box

The Graphics pane

By using the Graphics pane, you control how graphics are printed and how fonts are downloaded. The options here are meant for professional printing, such as to imagesetters, in situations where you're working with a service bureau or in-house printing department. This is also an expert area, so change these settings only after consulting with an experienced pro.

The Color Management pane

The Color Management pane is where you manage color output (apply color calibration). Most options should be changed only in consultation with your service bureau or production department.

One option you should be able to change on your own is Printer Profile. Use this pop-up menu to select the device to which the document will ultimately be printed. This is by default the same as the profile selected in the Edit Color Settings pane, which we discuss earlier in this chapter, in the section "Calibrating Color."

The Advanced pane

The options in the Advanced pane let you control graphics file substitutions in an Open Prepress Interface (OPI) workflow and also set transparency flattening, which controls how transparent and semitransparent objects are handled during output. Again, these are expert options you should change only in consultation with your service bureau or production department.

The Summary pane

The final Print dialog box pane is the Summary pane. It simply lists your settings all in one place for easy review. The only option — Save Summary — saves the settings to a file so you can include it with your files when delivering them to a service bureau or for distribution to other staff members so they know the preferred settings.

Creating PDF Files

Sometimes you want to create a PDF file for distribution on the Web, on a CD, on a corporate intranet, or even by e-mail. PDF creation is a really easy task in InDesign. First choose File➪Export or press ⌘+E or Ctrl+E. The Export dialog box appears, which like any standard Save dialog box lets you name the file and determine what drive and folder the file is to be saved in. The key control in the Export dialog box is the Formats pop-up menu, where you choose the format (in this case, Adobe PDF). Then click Save.

If you're working with the InDesign Books feature (see Chapter 9), you can export the book's chapters to PDF files from an open book's pane by using the Export Book to PDF option in its palette menu. (If one or more documents in the book are selected in the pane, the menu option changes to Export Selected Documents to PDF.) The setup options are the same as for exporting individual documents.

After you select Adobe PDF in the Export dialog box's Formats pop-up menu and give the file a name and location in the File Name and Save in areas, click Save to get the Export Adobe PDF dialog box shown later in this chapter in Figure 23-4.

The dialog box has six panes; the General pane is displayed when you open the dialog box. There are several options that are accessible from all six panes.

If you know how to use Acrobat Professional, you know how to set up your PDF export. If not, it's best to consult with a local expert because PDF export options are as complex and job-specific as the print options we covered earlier. Still, there are some basic options available in all the panes that you should feel comfortable setting on your own:

- **Adobe PDF Preset:** This pop-up menu lets you select from both predefined sets of PDF-export settings (similar to the printer presets covered earlier in this chapter), as well as any presets you may have created.
- **Compatibility:** This pop-up menu lets you choose which PDF file version to save the file as. Your options are Acrobat 4 (PDF 1.3), Acrobat 5 (PDF 1.4), Acrobat 6 (PDF 1.5), and Acrobat 7 (PDF 1.6). Choosing Acrobat 4 (PDF 1.3) is the best option for documents that you want to distribute on CD or over the Web because it ensures the broadest number of people will be able to view the file. Choose a later version only if you're certain that your intended recipients use that version of Acrobat or Adobe Reader. For example, if your company has standardized on Acrobat 5 and the document will be used only internally, picking the Acrobat 5 (PDF 1.4) option makes sense. Likewise, if you're sending the PDF file to a service bureau, use the version of Acrobat that the service bureau uses because later versions of Acrobat support more features, especially for commercial printing. (Versions 1.5 and later, for example, support native transparency.)
- **Save Preset:** Click this to save any settings made in the Export Adobe PDF dialog box as a new preset. (You can also define new PDF presets by choosing File⇨PDF Export Presets⇨Define.)
- **Export:** Click this to create the PDF file based on the settings that you selected in the various panes.

Using Distiller job options

InDesign CS2 also lets you import settings from Acrobat Distiller job-options files. You can load such job-option files by clicking Load in the Adobe PDF Presets dialog box (choose File⇨PDF Export Presets⇨Define).

You can use the Adobe PDF Presets dialog box to create and edit the job-option files for sharing with Acrobat Distiller and other Creative Suite 2 users; just click Save when you're done. When creating or editing these PDF presets, you get the same options that we describe in the previous section for the Export PDF dialog box.

The General pane

Use the General pane to determine what is exported. The Pages option gives you the same flexibility as the Print dialog box's Pages option, we cover in the earlier section "Choosing Print Options." Similarly, the Spread option works like the same-name option in the Print dialog box.

In the Options section, you can select the following options:

- **Embed Page Thumbnails:** Select this option if you're creating a PDF file to be viewed on-screen. Thumbnails help people to more easily navigate your document in the Adobe Reader program. However, if you're sending the PDF files to a service bureau or commercial printer for printing, you don't need to generate the thumbnails.
- **Optimize for Fast Web View:** Always select this option — this minimizes file size without compromising the output.
- **Create Tagged PDF:** Select this option to embed XML tag information into the PDF file. This is useful for XML-based workflows and Adobe eBooks. If you don't know what XML or eBooks are, you don't need to select this option.
- **View PDF after Exporting:** Select this option if you want to see the results of the PDF export as soon as the export is complete. Typically, however, you shouldn't select this option because you likely will have other things you want to do before launching Adobe Reader (or the full Acrobat program, if you own it) to proof your files.
- **Create Acrobat Layers:** If you selected Acrobat 6 (PDF 1.5) or Acrobat 7 (PDF 1.6) in the Compatibility pop-up menu, you can select this option, which outputs any InDesign layers to separate layers in Acrobat. (Acrobat 6 was the first version of Acrobat to support layers.) If you choose a different Compatibility option, Create Acrobat Layers is grayed out.

In the Include section, you set what elements of the document are included in the PDF file. You can select the following options:

- **Bookmarks:** This takes InDesign table-of-contents (TOC) information and preserves it as bookmarks in the exported PDF file.
- **Hyperlinks:** This preserves any hyperlinks added in InDesign. Otherwise, the hyperlinks are converted to standard text in the PDF file.
- **Visible Guides and Grids:** This includes the on-screen guides and grids in the output version — an option you'd use only when creating PDF files meant to be used as designer examples, not for readers or for prepress.
- **Non-Printing Objects:** This includes any objects marked as Nonprinting through the Attributes pane (choose Window⇨Attributes).

- **Interactive Elements:** This preserves interactive objects such as buttons rather than convert them to static graphics.
- **Multimedia:** This pop-up menu lets you control how embedded sound and video are handled. This option is available only if you choose Acrobat 6 (PDF 1.5) or Acrobat 7 (PDF 1.6) in the Compatibility pop-up menu. The options are Use Object Settings, Link All, or Embed All. In InDesign, you can embed a sound or movie file, or link to one. This option lets you override the individual settings and make all such objects embedded or linked.

The Compression pane

All the options in this pane compress your document's graphics. For documents you're intending to print professionally, make sure that for the Color, Grayscale, and Monochrome image types, the No Sampling Change option is selected, and that Compression is set to None. You don't want to do anything that affects the resolution or quality of your bitmap images if you're outputting to a high-resolution device.

But it's fine to select the Crop Image Data to Frames option because this discards portions of pictures not visible on-screen, reducing file size and reducing processing time during output. (Imagesetters and other devices usually have to process the entire image, even if only part of it is actually printed.)

You can also select the Compress Text and Line Art option. It compresses vector graphics (both imported and those created in InDesign) as well as text, but does so without affecting output quality.

For the rest, stick with the defaults based on the preset you chose, or check with your production department.

Marks and Bleed pane

The Marks and Bleed pane in the Export Adobe PDF dialog box works just like the Marks and Bleed pane in the Print dialog box, which we cover earlier in this chapter.

The Output pane

The Output pane has two sections — Color and PDF/X — where you control color calibration. Adjust these only if you're creating a PDF file meant to be used by a service bureau to print the final document on paper or to create plates for commercial printing. Ask the people at your service bureau what settings they prefer for this pane's options.

The Output pane is new to InDesign CS2, though its features existed in the Advanced pane in InDesign CS. Several of the options have been changed to reflect InDesign CS2's new color-management settings.

The Advanced pane

The Advanced pane in the Export Adobe PDF dialog box has the same options as the Advanced pane in the Print dialog box, which we cover earlier in this chapter. Like the Output pane, these options are relevant only if you're generating a PDF file that your service bureau or commercial printer will use to create the final printed output from.

Security pane

The Security pane, shown in Figure 23-4, has no relevance to documents intended to be output at a service bureau or commercial printer, so make sure the Require a Password to Open the Document and the Use a Password to Restrict Printing, Editing, and Other Tasks option are not selected in that case.

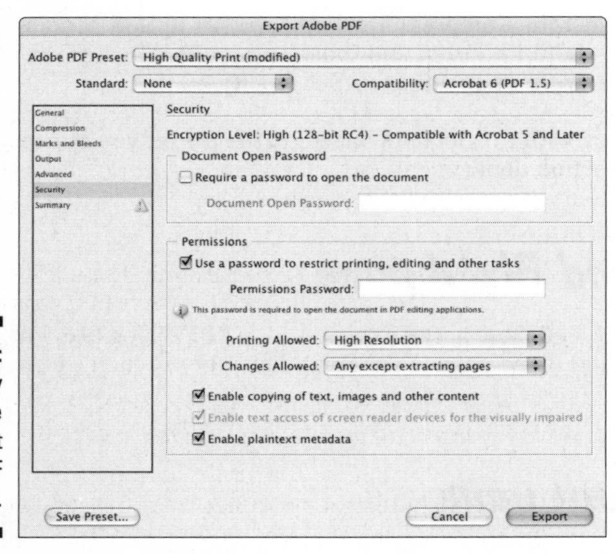

Figure 23-4: The Security pane of the Export Adobe PDF dialog box.

These settings are useful if you're publishing the document electronically, because they control who can access the document and what they can do with the document once it's open. Here's how they work:

- **Encryption Level:** This section's options depend on the option set in the Compatibility pop-up menu; Acrobat 5 (PDF 1.4) or higher use High (128-bit RC4) encryption, while earlier versions use 40-bit RC4.
- **Document Open Password:** In this section of the Security pane, you can require a password to open the exported PDF file by selecting this option and typing a password in the associated text field. If you don't type a password here, you're forced to type one in a dialog box that appears later. To access protected content, recipients must use the Security pane in Acrobat (choose File⇨Document Properties or press ⌘+D or Ctrl+D).
- **Permissions:** Here, you determine what restrictions to place on the PDF file. Note that the options will vary based on what version of the PDF format you selected in the General pane.
    - **Use a Password to Restrict Printing, Editing, and Other Tasks:** You can restrict recipients' actions by selecting this option and then specifying permissible actions by using the Printing Allowed and Changes Allowed pop-up menus, as well as selecting from among the options that follow (the number of options displayed varies based on the preset chosen). You can also require a password to allow editing of the file in another application. Your management options include the following:
    - **Printing Allowed:** You can select None, Low-Resolution (150 dpi), or High Resolution. You would disable printing to ensure that the material can be read only on-screen.
    - **Changes Allowed:** You can select None; Inserting, Deleting and Rotating Pages; Filling in Form Fields and Signing; Commenting, Filling in Form Fields, and Signing; or Any Except Extracting Pages. (*Signing* means using digital signatures to verify sender and recipient identities.)
    - **Enable Copying of Text, Images, and Other Content:** If it's okay for recipients to use the PDF file's objects, select this option.
    - **Enable Text Access of Screen Reader Devices for the Visually Impaired:** If you want the file to be accessible to visually impaired recipients who use text-reader applications, select this option. This option is available only if you are exporting to Acrobat 5 (PDF 1.4) or later.
    - **Enable Plaintext Metadata:** For documents with *metadata* — authoring information associated with XML documents and Web pages — you can make that metadata visible to Web-based search engines and similar applications by selecting this option. This option is available only if you are exporting to Acrobat 6 (PDF 1.5) or later.

Settings for on-screen usage

If your output is destined for use on a monitor — such as from CD, on the Web, or in a corporate intranet — use these settings when exporting to PDF files:

- In the General pane, select the Optimize for Fast Web View option. Also, check Spreads if your facing pages are designed as one visual unit.
- In the Compression pane, change the two Image Quality pop-up menus to Low. Also, choose any of the Downsampling or Subsampling menu options in all three image types' sections. The pixels-per-inch (ppi) value should be either 72 (if you intend people just to view the images on-screen) or 300 or 600 (if you expect people to print the documents to a local inkjet or laser printer). Pick the ppi value that best matches most users' printers' capabilities. For the Compression pop-up menus, choose Automatic (JPEG) for the color and grayscale bitmaps, and CCITT Group 4 (the standard method for fax compression) for black-and-white bitmaps. Set Quality to Maximum for color and grayscale bitmaps. Finally, select the Compress Text and Line Art option.
- In the Marks and Bleeds pane, make sure no printer's marks are selected.
- In the Security pane, select the security features (Document Open Password and Permissions) and the options for which you want to add security. Uncheck the Enable Copying of Text and Graphics option to prevent readers from copying and pasting your content, and select None from the Printing Allowed pop-up menu to prevent printing. The Changes Allowed pop-up menu options control whether readers can extra pages, add comments to the file, fill in forms, delete pages, or rotate pages. Typically, you'd choose either Filling in Form Fields and Signing (so readers could complete forms) or Commenting, Filling in Forms, and Signing (so readers can complete forms and add their own comments) — both options keep the user from accessing the underlying content of your PDF files.

The Summary pane

The final Export Adobe PDF dialog box pane is the Summary pane, which simply lists your settings all in one place for easy review. The only option — Save Summary — saves the settings to a file so you can include it with your files when delivering them to a service bureau, or for distribution to other staff members so they know the preferred settings.

Creating a Document Package

Have you ever given a page-layout document to a service bureau only to be called several hours later because some of the files necessary to output your document are missing? If so, you'll love the Package feature in InDesign.

This command, which you access by choosing File➪Package or by pressing Option+Shift+⌘+P or Ctrl+Alt+Shift+P, copies into a folder all the font, color-output, and picture files necessary to output your document. It also generates a report that contains all the information about your document that a service bureau is ever likely to need, including the document's fonts, dimensions, and trapping information. You can also create an instructions file that has your contact information and any particulars you want to say about the document.

When you run the Package command, InDesign preflights your document automatically and gives you the option of viewing any problems it encounters. If you elect to view that information, the Preflight dialog box appears. You can continue to package your document from that dialog box by clicking Package after you assure yourself that none of the problems will affect the document's output. If it finds no problems during the automatic preflighting, InDesign will not display the Preflight dialog box.

Before you can actually package the document, InDesign asks you to save the current document, and then fill in the Printing Instructions form. You can change the default filename from Instructions.txt to something more suitable, such as the name of your print job. Often, you'll leave the printing instructions blank — use it only if you have *special* instructions.

If you *don't* want to create an instructions form, don't click Cancel — that cancels the entire package operation. Just click Continue, leaving the form blank. Similarly, you must click Save at the request to save the document; clicking Cancel stops the package operation as well.

The next step is to create the package folder. You do this in the dialog box that follows the Printing Instructions form, which on the Mac is called Create Package Folder and in Windows is called Package Publication. Figure 23-5 shows the Mac version, which except for the name at the top is the same as the Windows version.

In the dialog box, you can select what is copied: the fonts, color-output profiles, and *linked graphics* (graphics pasted into an InDesign document rather than imported are automatically included). You can also tell InDesign to update the graphics links for those that were modified or moved; if this Update Graphic Links in Package option isn't selected, any missing or modified graphics files won't be copied with the document.

You can tell InDesign to include fonts and links from hidden layers (which you would do only if you want the service bureau to print those hidden layers or if you were giving the document's files to a colleague to do further work).

You also can specify whether the document should use only the hyphenation exceptions defined within it. This often makes sense because it ensures that the printer's hyphenation dictionary — which may differ from yours — doesn't cause text to flow differently.

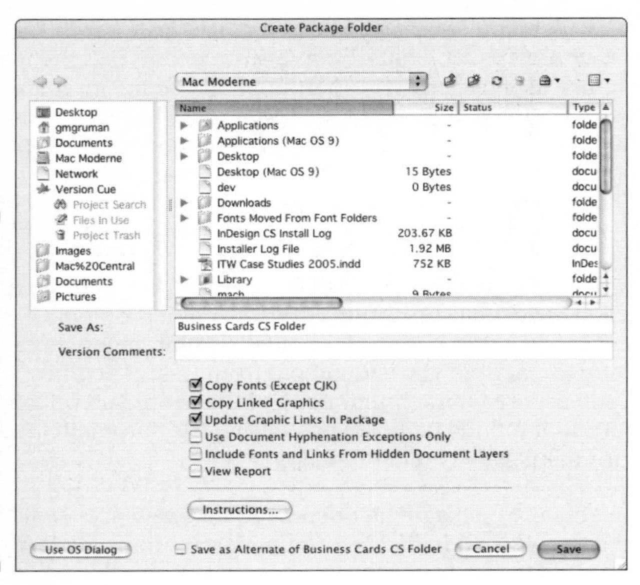

Figure 23-5: The Create Package Folder dialog box for Mac is called the Package Publication dialog box in Windows.

Finally, you can choose to view the report after the package is created — on the Mac, InDesign launches TextEdit and displays the report file, and on Windows it launches Notepad and displays the report file.

Click Save (on the Mac) or Package (in Windows) when everything is ready to go. Your document is placed in the folder you specify, as is the instructions file (the report). Inside that folder, InDesign will also create a folder called Fonts that includes the fonts, a folder called Links that has the graphics files, and a folder called Output Profiles that has the color output profiles.

We strongly recommend using the Package feature. It ensures that your service bureau has all the necessary files and information to output your document correctly.

Part VII
The Part of Tens

"...and here's me with Cindy Crawford. And this is me with Madonna and Celine Dion..."

In this part . . .

This part of the book gives you helpful Web sites, interesting books on InDesign and related publishing programs, and where to go to get InDesign information from Adobe. This part also shows you some important points to consider if you're switching from QuarkXPress or PageMaker to InDesign.

Chapter 24

Top Ten Resources for InDesign Users

In This Chapter

- Discovering useful Web sites
- Using Adobe Web resources
- Finding books to read

When you're ready to expand your horizons beyond what we can squeeze into the pages of this book, check out this chapter. No matter what type of information you're looking for, you can find it here among our handy list of InDesign resources.

Web Sites

Web sites are a great on-going resource, because they let you keep up with news, techniques, and product versions. Here are four sites that belong in your bookmarks:

InDesignCentral

`www.indesigncentral.com`

To help you keep up with the dynamic field of publishing, we've created an independent Web site that helps InDesign users stay current on tools and techniques. InDesignCentral provides the following resources:

- **Tools:** Links to plug-ins, scripts, utilities, and Adobe downloads.
- **Tips:** Our favorite tips, as well as reader tips.

- **Resources:** Print publishing links, Web publishing links, Mac OS X links, and Windows 2000/XP links.
- ***Adobe InDesign Bible* series and *QuarkXPress to InDesign: Face to Face*:** Excerpts from the books, including updates from after the books' releases and color versions of the screenshots from the chapters that cover color.

Figure 24-1 shows the site's home page.

The Adobe Web site

`www.adobe.com`

The friendly people at Adobe, who gave the world InDesign, recognize the value in providing useful information for users of their software solutions. The Adobe Web site offers InDesign tips and tricks, guides, interactive tutorials, and lists of user groups. It's worth your while to visit the site now and then to see what's new. Figure 24-2 shows an InDesign-related page from the Adobe site.

InDesign User Group

`www.indesignusergroup.com`

Seeking to help InDesign users share skills and tips, Adobe is sponsoring local user groups in many cities. Here's your chance to extend your InDesign knowledge and enlarge your personal network of graphics and layout experts.

You can also find links to several how-to guides from Adobe.

Creativepro

`www.creativepro.com`

Looking for the latest product and industry news? Go to Creativepro.com, an online magazine that also functions as a resource and reviews center.

Figure 24-1: Visit InDesign-Central for useful tips and tricks.

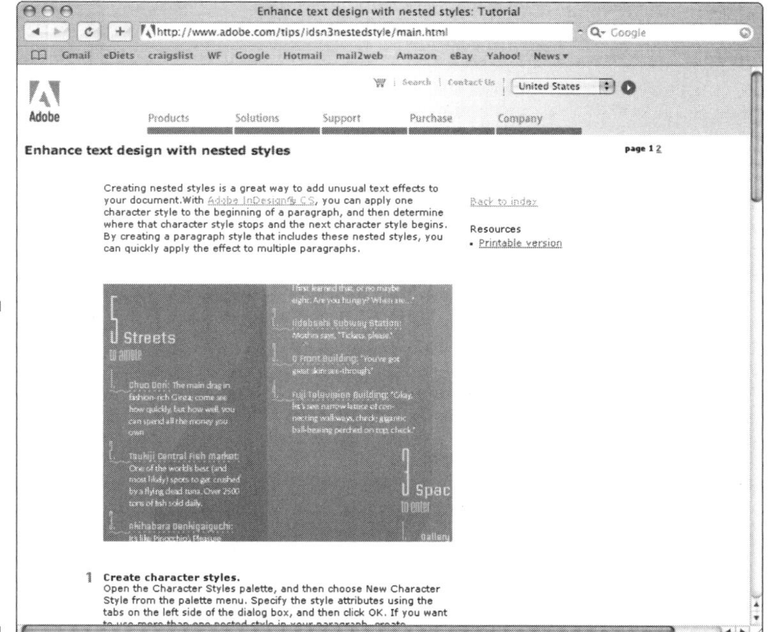

Figure 24-2: At the Adobe Web site, you can find useful information on InDesign, such as the tips page shown here.

Other InDesign Books We Recommend

Wiley Publishing, Inc., the publisher of this book, also offers a wide range of books to help layout artists and publication designers exploit publishing tools to the fullest. The following books could be of great use to you:

- *Adobe InDesign CS2 Bible,* by Galen Gruman, gives you extensive insight and tips on using the newest versions of InDesign in professional publishing environments.
- *QuarkXPress to InDesign: Face to Face,* by Galen Gruman, shows you how to make the move from QuarkXPress to InDesign. You'll be running at full speed in no time, leveraging your knowledge of QuarkXPress and translating it into InDesign's approach.
- *Photoshop CS2 Bible,* by Deke McClelland, provides an in-depth look at how to make the most of Photoshop's extensive image-editing capabilities. The *Photoshop CS2 Bible, Professional Edition,* also by Deke McClelland, goes even further, adding new and expanded coverage of high-end topics, such as creating and optimizing Web graphics, using filters, working with convolution kernels and displacement maps, harnessing actions and batch processing, and adjusting color. For quick techniques, *Photoshop CS: Top 100 Simplified Tips & Tricks,* by Denis Graham, provides clear, illustrated instructions for 100 tasks that reveal cool secrets, teach time-saving tricks, and explain great tips to make you a better Photoshop user. And *Photoshop CS2 For Dummies,* by Deke McClelland and Phyllis Davis, is a great way to quickly get up to speed on the newest version of Photoshop.
- *Illustrator CS2 Bible,* by Ted Alspach and Jennifer Alspach, includes extensive coverage on using Illustrator for print and Web graphics, as well as shows how to integrate Illustrator with Photoshop. And, of course, *Illustrator CS2 For Dummies,* by Ted Alspach, is a great way to quickly get up to speed on the newest version of Illustrator.
- *Adobe Acrobat 7 PDF Bible,* by Ted Padova, features complete coverage Acrobat and PDF for print prepress, the Internet, CD-ROMs, and all the new media.
- *Adobe Creative Suite 2 Bible,* by Ted Padova, Kelly L. Murdock, and Wendy Halderman, provides an all-in-one resource for users of Adobe's cornerstone tools (Photoshop, Illustrator, Acrobat Professional, and InDesign).
- *Digital Photography: Top 100 Simplified Tips & Tricks,* by Gregory Georges, provides clear, illustrated instructions for 100 tasks that reveal cool secrets, teach time-saving tricks, and explain great tips to make you a better digital photographer. To help you understand the implications of digital photography on the production process, *Total Digital Photography: The Shoot to Print Workflow Handbook,* by Serge Timacheff and David Karlins, offers complete, end-to-end workflow advice from shoot to print in a full-color presentation.

Chapter 25

Top Ten Must-Knows for QuarkXPress Refugees

In This Chapter

- Transferring QuarkXPress files to InDesign
- Understanding what works differently

You've jumped on the InDesign bandwagon after seeing everything it can do. Your problem is that a lot of QuarkXPress is still stuck in your brain. This chapter helps you make the mental switch so that you can become a native InDesigner.

Also, consider picking up a copy of *QuarkXPress to InDesign: Face to Face,* by Galen Gruman (Wiley Publishing, Inc.), which shows you side by side how to do in InDesign what you know how to do in QuarkXPress.

Opening Those Old QuarkXPress Files

InDesign opens QuarkXPress and QuarkXPress Passport files — but only in versions 3.3, 4.0, and 4.1. If InDesign sees any problems when opening these files, it gives you an alert so you know what to fix in the converted file. After the file opens, it is untitled, so you need to give it a new name.

Paying Attention to Selection Tool Differences

If you're a QuarkXPress veteran, the toughest thing about switching to InDesign is the set of tools. InDesign's Selection tool only lets you move and resize objects, and the Direct Selection tool lets you reshape objects and work with graphics. In InDesign, you use the Type tool to work with text, but you can't move or resize text frames while you're using it.

Using Keyboard Shortcuts for Tools

Because InDesign requires a lot more switching among tools than QuarkXPress, your mouse hand can tire very quickly. To avoid that, embrace InDesign's single-letter shortcuts for selecting tools.

Table 25-1 shows the shortcut translations for common activities.

Table 25-1 Keyboard Shortcuts Translated from QuarkXPress to InDesign

Action	*QuarkXPress Shortcut*	*InDesign Equivalent*
Preferences	Option+Shift+⌘+Y or Ctrl+Alt+Shift+Y	⌘+K or Ctrl+K
Get Text/Picture	⌘+E or Ctrl+E	⌘+D or Ctrl+D for Place
Paragraph formats	⌘+Shift+F or Ctrl+Shift+F	Option+⌘+T or Ctrl+Alt+T
Character formats	⌘+Shift+D or Ctrl+Shift+D	⌘+T or Ctrl+T
Style Sheets palette	F11	F11 (Character Styles), Shift+F11 (Paragraph Styles)
Spelling (word)	⌘+L or Ctrl+W	⌘+I or Ctrl+I
Modify dialog box	⌘+M or Ctrl+M	No equivalent
Duplicate	⌘+D or Ctrl+D	Option+Shift+⌘+D or Ctrl+Alt+Shift+D
Step and Repeat	Option+⌘+D or Ctrl+Alt+D	Option+⌘+U or Ctrl+Alt+U
Lock/Unlock	F6	⌘+L or Ctrl+L (lock), Option+⌘+L or Ctrl+Alt+L (unlock)
Ungroup	⌘+U or Ctrl+U	Shift+⌘+G or Ctrl+Shift+G
Send to Back	Shift+F5	Shift+⌘+[or Ctrl+Shift+[
Send Backward	Option+Shift+F5 or Ctrl+Shift+F5	⌘+[or Ctrl+[
Bring to Front	F5	Shift+⌘+] or Ctrl+Shift+]
Bring Forward	Option+F5 or Ctrl+F5	⌘+] or Ctrl+]

Thinking Panes, Not Dialog Boxes

Keep in mind that many InDesign menu commands simply display a pane (which may already be open) rather than show a dialog box. Get used to deciphering icons or using Tool Tips on the panes because InDesign doesn't have as many dialog boxes containing named fields as you're used to in QuarkXPress. Also, InDesign implements contextual menus on a broader scale than QuarkXPress, so you can Control+click or right=click objects, rulers, and more to make changes quickly.

Using Familiar Measurements

InDesign uses all of the QuarkXPress measurement abbreviations, as well as its own. For example, InDesign accepts QuarkXPress's use of " to indicate inches, as well as InDesign's own standard of `in` and `inch`.

Knowing Differences in Documents

By and large, documents in InDesign and QuarkXPress are the same. You have master pages, layers, and pages. You can also set bleeds for objects that go beyond the page boundary. The biggest difference is that InDesign's master text frame lets you automatically flow text from page to page, while the QuarkXPress equivalent automatic text box places an empty text box on each page for you to use as you see fit.

Working with Objects, Not Items

In QuarkXPress, you're used to distinct items such as text boxes, picture boxes, lines, and maybe text paths. In InDesign, you have more flexible objects such as paths and frames that can contain graphics or text.

Approaching Text from a New Perspective

In many cases, InDesign works with text very differently than QuarkXPress, even though the fundamental capabilities are the same in both programs. Veteran QuarkXPress users will be frustrated initially with InDesign's more-laborious approach to text flow and formatting, but will eventually appreciate some of InDesign's more powerful capabilities such as stroke formatting and nested styles.

Starting with the Direct Selection Tool for Graphics

Importing and manipulating graphics in InDesign is very similar to QuarkXPress. As long as you remember to use the Direct Selection tool to select a graphic rather than its frame, you and the InDesign graphics features will get along fine.

Paying Close Attention When Printing

InDesign and QuarkXPress offer many of the same output capabilities, such as print styles (called *print presets* in InDesign), PDF export, color calibration, and color separation support. But there are some notable differences beyond the different organization of their Print dialog boxes. For example, InDesign doesn't have any options to change image contrast or line-screen element for grayscale and black-and-white images, as QuarkXPress does. You need to apply such effects in an image editor.

Chapter 26

Top Ten Must-Knows for PageMaker Orphans

In This Chapter

- Transferring PageMaker files to InDesign
- Comparing how the two programs work

It's official: PageMaker is now part of history, formally discontinued by Adobe and lacking any updates since 1999. InDesign is Adobe's new — and only supported — publishing tool. So you're making the switch. Yet you have a lot of PageMaker still in your brain. This chapter helps you shift your mental gears so that you can become an InDesign user.

Fortunately, Adobe has retained a lot of PageMaker's approach in InDesign, so you can mainly focus on what's new rather than what's different. The basic methods for working with frames, lines, and pages are the same in both programs. What you get with InDesign is more control, with improved tools for drawing, formatting text, and manipulating objects.

Open Those Old PageMaker Files

InDesign opens PageMaker files saved in versions 6.0, 6.5, and 7.0. If InDesign sees any problems, it gives you an alert so you know what to fix in the converted file. After the file opens, it is untitled. You need to give the file a new name so that you don't accidentally overwrite that original PageMaker file.

You Now Have Three Selection Tools

The basic selection, object-creation, and navigation tools in InDesign are similar to those in PageMaker, but InDesign CS2 has *three* selection tools:

- Use the **Selection tool** to move or resize objects.
- Use the **Direct Selection tool** to reshape objects, change the endpoints of lines, and work with objects in groups. The Direct Selection tool also works like PageMaker's Crop tool, letting you move graphics within a frame.

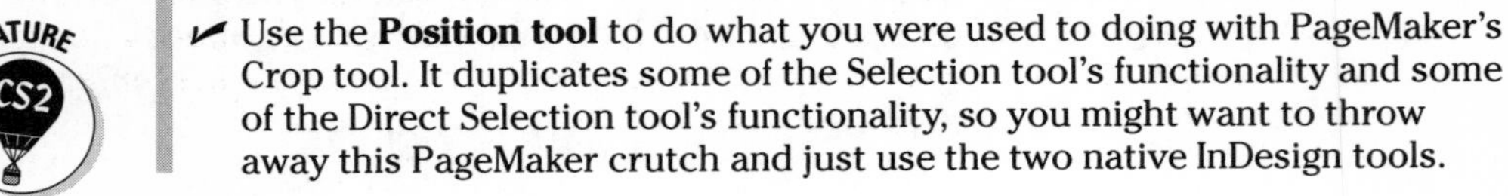

- Use the **Position tool** to do what you were used to doing with PageMaker's Crop tool. It duplicates some of the Selection tool's functionality and some of the Direct Selection tool's functionality, so you might want to throw away this PageMaker crutch and just use the two native InDesign tools.

Switching Your Shortcuts

InDesign uses many different keyboard shortcuts than PageMaker did, so be aware of the differences. Table 26-1 highlights the main differences.

Table 26-1 Keyboard Shortcuts Translated from PageMaker to InDesign

PageMaker Shortcut	*Result*	*InDesign Equivalent*
⌘+B or Ctrl+B	Styles pane	F11 (Character Styles), Shift+F11 (Paragraph Styles)
⌘+I or Ctrl+I	Indents/tabs dialog box	Shift+⌘+T or Ctrl+Shift+T
⌘+E or Ctrl+E	Edit in Story Editor	⌘+Y or Ctrl+Y
⌘+L	Spell-check	⌘+I or Ctrl+I
⌘+' (apostrophe) or Ctrl+' (apostrophe)	Control palette	Option+⌘+6 or Ctrl+Alt+6
⌘+J or Ctrl+J	Colors pane	F12 (Swatches pane)
⌘+8 or Ctrl+8	Layers pane	F7
Option+⌘+8 or Ctrl+Alt+8	Master Pages pane	F12 (Pages pane)
⌘+U or Ctrl+U	Fill and Stroke dialog box	F10 (Stroke pane)
Shift+⌘+E	Align dialog box	None
Option+⌘+E	Text Wrap dialog box	Option+⌘+W or Ctrl+Alt+W

Setting Aside Time to Set Preferences

You have so many preferences options in InDesign that you may wonder whether you'll ever leave the Preferences dialog box after you start setting them! Fortunately, you can set preferences at any time, so go ahead and start working with InDesign as it comes out of the box and then update preferences as specific needs arise.

Working with Objects, Not Elements

As with other aspects of InDesign, when you work with objects, you gain more than you lose. The types of objects (called *elements* in PageMaker) are similar — text frames, graphics frames, and lines — but InDesign offers more variations of them and more controls over their formatting.

Don't Worry Much about Text Differences

InDesign gives you more control over text formatting, such as the ability to stroke and fill characters in InDesign. Note that there are no type-style buttons — InDesign requires you to choose the appropriate version of a typeface rather than apply bold and italic to the general typeface. Other type styles are listed in the Character pane's palette menu.

Don't Worry Much about Graphics, Either

InDesign and PageMaker are very much alike when it comes to importing and manipulating graphics. InDesign lets you click and drag graphics files into a layout in addition to using the Place command (choose File⇨Place or press ⌘+D or Ctrl+D), as well as create clipping paths and automatically scale graphics or frames for you.

A Different Way to Change Pages

The one feature you'll miss about PageMaker is those neat little page icons in the lower-left corner of the document window. In shorter documents especially, the icons provided a quick, easy method for jumping to pages. Get used to using the Page Number text field and arrows at the bottom of the document window or the buttons at the bottom of the Pages pane instead.

Creating Colors Is Different

Most of your work with colors happens through the Swatches pane (choose Window⇨Swatches or press F5) — not through the Colors pane as PageMaker users might think. To share colors among documents, click and drag a colored object into another document window.

Using the PageMaker Toolbar

In addition to adding the Position tool, which acts like PageMaker's Crop tool, InDesign CS2 also adds the PageMaker toolbar, which provides 31 iconic buttons (see Figure 26-1) to allow quick access to various operations. You open and close this toolbar by choosing Window⇨PageMaker Toolbar.

Figure 26-1: The PageMaker toolbar.

Index

• A •

• B •

• C •

• D •

• E •

• F •

• G •

• H •

• I •

• J •

• K •

• L •

• M •

• N •

• O •

• P •

• Q •

• R •

• S •

• T •

• U •

• V •

• W •

• Y •

• Z •

USINESS, CAREERS & PERSONAL FINANCE

0-7645-5307-0

0-7645-5331-3 *†

Also available:

- Accounting For Dummies † 0-7645-5314-3
- Business Plans Kit For Dummies † 0-7645-5365-8
- Cover Letters For Dummies 0-7645-5224-4
- Frugal Living For Dummies 0-7645-5403-4
- Leadership For Dummies 0-7645-5176-0
- Managing For Dummies 0-7645-1771-6
- Marketing For Dummies 0-7645-5600-2
- Personal Finance For Dummies * 0-7645-2590-5
- Project Management For Dummies 0-7645-5283-X
- Resumes For Dummies † 0-7645-5471-9
- Selling For Dummies 0-7645-5363-1
- Small Business Kit For Dummies *† 0-7645-5093-4

OME & BUSINESS COMPUTER BASICS

0-7645-4074-2

0-7645-3758-X

Also available:

- ACT! 6 For Dummies 0-7645-2645-6
- iLife '04 All-in-One Desk Reference For Dummies 0-7645-7347-0
- iPAQ For Dummies 0-7645-6769-1
- Mac OS X Panther Timesaving Techniques For Dummies 0-7645-5812-9
- Macs For Dummies 0-7645-5656-8
- Microsoft Money 2004 For Dummies 0-7645-4195-1
- Office 2003 All-in-One Desk Reference For Dummies 0-7645-3883-7
- Outlook 2003 For Dummies 0-7645-3759-8
- PCs For Dummies 0-7645-4074-2
- TiVo For Dummies 0-7645-6923-6
- Upgrading and Fixing PCs For Dummies 0-7645-1665-5
- Windows XP Timesaving Techniques For Dummies 0-7645-3748-2

OOD, HOME, GARDEN, HOBBIES, MUSIC & PETS

0-7645-5295-3

0-7645-5232-5

Also available:

- Bass Guitar For Dummies 0-7645-2487-9
- Diabetes Cookbook For Dummies 0-7645-5230-9
- Gardening For Dummies * 0-7645-5130-2
- Guitar For Dummies 0-7645-5106-X
- Holiday Decorating For Dummies 0-7645-2570-0
- Home Improvement All-in-One For Dummies 0-7645-5680-0
- Knitting For Dummies 0-7645-5395-X
- Piano For Dummies 0-7645-5105-1
- Puppies For Dummies 0-7645-5255-4
- Scrapbooking For Dummies 0-7645-7208-3
- Senior Dogs For Dummies 0-7645-5818-8
- Singing For Dummies 0-7645-2475-5
- 30-Minute Meals For Dummies 0-7645-2589-1

NTERNET & DIGITAL MEDIA

0-7645-1664-7

0-7645-6924-4

Also available:

- 2005 Online Shopping Directory For Dummies 0-7645-7495-7
- CD & DVD Recording For Dummies 0-7645-5956-7
- eBay For Dummies 0-7645-5654-1
- Fighting Spam For Dummies 0-7645-5965-6
- Genealogy Online For Dummies 0-7645-5964-8
- Google For Dummies 0-7645-4420-9
- Home Recording For Musicians For Dummies 0-7645-1634-5
- The Internet For Dummies 0-7645-4173-0
- iPod & iTunes For Dummies 0-7645-7772-7
- Preventing Identity Theft For Dummies 0-7645-7336-5
- Pro Tools All-in-One Desk Reference For Dummies 0-7645-5714-9
- Roxio Easy Media Creator For Dummies 0-7645-7131-1

Separate Canadian edition also available
Separate U.K. edition also available

vailable wherever books are sold. For more information or to order direct: U.S. customers visit www.dummies.com or call 1-877-762-2974. K. customers visit www.wileyeurope.com or call 0800 243407. Canadian customers visit www.wiley.ca or call 1-800-567-4797.

SPORTS, FITNESS, PARENTING, RELIGION & SPIRITUALITY

0-7645-5146-9

Parenting For Dummies

0-7645-5418-2

Also available:

- Adoption For Dummies 0-7645-5488-3
- Basketball For Dummies 0-7645-5248-1
- The Bible For Dummies 0-7645-5296-1
- Buddhism For Dummies 0-7645-5359-3
- Catholicism For Dummies 0-7645-5391-7
- Hockey For Dummies 0-7645-5228-7
- Judaism For Dummies 0-7645-5299-6
- Martial Arts For Dummies 0-7645-5358-5
- Pilates For Dummies 0-7645-5397-6
- Religion For Dummies 0-7645-5264-3
- Teaching Kids to Read For Dummies 0-7645-4043-2
- Weight Training For Dummies 0-7645-5168-X
- Yoga For Dummies 0-7645-5117-5

TRAVEL

0-7645-5438-7

0-7645-5453-0

Also available:

- Alaska For Dummies 0-7645-1761-9
- Arizona For Dummies 0-7645-6938-4
- Cancún and the Yucatán For Dummies 0-7645-2437-2
- Cruise Vacations For Dummies 0-7645-6941-4
- Europe For Dummies 0-7645-5456-5
- Ireland For Dummies 0-7645-5455-7
- Las Vegas For Dummies 0-7645-5448-4
- London For Dummies 0-7645-4277-X
- New York City For Dummies 0-7645-6945-7
- Paris For Dummies 0-7645-5494-8
- RV Vacations For Dummies 0-7645-5443-3
- Walt Disney World & Orlando For Dummies 0-7645-6943-0

GRAPHICS, DESIGN & WEB DEVELOPMENT

0-7645-4345-8

0-7645-5589-8

Also available:

- Adobe Acrobat 6 PDF For Dummies 0-7645-3760-1
- Building a Web Site For Dummies 0-7645-7144-3
- Dreamweaver MX 2004 For Dummies 0-7645-4342-3
- FrontPage 2003 For Dummies 0-7645-3882-9
- HTML 4 For Dummies 0-7645-1995-6
- Illustrator CS For Dummies 0-7645-4084-X
- Macromedia Flash MX 2004 For Dummies 0-7645-4358-X
- Photoshop 7 All-in-One Desk Reference For Dummies 0-7645-1667-1
- Photoshop CS Timesaving Techniques For Dummies 0-7645-6782-9
- PHP 5 For Dummies 0-7645-4166-8
- PowerPoint 2003 For Dummies 0-7645-3908-6
- QuarkXPress 6 For Dummies 0-7645-2593-X

NETWORKING, SECURITY, PROGRAMMING & DATABASES

0-7645-6852-3

0-7645-5784-X

Also available:

- A+ Certification For Dummies 0-7645-4187-0
- Access 2003 All-in-One Desk Reference For Dummies 0-7645-3988-4
- Beginning Programming For Dummies 0-7645-4997-9
- C For Dummies 0-7645-7068-4
- Firewalls For Dummies 0-7645-4048-3
- Home Networking For Dummies 0-7645-42796
- Network Security For Dummies 0-7645-1679-5
- Networking For Dummies 0-7645-1677-9
- TCP/IP For Dummies 0-7645-1760-0
- VBA For Dummies 0-7645-3989-2
- Wireless All In-One Desk Reference For Dummies 0-7645-7496-5
- Wireless Home Networking For Dummies 0-7645-3910-8